Philip Thomas is a retired British Army warrant officer and published author.

In his memoir *Royal Engineer*, he shares his story and experiences of a fascinating 24-year military career that began on 6 June 1976, the day he first joined the Territorial Army in Llanelli, West Wales. In June 1977, he transferred across to the Regular Army and went on to serve for 23 years.

Totally absorbing from a historical perspective and fascinating in the way he shares numerous narratives and historical accounts, this is a fulfilling reading experience for anyone with a military background, or has an interest in modern history.

Ingeniously and creatively, the story centres on a journal written by the author during his six-month post-war operational tour of the Falkland Islands in 1983, whilst serving with 52 Field (Construction) Squadron, Royal Engineers.

From serving during the Cold War in the former Federal Republic of Germany to patrolling the streets of West Belfast in Northern Ireland at the time of The Troubles, and from qualifying as a Joint Service Mountain Expedition Leader in Norway to serving in post-war Bosnia, *Royal Engineer* has all the ingredients to make it a 'must' read.

Seeing US President Jimmy Carter at close hand in Berlin and catching sight of Rudolf Hess in Spandau Prison, exchanging letters with legendary comedian Eric Morecombe and confronting a black bear in the wilds of Canada's Algonquin Provincial Park, these are just some of the many experiences the author shares in a style of writing that is both captivating and enchanting.

To my son David and the memory of Alcwyn and Enid

"Writing a memoir is not saying goodbye, but hello."
Philip Thomas

Philip Thomas

ROYAL ENGINEER

A SAPPER'S MEMOIR

AUSTIN MACAULEY PUBLISHERS™
LONDON * CAMBRIDGE * NEW YORK * SHARJAH

Copyright © Philip Thomas 2023

The right of Philip Thomas to be identified as author of this work has been asserted by the author in accordance with sections 77 and 78 of the Copyright, Designs and Patents Act 1988.

All rights reserved. No part of this publication may be reproduced, stored in a retrieval system, or transmitted in any form or by any means, electronic, mechanical, photocopying, recording, or otherwise, without the prior permission of the publishers.

Any person who commits any unauthorised act in relation to this publication may be liable to criminal prosecution and civil claims for damages.

A CIP catalogue record for this title is available from the British Library.

ISBN 9781035821006 (Paperback)
ISBN 9781035821013 (Hardback)
ISBN 9781035821020 (ePub e-book)

www.austinmacauley.com

First Published 2023
Austin Macauley Publishers Ltd®
1 Canada Square
Canary Wharf
London
E14 5AA

To all who have supported and encouraged me to share the story of my time with the British Army, I extend my genuine heartfelt gratitude and special thanks must go to the following:

My greatest influencers, Alcwyn and Enid, who always encouraged me to chase my dreams and listen to my heart.

Irene Evans for telling me in 2019 "this is the book you should write" and for her constant encouragement.

The Army Personnel Centre at Kentigern House in Glasgow for kindly providing me with copies of my Service Records. Without these, writing my memoir accurately would have been much more difficult.

Austin Macauley Publishers for helping fulfil a writer's ambition.

Michael and Margaret Gimblett for their patience and true friendship.

My former British Army colleagues wherever you are.

And finally, to each and every member of the British Armed Forces both past and present, for their incredible service to our nation.

Table of Contents

Preface	**19**
Chapter One: Before the Falklands	**21**
Afternote	*41*
Chapter Two: From Canada to the Falklands	**43**
Foreword	*45*
Introduction	*60*
Afternote	*64*
Chapter Three: The Voyage South	**65**
Foreword	*67*
Afternote	*86*
Chapter Four: War and Peace	**89**
Foreword	*91*
Afternote	*103*
The Falklands War	*107*
Chapter Five: All Work and No Play	**115**
Foreword	*117*
Afternote	*136*
Chapter Six: Falklanders and Gurkhas	**139**
Foreword	*141*
The Falklands and Islanders	*144*

Afternote	*155*
Gurkha Heritage and Culture	*157*
Chapter Seven: The Rubb Hangar	**161**
Foreword	*163*
Afternote	*172*
Afternote	*180*
Chapter Eight: A Letter from Eric Morecombe	**181**
Foreword	*183*
Afternote	*188*
Afternote	*201*
Chapter Nine: Reach for the Sky	**203**
Foreword	*205*
Afternote	*220*
Chapter Ten: Falklands, South Georgia and Sir Ernest Shackleton	**221**
Foreword	*223*
Introduction	*226*
The Falkland Islands	*229*
South Georgia	*235*
Sir Ernest Henry Shackleton	*237*
Chapter Eleven: Patience and Progress	**241**
Foreword	*243*
Afternote	*260*
Chapter Twelve: A Show Comes to Town	**261**
Foreword	*263*
Afternote	*278*
Chapter Thirteen: Daffodils and Dilemmas	**281**
Foreword	*283*

Afternote	*289*
Afternote	*300*
Chapter Fourteen: Times Gone By	**303**
Foreword	*305*
Afternote	*316*
Afternote	*322*
Chapter Fifteen: Football's Coming Home	**327**
Foreword	*329*
Afternote	*337*
Afternote	*342*
Afternote	*349*
Chapter Sixteen: Work Hard and Play Hard	**351**
Foreword	*353*
Afternote	*360*
Afternote	*367*
Afternote	*370*
Chapter Seventeen: High Hopes	**371**
Foreword	*373*
Afternote	*388*
Chapter Eighteen: What Goes Up	**391**
Foreword	*393*
Afternote	*411*
Chapter Nineteen: No Stopping Now	**413**
Foreword	*415*
Afternote	*432*
Chapter Twenty: Sooner the Better	**433**
Foreword	*435*

Afternote	*451*
Chapter Twenty-One: Goodbye Kelly's Garden	**455**
Foreword	*457*
Afternote	*475*
Chapter Twenty-Two: Val and Rose	**477**
Foreword	*479*
Afternote	*494*
Afternote	*497*
Chapter Twenty-Three: June 1983 to October 1988	**499**
Foreword	*501*
Afternote	*509*
Afternote	*522*
Chapter Twenty-Four: October 1988 to August 1995	**525**
Foreword	*527*
Afternote	*544*
Chapter Twenty-Five: August 1995 to August 2000	**547**
Foreword	*549*
Afternote	*570*
Testimonial	**573**
Theatres	**574**
Specialist Qualifications	**576**

Illustrations

All images are the property of the author except:
*By kind permission of Air Vice Marshal David Owen Crwys-Williams (Retired)
**By kind permission of Colonel Wayne Robinson (Retired)

Disclaimer

This work depicts actual events in the military career of the author, as truthfully as recollection permits, and in part can be verified through his journal penned in the Falkland Islands in 1983, the Service Records provided by Disclosures 2 of the Army Personnel Centre, his own private collection of photographs, hand drawn maps and plans, research documents and notes he amassed throughout his career.

All persons contained within are actual individuals and no composite characters have been incorporated. Those who are known by the author to be deceased are mentioned by their true name as a gesture of respect.

For the author's part and under the Data Protection Act 2018 (DPA18), it was virtually impossible to obtain written permission from every single former colleague who may still be alive, to request and obtain permission to be named in this book therefore, no known full names have been used throughout however, this has not impacted in any way on the author's story.

Historical accounts, forewords, and afternotes were written by the author either during or after 1983 and all sources of information used are from the author's own knowledge of subjects, his penned journal and research notes, and documents collected over the years as a freelance historian.

All photographs, drawings, and plans contained in this memoir were taken and produced by the author and as such are the sole property of the author, with the sole exception indicated in the List of Illustrations.

The author accepts no legal responsibility for any inaccuracy contained within this book that relate to accounts written on matters not appertaining to his military career, and every effort has been made to present these as accurately as possible. Furthermore, the reader should consider this memoir to be a work of literature only, and not used as an official or public source of historical fact and information. As such, this memoir is not to be used or referred to in any private, public, written, or broadcast discussion or presentation without the sole written permission of the author himself.

Preface

Let me first say that everything I have written in this book actually happened.

For as long as I can recall, there have been two interests in life that I particularly enjoy and the first is writing. The second is history, whether it be ancient, middle, modern, cultural, political, or any other because in truth they all fascinate me. I inherited these interests from my mother Enid who actively encouraged me to read and then write accounts on historical characters and periods, and from an early age I was entering school and local newspaper writing competitions. Even when I joined my local Territorial Army Unit in May 1976 and subsequently the British Regular Army in July 1977, I already had a burning ambition to write about my experiences with the military at some point in my life. In January 1983 and only five months after the Falklands War concluded in a decisive British victory over the unlawful invasion by Argentine forces, I deployed on a six-month operational tour of duty to the Falklands and from the very first day I began to write a journal. This was something I had never done before yet something was compelling me to record the events of each and every day, and it wasn't too long before I worked out the reason why. In a light bulb moment I realised that my journal would one day prove pivotal in writing my military memoir and so important was the journal to my ambition, I looked after it like gold dust and kept it close to me no matter where I served. To this day it remains safe and a treasured part of my private library.

In June 2019 and after having relocated back to my hometown of Llanelli after almost 30 years, I was writing an eighteenth century fictional drama that I had been planning for some time. One sunny Sunday afternoon, Irene happened to notice my Falklands journal sitting on a shelf amongst numerous photograph albums and research folders which I had spent years compiling, and she asked to see it. Within a few minutes she looked at me and said, "this is the book you should write."

I explained that for decades an ambition of mine was to write a military memoir and her words immediately rekindled that aspiration. I had already obtained copies of my military Service Records from the Army Personnel Centre in Glasgow and had accumulated a private library of photographs, documents, research papers, and accounts that I had written and all bore relevance to my military career. Indeed, I had written bundled notes and historical references about my time in Germany during the Cold War, my experiences in West Belfast, Canada, and Bosnia, and articles centred on the politics and events in Argentina leading up to the Falklands War.

Because of my keen interest in early polar exploration and expeditions, I had also written notes on Captain Robert Falcon Scott and a true hero of mine namely Sir Ernest Henry Shackleton, but for me the most important archive of all was my hand-written journal from the Falklands along with all my hand-drawn maps and charts. All in all, I had everything I needed to start writing a military memoir, and this is it.

The author
2023

Chapter One
Before the Falklands

My army career first began in Llanelli in 1976 and the date was Tuesday 4 May.

Enid, my mother, had served as an army pay sergeant while serving with the Auxiliary Territorial Service (ATS) during World War Two at Phoenix Garden in London, and it was she who first suggested that I consider joining the British Army. This came about after I mentioned to her one day that I wanted to change my job and travel the world. I explained as honestly as I could that I needed a new beginning that would bring with it adventure, good career prospects, excitement, opportunities, and most important of all job security. She and my father Alcwyn, and my wonderful grandfather Benjamin had provided me with a private education at Saint Michael's School in Llanelli and at the age of 19, I was employed as a Slab Bank Inspector with Duport Steelworks, a company that no longer exists.

Although earning a decent salary and actively involved in local sport such as boxing and rugby, for some reason I felt that life had more to offer and I desperately wanted to do something about this as soon as I could. Around that time I was a frequent visitor to London and enjoyed going to see the art galleries and museums, and also famous places such as Carnaby Street and Covent Garden. And just like my mother, I had a passion for theatre and musicals and so I would go to West End shows such as Richard O'Brien's Rocky Horror Show, and Andrew Lloyd Webber's Jesus Christ Superstar and Evita. London in those days was so very different and there was a sense of excitement everywhere you went.

My parents clearly understood how I was feeling because they too had gone through a similar experience when they were young, and indeed my father relocated to Edgbaston in Birmingham at the age of 19 and it was only when he returned to Llanelli in 1946, that he met and married Enid on 2 August 1948.

After listening to what I had to say, my mother who I absolutely adored suggested that I consider joining the British Armed Forces but in order to find out more about what they had to offer, she recommended I first visit the local Territorial Army Unit in Llanelli's Drill Hall on Murray Street where it just so happened that 'A' Company, 4th Battalion Royal Regiment of Wales were conducting a recruiting campaign at the time.

I was interviewed by a young officer who told me that if my application proved successful, I could expect an exciting part-time career as a Territorial infantryman and that I would make new friends while earning a second salary. Furthermore, if I were to attend a certain number of weekly parades each year as well as an annual camp on the Brecon Beacons, I would qualify for an annual bonus but all of this sounded too good to be true and just as I was contemplating whether or not to enlist, out of the blue he mentioned an added incentive which was a flight in a Westland Army Scout helicopter. As there were only 12 vacancies and having never before flown in a helicopter, I jumped at the chance and not long after attending a formal interview and passing my entrance exam, an official brown envelope arrived at my parents' house at 23 Cornish Place.

Inside was a letter formally inviting me to report to the Drill Hall on Tuesday 11 May and to my absolute delight, I had been selected but first I needed to sign the Official Secrets Act and swear an Oath of Allegiance. On Saturday 15 May 1976 at 11.00 precisely, I reported again to the Drill Hall where I was issued a full set of military clothing and equipment. Feeling apprehensive yet very excited, I had joined the Territorial Army and two weeks later on Friday 28 May, I was waiting at the edge of Peoples' Park in Llanelli along with fellow new recruits and we were each wearing full combat dress, Frank Spencer type berets, and carrying backpacks that were packed to the hilt. As we listened for the sound of military aircraft approaching our location from the west, it was then that the nerves kicked in.

What we had not been told was that our helicopter flight was a one-way trip only, and that we were being airlifted to a remote part of Sennybridge Military Training Area on the Brecon Beacons in South Wales where we would undertake a weekend's crash course on Basic Infantry Skills. The area where the helicopters touched down was Dixies Corner and over the course of the next 48 hours we were taught various field craft skills such as first-aid, patrol formations, hand signals, how to build a survival trench, camouflage techniques, map reading, weapon handling, and military aircraft recognition. Our Final Training Exercise (FTX) involved a nine-mile night patrol to an enemy location where we carried out a surprise attack and captured three hostile combatants, before moving on to a secure Harbour Area where we had to take it turn to debrief our instructors. After completing a written test on everything we had learned over the weekend and feeling exhausted yet elated, we eventually climbed onto the back of a Bedford 4-ton truck and were driven back to Llanelli Drill Hall. It was a superb introduction to a brand-new world and despite being extremely challenging and demanding, I enjoyed every minute and wanted more.

My mother, Enid

That brief welcome to army life took me completely out of my comfort zone yet I was totally gripped by the whole experience because it had taught me a lot about myself such as how far I could be pushed mentally and physically, and I discovered what I could achieve simply through believing in myself. More importantly and for the very first time in my life, I experienced military discipline and what true team-play is all about, and this alone completely opened my eyes. At that time I played scrum-half with Bynea Rugby Football Club and was running an average of 30 miles every week, plus I was regularly training with Trostre Boxing Club and so naturally I considered myself to be reasonably fit then one day, I was invited by my officer commanding to take part in the 1976 Welsh 1000 Peaks Race.

Knowing absolutely nothing about this event, I was told that the military race involved teams of four racing against each other across the three highest peaks in Snowdonia and over a distance not far short of a full marathon. The event attracted military teams from across the NATO member countries and it proved to be one of the hardest challenges I have ever undertaken.

Without hesitation I agreed and over the course of the next five months, our squad was put through the most intense physical training programme along local beaches and hills, in gymnasiums, on the Brecon Beacons, and in Snowdonia itself. Our Team Leader was Staff Sergeant Richards whose standard of fitness was incredible, as was the fitness levels of Sergeant Cliff Williams and Private Fyfield. Looking back at it now, this competition proved one of the most brutal and physically demanding events I have ever participated in and still to this day, I bear the scar on my left shin to prove it.

The Welsh 1000 Race started in a small car park in the village of Abergwyngregyn on the west coast of North Wales. From there, the race followed a 32-kilometre route of which the first three followed a narrow road that had a gradual incline before veering off and following a very steep climb into the mountains of Snowdonia. The race then took us over the peaks of Carnedd Llewellyn and Carnedd Daffydd before heading down a long descent covered in loose rocks and stones, and from there we could see the glistening water of Llyn Ogwen at the foot of Tryfan. It is reputed King Arthur's sword Excalibur sits on the bottom of this lake.

We then crossed the A5 road after passing through one of the many checkpoints along the route, and from there we made our ascent along the east face of Tryfan before heading across boggy terrain that led to the peak of Glyder Fawr. It was at this juncture that we picked up the pace and continued until we could see Pen-y-Pass Car Park, and yet another checkpoint off in the distance. After passing through Pen-y-Pass we joined the famous Pyg Track and made our way along the path while keeping Crib Goch to our right, and continued until we had the famous Zig Zags clearly in our sight.

This steep footpath proved quite demanding and took us up to a well-known feature called the Gate Post, which is a magnificent slab of slate standing some eight feet in height and overlooks the mountain rail-track below. At this point we knew our race was nearly over and all we had to do was follow the path to the finishing line at the old railway station on the summit of Snowdon, and at a height of 1,085 metres. Each team was required to wear military dress, army boots and webbing, and at various stages we all competed in some of the worst weather conditions imaginable, but the one thing I will never forget was the sheer sense of elation when I crossed the finishing line.

'A' Company completed the event in a time of 7 hours 58 minutes, but our biggest achievement was coming close to overtaking a team from the Gurkha Regiment. Whilst scrambling up Tryfan, I lost my footing and fell heavily against a large boulder. The pain that shot up my left shin was unbearable at first and as I tore open my trousers leg, I saw a gaping wound over which I poured ice-cold water and applied a thick dressing. I then changed my trousers and was soon back in the race. On returning to Pen-y-Pass car park after the race, I was taken to Llanberis Medical Centre in an army Land Rover where my wound was treated before re-joining my colleagues in a pub in Llanrwst, for a well-earned beer.

The finishing line on Snowdon, 1976

Another special moment during my 12 months with the Territorial Army was taking part in the Queen's Silver Jubilee Armed Forces Parade at Wembley Stadium in early 1977. Thousands of part-time servicemen and women proudly marched onto the famous Wembley turf to the inspirational music of the Massed Band of the British Territorial Army, and everyone on parade grew a couple of inches as HM Queen Elizabeth II inspected her troops from the back of an immaculate army Land Rover.

I thoroughly enjoyed my time with 'A' Company. I qualified as a Physical Training Instructor and passed a 14-day cadre at the former Cwrt-y-Gollen Army Training Camp near Crickhowell, but after 12 months I felt it was the time to consider transferring across to the British Regular Army to start a new career as a full-time professional soldier. Following an interview at the Army Recruiting Office on Swansea's High Street, I was selected to attend an Assessment Weekend at the Army Personnel Selection Centre in St George's Barracks, Sutton Coldfield where I underwent a series of assessments including a full medical examination, physical fitness and mental agility tests, team problem solving exercises, a written and numeracy exam, and finally I attended a career interview with a Selection Sergeant.

Instead of opting to stay with the Infantry and in particular the Royal Regiment of Wales, I decided to enlist into the Corps of Royal Engineers which is a branch of the British Army that can trace its origins back to William the Conqueror, and my main reasons for choosing the Sappers were:

a. More choice of trades such as artisan and technical.
b. Better promotion prospects.
c. Guaranteed worldwide travel.
d. Better rates of pay.

I signed-up there and then and exactly one week later I was back in Swansea swearing a second Oath of Allegiance but this time, with my proud father in attendance. I was issued a single rail-ticket to Farnborough in Hampshire and handed a booklet containing all the information I needed to prepare myself for my Basic Army Training Course, and it was while serving with the Territorial Army that I decided to adopt the nickname Pip because Philip Pirrip was a favourite Charles Dickens character of mine from *Great Expectations*. Several years before retiring from the army in August 2000, I reverted to my birth name of Philip.

Too upset to leave the house, my mother and I said our farewell in private inside the front parlour of 23 Cornish Place, and it was there that we shed our tears and hugged each other until it was finally time to say goodbye. The date was Wednesday, 22 June 1977 and some 20 minutes later, my father and I were standing on Platform One of Llanelli Rail Station shaking hands and as the train began to pull away, I suddenly saw something I had never witnessed before.

My father Alcwyn discreetly wiped away a tear from his eye and seeing this upset me more than I dare to admit, because he was the toughest man I knew and always kept his emotions to himself. Yet for the first time ever, he could not conceal his feelings and all I wanted to do at that moment in time was to hug and tell him how much I loved him, but the words would not come out. As the train pulled further away, he smiled and waved goodbye to me and all too soon both he and Llanelli were out of sight. My new life with the British Regular Army had begun, and my sentiments that day were somewhat muddled yet deep down inside I knew that I was doing the right thing, and I have never ever looked back.

As anyone who has served with the British Army will tell you, Basic Military Training is hard and indeed it is bloody tough! At times, your instructors will push you beyond your limits and that is not a bad thing because military training is not meant to be easy, and for very good reasons. My nine-week course took place at 1 and 3 Training Regiments Royal Engineers (TRRE) which was based at Southwood

Camp in Cove, a small suburb on the outskirts of Farnborough in Hampshire. On reporting to the guardroom, I was directed to an old wooden billet that had been assigned to Training Party 77/08 and inside the powerful aroma of wax polish was overwhelming, and there were lockers and beds neatly lined up along both sides. And it was inside this building that I first met my fellow recruits who judging by their appearance and bearing, had no previous military experience of any kind and it was their length of hair that gave the show away.

We were 14 in total and everyone had a completely different character yet overnight we gelled to become a team of loyal, trustworthy, and true friends who were absolutely determined to pass the course and win the prize for Best Training Party. All privileges and freedoms that my new colleagues had taken for granted as civilians were taken away in an instant by three corporal training instructors who put the fear of God into us, and regularly put us through our paces yet in doing so, they made it abundantly clear as to who wagged the tail.

No one dared answer back or contradict an order for fear of being marched to the guardroom and 'beasted' on the Parade Square in full view of others, and in no time they won our respect because quite simply they were exceptional and so very good at their job. At times they made us laugh but every single day they drove us so hard that it genuinely hurt, but we all totally believed in them and knew that through dogged determination and perseverance, they would get us through the course.

Sometimes they pushed us too hard if truth be told, but this was only to be expected and not one of us was going to be beaten because we were a team, and instead of moaning and groaning, we made a pledge that we would help each other at all times and ensure we all made it through to the end. We also agreed to see the funny side to life and I truly believe that our instructors picked up on this, because they encouraged and motivated us even more until eventually they achieved their aim, and turned us into a squad of highly disciplined soldiers. One day during an intense training session on the Regimental Square, one of the instructors said something profound which I have never forgotten to this day. "My job," he barked, "is to break you and then I am going to make you!"

On Thursday, 13 October 1977 Training Party 77/08 proudly marched onto the Regimental Square at Southwood Camp for the very last time, along with seven other training parties and to the sound of the Band of the Royal Engineers. I felt seven feet tall. This was our Passing Out Parade and during the ceremony, speeches and presentations were made in front of proud parents, families, and friends and at the post-parade buffet my parents spoke with both the Commanding Officer 1 and 3 TRRE and the Officer Commanding 28 Training Squadron.

One hour later, they drove back to Llanelli but for me it was time for the next stage in my Royal Engineer training, and so I moved across into 55 Training Squadron's accommodation for my Combat Engineer Class 3 Trade Course. This was meant to finish on 13 January 1978 however on 17 November 1977, Britain's fire fighters went on national strike and as a result some 10,000 troops including my colleagues and I were deployed on Operation Burberry, to provide emergency fire-fighting cover. All leave and military training courses were cancelled and I was assigned to Banbury in Oxfordshire where I remained until 4 January 1978. Throughout the whole of the strike, food parcels were generously gifted to the troops across the country by local communities who appreciated us more than we had expected, and at the TA centre where I was billeted my team were frequently visited by the Town Mayor, local councillors, and other dignitaries.

It was an incredible time and being part of a Green Goddess fire-fighting crew was not only an exciting experience, it also gave us a real chance to truly understand why Military Aid to the Civil Authorities plays such an important role for the members of Britain's Armed Forces. The Green Goddess was not a modern fire-fighting vehicle by any means because they were first built in 1953 and had a hand-rung bell instead of an air horn, and the only flashing light was a borrowed yellow road hazard light which we kept inside the cabin. Looking back at it now, the experience was as hilarious as it was surreal and I often think we must have looked like the Keystone Cops in old black and white movie, and yet I enjoyed every single minute of my time on Operation Burberry. When the strike ended, I was told that I had been awarded my Combat Engineer Class 3 qualification and with that, I was posted to my first Regular Army unit.

Top Left: FTX at Hawley, 1977
Top Right: Training Party 77/08 (I'm front row 3rd from right)

For any new soldier reporting to his or her first unit after passing Basic Military Training, the experience is both exciting and somewhat daunting because every military barracks will have a guardroom located at the main entrance, and soldiers on guard duty can smell a recruit fresh out of training a mile away. They stand out like a sore thumb and all too often try too hard to impress, or at least that was how it was back in 1978 and as such, they always provided good entertainment for the guard commanders and their teams.

My first regular army unit was 26 Armoured Engineer Squadron which was based at Dennis Barracks in the beautiful Lower-Saxony town of Munsterlager, in what was then the Federal Republic of Germany or West Germany, as it was better known. I reported for duty on Wednesday, 15 February 1978 and as the white Royal Corps of Transport 52-seater bus pulled up outside the guardroom, the German civilian driver without even looking at me said, "viel glück, du wirst es brauchen" which translated means "good luck, you'll need it."

Inside the guardroom and standing behind a counter which looked like a magistrates' bench, I could see a corporal and two sappers and I just knew they were going to make my life hell. To the right of the guard commander was Jim Pridding and as I stepped down off the bus, I heard him say something to the other two who were giggling away. I was wearing a dark brown suit with the widest collars imaginable and flared trousers, a multi-coloured shirt and matching tie, purple wetlook shoes, and bright yellow socks and in my eyes I looked trendy and so very cool. This was after all the 1970s.

As they watched me collect my army suitcase and military holdall from the rear of the bus, they must have been rubbing their hands in glee. I approached the entrance to the guardroom and was immediately overcome by the smell of furniture and metal polish and while everything inside looked meticulous, it was nevertheless extremely intimidating but right then I was ordered by the commander to approach the counter and stand to attention. He was obviously perched on a raised platform because he towered above me, and looked down as if I was a criminal on trial for murder and with that, he snarled a command for me to state my number, rank, and name. I started to answer but he immediately stopped me and screamed "Silence! You're in Krautland now so speak the bleeding local lingo!" Nervously I apologised and started to answer in German.

"Entschuldigen Herr Korporal, aber mein Deutsch ist nicht gut" which roughly translated means "Forgive me Corporal, but my German is not good."

Jim smiled and gave a playful wink as the guard commander started to laugh. I had been well and truly set up by all three and after we had a good laugh, I was given the warmest of welcomes by the guard commander who came out from behind the counter and shook my hand, then left to go about his duties. From that very moment we all became the very best of friends.

My employment with 26 Armoured Engineer Squadron was that of an Armoured Vehicle Launched-Bridge (AVLB) driver and crewman. The AVLB vehicles in those days were Centurion and Chieftain tanks that weighed 40 tons and when laden with a Number 8 Scissor folding bridge, would weigh up to 60 tons and were capable of spanning a gap of up to 75 feet.

Built between 1935 and 1938, Dennis Barracks served as a Nazi chemical weapon test centre during World War II and close to the tank park were several former gas storage chambers that were now derelict and starting to fall apart. The barracks was 33 kilometres north of Hohne Garrison which was located close to the site of the infamous Nazi concentration camp called Bergen-Belsen, a place I visited many times with friends to pay respect to the memory of tens of thousands of innocent people who suffered horrifically at the hands of their captors between 1940 and 1945. The inmates included Jews, Polish, Soviets, Austrians, and even Germans. In Hohne camp itself was a former World War II building that was turned into a well-known NAAFI shop and restaurant called The Roundhouse, and inside was an original German swastika from World War II that had been discovered beneath the floor boards.

Former Nazi gas storage chambers at Dennis Barracks, 1978

In July 1978, my troop was deployed on a 10 day Heavy-Ferry Training Exercise in what was then the British sector of West Berlin, and being British servicemen stationed in West Germany during the Cold War we were required to travel by rail on a military train that was called The Berliner. The 145-mile journey was quite simply fascinating to me as a keen historian because it started at Braunshweig in the west, and ended at Charlottenburg Station inside West Berlin, after passing through a wire-fenced area of land that was famously called 'The Corridor.'

At Marienborn Station, the British officer-in-charge and interpreter would disembark The Berliner to present all passenger passports to a Russian officer for inspection, and when satisfied that all paperwork was correct, the train would be allowed to continue on its journey. All British service personnel travelling on board had to wear full No 2 Service Dress because of an agreed Cold War protocol, and I can only describe the experience as being surreal. As soon as the train entered The Corridor it was required to slow down until it exited the other side.

Everyone was given a map which pointed out all special places of interest between Braunshweig and West Berlin such as Magdeburg Cathedral and the political prison, the Soviet tank workshops at Kirchmöser and a Soviet engineer camp, and the many eastern bloc armed watch towers that lined the route. It was rumoured that Soviet soldiers often resorted to drinking anti-freeze fluid whenever they ran out of money, but whether or not this was true will remain speculation. What was certainly clear to everyone however, was that the Soviet camps we saw for ourselves all looked badly run down, disorganised, and some had roofs collapsing.

I was accommodated at Smuts Barracks which is just off Heer Strasse and the perimeter fence of the camp ran immediately adjacent to Spandau, the famous prison where former Deputy Führer Rudolf Hess was serving a life sentence for crimes against peace, and conspiracy with others to commit crimes. One afternoon and through a broken window in the loft of an old stable block in Smuts Barracks, I saw and took photographs of the garden in Spandau Prison and quite unexpectedly, I caught a glimpse of an elderly man walking back into the prison through a tall arched door and I truly believe it was Rudolph Hess himself.

On 17 August 1987, Hess committed suicide and Spandau Prison was demolished for fear of becoming a neo-Nazi memorial. During my time in Berlin I saw US President Jimmy Carter at close range. The Heavy Ferry training was carried out on a stretch of water called Havel which flows through West Berlin and during one particular phase, we passed close to the site where on 20 January 1942, the Wannsee Conference was chaired by SS Officer Reinhard Heydrich on the direct order of Adolf Hitler. Selected senior officers from both the SS and State Departments met to discuss and approve the implementation of part of Hitler's plan to bring about a 'Final Solution to the Jewish Question.' As history shows, this meeting ultimately resulted in the mass killing of so many innocent people.

Spandau Prison, 1978   US President Jimmy Carter

Also stationed at Dennis Barracks in 1980 was 2 Squadron Royal Corps of Transport, and they extended an invitation to 26 Armoured Engineer Squadron for six volunteers to deploy with them as Armoured Fighting Vehicle (AFV) drivers on a five-month operational tour of duty in West Belfast. I successfully applied and this officially became my first tour of duty with the British Army in a military operational theatre, and after weeks of intense training which included riot control, convoy drills and urban patrols, we deployed on 4 October 1979 and returned to Munsterlager on 23 February 1980.

Throughout my time in Northern Ireland I drove a Humber 1-ton Armoured Personnel Carrier (APC) which was affectionately nicknamed The Pig by British troops, because of its similarity in appearance. I was stationed at Woodbourne Camp which in those days was a high corrugated iron-fenced British Army base located on the junction of Blacks Road and Stewartstown Road. In later years, the base was demolished to make way for a new building that would serve as Woodbourne Police Station. My tour coincided with the time when hundreds of convicted paramilitary-linked prisoners were interned in the H-Block Cells at HM Maze Prison, on the outskirts of Lisburn. I was awarded the General Campaign Medal (GCM) for this tour.

Woodbourne Camp, West Belfast, 1980

Back in Munsterlager in March 1980, I was selected to attend a three-week Regimental Junior Non-Commissioned Officer Cadre and after finishing runner up to the Top Student who ironically was a very good friend, I was promoted to lance corporal and over the course of the following year I participated on several military exercises on Soltau and Sennelager Training Areas. On 9 July 1981, I flew out to Calgary in Alberta, Canada for four months on Exercise Medicine Man. This was one of a series of large-scale live battlefield training manoeuvres that still take place each year at the British Army Training Unit Suffield (BATUS), which is some 30 miles north-west of Medicine Hat that sits close to the bank of the South Saskatchewan River, and remains very popular with British and Canadian troops.

BATUS covers an extensive area of almost 2,700 square kilometres and it is the largest military training area in the whole of Canada. I was taking part on Medicine Man 4 which involved approximately 1,400 troops and during the live enemy phase, I drove a FV432 Armoured Personnel Carrier that towed a large wheeled trailer containing a mine clearing device called 'Giant Viper'. In essence, the Giant Viper is a 250-metre-long hose that is packed with live plastic explosive and attached to six rockets which when fired, launches the hose into the air at an angle of 45° and directly over the top of the APC.

The rockets automatically shut down 10 seconds after firing and parachutes deploy to slow down the speed of descent. The Giant Viper was designed to land along the ground in a straight line and across a minefield, and the ensuing explosion would destroy all mines to create a safe corridor some 200 metres long and six metres wide. As I manoeuvred the FV432 into position, my vehicle commander spoke to me over the radio and calmly said, "right Pip, fingers crossed this piece of crap doesn't land on top of us."

With the whole battlegroup looking on, thankfully everything went according to plan and the explosion was of such magnitude that the sound rumbled into the distance for what seemed an eternity. It was the first and last time that I was ever involved in the live firing of a Giant Viper, and it was mightily impressive.

HRH Prince Charles married Lady Diana Spencer at St Paul's Cathedral on Wednesday, 29 July 1981 and as 740 million viewers around the world watched the historic ceremony on their television sets, and over 600,000 people lined the streets of London, Exercise Medicine Man 4 continued into the early hours of the evening. Around 19.00 the battlegroup was called to a halt after permission had been granted for the troops to celebrate the royal wedding, and I vividly recall the moment I photographed a commander sitting in the turret of his Ferret Armoured Vehicle while silhouetted against the backdrop of a most perfect Canadian sunset.

After Medicine Man 4 concluded, the Main Party returned to Germany but I stayed on at BATUS as a volunteer on the Rear Party for three weeks, and during this time I visited Calgary and its famous stampede and also Vancouver, where I stayed with my cousin Roger and his family at their home on Blundell Road in Richmond for 10 days.

My cousin's wife Christine took me to the summit of Grouse Mountain in the cable car, and to Stanley National Park and Gastown to see the famous steam clock. I also visited Victoria on Vancouver Island which is the beautiful capital of British Columbia where my Aunt Mair and Uncle Michael are buried. One memorable day was spent at the Pacific National Exhibition watching lumberjacks compete in the most incredible timber sports ever, but sadly my final weekend on Exercise Medicine Man 4 soon came and it was spent in Medicine Hat and the renowned hotel and bar called Assiniboia, which was affectionately known by visiting troops as the Sin Bin and still stands on the corner of 3rd Street.

I never took part on another Medicine Man exercise but I will always fondly remember the wonderful names given to the long dirt tracks that crossed the prairie, such as Rattlesnake and Kangaroo Rat Road, and the ancient burial sites where I was told members of the Cree and Blackfoot native tribes are laid to rest. I literally fell in love with Canada in an instant and that loves still lives inside me to this day.

BATUS Canada, 1981

Armoured Engineers on Ex Medicine Man 4, 1981

On 4 September 1981 and back serving with colleagues at 26 Engineer Squadron in Munsterlager, I deployed as an AVRE crewman on Exercise Certain Encounter. This was yet another large-scale military manoeuvre and involved around 71,000 NATO troops of which 17,000 were airlifted from the United States of America, in what was the largest military operation since World War II. The aim of Exercise

Certain Encounter was to pitch an invading Orange Force against the might of a friendly Blue Force that was defending the territory of Northern Hesse, a central German state of which Wiesbaden is the capital. During the two-week Joint Service Exercise on Sennelager Training Area, my location was visited by a RAF Harrier Jump Jet pilot who asked if he could look inside my Chieftain AVLB.

More than happy to oblige I explained that the armoured vehicle was a combat support tank that weighed 60 tons when fully laden, and that its primary role was to bridge gaps such as large craters and rivers by dropping a 26-metre-long scissor bridge inside four minutes. Instead of just showing him how the vehicle was operated, I took him for a drive and he sat in the commander's seat. For me, it was a pleasure and I literally left it at that but the very next day and without prior warning, he pulled up in his Land Rover at my location and said that he had arranged for me to be his guest for the afternoon, and that he was going to take me on a flight in his T-Bird Harrier Jump Jet as a thank you for my hospitality the previous day.

In no time at all, I was whisked to the RAF location which was hidden under camouflage nets and after putting on a flight-suit, I was given a pre-flight briefing and escorted across to the waiting T-Bird Harrier Jump Jet. I was talked through the controls and head-up display, the ejector procedure and safety controls, and then I climbed into the navigator's seat which was behind the pilot's cockpit, and after being strapped in by the ground crew I was told not to touch any equipment coloured black and yellow, as these were all part of the highly explosive ejector seat system.

If there was a genuine need to eject mid-flight I was told that Tim would say over my headphones "prepare to eject – eject – eject now!" Our flight followed the same path that Wing Commander Guy Gibson's 617 Squadron flew in their daring 'bouncing bomb' attacks on the Möhne, Eder, and Sorpe Dams in Nazi Germany during World War II on Operation Chastise. We flew over all three Ruhr Valley dams at low altitude and during our return flight back to Sennelager Training Area, I was handed control of the aircraft and guided through a series of manoeuvres before Tim eventually took back control of the aircraft. It was an experience I will never forget.

In my Harrier flight suit

I also deployed on Exercise Red Claymore with 26 Armoured Engineer Squadron however, it was after this particular military manoeuvre that I started to lose interest in armoured engineering as a career, and so being a qualified Physical Training Instructor I successfully applied for the vacant post of Regimental PTI, and this is what I did for the remainder of my tour. As a keen sportsman my disciplines varied from rugby union to gymnastics, and from basketball to cross-country but the one sport in which I excelled was tennis and I was given lessons by a former German National tennis coach.

Over three months he improved both my game and serve that excelled even my own wildest expectations. At weekends I would often drive to Bergen-Belsen with colleagues to visit the former concentration camp where tens of thousands of defenceless victims died so horrendously at the hands of the German Nazis during World War II. In the silence of the camp, we would walk around the burial sites and I recall vividly one in particular which bore the simple but heart-breaking inscription 'Hier Ruhen 5,000 Toten. April 1945.' Translated it read 'Here Lie 5,000 dead. April 1945.'

On my first visit to Bergen-Belsen, I nearly missed the entrance as it was not as well sign-posted as I would have imagined, yet maybe there was a reason for this but the one thing I clearly remember as we approached Belsen, was an old railway siding that had a platform which had a distinct 1940s look about it. Later, I was informed that this platform was one of the actual drop-off areas used by prisoners and back inside the museum I viewed maps, images, artefacts, and read the history of the concentration camp and the horrific accounts of what took place. On the afternoon of 15 April 1945, British troops from the 63 Anti-Tank Regiment and 11 Armoured Division entered Bergen-Belsen and liberated 60,000 starving prisoners many of whom were very close to death.

One of the survivors was Anne Frank and it is estimated that between 1943 and 1945, close to 50,000 prisoners died. The narratives I read literally appalled me as to the level of cruelty and inhumane treatment meted out on innocent and defenceless adults and children, and all in the name of Hitler's German Nazi obsession to commit genocide.

It was during a live firing day at Bergen-Hohne Tank Range that I and fellow AVRE crew members were told about a concrete bunker that was located about a mile down the range, and it was called the Hitler Hoff or Hitler's House. This according to one of the range staff team was a building in which Adolf Hitler himself would sit with panzer commanders to observe and discuss tank manoeuvres and tactics is some detail. Through my binoculars I could see the bunker and on one occasion during a lull in live firing, I visited the building along with colleagues courtesy of a ride in the Range Safety Officer's vehicle and it was an incredible experience being so close to a piece of World War II history. The information the safety team provided us with was better than any tour guide.

My time in Munsterlager was exciting and very enjoyable because I achieved so much in just three years, and I did not waste a single opportunity to see as much of the former West Germany as I possibly could. But towards the end of 1981, my time with my first British Army regular unit was almost up and I was expecting a posting order at any time. This arrived sooner than I expected and on 30 November 1981, I drove out of Dennis Barracks to return to the United Kingdom and report to my next unit which was 22 Engineer Regiment and based at Swinton Barracks in Tidworth, Wiltshire.

Afternote

What I liked most about my first Regular Army unit was being stationed in the former West Germany during a period of geopolitical indifference between two superpowers, namely the United States and its allies, and the Soviet Union and its allies. Basically, this was a case of east versus west or better still Warsaw Pact versus NATO. The Warsaw Pact comprised of the then Union of Soviet Socialist Republics (USSR) and its allies while NATO was made up of the United States of America and her allies, and this period in history was called the Cold War which first began in 1947 and ended on Boxing Day 1991.

For me, being based in Germany at that time was just perfect because of my keen interest in history and world politics, but there was also another reason. Over time I genuinely became very passionate about the heritage and culture of the country, its people who were so very friendly as I quickly discovered when visiting the historical and beautiful cities of Berlin, Hamburg, Hannover, and the ancient traditional Lower-Saxony towns of Celle, Hamelin, Uelzen and Walsrode.

I also realised that I was being re-assured that this was one of the reasons why I wanted to make a new start in life back in 1976, and that the advice my mother Enid gave me to join the British Army was the best ever. For that reason alone, I am still so grateful to her even though she sadly passed away in March 1984. I miss Germany more that I dare admit and often I think about revisiting those old towns and one day, I am sure I will.

Prost!

**Chapter Two
From Canada to the Falklands**

Foreword

No matter how many plans a person will make during their lifetime, not all happen straight away no matter how motivated that individual may be, and a prime example is this memoir. I knew back in 1983 that I wanted to write the story of my military career at some point in my life yet in reality, it has taken 40 years to accomplish because before I could even begin to put a structure in place, first and foremost I needed to have a career that was worthy of writing about and in 1983, I had no idea as to how long my time with the British Army would actually be.

For a British non-commissioned soldier, the 'full career' is defined as being 22 years unbroken service commencing from date of enlistment or 18th birthday, yet not everyone goes on to achieve this and for a number of reasons. Medical discharge, personal choice, the needs of the Service, and so the list goes on and many will simply decide to serve 3, 6, or 9 years while others go on and complete 12 or more, depending on individual circumstances such as an offer of civilian employment.

Even marriage and a relationship can dictate the length of a military career because not all spouses or partners are able to tolerate the lengthy periods of separation, and especially six-month operational tours of duty and back-to-back deployments which in the 1990s were increasingly becoming more frequent. Families are meant to be together and so quite understandably, life as a partner of a member of the Armed Forces is not everyone's cup of tea.

During my time between July 1977 and August 2000, the responsibility for managing army careers in the Royal Engineers was that of Personnel Branch 7 (PB7) at MoD Stanmore for officers, while RE Manning and Records Office (REMRO) at Glasgow looked after all other ranks who are otherwise known as (ORs). Both MoD departments worked closely with Divisions and Units and maintained an excellent working partnership with Commanding Officers, Staff Assistants and Regimental Chief Clerks.

The biggest incentive back then for troops to complete a 22-year career was the receipt of an immediate full army pension that was payable from date of discharge. Personally, by the time I completed my 22 years I was still enjoying military life too much to even think about retiring, and so I successfully applied to be transferred across to a career stream that was called 'Extended Continuance Service.' One condition of serving on extended continuance was that I was no longer eligible for further promotion yet on the other hand, my pension would increase with each additional full year served beyond 22 years, and being more than happy with this, I signed on the dotted line without hesitation. Another condition that appealed to me was that I would automatically qualify for a free discharge whenever I decided to terminate my service, and so I was quite literally in a win-win situation.

In July 1997, an application to serve on Extended Continuance would first need to have the support of a commanding officer who would then pass it to Division for further consideration. If approved, the application would be submitted to APC Glasgow where each would be presented to a selection panel. This panel's main responsibility was to assess the applicant's age, substantive rank, work experience and qualifications, suitability, confidential reporting history, and finally the needs of the Corps. On being accepted for Extended Continuance, I was invited to remain in my post as Staff Assistant to the Commander Royal Engineers (CRE) of 3 (UK) Division which was based at Bulford and then in 1999, I was offered a further two additional years in the role of Regimental Administrative Office Warrant Officer (RAOWO) with 9 Supply Regiment, Royal Logistics Corps (RLC) at Hullavington Barracks in Wiltshire.

Whilst at Hullavington, I was approached and interviewed for the post of Accounts and Office Manager with a civilian logistical planning consultancy based in Dyer Street, Cirencester and for me personally, the timing could not have been better. I was already considering my career options outside of the Armed Forces and by retiring from the British Army in 2000, it meant that I was in a position to start putting together my memoir, or so I thought.

Another reason why it took so long for me to start writing my memoir was because my new civilian career quite literally accounted for almost every single minute of every day, and genuinely left me no spare capacity of any kind to even think about starting a time-consuming project such as writing a book. In February 2013, I established a self-employed bookkeeping business and in 2016 finally had my first book published which was 'The Story of Parc Howard' albeit, this was only a short book of 84 pages yet it still took eight months to draft, edit, and have printed.

Also, in 2016 I was presenting two weekly radio programmes with Radio Tircoed near Swansea in South Wales and in 2017 I received a commission to research the British Red Cross Hospital at Parc Howard in Llanelli' as part of the National First World War at Sea Exhibition. I was also giving public talks and presentations to *local groups and historical societies on my book and other historical subjects such as 'The History of Welsh Castles' and 'The Aviator Amelia Earhart'.*

All of this was proving invaluable to me because I was learning new skills and so much so that by 2019, I was ready to start work on putting together my memoir. In September 2020, I closed my self-employed business to focus on becoming a full-time writer and author and it has been and still is, a most fulfilling and enjoyable experience.

Royal Engineers are posted as individuals and not as a regiment. The average length of a posting is between two and three years and this in part is to help develop the officer or soldier's career and progression and on 1 December 1981, I was posted to 52 Field (Construction) Squadron which was a sub-unit of 22 Engineer Regiment based at Swinton Barracks, Perham Down in Tidworth. Just seven months later on 5 July 1982, I was back in Canada but this time as a section commander with 3 Troop on Exercise Waterleap which was a four-month military engineering project at the Canadian Forces Base (CFB) Meaford, located in the beautiful province of Ontario and on the eastern edge of Lake Huron. 52 Field Squadron flew to Canada from RAF Brize Norton in a C-130 Hercules transporter plane and during our flight to Toronto International Airport, we stopped off at Keflavik in Iceland and Gander in Newfoundland for refuelling after flying over the site where *RMS Titanic* sank on 15 April 1912.

Eventually we touched down at Toronto International where it was so hot that the aircraft had to taxi along the runway with its rear ramp half-lowered, in order to allow everyone inside to cool down. 3 Troop's primary task on Exercise Waterleap was to dig and lay a three-mile-long water pipeline from the Pump House at the edge of Georgian Bay, up a steep gradient of some 200 feet in length, and then along an extensive area of open land to be connected to a redundant water pipe. All of this was at a depth of five feet.

Some of my colleagues were assigned to support the construction of a new Ablution Block, and this particular tour was without doubt one of the best I ever served on and still to this day, I look back with fond memories of those I worked with, the adventures we undertook, and the special moments we enjoyed on hot sultry evenings such as BBQs with our Canadian Army friends. The camp itself had just a couple of basic wooden billets and an old rundown fire station that had a bright red roof, and basically this was just the beginning of the preparations of a site on which a large-scale permanent Canadian Forces Base would be established over the next few years. The project also involved several civilian construction companies and local artisans with whom we became good friends.

Enjoying a packed lunch on the sun-kissed shore of Georgian Bay with members of my section still stand out in my mind as being a time I would dearly like to relive. Every day we swam in Lake Huron and often worked with wonderful subcontractors such as Mitch who operated a mechanical digger, and lived in Collingwood which was 33 kilometres from the base. Because of the extreme gradient of the hill, we eventually had to dig the trench by hand which proved exhausting given that in 1982, Canada was having one if its hottest summers on record and to its credit, 3 Troop managed to complete the task within five days.

With temperatures soaring, one day I decided to drive a Canadian Army Deuce and a Half Truck along a deserted track that nobody had driven down in years, or so it seemed, and it led me and my section to a small waterfall where we decided to take a cold shower and this soon became a regular jaunt after work.

Halfway along the old dirt track which went on for about 2 miles, we came across an abandoned wooden cabin which stood next to a small overgrown cemetery that fascinated me beyond words. It was just like walking into an old western movie set that took you back to the early 1800s, and it was all so very atmospheric. The views of Lake Huron from the main track were quite breathtaking and on weekday evenings, I would often run down to the edge of Georgian Bay and then back up the hill to camp which was always a real challenge. I emailed the Canadian Base Commander when I was writing my memoir in 2021 to ask if I could visit CFB Meaford, and his agreement was very warm and welcoming.

Hand dug trench at CFB Meaford

Everyone worked and played hard on this tour and at weekends, many of us took a taxi along Highway 26 to the small city of Owen Sound some 28 kilometres west of CFB Meaford, to meet with locals we had befriended at a wonderful venue called the Harbour Inn. Sadly, Harbour Inn no longer exists but I saw some incredible live rock bands perform there in 1982, and it was on this tour that I first heard the wonderful American rock band Billy Squier who wrote 'Lonely is the Night' and 'Everybody wants You'. I watched the Toronto band Sheriff perform their great hit 'You Remind Me' and 'When I'm With You', and it was also at the Harbour Inn that I first heard Asia's incredible song 'Heat of the Moment.'

This was my second military tour of Canada and again the scenery was just breathtaking. Canadian provinces are vast and no matter where we went, the hospitality we received was superb.

The old dirt track that connected Highway 26 to CFB Meaford was lined on one side with old telegraph poles that leaned slightly after years of being blown by strong winds, and it was the same time that British rock band Dire Straits brought out their brilliant record 'Telegraph Road'. Every time I hear this song the memories come flooding back of those joyful days in 1982.

Other places that 3 Troop visited included CFB Borden which was a large military base and the birthplace of the Royal Canadian Air Force. There was also the Labatt Brewing Company in Toronto and the world-famous Niagara Falls on the American-Canadian border, where I met and spoke with Sandy Allen who was the tallest woman in the world at that time. Standing 7 feet 7 inches tall and working as a live exhibit in the Guinness World of Records Museum, Sandy told me that being in such shows was one way she could make a living and that upset me. It was also around that time that the New Zealand rock band Split Enz released their song 'Hello Sandy Allen.'

Her incredibly deep voice sounded very masculine and I was lucky enough to have a private moment with her during which she told me that her unprecedented height, voice, and short life expectancy of approximately 45 years was all down to a pituitary gland tumour she had suffered since childhood. We had a photograph taken together but over the years it was mislaid. I really enjoyed speaking with Sandy because she was so open, honest, and friendly, and sadly she died at Shelbyville in Indiana on 13 August 2008 at the age of 53.

Niagara Falls and Maid of the Mist 1 and 2

On 2 August 1982, I watched British rock band Queen perform live at Maple Leaf Gardens which was then an ice-rink and home to Toronto's Maple Leafs Ice-Hockey Team. The building stood on the northwest corner of Church Street and Carlton Street and Queen were on their 'Hot Space' World Tour, and to my total disbelief but absolute delight, they were supported by none other than Billy Squier. The concert was as memorable as it was incredible and another highpoint of my time on Exercise Waterleap was the 14-day portage expedition I took part in, along with seven colleagues in the beautiful Algonquin Provincial Park in south-eastern Ontario.

One member of my section was also a good friend by the name of Kevin Diable who I will speak more about later in this chapter. Once home to the Canadian indigenous Mohican Native Indian, the Algonquin is Ontario's oldest provincial park and sits in 7,000 square miles of deep forest, lakes, small islands, and the portage trails are in abundance as are black bears and moose that freely roam the park. For two weeks we explored the islands and canoed many of the beautiful lakes such as Hogan, Little Crow, Big Crow, Nool, and Opeongo and throughout the entire expedition, my expedition partner was Sapper Yuille.

One day we were leisurely portaging our canoe above our heads and along a well-worn track that connected Little Crow Lake to Big Crow Lake when suddenly out of the blue, we encountered a large magnificent adult black bear sitting on its rear and blocking our path, and it clearly had no intention of moving. We were the only people on this particular trail at the time and had no support or back up of any kind, and because I was walking at the front, I was naturally the closest to the bear yet from beneath the cover of our canoe I had the most spectacular sighting of my first ever encounter with a bear in the wild, and it was an incredible experience.

Free to do whatever it wanted, we remained perfectly still and unfortunately my camera was packed inside my rucksack which was wedged under an upside-down seat. Eventually the bear decided to get back on all fours and then sniffed the air that was coming from our direction, and with that it stood on its hind legs and tossed its head from side to side, then slowly made its way back into the forest. Relieved but sad to see it disappear out of sight, we had witnessed a truly remarkable wildlife experience and could not wait to tell the others. I suspect this was the same bear that later that day tried to steal our food rations which were stored in an old milk crate suspended from a tree on a small island on Big Crow Lake.

Big Crow Lake

British soldiers can be creative when it comes to cooking out in the wild and on the penultimate day of the expedition, I decided to give our chef 'Noz' a break by offering to cook a meal for the team and it was baked spam slices, mashed potato, tinned carrots and peas, and flavoured with mint. However, there was no natural mint available which posed a problem so without telling any of my colleagues, I discreetly squeezed spearmint toothpaste into the mashed potato and then dished out the food into each mess tin and at first, everyone remarked on how delicious my meal tasted and I felt great.

Several minutes later and while we were sitting around the fire chatting away near the water's edge, one of my colleagues named Paul started to turn a peculiar colour and suddenly made a dash for the lake with his hands covering his mouth. He fell violently sick for several minutes and just then, our chef Noz did exactly the same and he was quickly followed by a third member of the expedition. While all this was happening, the rest of us looked at each with expressions of subdued puzzlement, then shrugged our shoulders and carried on eating. After breakfast the next morning, Paul who was looking delicate approached me as I was packing my canoe and in a quiet voice whispered, "sorry about yesterday Pip, but carrots and I don't get on."

I didn't have the heart to tell him what was in the mashed potato but instead, I gave him a warm empathetic smile. Our time in Algonquin was a true adventure in every sense and it could not have been spent in better company, because between us all we were a great team who had the experience of a lifetime, and so much so that a couple of weeks later Dave, Kevin, Paul, Jock and I returned for a second expedition but this time it was only for five days.

Everyone's favourite in 3 Troop was a character I mentioned earlier by the name of Kevin, or Dibs as he was affectionately known and as his section commander, he and I became very good friends. Not only was Kevin comical and superb company to be with, but he was also highly intelligent and very knowledgeable on so many subjects and it was an absolute delight having interesting discussions with him. He was naturally good at everything he turned his hand to, a true prankster and always outrageous at parties, and I have never met anyone since who laughed as much as he did.

At a BBQ one evening at CFB Meaford, Kevin passed a comment that took us by surprise when quite unexpectedly he said, "I hope I never see my 30th birthday." Naturally, everyone put this down to the fact that he was either inebriated or quite simply fooling around and we left it at that, but when I was serving again in Munsterlager having left 52 Field Squadron in 1983, I was given the heart-breaking news that he died while serving at Barton Stacey. It was said he drowned in a river near his barracks but for several months after hearing the news, I just could not accept that he lost his life at such a young age.

Alberta has and always will be my favourite Canadian province and for a number of reasons such as its breathtaking scenery, the beautiful ranches and roads that seem to go on for as far as the eye can see, the incredible sunsets over magnificent snow-capped mountains, the cowboy culture, and the indigenous people that descend from the Blackfoot, Cree, and Chipewyan nations. There are also the National Parks of Banff, Jasper, Waterton Lakes, and Elk Island, and it was while I was on Exercise Waterleap in Ontario in 1982 that 52 Field Squadron began to monitor concerning events that were taking place in the South Atlantic. Prime Minister Margaret Thatcher deployed British troops to South Georgia and a tri-service Task Force to the Falkland Islands to recapture both British Overseas Territories following an illegal Argentine invasion.

Accommodated for our final two weeks in a large Canadian RAF aircraft hangar near Toronto, we followed the news every day and 52 Field Squadron eventually returned to the United Kingdom on 2 October 1982. For the next four weeks we heard continuous talk of a possible deployment to the Falkland Islands to support the essential repair programme of a war-damaged infrastructure and, to establish a Defence Base on East Falkland Island. Back in Tidworth on 6 November 1982, 52 Field Squadron was officially put on notice to deploy to the South Atlantic on 4 January 1983, on a six-month operational tour of duty.

Up until that moment in time, I had never written or kept a diary or journal of any kind yet something was telling me that this particular tour was going to be very different from all the others, and so for this very reason I needed to record the events of each and every single day, and that is exactly what I did. Ever since the tour finished in June 1983, my handwritten journal has been safely stored away but after almost 40 years some of the writing was starting to fade.

As a published author, in 2019 I was already working on a new book but that was immediately put on hold one Sunday afternoon after deciding it was time to finally write my military memoir. Part of the reason why I decided to do this was because in the introduction which I had hand-written inside the journal cover, were the words "in future years I will look back at this journal and hope that others will also have read my story."

In 1983 and without having any knowledge of how my army career would progress, or indeed how long it would last, deep in my heart I had the burning ambition to write a memoir at some point in my life and instantly, I felt the journal would be the perfect core content around which to write my story. Everything made sound common sense but what was even more ironic, was that at the time of writing my journal in the Falklands I also decided to write my own account of the political and military events that led to the war, and also to explain how the conflict was fought and won. What follows next is a synopsis of those events.

Since 1833, Britain and Argentina had been locked in a long-standing dispute as to who had rightful sovereignty over the Falklands and although the majority of South American countries supported Argentina's claim, the fact is that the Falkland Islands were and still are a British Overseas Territory. Furthermore, the islanders themselves freely swear allegiance to Great Britain and whilst armed conflicts over sovereignty are not new, in 1914 the British Navy fired its guns in anger at a German Imperial Navy during the Battle of the Falklands.

Two years into her first term as British Prime Minister, a resolute Margaret Thatcher found herself under increasing pressure from Her Majesty's Treasury to address concerns over the escalating costs of administering the Falkland Islands, and pressure was also growing on her to consider implementing austerity measures as a means of safeguarding the British economy. One favoured suggestion was to hand over the Falklands to Argentina and after considering this initiative, a series of meetings was planned and negotiations between both countries began, but by 1981 Argentina was in crisis.

Following unprecedented economic failings and with inflation spiralling out of control, the people of Argentina were becoming increasingly angry and in addition to this, serious questions were being asked of its governing military junta over historic Human Rights abuses and violations committed against 30,000 young Argentinian males, all of whom suddenly disappeared without a trace in 1977.

Unsurprisingly, public disorder broke out across the country as people took to the streets in their tens of thousands, while anger and outrage was openly directed at the now highly unpopular dictatorial military junta led by a newly appointed President General Leopoldo Fortunato Galtieri. In March 1982, this same government approved a plan that would not only enrage Great Britain but also all NATO member countries and others from around the world, and that plan was to invade South Georgia and the Falklands Islands.

The architect of the plan was Admiral Jorge Anaya and his aim was to divert public anger away from the political and economic crisis that was now consuming Argentina, but before Galtieri authorised the invasion a group of 40 Argentine scrap metal workers illegally landed on South Georgia on 19 March 1982. In an act of open and international defiance, they took down the Union Jack and replaced it with the flag of Argentina. As the events unfolded, word reached London that the scrap workers were in fact Argentine Special Forces and back in 10 Downing Street, Prime

Minister Thatcher expressed her anger at Argentina by branding the country an 'armed aggressor.'

Thatcher's Cabinet unanimously agreed that Argentina had breached international law and as a military response, Captain Nick Barker of the Royal Navy was commanded to sail the Royal Naval ice-patrol ship *HMS Endurance* to South Georgia to reclaim the island. With the world looking on and as tensions intensified between the two countries, the War Office in London monitored the situation and late in the evening of 1 April 1982, the unexpected happened. President Galtieri issued the order to put into action an invasion of the Falkland Islands by launching Operation Rosario.

As Argentina's amphibious task force landed close to Stanley Airport on 2 April 1982, its troops were met by an unprepared Falklands' Defence Force commanded by Major Mike Norman of the Royal Marines. Sir Rex Masterman Hunt, Governor of the Falkland Islands knew that there was nothing he or Major Norman could do to repel the invading troops and despite putting up courageous resistance, Port Stanley was eventually overrun by Argentine soldiers and a surrender of the islands was reluctantly agreed at Government House.

Britain reacted to the events taking place on South Georgia by deploying two nuclear submarines namely *HMS Spartan* and *HMS Splendid*. Both were armed with long-range Tomahawk Cruise missiles and manned by a crew of 116 submariners. An exchange of electronic messages between London and Government House confirmed that the invasion had taken place and the United Nations (UN) imposed crippling sanctions and embargoes on Argentina, with immediate effect. For Prime Minister Thatcher, in her mind she had only one option and that was to seek approval from her Cabinet to strike back at Argentina and on 3 April 1982, the British parliament unanimously approved her plan.

On 6 April, a British War Cabinet was established to act as Joint Service Control Centre (JSCC) of Operations from which the recapture of the Falkland Islands would be directed.

The Falklands War lasted 74 days and it was fought in freezing cold temperatures and extremely hostile conditions, while out at sea and in the air battles raged and images captured by war correspondents were flashed across the world. At an emergency meeting on 3 April, Sir Anthony Parsons the British Ambassador to the UN secured a resolution that demanded the immediate withdrawal of Argentine troops from the Falklands. European and commonwealth leaders offered joint support and condemned Argentina's action as being a breach of international peace.

Because 8,050 miles separated Great Britain from the Falkland Islands, some allied countries and several politicians at Westminster considered Thatcher's plan to be doomed to fail. The military, logistical, and technical resources needed to support such a large military operation deep in the South Atlantic presented enormous challenges to the Commanders in Chief of all three Armed Services however, comprising of a fleet of 120 ships and 9,000 soldiers, sailors, and airmen, a British Task Force was finally deployed to the Falklands. Operation Parquet meanwhile was brought to a successful conclusion when South Georgia was recaptured on 25 April 1982.

21 May 1982 saw the first British troops land at Ajax Bay and Port San Carlos, together with members of the Parachute Regiment, and with it were members from 3 Commando Brigade. Over the next few days the Battle of San Carlos was fought and a nearby grassed plain famously became known as 'Bomb Alley.' Argentine air strikes targeted the British naval ships *HMS Antrim*, *Argonaut*, *Ardent*, *Brilliant*, and *Broadsword* and also, members of the British Royal Marines and Parachute Regiment started their legendary 56 mile Yomp across East Island to Port Stanley, which took three days to complete. The photograph of a Royal Marine flying the Union Jack from his radio aerial while acting as 'tail-end Charlie' is still considered one of the most famous images from the war. Out at sea six British naval ships were lost:

- *HMS Sheffield* – attacked May 4
- *HMS Ardent* – attacked May 21
- *HMS Antelope* – attacked May 23
- *HMS Coventry* – attacked May 25
- SS *Atlantic Conveyor* – attacked May 25
- Sir *Galahad* – attacked June 8

Of the Argentine losses, the most significant was the sinking of the naval light cruiser *General Belgrano* by the British nuclear submarine *HMS Conqueror* on 2 May 1982. Some 324 crew were lost at sea while 700 were rescued however, controversy ensued when Argentina claimed that two international violations had taken place.

Firstly, it was claimed *General Belgrano* was returning to Argentina at the time of attack and as such, was no longer an enemy threat and secondly it was alleged that *Belgrano* was attacked outside the 200-mile Maritime Exclusion Zone (MEZ). In its defence, Britain justifiably contested that Argentina had been forewarned that the MEZ was no longer deemed an acceptable boundary for military action. On land the key battles that were fought included:

- Battle of Goose Green (during which Lt Col H Jones VC was killed.)
- Battle of Two Sisters.
- Battle of Mount Longdon.
- Battle of Mount Harriet.
- Battle of Mount Tumbledown.

On 14 June 1982, the Falklands War ended when General Mario Menendez surrendered to General Sir Jeremy Moore, Commander British Land Forces. Argentine troops were rounded up, disarmed, and the Falkland Islands were once again under British protection.

Some three months later and back at Swinton Barracks in Tidworth, 52 Field (Construction) Squadron began its preparation for our six-month tour and this involved taking refresher courses on combat and military engineering skills, servicing engineering equipment that would be deployed with the squadron, loading equipment into containers, carrying out personnel documentation checks such as verifying Next of Kin details, and undergoing dental and medical inspections.

Everyone attended briefings and presentations on what to expect during our forthcoming operational tour, and checks were also made on personal weapons, NBC respirators and protective clothing, renewing old or damaged military equipment, and boxing all personal possessions that would be put into storage during our absence.

I spent Christmas 1982 with my parents back in Llanelli and on Tuesday 28 December, I drove to Tidworth to rejoin 52 Squadron ahead of its deployment on 4 January 1983. For any military personnel deploying to a theatre of war or conflict so soon after the fighting has ended, the experience and emotions can vary considerably because in reality you do not truly know what lies ahead of you. My colleagues and I genuinely could not wait to deploy and my final few days were spent working-out in the gymnasium, stocking up on free blue-coloured Forces Air letters otherwise known as 'blueys,' making final phone calls to my parents and friends, and packing away last-minute personal belongings.

Eventually and with everyone ready to deploy, it was now a case of waiting to board the coaches that would take us to RAF Brize Norton in Oxfordshire. The first couple of paragraphs that I wrote in my journal were penned on the inside cover and served as an introduction, and this was followed by my personal details and the first day's entry, and this is all transcribed below.

What I have not included however, are the names of my colleagues from 3 Troop or the management, as I have not been able to make contact with any to ask for their permission to have known names published. There are simply far too many legal hurdles involved such as obtaining contact details from the Ministry of Defence because of understandable security reasons, not knowing if my colleagues are still alive, the formal process of corresponding with each to seek written permission, and so much more.

The golden rule with publishing names is either to replace a known name with a fabricated name, or simply not to use either. As a historian who has no desire to distort facts by making up or replacing a name, I have decided that where a former colleague or person is known to have passed away, then I have used their known name as a mark of respect. Where I do not know if a colleague is alive then I have used either their forename or surname only, but not both. In some instances I have simply referred to them as 'colleague.'

Introduction

We all at some stage in our lives experience happenings and events that mean a lot, not only to ourselves but also to those who are forever close to us, be it in presence or in thought. To tell our story accurately and as events actually happened, this can present us with a problem because we do not always remember each and every single detail and from time to time, some occurrences and facts will elude us. Nevertheless, our accounts should always be as close to the truth as is possible, and our stories told as candidly as we can, and always with sincerity.

Before the start of my six-month operational tour of the Falkland Islands, I have decided to record the events of each and every day as they take place, and without exception. It is to be a project and a work of literature that will prove invaluable to me in the years to come, both from a historical and personal perspective, and hopefully for others whether it be just for recollection of times spent together as a troop, and as comrades in arms. Also, I hope it will provide a clear understanding of the reasons why the Falklands War came about to those who are too young to remember the conflict, and to explain how it was concluded. More importantly, we should never forget the true human cost of conflict and what happens after a war has been fought.

Already, I feel fully totally committed to seeing my project through to the end because no-one can foretell what the future holds or what will happen. Unexpected events can arise at any time, and extraordinary moments may occur without warning, and even humour can bring about a fascinating story. I suppose it is all part of life and the lives we in the military lead. In future years I will look back on my journal and hope that others will have read my story.

Hopefully some will have learned from what I have written, and so it is for you the reader that I have decided to take upon my shoulders the task of writing this account of my six-month operational tour in the Falkland Islands, just five months after the war ended on 14 June 1982. And it is for you also, that I will persevere to record accurately every day, the events as they truly happen.

L/Cpl Thomas 24423809 (Zap No: 766), 3 Troop, 37 (FI) Engr Regt, BFPO 666

Tuesday, 4 January 1983

At 03.00 precisely, the silence inside 52 Field (Construction) Squadron's single soldier accommodation block at Swinton Barracks in Tidworth was shattered by members of the regimental guard, knocking loudly on every door and shouting down the corridors that breakfast would be served in the cookhouse in one hour. My roommates David and Kevin will both be deploying to the Falkland Islands however, Ishmael sadly has been assigned to work with the Rear Party which he is not very happy about being a bachelor, and understandably wants to be with his fellow colleagues.

Everyone quickly showered, shaved, and then headed to the cookhouse for breakfast after which we reported to 3 Troop Office. Last minute phone calls to families and friends all took place last night and just a few hours earlier, I was speaking with my parents from inside the red phone box at the far side of the Regimental Parade Ground at 23.00. As I inserted my last coin, I quickly bid them both an emotional farewell. The time to deploy on our six-month operational tour to the war-torn Falkland Islands had finally arrived, and I was eager to get going.

No sooner had I collected my personal luggage from the Quartermaster's Department, word reached 3 Troop that three 52-seater coaches from the Royal Corps of Transport were parked outside our accommodation block, and close to the Regimental Guardroom. As we boarded the lead coach, the civilian bus driver shook each of us by the hand and wished us good luck on the tour and as dawn began to break, the convoy slowly made its way out of Swinton Barracks.

At long last, 52 Field (Construction) Squadron was on the road to RAF Brize Norton in Oxfordshire, just 90 minutes' drive away. Some of my colleagues tried to catch up on lost sleep while others stared out through their window in total silence and soon we arrived at the main gate to Brize Norton, and as we drove into the airbase I could see two rows of grey RAF C-130 Hercules transporter planes neatly lined up while at the very far end, was a British Caledonian McDonnell-Douglas DC10 which would be our plane for the flight to Ascension Island in the South Atlantic Ocean.

After collecting our air tickets we reported to the departure lounge where we were briefed by a RAF sergeant and informed that the flight to Ascension Island would take approximately nine hours, and en route we would be stopping off at Banjul International Airport in Gambia, West Africa for one hour to refuel. Although a civilian aircraft, we were informed that the Gambian government considered our flight to be a 'foreign military operation' and as such, we would need to disembark on arrival and remain at the side of the runway while under the protection of an armed Gambian military escort.

Upon boarding the aircraft we were warmly greeted by the cabin crew and after settling into our seats and fastening our seatbelts, we were given a pre-flight safety briefing and during the flight south to Banjul, we were served a meal and hot and cold drinks, and also a snack from time to time. For those who managed to stay awake, we watched a movie called 'The Gods Must Be Crazy' which was quite bizarre, while others read books and magazines to pass away the time.

Six hours after departing RAF Brize Norton, we touched down at Banjul International Airport and taxied to the far south-eastern end of the runway where the aircraft was turned through a full 360°. There, the engines were shut down and we awaited the arrival of the refuelling tanker and as forewarned, we were asked to disembark the aircraft and stand at the side of the runway.

We were surrounded by approximately 30 armed Gambian soldiers and a young officer who to our astonishment appeared unprofessional and somewhat confused. The time was 16.45 and for many of us the sun was getting so hot that we had no option but to take shelter under the aircraft's wings, while others ventured across to the other side of the runway to take photographs of tall terracotta coloured termite hills. Some even tried to take photographs of the distant white painted air-terminal which was about half a mile away, but they were immediately ordered to put their cameras away by members of the armed guard.

After 45 minutes had passed, two Gambian army trucks approached our location at speed and in doing so, kicked clouds of orange coloured dust up into the air. They parked close to the aircraft and the armed soldiers boarded the vehicles while the young officer radioed for permission for us to board. With permission granted, we began to climb the steps but just then the two military trucks drove off with the soldiers in the back waving their rifles excitedly in the air, as if to wish us luck. It was a surreal moment and not long after that, the DC10 was back in the air and heading south on the final leg of our journey to Ascension Island. Approximately one hour later we were toasting Father Neptune to celebrate crossing the equator.

Three hours later we touched down at Wideawake Airfield on Ascension Island and after thanking the crew, everyone disembarked the aircraft and was escorted by RAF personnel across the runway and towards a large green military hangar, from where we were air-lifted across to the cruise liner *Cunard Countess* by RAF Wessex helicopters. The ship looked incredibly sleek and graceful as she sat berthed at the end of a jetty, and once on board we were shown to the Galaxy Lounge to await the arrival of the rest of 52 Field Squadron. It was while I was sitting inside the lounge that I caught up with a former colleague from 26 Armoured Engineer Squadron in Munsterlager.

Mick and I chatted for ages and arranged to meet up again during the voyage south. We shook hands and I was shown to cabin 3096 on Deck 3 along with Paul who would be my cabin mate.

Banjul International Airport

Afternote

*S*tanding alongside the plane at Banjul International Airport while dressed in my army clothing and under the heat of a high sun, reminded me of the 1978 film 'The Wild Geese' starring Richard Burton, Roger Moore, and Richard Harris. The movie tells the story of a group of British mercenaries hired by a retired British army colonel to rescue the imprisoned president of a South African country by the name of Julius Limbani. Their training takes place in Swaziland and the mission is fraught with danger, as the heavily armed and totally outnumbered merceraries venture deep into the African bush. Eventually they manage to rescue Limbani after carrying out a daring raid on the heavily guarded prison and in the ensuing chase to rejoin their aircraft, the mercenaries are drawn into a long and deadly fire fight and as the depleted team desperately attempt to board the taxiing aircraft which is piloted by Roger Moore, Richard Harris is shot while carrying a wounded Julius Limbani. Fierce fighting continues along the runway and eventually the mercenaries and Limbani make their escape. Standing on the runway at Banjul International Aiport felt just like being on the film set of 'The Wild Geese', and I enjoyed every single second.

Operational tours can differ significantly both in purpose and duration and within just five years of serving with the British Army, I was already serving on my third. By being posted to the former West Germany in February 1978, I was directly at the heart of the Cold War whereas serving in Northern Ireland, my role was to support the Royal Ulster Constabulary in their policing of The Troubles. But by being in the Falkland Islands so soon after the war had ended was a completely different operation, because our purpose was to support the recovery of the island's infrastructure, such as repairing the runway at Port Stanley Airport and establishing a Defence Base at Kelly's Garden.

Chapter Three
The Voyage South

Foreword

I have never really found my sea legs despite having sailed on a school cruise to Madeira, Tenerife, Lisbon, and Gibraltar on board the SS Nevasa in 1967 and it was quite ironic that in 1982, her sistership SS Uganda was requisitioned and served during the Falklands War as a hospital ship for the British Task Force. Designated the radio call-sign 'Mother Hen' the SS Uganada steamed south to the Falklands and in November 1982, she was used as a supply ship for a further two years. Both Nevasa and Uganda were first ownd by the British-India Steam Navigation Company which was taken over by P&O in 1972, but they were always easy to recognise because of their distinctive black funnel with double white stripes at the top. The most distinguishing feature however was that SS Nevasa had a rounded funnel whereas the SS Uganda's was flat. The first chart I drew in my journal was the route that 52 Field Squadron followed both by air and sea during our journey south, which took 12 days during the period 4 to 15 January 1983.

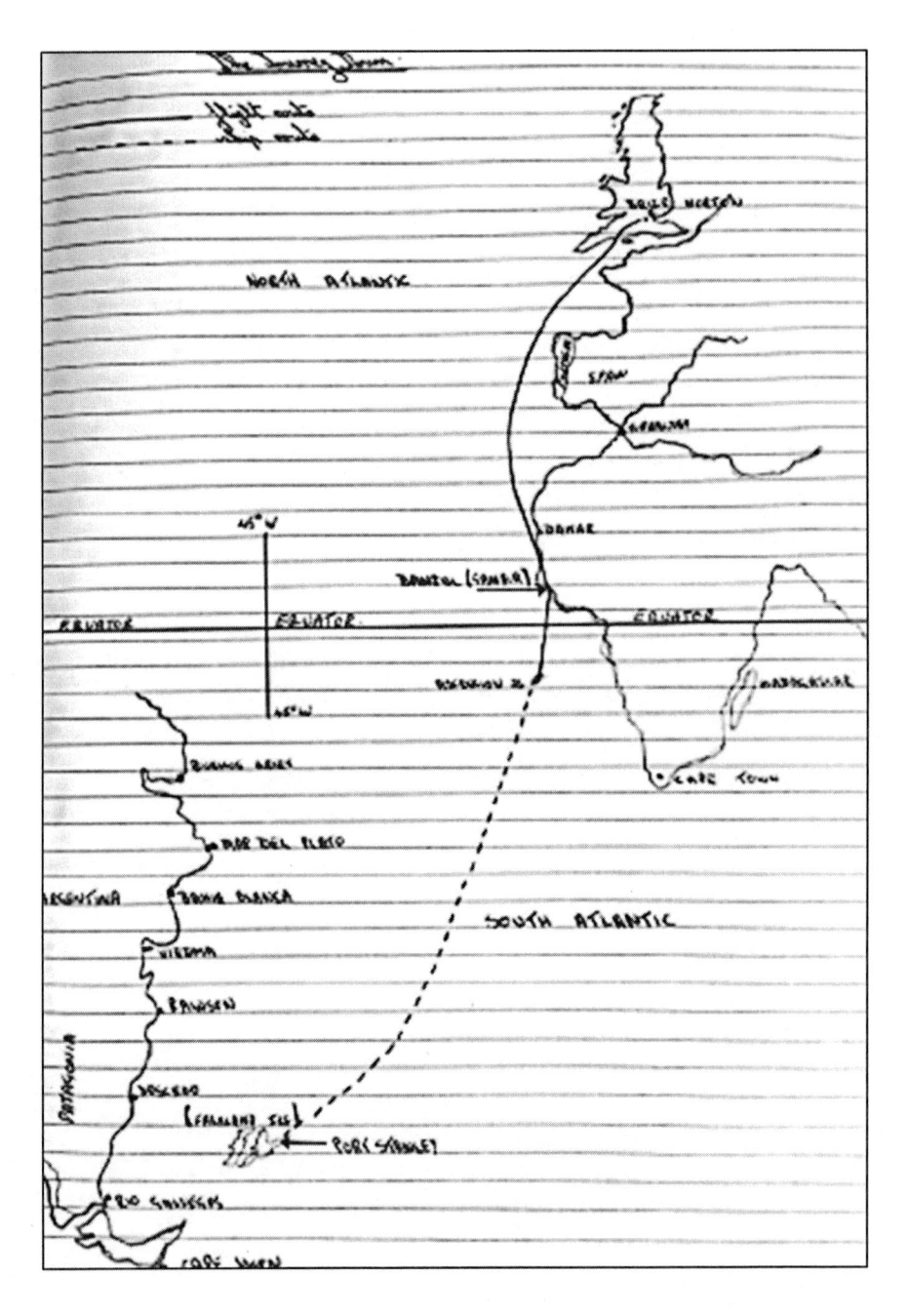

The route I drew in my journal

Wednesday, 5 January 1983

Rising at 07.00, I quickly showered and dressed then proceeded to make my way to the main restaurant where I joined colleagues from 3 Troop for breakfast and at 08.30 precisely, the whole of 52 Field Squadron and all other troops on board *Cunard Countess* reported to the Galaxy Lounge for a presentation by a senior officer from the ship's crew. We were given clear instructions on the daily routine while at sea and also, what actions needed to be taken on hearing alarms such as fire and general emergency, and blasts of each were sounded so that everyone knew them inside out.

Finally we were shown around the ship in small groups and briefed on the various types of lifeboats, how to correctly fit a lifejacket, how to use the fire extinguishers, and where our nearest Muster Station was located. The briefing finished at 09.15 and up on the sundeck the air temperature was already hitting 32°C. Thankfully, 3 Troop was among the first to be allowed to collect their personal luggage from the security store which was located on Deck 4 and after unpacking and putting away my belongings, I headed for the top sundeck to take photographs of Ascension Island for my journal, and also of the South Atlantic Ocean.

Ascension Island and Green Mountain

Ascension is a volcanic subtropical island that sits 8° south of the equator and is almost in the middle of the South Atlantic, halfway between Natal on the east coast of Brazil in South America, and Luanda the capital of Angola on the west coast of Southern Africa. The island has a fascinating geographical feature called Green

Mountain which is the highest peak at 859 metres, and just 226 metres lower than the summit of Mount Snowdon in North Wales. Green Mountain is covered by a cloud and the forest and certain types of crops and plants that grow on its slopes are not indigenous to the island but instead, were introduced from other countries. There are several levels of differing types of vegetation and the island is truly fascinating.

In 1836, Ascension Island was visited by the famous Shrewsbury born biologist and naturalist Charles Darwin during his five-year exploration of the 'New Worlds' whilst on board *HMS Beagle*.

The island's capital is Georgetown and named after King George III who was married to Queen Charlotte and said to have suffered from a madness caused by porphyria, a hereditary disorder. The landmass forms part of the British Overseas Territory of St Helena, Ascension, and Tristan da Cunha. For most of the day this beautiful island sits majestically beneath a low motionless cloud that nearly always covers the summit of Green Mountain, and as I gazed across at the breathtaking scene before me, I was joined by several of my colleagues on the sundeck and together we soaked up the sun, sipped on ice-cold juices, and chatted about our forthcoming six months in the Falklands. Meanwhile, others either slept or were taking photographs and the time now was 11.15 and the air temperature hitting 38°C.

Afternoon siestas and sunbathing sessions were frequently interrupted by the loud roar of RAF C-130 Hercules and Vickers VC10 transporter planes flying in and out of Wideawake Airfield, and as we watched the activity that was taking place, it suddenly made us realise that at long last we really were part of this large-scale military operation. That feeling instantly excited and inspired me beyond words as I continued to follow the arrival and departure of the British military aircraft, through a pair of binoculars which I had borrowed from a member of the ship's crew.

Helicopters continued to airlift newly arrived troops to the stern of *Cunard Countess* where the helipad was located while along the starboard side of the ship, soldiers looked down to watch the abundance of marine life that was swimming alongside, such as hammerhead sharks that glided gracefully through the clear azure-coloured water close to the ship's stabiliser. From time to time, we watched as large shoals of black triggerfish frenzied and devoured food and fruit that was thrown overboard by the crew for us to watch these fish in action, and for me they were as fascinating as the scavenger piranha.

Cunard Countess at sea

It was now 17.30 and soon *Cunard Countess* would begin its voyage to Port Stanley some 3,348 miles south-west of our location and at 18.00 precisely, the famous red and black funnel burst into life and with it a long deep blast was sounded from an air horn which took many on board by surprise. It was then that a voice was heard over the tannoy system announcing that the ship was ready to set sail. Inside the Kensington Restaurant, I rushed my evening meal and headed back to the sundeck to join my colleagues and as we stood there in silence, we gazed in wonderment as the tropical island gradually grew smaller and smaller as *Cunard Countess* gathered speed.

After an hour at sea and with the daylight beginning to fade, some of my friends went below but I decided to stay on deck with Paul and Kevin, and together we stood totally captivated by the magnificence and stillness of the South Atlantic Ocean. By now Ascension Island was just a small blot on the horizon and then suddenly, it was completely out of sight. I was spellbound and yet there was another sensation I felt, and that was the ever-decreasing air temperature of the South Atlantic sea-air.

Ahead of us are 10 days at sea and already my parents and friends seem so very far away and although I miss them all, I felt very excited about the six months I am going to spend on operational duty in the Falkland Islands. It is still hard to comprehend that just five months ago, a bloody and bitter war was being concluded while I and my colleagues were serving on a sun-baked military operation in Canada, and under such very different conditions. My parents will never know this but at that very moment in time, I sent them a prayer.

Thursday, 6 to Friday, 14 January 1983

Cunard Countess is a magnificent cruise liner that is 537 feet in length. Her gross registered tonnage (GRT) is just short of 18,000 and the ship has 7 passenger decks, 3 sun terraces, a shopping gallery, wellness centre, an outdoor heated swimming pool, 2 restaurants, a luxurious lounge, and a theatre. Built in Denmark in 1976 and fully air-conditioned, she made her way south with ease and at an average speed of 13 nautical knots.

As a qualified Physical Training Instructor I was tasked with organising and supervising 3 Troop's fitness programme throughout the voyage while others supervised military skill sessions such as minefield clearance, weapon handling, First-Aid, combat engineering skills, aircraft recognition, radio communications, NBC, and more. At 08.30 each day our new troop commander carried out a cabin inspection and at 11.00, a ship's nominated officer would conduct a further inspection because the ship had been requisitioned by the Ministry of Defence to serve as a troop carrier specifically for the Falkland Islands.

A calm South Atlantic

During the voyage south, 52 Field Squadron organised and presented a Cabaret Evening in the Holyrood Show Lounge for all troops on board, and the guest of honour was the ship's captain. The show was compered by two sergeants and an amusing character called 'Exocet Benny,' who was named after the French anti-ship Exocet missile. Various popular songs were sung and several comical sketches performed such as 'Shakespeare's Unknown Masterpiece,' 'A Day in the Life of Air-Trooper Hooper', and a hilarious skit that was presented by 3 Troop based on a Mr Universe Contest which my cabin mate Paul won, even though the obvious winner should have been a fellow lance corporal who was an actual body builder. To bring the show to an end, one of the sergeants sang 'Yesterday' by the Beatles while the other performed an emotional version of Harvey Andrew's song 'Soldier.'

Throughout the voyage we encountered good sea conditions despite the famous reputation of the South Atlantic and its treacherous easterly winds called the 'Roaring Forties,' and I met up again with Mick and another former colleague from 26 Armoured Engineer Squadron by the name of Sapper Baker. I also met up with a lieutenant from 2nd Squadron Royal Corps of Transport with whom I served in West Belfast in 1978, and on the penultimate morning of our sea-journey I went along with five colleagues on a guided tour of the ship's bridge. As we listened to the ship's captain explain how the navigation, radar, and steering systems worked, he told us that we were exactly 239 miles north of Port Stanley and that our expected time of arrival was 06.00 the next morning.

Saturday, 15 January and Sunday, 16 January 1983

Waking up at 05.00 on Saturday 15 January, Paul and I quickly prepared our cabin for the final inspection before going up on deck to see the Falkland Islands for the very first time, and when we got there we were not alone. A strong icy sea-breeze was blowing hard as more colleagues from 52 Field Squadron joined us while at the same time, coming astern of *Cunard Countess* was the British Naval Replenishment Auxiliary ship *Port Grange* as she prepared to come alongside our starboard.

Once she had completed this manoeuvre, both ships sailed in tandem while maintaining the same speed, and they kept their course for some 45 minutes. This was something none of us had ever witnessed before and the skill involved and the way in which the exercise was executed impressed everyone, and during one particular phase a refuelling pipe was winched across from *Port Grange* as waves crashed between the two ships.

Port Grange coming alongside *Cunard Countess*

Some minutes later, a RAF Sea King helicopter slowly approached our stern and hovered as two passengers were carefully lowered onto the *Cunard Countess* after which, the aircraft headed back to Port Stanley. With daylight becoming increasingly brighter, Paul and I returned to our cabin for the inspection and then headed to the Galaxy Lounge where we sat with others to listen to Major General Sir David Thorne, Commander British Forces Falkland Islands who was giving a welcoming presentation.

As soon as he started to talk he made an instant impression on everyone and his first words were, "You troops must be ready to fight again, should Argentina ever decide upon another foolish attempt to invade the Falkland Islands." The way in which he delivered his words was truly inspiring and everyone inside the room felt proud to be a part of this military operation.

RAF Sea King approaching *Cunard Countess*

When we eventually sailed into Port Stanley Harbour, the capital of the Falkland Islands was not as big as I had expected and indeed, it reminded me of a town you would expect to find on a Scottish island such as Shetland, and whilst looking across to the far right of the harbour I could make out *Sir Tristram* which was attacked by Argentine Skyhawks during the war. I could also see Government House and Christ Church Cathedral, and the houses that lined Ross Road and the quay to the right of East Jetty. Everything looked typically British while to my left and out in the distant waters of Whalebone Cove, I saw the blue and red floating accommodation block which is called Coastel.

Not far from her was the ghostly wreck of a three-masted trading ship which I know is the *Lady Elizabeth*, a rusting relic from the past and one that I have always wanted to see because of its historical interest. Already I feel very much at home, but I do sense that some of my colleagues are somewhat surprised by what they have seen since we arrived. Berthed out in the harbour and not too far from our location is the former Sealink car ferry *St Edmund* and close to her, is the roll-on/roll-off ferry *TEV Rangatira*.

Despite the Ministry of Defence's original plan to use her as a hospital ship, the *Rangatira* is now used as accommodation and if my bearings are correct, approximately one kilometre beyond the Coastel should be the north-west end of

Stanley Airport runway. This was purposely damaged during a series of seven long-range sorties involving British RAF Vulcan Bombers during the war called Operation Black Buck, and their mission was to directly hit the runway and surrounding installations to deny the Argentinian fighter aircraft use of the facility. Operation Black Buck was both daring and highly dangerous, and the courage shown by the pilots crossed new boundaries.

Not long after *Cunard Countess* dropped anchor, 52 Field Squadron was ferried across to the *St Edmund* by Royal Navy Kiwi landing craft and once on board, we made our way along the lower car deck and shown to an area where we would set up our camp beds for the night. Our staff sergeant informed us that cabins would be allocated the next morning but for now, the rest of the day was ours to do with as we please. Around 18.00, I went ashore and for the first time in 11 days I was back on dry land and as I walked the streets of Port Stanley, I could see for myself some of the aftermath from the war. I hardly met any locals but to my pleasant surprise, I bumped once again into Sapper Baker who I had met a few days ago on *Cunard Countess* and we chatted about our time with 26 Armoured Engineer Squadron.

After I finished my walk I headed along Ross Road and towards Christ Church Cathedral but it was now getting late and around 21.45, I made my way back to East Jetty where I boarded another Kiwi landing craft that took me across to *St Edmund*. While standing on deck before retiring for the night, I looked out across Port Stanley Harbour one more time and thought about the recent war with Argentina. Prime Minister Thatcher had no option but to recapture this British Overseas Territory and of that, there can be no doubt whatsoever and her response was as justified as it was admirable, because it cost and humiliated Argentina and President Galtieri far more than they had expected.

Tragically as with any war, hundreds of lives were needlessly lost on both sides but there was only one country that carried the blame, and that was Argentina. Thatcher had the full backing of parliament and the British people, as well as every NATO member country and indeed the United Nations and the British Commonwealth. I looked across one more time at the street lights along Ross Road and the night sky above, and there was an eerie silence all around but it was all so very beautiful and magical.

Farewell *Countess Cunard*

My plan tomorrow is to visit *Sir Tristram*, Christ Church Cathedral, Government House, and the site where captured and deserted Argentine artillery and military equipment are stockpiled on the high ground close to the meteorological station but right now, my mind is focussed on Galtieri's inexcusable actions last year. Surely he must have known that the invasion of South Georgia and the Falklands would end in failure, and I find it hard to understand why some people believe they have the right to threaten, persecute, and invade another country or territory without a care or concern for the people, or their express wish to live in peace.

All too often it is done to demonstrate geopolitical and military might and to enforce economic hardship and dominance upon the innocent and vulnerable. Such leaders are enemies of democracy and freedom, and rarely do they play by the rules and that is why sometimes, it is justified and necessary to fight fire with fire and show that such illegal action is unacceptable and will not be tolerated. Sadly however, history shows that there will always be cruel and mindless dictators for as long as mankind exists.

East Jetty, Port Stanley Harbour

On Sunday, 16 January I was allocated cabin 140 along with my fellow lance corporal who is the body builder and although it is tiny in comparison with the cabin I occupied on *Cunard Countess* with Paul, it is comfortable and has an ensuite shower and toilet. Up on deck a pleasant easterly breeze gently blew across Port Stanley Harbour which shows that this really is the beginning of another summer here in the southern hemisphere, and I went ashore again after lunch but this time with several colleagues from 3 Troop. We arrived at East Jetty in a Royal Naval Kiwi landing craft around 14.30 and after stepping ashore at the bottom of Philomel Street, we headed for the General Store.

After buying something to eat and drink we made our way along Fitzroy Street and to the junction of Villiers Street, and it was from here that we could see both Government House and Christ Church Cathedral. The latter has an arch that is made out of two sets of Blue Whale jawbones and stands directly over the footpath that leads to the main road, but what I wanted to see more than anything was *Sir Tristram*, to take photographs for my journal and to pay my respect to those who lost their lives. On seeing her at close hand, I was genuinely astonished at how anyone could have survived such an attack.

Our walk back to East Jetty followed the exact same route that British troops marched into Port Stanley following the Argentine surrender which was handed over by General Menendez just six months earlier. Above Port Stanley Harbour, military helicopters filled the skies and as I took more photographs, I began to wonder if life will ever be the same again for the islanders.

To the west I could see two prominent geographical features namely Twin Sisters and Sapper Hill and as I looked at their distant beauty, the realisation finally sunk in that I was at long last in the Falkland Islands and for the next six months, this would be my home. I walked with colleagues back to East Jetty and met two other members from 3 Troop and together, we ventured up to the meteorological station that overlooks Port Stanley and to the site where the deserted and captured artillery and relics from the war were kept. As we approached the compound, I was surprised at the quantity and different types of Argentine equipment that was there because all around us, was literally pile upon pile of clothing and personal equipment, ammunition stock, items of artillery and destroyed Pucara aircraft, helmets, and so much more. For over an hour we roamed freely around the site and took as many photographs as we could.

Sir Tristram

Ross Road and Christ Church Cathedral

Back on board *St Edmund* my colleagues were either sleeping or watching a movie, while some had gone on a fishing trip that was organised by members of the ship's crew. I returned to my cabin and started to log today's events in my journal as I listened to pieces of classical music by Grieg, Vivaldi, and Handel on my cassette player. Writing while listening to such music is something I have always found enjoyable and comforting and around 20.00, my troop commander visited my cabin to show me a map which I quickly copied into my journal.

At 21.30, 3 Troop paraded on the car deck to be given a SITREP (Situation Report) and we were notified that many members of 52 Field Squadron would be attached to 8 Field Squadron, while we in 3 Troop would deploy to a remote location on the far western side of East Falkland Island called Kelly's Garden. This is near San Carlos Settlement on the southern edge of Bonners Bay, and our role would be to support 51 Field Squadron in constructing a brand-new Defence Base. San Carlos Settlement is a very small and remote community so I cannot wait to see it for myself, and as if willing it all to happen as quickly as possible, at 22.00 I was informed that I would fly out to Kelly's Garden tomorrow morning as part of 3 Troop Advance Party.

Elated and excited, I spent the remainder of my evening writing up today's entry in the journal after which I packed up my personal belongings, and then had a shower before setting my alarm for 05.30.

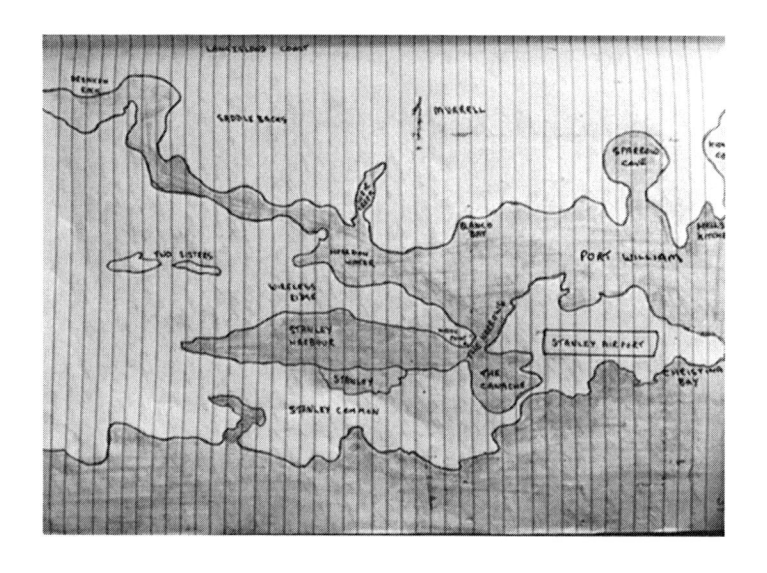

The map I copied of Port Stanley

Monday, 17 January 1983

The time is 20.35 and it is a most perfect evening as I sit here alone on the southern edge of Bonners Bay, on a large boulder while gazing across the calm blue water to the tiny community that is San Carlos Settlement, some 800 metres to the north. I arrived in Kelly's Garden about four hours ago courtesy of a RAF Sea King helicopter along with five colleagues from 3 Troop, and already I feel as if I truly belong here. San Carlos Water is out in the distance and just west of San Carlos Settlement, I am told a British Union Jack flies at the entrance to Blue Beach Military Cemetery, the tranquil and final resting place of 14 British officers and soldiers who lost their lives during the Falklands War.

Unfortunately from where I am sitting, I cannot see the flag but I am also told that each grave within the cemetery is marked by a simple white wooden cross, and among them is the grave of Lieutenant Colonel H Jones VC who commanded the 2nd Battalion Parachute Regiment and was killed in action at the Battle of Goose Green. My plan is to visit Blue Beach Cemetery at the earliest opportunity because I want to pay my respect to all who lay there, and because I have studied in quite some detail the events that took place during that battle.

Some 250 yards behind me is the Defence Base at Kelly's Garden and I can think of no better place to write today's events in my journal, especially as the early evening sun is shining down on the gentle waves that sleepily lap the craggy shore. There is no sand to be seen anywhere, just small stones and a narrow footpath that skirts the edge of this beautiful secluded bay and leads to San Carlos Settlement. The peace and quiet here is unlike anything I have experienced before and I feel as if I am in heaven, and so grateful to be where I am right now.

Earlier today at around 08.00, I was ferried across from *St Edmund* to East Jetty while weighed down under my backpack, personal weapon, and a small number of items of engineering equipment. Sapper Williams kindly drove me and five colleagues to the same compound that I visited yesterday near the meteorological centre but this time, we had to keep an eye on the time. After disembarking the Bedford 4 Ton truck, I took more photographs of deserted Argentinean field cannons and rusting captured military equipment, and according to my map we were close to a large minefield.

I decided to venture a little further afield and came across the carcass of what was once a young horse which, I presume had been killed by an anti-personnel mine and quickly realised that I had walked into an unmarked section of the minefield. Slowly turning around and carefully re-tracing my steps back to the small track, I was once again on safe ground and around 13.30 we all headed for 60 Field Squadron's location from where we were to be airlifted by the RAF to Kelly's Garden. We reached the helipad around 14.45 and met up with the rest of the Advance Party who were sitting down on the grass, while enjoying their lunch and chatting away.

Argentine field cannon

At around 15.30, the unmistakable sound of a RAF Sea King helicopter was heard approaching our location from across Port Stanley Harbour and it was soon hovering directly above us, and with its rotor blades created one almighty downdraft. We covered our faces as the aircraft began its descent and as soon as the pilot shut down the engine, the side door was opened by a sergeant loadmaster who gave us the thumbs-up to approach and pointed to the door by which we were to board the aircraft on the port side. I was directed to the rear window seat and as soon as we were strapped in, we were quickly briefed on how long the flight would take, the route, altitude, and direction of approach into Kelly's Garden.

The pilot then fired the Rolls-Royce engine into life and as the power increased the aircraft began to gently rock from side to side however, there was a problem. After two failed attempts at take-off it was clear the aircraft was too heavily laden and so after helping the loadmaster offloaded several heavy boxes of stores, the aircraft was again ready for take-off and this time it climbed effortlessly to about 40 feet, then turned through a full 360° and headed north-west as it slowly climbed to an altitude of around 100 feet.

Dropping the nose of the Sea King to gain forward acceleration, the pilot opened the throttle and en route across East Falkland Island he put the aircraft through a series of manoeuvres, one of which one was a tactical approach and exit that involved putting the aircraft into a steep turn, and also a low-level manoeuvre where the tip of the rotor blades was just metres from the ground. This was white-knuckle flying yet totally thrilling and exhilarating and eventually we landed at Kelly's Garden at around 16.20, after circling the Defence Base twice to take photographs. Safe on the ground, we disembarked the Sea King and gave a thumbs-up to the pilot who waved back and headed south-east to Port Stanley.

The Sea King preparing to leave Kelly's Garden

Waiting our arrival at the temporary helicopter landing site was a staff sergeant from 51 Field Squadron who gave us a warm welcome and as he escorted us to our portakabin, he gave a SITREP on the progress being made at Kelly's Garden, the facilities that were operational, and a quick brief on the tasks he wanted us to undertake the next day. He then said that the only house rule we needed to know was "whatever you do, just keep it under control." That sounded more than reasonable and it made us even more grateful that we had been assigned as 3 Troop Advance Party, because we now understood the type of the work we would be undertaking together with timeframes, and the different types of equipment we would be operating.

More importantly, we were assured that we would be allowed to get on with our work unhindered. As a work in progress, there is much that still needs to be done at Kelly's Garden because it only has 25 white portakabin accommodation units installed at present, one small cookhouse, a POL Point (Petroleum, Oil, and Lubricants) and Bulk Fuel Store, a partly completed water supply pipeline, a fully operational Generator House, and one Ablution Block. The First Aid station is very basic and there is a laundry facility and small bar, and the one temporary helipad where we landed earlier but at least the camp has the makings of a much larger Defence Base in time. We were also informed that this part of East Falkland Island is clear of minefields and that we are protected by several concealed Royal Artillery Rapier surface-to-air missile sites that are dotted all around.

Out in San Carlos Water lays the wreck of *HMS Antelope*, a British Type 21 Frigate which was attacked on 23 May 1982 by four Argentine Skyhawk fighter aircraft however, two bombs failed to explode. Brought closer to shore for Royal Engineer Explosive Ordnance Disposal (EOD) technicians to make safe the two shells, one unfortunately detonated and the ship's fate was sealed. *HMS Antelope's* sister ship *HMS Ardent* was also sunk during the war and she lays at the bottom of Grantham Sound which is out to the west. To the east and overlooking Kelly's Garden are the beautiful Verde Hills, which I plan on trekking as soon as I can to take photographs of the surrounding area and to better understand the layout of the land.

My first engineering task is to assist a Royal Engineer Clerk of Works staff sergeant with surveying and marking out the site for three RAF helipads, and a connecting taxiway which will run east to west. This work will begin tomorrow morning so that the temporary helipad can then be dismantled and stripped out at the earliest opportunity. Three of our Advance Party will be assigned to Blue Beach Military Cemetery to help prepare the foundation for a memorial stone wall. Seeing the Union Jack fly above the cemetery makes it a sombre sight and having carried out some research before we deployed, there appears to be some confusion over the circumstances that led to the death of Lieutenant Colonel H Jones at the Battle of Goose Green.

I have read that he led his men into an assault on the enemy's position from the front which as most soldiers will know, is not really the role of a commanding officer in any combat situation nevertheless, whatever the circumstances were on that fateful day the loss of all those killed in the fighting was both truly devastating and so very tragic.

Around 20.35 and after buying refreshments over at 51 Squadron's bar, I returned to my portakabin to prepare my sleeping bag for a good night's sleep but rather than stay and chat with colleagues, I have decided to bring my journal down to the edge of Bonners Bay where I am now writing up the rest of the events of this very long and exciting day. Later the movie 'Papillion' which stars Dustin Hoffman will be shown but first I need a hot shower plus, I want to prepare my works dress ready for tomorrow and then finish this log.

The time now is 22.35 and it is very dark outside. I did not bother going to watch the film and the stars sparkle in the night sky above like tiny diamonds while deep in my thoughts, is the fact that I am so close to Blue Beach Military Cemetery. This fills me with a feeling I cannot even begin to describe because of its importance to me, and because the emotions of the day are still racing through my mind. I feel as though I really do belong here and I could not be any happier than I am right now. The night sky is truly beautiful, captivating, and so marvellous to look at. I feel very blessed.

Afternote

I have a number of relatives who served with the British Armed Forces on my adopted side and having only a limited knowledge of my biological family, an ancestral research was very kindly undertaken by Irene that has proved remarkable and fascinating, and I am so very grateful to her for all her incredible work. As a result, I have met one of my biological cousins and in July 2020, Irene discovered that I have a 3rd cousin by the name of David Crwys-Williams. David is a retired Air Vice-Marshal and trustee with the Falkland Islands Conservation, a charitable organisation that helps protect both the environment and wildlife of these remarkable islands. But what truly fascinated me was that from 1988 to 1989, David served as Commander British Forces Falkland Islands (CBFFI) and so I wrote an email to introduce myself, and explain how we are related. I mentioned that I was writing a military memoir and to my absolute delight, he replied and after further exchanges of emails he generously contributed the photograph below to my memoir and for this, I am extremely thankful.

Air Vice-Marshal David Crwys-Williams*

Even after almost 40 years, I still reflect on my time in the Falkland Islands as if it only happened yesterday and given my keen interest in history, what truly fascinates me about these islands are its relics from the past such as the Lady Elizabeth which I researched long before my deployment. Much closer to home is another piece of maritime history that has links with the Falkland Islands, and that is Isambard Kingdom Brunel's gigantic ship SS Great Britain which was eventually returned to Bristol in 1970 after Sir Jack Arnold Hayward paid to have her repaired and towed across the Atlantic Ocean. Her mizzen mast rests on its side along the quay of Port Stanley Harbour and I could not wait to see it for myself. When that moment finally came and I touched this remarkable piece of history, the shiver that raced through my body is something I will never forget.

Just two days into our six-month tour I was already spellbound by the Falklands, but what I did not realise was that over time that feeling would grow even stronger with every day until eventually, I reached the point where I did not want to leave Kelly's Garden. Such an emotion can be extremely powerful yet ultimately worrying if truth be known, because once a place becomes a part of you, it is very upsetting when you have to leave and that is how it genuinely was with me and Kelly's Garden in 1983.

Between 10 and 14 of September 2022, I had the privilege to be part of the Welsh Guards 78th Anniversary of the liberation of Hechtel, Arras, and the Somme, along with my son David who is himself a former Welsh Guardsman. Superbly organised by Major Lyndon Davies QARANC (Battlefield Tour Project Officer), the places we visited included Hechtel-Eksel and Ypres in Belgium, followed by Arras in France via Loos and Souchez, then the Somme area, Beaumont-Hamel, Ginchy, the Thiepval Memorial, Mametz Wood, and finally Vimy Ridge.

Several wreath laying ceremonies took place to remember those Welsh Guards who gave their lives during the Great War of 1914-1918, and it was a truly emotional experience and one I will never forget. Also on the tour was Colonel Wayne Robinson (late RAMC) and together we shared stories and experiences and one day, he showed me a photo of a watercolour he painted whilst serving in the Falkland Islands. To my total disbelief, it was of Ross Road and Christ Church Cathedral in Port Stanley and the angle, parked Land Rover, telegraph poles and background was identical to the photograph I took on 5 January 1983, as can be seen earlier in this chapter. As soon as I returned to Llanelli, I emailed Colonel Robinson a copy of my photograph and he replied that "the similarity is extraordinary."

The watercolour of Ross Road painted by Colonel Wayne Robinson**

Chapter Four
War and Peace

Foreword

For as long as I can recall, I have always been at my happiest when walking along the shore of a quiet secluded bay while looking out to sea, visiting historical places of interest such as Rome, Pompeii, Venice, and Berlin, and spending time in castles, museums, galleries, and cathedrals. They all touch nerves inside me that immediately generate feelings of awe, wonderment and interest, but I am also at my happiest when I listen to others who with a passion share their incredible knowledge of ancient civilizations and cultures.

As a proud Celt, I am extremely blessed to live in West Wales because there is so much history on my doorstep and still today, I am forever captivated when I drive through the magnificent Welsh countryside and see castles in abundance, and scenic locations such as Crai Reservoir in the Brecon Beacons, Burry Port Harbour, the famous cockle village of Penclawdd on North Gower, the old drover towns of Llandovery and Brecon, and the remote Capel y Baran that sits on Betws Mountain where my great grandfather Noah Williams was laid to rest with his second wife Elizabeth, in 1893.

Each time I walk along my local promenade, I gaze across to the derelict Whitford Lighthouse where I have often given guided tours to international students from Swansea University and in one hour, I can be in the harbour town of Tenby or on a boat to the monastic island of Caldey which has a 1,500 year history of holy orders and where Cistercian monks still worship to this day. What more could anyone wish for if they truly enjoy history? Yet despite having no historical building, church, or museum at Kelly's Garden or indeed San Carlos Settlement, I was nevertheless fascinated beyond words from the moment I stepped out of the RAF Sea King on Monday, 17 January 1983.

I was completely obsessed with these locations and the Verde Hills, the expanse of wild open grassland and the tiny cove that nestled quietly on the eastern edge of Bonners Bay. Everything reminded me of my childhood days and the safe and open places where friends and I played near the small coastal communities of Machynys and Bwlch-y-Gwynt, and even the sweet aroma of fresh sea-air and the sharp shrill of seabirds reminded me of those wonderful days.

After the Falklands War ended, a decision was made to construct and establish a British military base on the far western side of East Falkland Island to provide a frontline defence against future possible Argentine aggression, and the site chosen was Kelly's Garden. Work began immediately and the location had several geographical features that made it the ideal choice, because not only did it provide strategic positions for Royal Artillery Rapier surface-to-air missile systems, but Bonners Bay itself was also a natural supply of water and offered quick and easy access to San Carlos Water for shipping, and the shallow cove was suitable for Mexeflotes and offloading military equipment, supplies, and vehicles. And also, the ground was suitable for the construction of permanent buildings and establishing a RAF Chinook Detachment. Kelly's Garden had it all.

Llanelli coast at dawn

Tuesday, 18 January 1983

The portakabin I am sharing with colleagues from 3 Troop Advance Party is extremely basic but at least it is comfortable, and my bed space is small and has furniture constructed from old wooden pallets and storage boxes. I will definitely need to make myself a writing table to update my journal and also a wardrobe, chair, and book case. Outside the ground is extremely damp and we have been advised to wear our military issued wellingtons for today's schedule of tasks. I missed breakfast in order to report to 51 Field Squadron Office by 07.00 and meet with the Clerk of Works staff sergeant who is a very cheerful person and forever smiling, and wears very large spectacles.

He is also a great conservationist and together we walked across to the section of open ground on which the three helipads will be laid, and after an hour's work we quickly went on a walkabout of Kelly's Garden so that he could familiarise me with the layout of the Defence Base, and the facilities that are already in place and operational. It is quite clear that a tremendous amount of hard effort and work has already been put into getting Kelly's Garden to its current status, but there is still so much that needs to be completed before troops can be stationed here on six-month operational duties.

As we approached the cookhouse, I came across a colleague who had been given a small concreting task near the Laundry Block, and when we returned to the helipad site we surveyed and marked out more sections of ground but very quickly we started to run out of stores. To make best use of my time I went and searched for as many panels of Perforated Steel Planking (PSP) as I could find, to determine the actual quantity that was on site and to make a record of their location by painting a number on each.

These will be used to make the floor sections of the three helipads and connecting taxiway, and I am reliably informed that the estimated value of PSP matting here at Kelly's Garden is around £3 million. Given the value of these panels, I made it my primary role to find and inspect as many as I can and this work took up until lunchtime to complete.

Not exactly the Ritz

During my search for the PSP panels I was told that many would be found near the edge of Bonners Bay, and so I decided to look for these and also visit San Carlos Settlement and Blue Beach Military Cemetery for the very first time. I followed the narrow stony path next to the bay and as I approached the wooden jetty that was located to the east of the settlement, I came across 51 Squadron's staff sergeant who was making his way back to Kelly's Garden, and so we chatted for a while. An interesting and pleasant SNCO, he pointed out various sites in the distance and said that we were not far from where British Royal Marines and members of the Parachute Regiment first landed in 1982. He also told me that Blue Beach Cemetery was roughly a twenty-minute walk from where we were stood. We said goodbye to each other and I continued on my way to San Carlos Settlement but when I arrived some five minutes later, there was not a soul to be seen anywhere and it was as if the entire village was completely deserted.

To my surprise, there were no more than a dozen wooden houses and outbuildings and they were mostly painted white and had red or grey corrugated tin roofs, and were beginning to look quite weathered. I hope I get to speak with one or two settlers at some point during my time here at Kelly's Garden to ask about their lifestyle, and how difficult life can be living in this remote part of the island. I carried on with my walk to Blue Beach Military Cemetery which was about 15 minutes west of the settlement and when I eventually reached the perimeter fence, my emotions kicked in immediately, because I knew only too well the story of those who were laid to rest in this simple yet beautiful graveyard.

Surely, this had to be one of the most remote British military cemeteries ever and the stillness and tranquillity was overwhelming and so much so, that it took about 10 minutes for me to take it all in. At long last I was standing at the entrance to a cemetery that I had wanted to visit ever since the war finished for reasons that were personal to me, and as I looked around the site I waved to my colleagues who were working at the far eastern side. At that moment, I said a quiet prayer.

I entered and visited each grave in turn, then went to speak with my friends from 3 Troop who were hard at work on the foundation for a commemorative stone wall. All through my visit the atmosphere was unlike anything I had ever experienced before.

Blue Beach Military Cemetery, January 1983

The white painted wooden triple-railed perimeter fence that surrounds the cemetery gives it a British colonial appearance of old, while inside are 14 white crosses that mark the graves where some of those killed during the fighting in 1982 are laid to rest. Their graves are contained in two memorial gardens and each cross bears the name of the individual in black lettering. It all looks very basic yet it is also extremely respectful and poignant.

The entrance is a double gate which has a flagpole to its right and from which the Union Jack flies at full mast, while at the centre of the furthest fence is a large brown wooden cross and everything about this place looks perfect. Also working inside the cemetery were a few members of 51 Engineer Squadron and after a brief conversation with them, I recorded all 14 names on the white crosses for my journal and ventured up onto higher ground to take photographs. Back inside the cemetery, I took a photograph of the windswept grave of Lieutenant Colonel H Jones VC and as I looked out towards San Carlos Water, I spent several minutes reflecting on life and how the families and loved ones must still be feeling given it has not been a year since these officers and soldiers were killed, and my heart went out to each and every one of them.

Grave of Lieutenant Colonel H Jones VC

The names I recorded in my journal are:

Lieutenant Colonel H Jones VC OBE 2 Para.
Captain C Dent 2 Para.
Private F. F. Slough 2 Para.
Private M Holman-Smith 2 Para.
Staff Sergeant C A Griffin 656 Squadron Army Air Corps.
Major M L Forge Royal Signals.
Staff Sergeant J I Baker Royal Signals.
Lance Corporal C Davidson Commando Logistic Regiment.

Sergeant R A Leaming RM 45 Commando.
Corporal A B Uren RM 45 Commando.
Corporal K Evans RM 45 Commando.
Marine K Phillips RM 45 Commando.
Marine D Wilson RM 45 Commando.
Lieutenant R J Nunn DFC RM Brigade Air Squadron.

Fought on 28 May 1982, the Battle of Goose Green was the longest land engagement of the Falklands War and involved officers and soldiers from 2nd Battalion, the Parachute Regiment, otherwise known as 2 PARA. With the enemy clearly having the advantage, against all odds the battle proved a turning point in the conflict when 2 PARA claimed a remarkable but costly victory. The fighting at Goose Green was ferocious and during a frontal assault on an Argentine trench, Lieutenant Colonel H Jones was fatally wounded and posthumously awarded the Victoria Cross. The British victory at Goose Green was not only extraordinary, but it also changed the course of the Falklands War.

San Carlos Settlement

Leaving San Carlos Settlement

After checking the land immediately around the cemetery for PSP panels, I said goodbye to my friends and colleagues and started to make my way back to Kelly's Garden, and as I walked through Port Carlos Settlement I met and spoke with a settler who was making repairs to his roof. I am completely gripped by the tiny size and sheer remoteness of this very basic community, and the rudimentary lifestyle they appear to lead. After we chatted for some 15 minutes during which time we introduced ourselves and gave a summary of our background, I continued on my way back to the Defence Base.

The settler's name was Ron and he told me that he was married and had one son. Soon I was about 200 metres further along the track and I stopped to look back at the settlement, and it was then that I made myself a promise to visit both San Carlos Settlement and Blue Beach Military Cemetery as often as I could during my time here at Kelly's Garden. On the jetty just a few minutes later, I gazed out across Bonners Bay to Kelly's Garden while to my left and looking magnificent in all their glory, were the Verde Hills and directly to the south was the extensive open ground that is now called Bomb Alley.

Everything seemed just perfect and as it should be, but I needed to get back to the Defence Base and as soon as I reached the footpath that led from the water's edge and into Kelly's Garden, I was greeted by two colleagues and we headed to the cookhouse for lunch. Just then the heavens opened and it poured with rain. The weather here seems to change from one extreme to the other within seconds, and so it was decided that before we finish our work for the day, we would split the Advance Party into two small sections ahead of tomorrow's task which is to complete the anchoring and fitting-out of four newly-sited white accommodation portakabins.

Kelly's Garden from San Carlos Settlement

The dreadful weather killed off any chance of working this afternoon which meant we had lost six hours and this frustrated us, because we could have completed much of tomorrow's tasks ahead of schedule. Around 18.55, we went for dinner after which I returned to my portakabin and wrote letters to my parents and friends back home in Llanelli and Tidworth, and I took these across to 51 Field Squadron's office just as Captain Williams arrived from Port Stanley. He is here to replace an officer who I do not really know while over in the small squadron bar, I cashed my first cheque since arriving here in the Falklands and was given ten Falkland Island £1 banknotes which are surprisingly large, and only just fit inside my wallet.

At the other end of the bar, a few colleagues from 51 Squadron were watching the 1974 movie 'Thunderbolt and Lightfoot' starring Clint Eastwood but feeling tired, I returned once again to my portakabin and wrote up today's entry. The time here passes quickly and 3 Troop will need to work 11 hours each day, 7 days a week if we are to complete our schedule of work within the deadline given, and having nearly finished my writing for the day I am now more than ready to slip inside my sleeping bag. It has been a long but very enjoyable first day here on the Defence Base and what an introduction we have had to the Falklands' weather.

Wednesday, 19 January 1982

It took me less than 15 minutes to get showered and dressed before joining my colleagues for breakfast. Our chef is Private Hollings and he is one of six chefs working in the cookhouse and they are providing us with such excellent meals. We paraded at 07.30 and were given a SITREP on what was happening here in the South Atlantic and during the briefing, we were told of an incident back home which involved the shooting by police of an innocent man in London who apparently was sitting inside a car and mistaken for the escaped prisoner David Martin.

With the work of anchoring and fitting out the four portakabins assigned to number one section, Paul and I headed for the Generator House where we have been tasked with driving a series of five-foot earthing spikes into the ground and when we reported to the sergeant from 51 Field Squadron, he explained how he wanted the work carried out. I instantly had reservations and after he left, I sent Paul to collect a small list of equipment from 51 Squadron's G1098 Engineering Store. The ground at Kelly's Garden varies considerably and it was obvious that we would need the support of a mechanical digger to complete this task, especially after hitting an unexpected layer of rock at a depth of around 18 inches.

Within 10 minutes, the digger arrived and I could not believe who the Plant Operator Mechanic (POM) was, because it was none other than an old friend from 26 Armoured Engineer Squadron. After a quick catch up, I explained the briefing I had been given by the sergeant and then listed my reasons why I believed his idea would not work. To my relief both Paul and Steve fully agreed, and so we decided to run with my plan.

At around 11.43 an unexpected air-raid alarm was sounded throughout Kelly's Garden and the three of us hurried to 51 Squadron's office however, when we got there were no colleagues from 3 Troop, and we were informed that they were still working over at Blue Beach Cemetery. The order was given for everyone on site to immediately wear their combat helmets and to have our NBC respirators at the ready because this was a 'State Yellow' warning, which meant that the Defence Base could be the target of an Argentine air strike at any time.

The alarm was cancelled after just ten minutes and everyone was stood down when the state of readiness reverted back to 'White'. Four aircraft had been observed by the Royal Artillery but only three were recognised as friendly forces and quite rightly, their only option was to instigate the alarm and it was a good call on their part. Paul and I continued with our work in windy conditions and managed to sink four earthing spikes to a depth of five feet before stopping for lunch, but by 13.45

heavy rain was falling once again which started to turn the camp into one giant mud field.

During the afternoon and early evening, we sank a total of 12 earthing spikes and eventually completed the work at around 19.00. Over dinner at the cookhouse, we discussed the events of the day and then I went for a shower and across to the bar to join colleagues who were watching the movie 'Towering Inferno.' Outside a cold wind was blowing through Kelly's Garden and already some of my colleagues were either fast asleep or reading their books, and so I decided to review my journal from the very beginning.

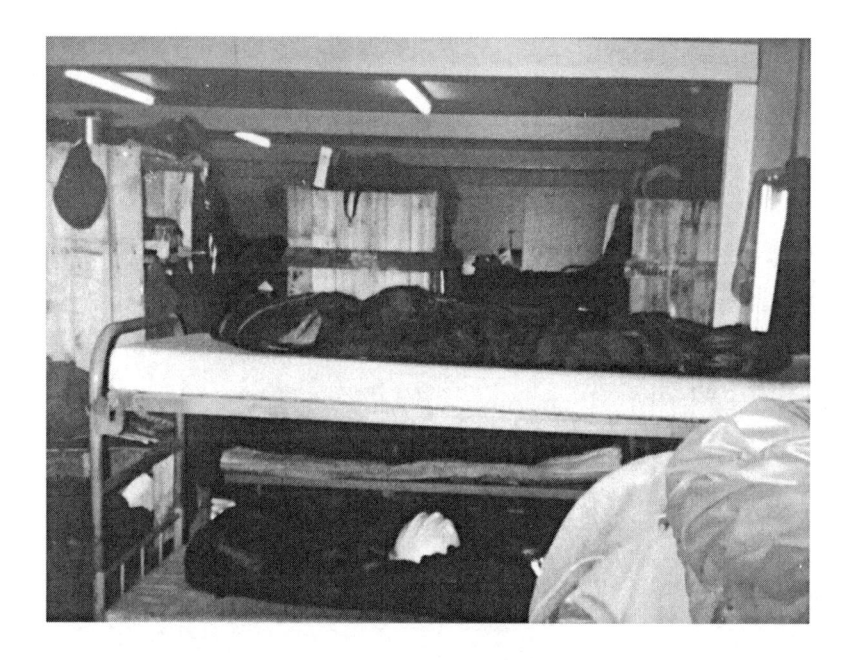

3 Troop's portakabin

We are starting to feel somewhat crammed inside our portakabin because there is hardly any room in which to swing a cat as we have now made three more wardrobes out of old wooden storage boxes, and they are certainly making a difference to our quality of life. We have also managed to acquire eight bunk beds and still only have bare mattresses on which to place our sleeping bags, but at least we are dry and out of the cold.

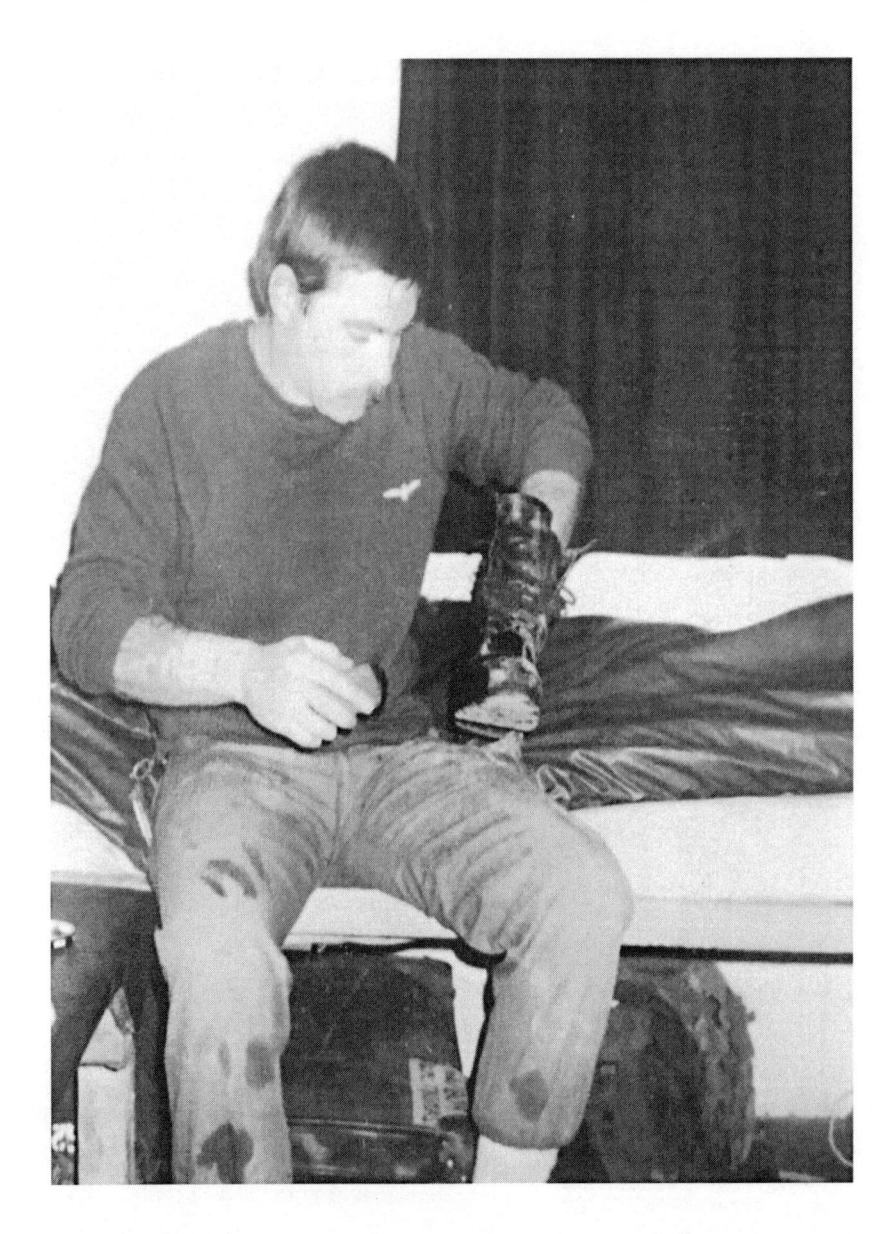

Polishing my boots

Afternote

After serving in the Falklands for six months, I can best describe the experience as 'unique' and 'memorable'. Not only were we based in a demanding environment with vast expanses of open grassland all around, but the day-to-day life in the local settlement was the most basic I had ever come across and the weather conditions were extremely challenging at times. For anyone who loves the secluded life then Kelly's Garden and San Carlos Settlement would be your dream location and indeed, it was very much my kind of place. 1983 was a period when recovery and repairing the post-war infrastructure was pretty much in its infancy, and further permanent military defence bases were being either considered or planned for other locations. The Falklands was genuinely like no other place I had visited and still it remains an ambition of mine to return there one day, to re-visit Kelly's Garden where sadly hardly anything exists of the former Defence Base.

It is now over 40 years since the Falklands War ended and during the fighting, 255 British troops gave their lives in the recapture of this British Overseas Territory. It is accepted by those who serve in the Armed Forces that they could be called upon to fight in an armed conflict at any time during their career, and it is also a fact that war is a very bloody and terrible business. All armed conflicts can be avoided but only if the aggressor chooses to do so.

At the time of writing this memoir, Russia's President Vladimir Putin launched an invasion of Ukraine and under the absurd assertion that it was a "special operation to demilitarise and de-Nazify" the country. A more outrageous and highly offensive statement could not be made because the plain truth is that Putin was deliberately misleading the world, and more worrying, the Russian people were being fed with state-sponsored propaganda of the very worst kind.

The Soviet Union collapsed in 1991 and 15 independent republics formed and secured full sovereignty along with Ukraine, and these included Armenia, Estonia, Georgia, Kazakhstan, Latvia, Lithuania, Moldova, and Uzbekistan. Since then, Ukraine has never expressed any intention or desire to return to the past and this is officially on record after repeated public statements made by its President Volodymyr Zelenskyy.

Russia is a beautiful country that is steeped in culture and a history that is as fascinating as its architecture, and millions of tourists used to visit each year up until Putin's illegal invasion of Ukraine on 24 February 2022. The people of Russia are being punished economically and exiled from so many global events because of their leader who undeniably rules by fear, and they deserve better than a controlling president who for no known reason is totally obsessed with a deep-rooted fear of the West. His vanity is such that he even compares himself with Peter the Great.

After every military conflict there is a 'clean-up' operation, and I wanted to play my part in 1983 regardless of the fact that hostilities could have broken out at any time, and everyone in 3 Troop was more than prepared for such an event. Something that surprised me both during and after the Falklands War was the fact that not many people actually knew where the Falkland Islands were. While in Canada in 1982, many people I spoke with genuinely thought the Falklands belonged to Scotland, as indeed did many British people, but by the time the Task Force set sail from Portsmouth on 5 April 1982 the whole world knew exactly where these islands were on the map.

The realities of war only hit home when news presenters and journalists start to report fatalities and casualties in television and radio broadcasts, on social media, and in the tabloids but by then it is already too late. The brutality of war is very real and it can be horrendous and extremely distressing to those involved and also, for their families and friends.

As a retired soldier, Remembrance Day for me is always an important time of the year because we reflect on past conflicts and wars, and people remember those who gave their lives while attending memorial ceremonies around the country. During these services we repeat the same words year on year, "We Will Remember Them" while on cenotaphs we read the inscription 'Lest We Forget' but have these words simply become part of a ritual?

Of course we remember the fallen and yes, we will never forget but for me, the most important question is do we learn? This in part is the reason why I am driven to despair by leaders who are hell bent on showing aggression towards others, and believe it is their divine right to enforce their authority and control over others.

I was shocked to learn that in 2023 alone, there are 57 dictatorships worldwide and apart from just four that are in Central and South America, the remaining 53 are in Africa, the Middle East, Asia, Central Asia, the Russian Federation, China, and North Korea. Although there are different types of dictatorships, the three main categories are 'Military' such as Brazil, 'Single Party' such as China and North

Korea, and 'Royal' such as Saudi Arabia and of these three, the largest is 'Single Party'. Also, in the one hundred year period between 1900 and 2000, some 38 separate wars and conflicts have been fought including:

- *South African War.*
- *Boxer Rebellion.*
- *World War I.*
- *World War II.*
- *Russian Civil War.*
- *Spanish Civil War.*
- *Korean War.*
- *Vietnam War.*
- *Six-Day War.*
- *Yom Kippur War.*
- *Bosnian Conflict.*
- *Persian Gulf War.*
- *Falklands War.*

Not only was constructing a Defence Base at Kelly's Garden key to Britain's post-war military plans for the Falkland Islands, it also needed to be fully operational as quickly as possible and in addition to Rapier ground-to-air missiles sites manned by members of the Royal Artillery, there were daily foot patrols and a RAF ChinDet (Chinook Detachment) made up from Numbers 7 and 18 Squadron. Two roles of the RAF at Kelly's Garden were to provide a logistical supply chain, and an air-trooping service between Kelly's Garden and Port Stanley, and other locations.

For the first few weeks 3 Troop worked in support of 51 Field Squadron and soon our work schedule increased considerably, albeit the vast majority of tasks were routine and pretty much basic military engineering, however, one of our main tasks was top priority and that was the installation and fitting-out of 40 white portakabins. Each needed anchoring to a concrete base due to the powerful South Atlantic crosswinds that frequently blew in from the open waters of Falkland Sound, and these portakabins would serve as accommodation and offices for troops deployed to Kelly's Garden on future operational duties.

Other small tasks assigned to 3 Troop included commissioning a Bulk Fuel Store pipeline, assembling and installing a fresh water supply system that converted seawater from Bonners Bay into fresh drinking water, building an incinerator, and setting up a Ration Store and Field Medical Centre. But one day and completely out of the blue, 3 Troop was given the task of assembling and erecting a large Rubb hangar that was capable of housing a Boeing CH-47 Chinook helicopter, and connected to three helipads and a central taxiway.

With regards to the Falklands War and as mentioned earlier in this memoir, I decided to write an account of the political events that led to the conflict in my journal, and that account is transcribed in Chapter 2. I also decided to write another account but this time, covering the actual events of the war that took place during the 74 days leading up to the Argentine surrender. For my part I knew that this was a complex subject yet even back in 1983, I felt a burning compulsion that this was something I needed to produce for anyone who wanted to know what really happened, and I also knew that this would be included in the military memoir I was determined to write at some point in my life.

While stationed at Kelly's Garden, I genuinely felt that I was in the best possible location to write that account because everything was still fresh in my mind, and while serving in Canada in 1982, I was following and recording the events taking place in the South Atlantic every day. By the time I reached the Falklands, I had completed my research and so it is fitting that at this juncture in my memoir, I transcribe that account.

The Falklands War

(Compiled by Philip Thomas at Kelly's Garden in 1983)

In 1982, Argentina was once again in dispute with Great Britain over sovereignty of South Georgia and the Falkland Islands, even though the latter became a British Crown colony in 1841. As tensions intensified in 1982, many considered the disagreement as being just another heated exchange between the two countries but this time, Argentina made the fatal mistake of committing an unprecedented violation of international law. It cannot be denied that the United States of America fully supported the appointment of General Galtieri as President of Argentina in December 1981 however, the mood of the Argentine people quickly turned against the unpopular and undemocratic junta and very soon, public anger and unrest spilled onto the streets of Buenos Aires.

With no real prospect of a peaceful resolution to the question of sovereignty, Prime Minister Thatcher recognised that Galtieri was a wounded president and desperate to win back the support of his people, but not even Thatcher could have imagined that he would use his armed forces to invade a British Overseas Territory. For his part, President Leopoldo Galtieri had quite simply committed military and political suicide, because even he would have known that by ordering the invasion it would inevitably trigger international condemnation.

At Government House in Port Stanley on the evening of 20 March 1982, Governor Sir Rex Masterman Hunt alerted Captain Nick Barker of the British Royal Navy Ice patrol ship *HMS Endurance* that a group of 40 illegal Argentine scrap workers had landed on the frozen island of South Georgia, some 800 miles to the east. Captain Barker had heard talk of a 'planned' Argentine invasion whilst attending a dinner party held in Buenos Aries however, after passing this information to British Defence Secretary John Nott, to his astonishment the report was dismissed.

Sir Rex Hunt consulted with London and was instructed to deploy *HMS Endurance* to South Georgia under the command of Captain Barker himself. Lieutenant Keith Mills and 22 Royal Marines were also deployed and their objective was to arrest all 40 Argentine scrap workers who by now, were heavily suspected by the Ministry of Defence in London of being members of the Argentine Special Forces. *HMS Endurance* arrived at Grytviken on 24 March by which time, the scrap workers were well established at Leith, some 40 miles away and under the command of Captain Trombetta on board *ARA Bahía Paraíso*. At 07.30 on 2 April, Captain Trombetta radioed Lieutenant Keith Mills and said that both he and his men would surrender to him at the local jetty.

Out at sea Captain Nick Barker received an order from London telling him to reach South Georgia as soon as he could because of the events that had taken place. Armed with two 20mm cannon and a Westland Wasp helicopter which was fitted with AS-12 air-to-surface missiles, *HMS Endurance* was ready for action. Lieutenant Keith Mills' instruction was to protect the British Antarctic Survey Team and resist any fighting, to which it is said that his response was simply "sod that, I'm going to make their eyes water."

On 3 April at 11.30, an Argentine Puma helicopter landed 15 marines on South Georgia and on its second sortie to land additional troops at King Edward Point, it was spotted by Lieutenant Mills' section and brought down by gunfire. They also successfully holed the Argentine ship *ARA Guerrico* and for two hours were involved in fierce fighting.

At Government House on 2 April, Colour Sergeant John Noone heard gunfire and realised that the 61 members of Naval Party 8901 had no chance of stopping the advancing Argentine soldiers. Major Mike Norman had earlier lifted spirits by telling his men, "Remember you're not fighting for the Falkland Islands this time, you're fighting for yourselves."

The marines put up an incredible resistance while out in the bay, the Argentine aircraft carrier *ARA Veinticinco de Mayo* sailed past the lighthouse. Governor Hunt was left no option but to order the Royal Marines to surrender even though the fighting continued for some time.

On 5 April, the British Naval aircraft carriers *HMS Invincible* and *HMS Hermes* and the amphibious assault ship *HMS Fearless* sailed out of Portsmouth Harbour, bound for the Falkland Islands and on Friday 19 April, the luxury liner *SS Canberra* set sail carrying Royal Marines and members of the Parachute Regiment. More British troops sailed south on board the P&O Ferry *MV Norland* and on 12 May 1982, the Cunard cruise liner *Queen Elizabeth II* sailed out of Southampton with 3,000 troops on board from the 5th Infantry Brigade, which included members of the Guards Division and Gurkha Rifles.

Also on board were 600 volunteers and the total strength of the British Military Task Force was now 127 ships including fishing trawlers from Hull, British Rail car ferries, and 46 requisitioned Royal Merchant vessels of various types. Commander of the Fleet, First Sea Lord Sir Henry Conyers Leach had discussed a plan with Prime Minister Thatcher to deploy this powerful Task Force and as such all postings, operational tours, and periods of leave were cancelled. Meanwhile, the Falkland Islanders were now living in fear amidst the presence of an uninvited Argentine invasion force, and on the same day that the first ships sailed out of Portsmouth Harbour, the British Foreign Secretary Lord Carrington resigned after accepting full responsibility for failing to recognise the significance of Argentine's escalating hostility towards British sovereignty over the Falklands.

General Mario Menendez was sworn in as the new Military Governor of the Falkland Islands by President Galtieri, and martial law immediately ensued. Life for the islanders was thrown into chaos as curfews were put in place and an order issued by President Galtieri himself, that Spanish was to be recognised as the official language of the Falkland Islands. Prime Minister Thatcher and the British parliament were horrified at the events taking place in the South Atlantic while outside the presidential palace at Casa Rosada in Buenos Aries, thousands of elated Argentinians gathered to show overwhelming support for President Galtieri and his military junta, and for the military invasion of the Islas Malvinas.

On 7 April, Great Britain declared a 200-mile Military Exclusion Zone (MEZ) around the Falklands and American Secretary of State Alexander Haig was appointed official diplomat by both Argentina and Great Britain. Tensions intensified and during the first four days of diplomatic talks, a series of events took place that shocked the world when the Argentine naval light cruiser *ARA Belgrano* was sunk by the British Naval submarine *HMS Conqueror*. Furthermore, the British Type 42 Destroyer *HMS Sheffield* was badly damaged by an Argentine Exocet missile and later sank as she was being towed to South Georgia.

Unbeknown to most people back home, British troops had already landed on East Falkland Island near San Carlos and on 1 May, members of Britain's elite Special Air Service and Special Boat Service were air-lifted by helicopter from the aircraft carrier *HMS Hermes* to carry out surveillance on Argentine activity. On 18 May, British ships entered the MEZ and were now within striking distance of the Argentine Air Force. Prime Minister Thatcher who was now desperate for favourable results handed full command of the British Military Task Force to Rear Admiral John Sandy Woodward, and his first task was to identify a base from which to launch his attack on the Argentine invasion force.

He ruled out Port Stanley and six other locations including Cow Bay, Uranie Bay, and Port North until eventually, it was San Carlos that was beginning to look like the favoured option from where to launch the recapture of the Falkland Islands.

Back on South Georgia, Major Guy Sheridan issued an order for a reconnaissance by members of the Special Air Service and Special Boat Service however on 21 April, deteriorating weather conditions caused two British helicopters to crash into the Fortuna Glacier, and so the Special Air Service troops hid on the rocks for seven days. The recapture of South Georgia was supported by *HMS Plymouth* and *HMS Brilliant*.

The Argentine submarine *ARA Santa Fe* was spotted by a Lynx helicopter and attacked with rocket and heavy machine-gun fire. *HMS Antrim* immediately deployed 60 Royal Marines and with the support of 45 members from the Special Air Service and Special Boat Service, they successfully captured the enemy's position behind Grytviken as *HMS Plymouth* launched an attack using her 4.5-inch guns. Surrender was secured and both the British Union Jack and British White Ensign were hoisted. The operation of recapturing South Georgia was codenamed Operation Paraquat.

'Palpas' was the pre-arranged codeword which London now eagerly awaited. This would authorise the landing of British troops at San Carlos Bay as soon as South Georgia had been recaptured. When the order was eventually received on 20 May at 23.25, Commander 3 Commando Brigade namely Brigadier Julian Thomson told his staff, "Gentlemen, we go!"

Royal Marines and members of the Parachute Regiment at San Carlos took up four pre-determined positions and while all this was happening, a convoy of 11 British vessels led by *HMS Fearless* and *HMS Intrepid* sailed towards Port Stanley but after nightfall, they would turn around and head straight back to San Carlos Water. In anticipation of an Argentine surrender, the British Military Task Force needed someone to act as official interpreter and the person chosen was Captain Roderick Bell of the Royal Marines, who was fluent in Spanish.

Members of 3 Special Boat Service landed by helicopter on Fanning Head which was a high point overlooking San Carlos Water and from there, they opened fire on the occupying Argentine forces. The ensuing fire fight was ferocious and Captain Roderick Bell shouted to the enemy to surrender, however, they refused and instead returned heavy gunfire.

Back at San Carlos 2 Para and 40 Commando Unit went ashore approximately one hour behind schedule and with them were members of 3 Para, who had encountered considerable difficulties when trying to land. All three units were now ready and in place to launch their assault. Lieutenant Colonel Nick Vaux of the Royal Marines was the commander of 42 Commando, a sub-unit of 3 Commando Brigade, and he went straight to Lieutenant Colonel Malcolm Hunt who was planning a combined advance.

The resistance by members of 43 Argentine Marines proved extraordinarily weak and as they withdrew from Port San Carlos, they opened fire on a British Westland Wessex helicopter that was carrying a Rapier Battery to a nearby hilltop. They also opened fired on two British Gazelle helicopters killing three crew members. Inside 24 hours San Carlos was turned into a British military stronghold with troops dug in, Royal Artillery Rapier surface-to-air missile sites positioned along the high ground, and a headquarters established however, Argentine forces gained strength and almost to the extent that they had victory within their grasp. British victims of Argentine air attacks were as follows:

1. 21 May – *HMS Ardent* sunk and *HMS Argonaut* badly damaged. *HMS Antrim, Brilliant,* and *Broadsword* hit by enemy missiles, but not all exploded.
2. 23 May – *HMS Antelope* sunk by a delayed explosion. *HMS Glasgow* hit by a missile that failed to explode.
3. 24 May – RFA *Sir Galahad* hit by a 1,000lb bomb that failed to explode, and sustained heavy air attack. RFA *Sir Lancelot* also hit with a 1,000lb bomb that failed to detonate.
4. 25 May – *HMS Coventry* sunk by Argentine Skyhawks and the British merchant naval ship *SS Atlantic Conveyor* hit by Exocet missiles. She sank three days later.
5. 8 June – *HMS Plymouth* attacked by Argentine Nesher fight bombers and hit by four 1,000lb bombs. The ship only just survived. RFA *Sir Tristram* attacked by A-4 Skyhawks while transporting British troops and military equipment to Fitzroy Cove. The vessel suffered a series of hits but thankfully, the 500lb bomb that penetrated her decks failed to detonate at first. The crew managed to disembark before she exploded.
6. 12 June – *HMS Glamorgan* hit by an Exocet missile but survived the attack.

Argentina's invasion force made two critical errors. Firstly, it failed or quite possibly chose not to attack three significant targets namely *SS Canberra*, *HMS Intrepid*, and *HMS Fearless*. Had these three been destroyed by enemy air strikes then the outcome of the war could have been a completely different story. Secondly, Argentine fighter pilots fired their missiles within 50 metres of their target despite the fact that the fuses were set to explode after a distance of 150 to 200 metres.

On 23 May and whilst on board *HMS Intrepid*, Lieutenant Colonel H Jones Commanding Officer 2 Para was informed that Goose Green had been identified as an enemy position that would be subjected to a British assault on 25 May. London however did not support this plan and on 24 May, an order was given to cancel the operation but on 26 May, this order was reversed and the planned attack was to go ahead immediately. 2 Para set off for Sussex Mountain but both the press and television reporters were divulging crucial British military intelligence at an alarming rate.

This understandably enraged Lieutenant Colonel Jones who heard of these leaks while at Camilla Creek House, the location where 2 Para planned their assault but deciding that the intelligence leaks would not jeopardise his plans, it was decided that the attack could proceed. On 27 May, eight men from 'C' Company undertook a reconnaissance of the Argentine defence positions as far south as Boca Hill, and it was from these reports that Lieutenant Colonel Jones finalised his plan of attack.

Fatefully what the reconnaissance had failed to highlight, was that a single enemy trench situated on Darwin Hill was concealed by dead ground and this presented the Argentine troops with a natural defensive position. It was during the charge on this very trench that Lieutenant Colonel Jones was fatally wounded by enemy gunfire. The hidden trenches were six in total and 'A' Company used 66mm anti-tank rockets in their attempt to neutralise these positions.

Some 20 minutes after Lieutenant Colonel Jones was killed, Argentine troops surrendered Goose Green to 2 Para and Darwin was once again back in British hands. At Bluff Cove on 8 June, Argentine aircraft attacked a British position held by 2nd Battalion Scots Guards, while another wave of Argentine air attacks claimed *Sir Galahad* which had a company of Welsh Guards on board, plus members of 16 Field Ambulance. 53 lives were lost and 46 British soldiers seriously wounded and suffered extensive burn injuries.

It is said that the Welsh Guards failed to listen to a Royal Marine officer who pleaded with them to disembark because *Sir Galahad* was like a sitting duck to the attacking Argentine Douglas A-4 Skyhawks fighter aircraft. Some 20 minutes later, two Argentine fighter aircraft attacked *Sir Tristram* and inflicted heavy damage upon her. At 17.15, BBC World News reported the events as pictures and footage of both attacks were flashed around the world, and for those who saw the images on television screens and in the newspapers, they will never forget what happened.

Between 11 and 14 June, 3 Para and 45 Commando marched from Ajax Bay and headed east to Estancia House and from there, on to the hills overlooking Port Stanley. The term 'Yomping' had entered the English language and the march to recapture Port Stanley was now in its final stage. Lieutenant Colonel Andy Whitehead, Commanding Officer 45 Commando told his troops, "In 1945, the infantry marched from Normandy to Berlin, so we can walk to Stanley."

On 13 and 14 June, 5th Infantry Brigade Tactical Headquarters established a position on Goat Ridge. From Mount Harriet and towards Mount William, 2nd Battalion Scots Guards supported by the Blues and Royals made their diversionary attacks and claimed Mount Tumbledown, while 1/7 Gurkha Rifles attacked Mount William after running through the Scots Guards' position as the enemy reportedly fled in a blind panic.

The Welsh Guards captured Sapper Hill and in Port Stanley, the Falkland Island's capital, spirits were boosted when British troops and locals witnessed the Argentine waving a white flag of surrender. At 09.00 on 15 June, Argentine General Mario Menendez signed the document of surrender which was presented to him by Major General Sir Jeremy Moore and with that, British troops were allowed to march into Stanley as the following message was transmitted to London:

'The Falkland Islands are once more under the government desired by their inhabitants, God Save the Queen.'

The Falklands War was over and yet again, the world had witnessed another tragic and needless armed conflict which ultimately claimed the lives of so many young servicemen on both sides, and all in the name of international territorial disagreement. The bodies of those who had been killed would either need to be repatriated to their homeland or buried in the Falkland Islands. British Defence Bases needed to be planned and built as a priority in order to protect the British Overseas Territory from any further attack by Argentina's armed forces.

This would prove costly and require military camps to be established at strategic locations across East Falkland Island, while the runway at Stanley Airport would also need urgent repairs by Royal Engineers in order to facilitate crucial RAF air patrols and long-haul flights. An extension to the runway was another priority, to accommodate larger and much heavier military and commercial aircraft needed to deliver air freight on an unprecedented scale, and for future air-trooping flights between Great Britain and the Falkland Islands.

It is for essential tasks and military needs such as these that 52 Field (Construction) Squadron and I now find ourselves on this six-month 'post-war' military engineering tour of duty in the South Atlantic, and I relish the challenge this presents to each and every one of us.

Chapter Five
All Work and No Play

Foreword

British Royal Engineers are also known as 'Sappers'. This originates from the antiquated French term 'sappe' meaning 'spade' and with regards to early military engineers, it referred to the technique of tunnelling beneath the outer or curtain walls of a castle, battlement, or any other aspect of an enemy's fortified position in order to breach and collapse the defence structure. The word first entered the English language during the 17th century and such was the barbarity of 12th century warfare, that early combatant engineers were known to have herded large numbers of pigs into hand dug tunnels beneath structures such as a castle gatehouse or turret, for the sole purpose of mass incineration. The fat produced fuelled huge fires that would blaze away for days and when fanned, would eventually crack and weaken the stones until the outer defences collapsed.

Prior to the 11th century, military engineers were highly skilled in building mighty siege engines such as the battering ram and the catapult, and the ballista which was a large powerful crossbow but one of the most famous pieces of military equipment was the siege tower. Over time sappers became efficient in other military and technical skills such as bridge building, road construction, explosives, demolition, laying and clearing minefields, water purification, cartography, surveying, and general construction.

They also made access and egress to and from the field of battle more organised through creating trench networks that provided overhead protection, while in camps the day-to-day life of soldiers was made far more comfortable and safe. Troop mobility was also improved due to the skills of these combatant sappers and by the turn of the 13th century, no army could function without them. Their support and ever-increasing areas of expertise eventually made them an invaluable branch of any fighting force, and crucial to almost every aspect of warfare.

The earliest recorded combatant engineers in Britain date back to the 11th century and in particular to the Norman conquest when William I, or William the Conqueror as he is better known, brought with him French 'sapeurs' to construct halls of administration, castles, churches and other remarkable buildings such as the White Tower which is also called the Tower of London. So important was the role and need for sappers to the British Army, in 1717 the first Corps of Engineers was formed but this was only made up of commissioned officers who brought with them their own private artificers and skilled workers.

55 years later in 1772, the first British Artificer Company was established and this time it comprised of both commissioned and non-commissioned tradesmen and 15 years later in 1787, the first Corps of Engineers was renamed the Corps of Royal Engineers. Because of its ability to work in various types of terrain and environment, in 1832 the British Corps of Royal Engineers was granted two mottos that still exist to this day.

The first is 'Ubique' which is the Latin for 'Everywhere', while the second is 'Quo Fas et Glorai Ducunt' which again is Latin translates as 'Where Right and Glory Lead.' The British Corps of Royal Engineers has seen action in every single military campaign and conflict since its formation and as such, it has no single battle honour because in reality they have literally served 'Everywhere'.

On parades and at ceremonial functions, King George VI was known to address his Royal Engineer non-commissioned ranks as 'Gentlemen of the Royal Engineers' and between October 1988 and October 1991, I had the honour to serve as the Chief Clerk of 5 Field Squadron which was a sub-unit of 26 Engineer Regiment based in Iserlohn, Germany.

5 Field Squadron prided itself on its historical connection with Lieutenant John Chard VC who was the Royal Engineer officer that served in Natal in 1879, and went on to play his part in the defence of Rorke's Drift during the Anglo-Zulu War. His character was portrayed by the Welsh actor Sir William Stanley Baker in his block buster movie 'Zulu' of which, he was also the producer.

London's iconic Royal Albert Hall was designed by two Royal Engineer officers namely Major General Henry Scott and Captain Francis Fowke, as a memorial to Prince Albert who died in 1861. The present-day Royal Engineers Museum is housed within Ravelin Building which was also designed by a Royal Engineer architect, and this is based at Brompton Barracks in the historic dockland town of Chatham in Kent. Brompton Barracks is also home to the Headquarters School of Military Engineering where I attended and passed my crucial RE SCNO Course in 1989.

Today's Royal Engineers operate some of the most advanced and sophisticated military engineering equipment in the world including armoured bridge-layers, heavy plant machinery, amphibious rigs, mine-clearing equipment such as the Dragon Runner, survey equipment, and much more.

A total of 36 Royal Engineers have won the Victoria Cross and in 1911, the Air Battalion Royal Engineers went on to form the Royal Flying Corp which in 1918 *became better known as the Royal Air Force. The Royal Engineers Military Band was originally called the RE Symphony Orchestra and was first formed in 1880. In 1897, it received a royal command from Queen Victoria to perform at her Diamond Jubilee Celebration and in 1953 the band also played at the Coronation of Her Majesty Queen Elizabeth II. It has performed to audiences around the world and at large Military Tattoos, sporting events and public concerts, and even the opening of the Channel Tunnel in 1994. The official Regimental March of the Corps of Royal Engineers is a piece of music called 'Wings' which was composed by Bandmaster William Newstead in 1870.*

The Corps of Royal Engineers also has an impressive sporting history and in 1875 it became the first football team ever to win the FA Cup Final. The Corps also came runner up in 1872, 1874, and 1878 while in Rugby Union, two officers namely Lieutenant Charles Crompton and Lieutenant Charles Sherrard played in the first ever England Rugby International.

Thursday, 20 January 1983

It was announced during 51 Field Squadron's morning parade that a camp walkabout would take place at 07.30 precisely, and that every available Royal Engineer on site would take part. Its purpose was to have teams visit and inspect every single work site in Kelly's Garden irrespective of whether or not the sites were finished or still ongoing, and then compile a detailed schedule of snagging, observations, and general comments. The aims of this exercise are to assess which sites can be signed off immediately and also, to create an itinerary of all outstanding work in descending order of importance. The final list would need to be submitted to RE Works back at Port Stanley by no later than 21.00 today.

Everyone agreed that this made sound common sense and that it would help 3 Troop significantly with signing off completed tasks, and to establish a logical starting point from which we can continue the work that 51 Field Squadron has assigned to us. We 'guesstimated' that this morning's snagging inspection should only take approximately two hours to complete and so we divided ourselves into two teams, with a corporal in charge of each. Two fellow lance corporals from 3 Troop and I worked as a team and around 10.40 and after compiling and submitting our report to 51 Squadron's staff sergeant, we headed across to the cookhouse for a late morning tea break. I then worked with Gerry and together we started to fit out seven newly installed portakabins, while four members of 3 Troop team returned to Blue Beach Military Cemetery to continue preparing the foundations for a memorial wall. The remainder of 3 Troop carried on working over at the helipad site and we were informed that for the remainder of this tour, everyone will work 12 hour shifts each and every day and there is no doubt in anyone's mind that this is going to be extremely demanding both mentally, and physically.

An electrician by trade, Gerry is as good as they come and today he installed light switches, cable trunking, power sockets, fuse boxes, and fluorescent lighting inside portakabins numbers 5 to 11. For my part, I fitted security locks to the portakabin doors and checked the tension of each anchor strop after which I secured notice boards and signage to the portakabin walls, and then carried out a final inspection of each portakabin.

All seven units had been flown in two weeks earlier and have been placed on concrete bases immediately adjacent to the partially completed REME Workshops, which is at the north aspect of Kelly's Garden. At 12.45 we went for lunch and for the remainder of the day, we worked on minor snagging that had been earlier identified in the new portakabins. This work took us right up until 19.45 to complete and over a late evening meal in the cookhouse, a member of 51 Field Squadron informed us that our troop commander had visited Kelly's Garden earlier in the day, but only stayed for approximately 15 minutes before being flown back to Port Stanley. This puzzled us at first but we left it at that.

We also heard that 51 Squadron's staff sergeant is to double up as Acting Sergeant Major while at Kelly's Garden and it seems that everyone has really taken a huge liking to him, because of his excellent man-management skills, approachability, and overall sense of fairness. He also listens before reaching a decision and I have to say that we in 3 Troop hold him in very high regard, because he is genuinely an exceptional Senior Non-Commissioned Officer. He is a soldier who is consistent in all dealings with both work and personal matters and as such, nobody feels apprehensive if they ever need to speak with him about a concern they may have.

After dinner, I returned to my portakabin to read a few pages of Gerald Seymour's thriller 'Harry's Game' which ironically, was made into a television drama series just before our operational tour began. Based on the fictional assassination of a British Cabinet minister in London during the time of The Troubles in Northern Ireland, the story tells of the search for the hitman in Belfast by an undercover agent named Harry Brown. It is a superb read and I am thoroughly enjoying it.

At 20.15, I went across to 51 Field Squadron's bar to relax with colleagues from 3 Troop but all too soon tiredness took its hold, so most of us returned to our portakabin and as I slowly trundled my way along the partly paved footpath, I was completely overwhelmed at how beautiful the evening sky looked. It does not get dark until around 22.00 and the southern hemisphere night-sky is so magical at times, and as odd as this may sound, the stars look so much closer than they do back home in Great Britain. They really are magnificent and so very perfect in every way, and I am always left speechless by their beauty and splendour and also the other celestial bodies that hang high above Kelly's Garden.

This is only possible because there is no light pollution of any kind here or anywhere else you look, and I find it all so very humbling and a true privilege to be able to feel so connected with this place. Suddenly, I sensed a storm approaching as the wind began to rise and the sky clouded over.

Typical of the unpredictable South Atlantic weather, hailstones suddenly lashed down on the Defence Base and within a matter of seconds the air temperature dropped significantly. Back inside my portakabin it was warm and unusually quiet, yet very comfortable and some of my colleagues were reading their books. All of this gave me a sense for how Captain Scott and his team must have coped with their long periods of isolation during the ill-fated 1913 Terra Nova Antarctic Expedition.

Robert Falcon Scott, just like Sir Ernest Shackleton was an exceptional polar expedition leader who fascinates me greatly, so I may well decide to write an account of the latter in my memoir, whenever that opportunity arises. Right now, I am busy updating my journal as one of my colleagues looks through a window and out into the storm. Shortly, I will write a letter to my parents back home in Wales and for me this is always the best time of day because of the peace and quiet I have come to know and appreciate so much. It is the time of day when you can truly be left alone with your own thoughts, and to read or write, or completely forget about the next day until it arrives and also, to think about those who are so very special in our lives.

Before I go to sleep, I need to finish updating my journal and even though our portakabin is a well-organised mess with its makeshift furniture and clothes hanging everywhere, it is nevertheless home sweet home and we appreciate it more than ever. The storm outside continues to blow as I listen to Grieg's Piano Concerto in 'A' minor on my headphones, but I can feel my eyelids grow heavier with every passing minute and so I shall finish my writing shortly. This has been another long hard day but at least it is nearly over.

Friday, 21 January 1983

The weather here no longer surprises any of us and today the conditions were just perfect. In fact, it is the best weather we have encountered so far because the sun shone throughout the whole of the day. My section's first task was to dig a 40-foot-long French drain immediately adjacent to the portakabin which we in 3 Troop occupied when we first arrived at Kelly's Garden, but around 11.00 one of my team was reassigned to another section to help with placing newly delivered portakabins onto their allocated concrete base using a Coles Crane.

As such my section was reduced to just me plus one, so we continued and as soon as the trench was dug, we laid three courses of finely crushed rock and then tested a submersible pump which had been reported as faulty. To our pleasant surprise it was in good working order, and so the drain was completed and the task signed off but before going to lunch I went across to the helipad site to lend a hand and around 13.30, I was informed that my colleague and I are to inspect a newly installed sewage pipeline.

This runs from an ejector pump building located immediately behind the ablutions, and all the way down to the edge of Bonners Bay from where it lays submerged along the seabed and out towards San Carlos Water. This particular work will involve inspecting the pipeline for any damage such as leaking joints, and if any are identified they are to be either repaired or stripped completely and replaced. I estimate the work would take three days to complete and after several wooden crates filled with seals, joints, bolts, and washers had been delivered to the allocated sites along the pipeline, we began the work by carrying out a thorough inspection beginning at the ejector pump building.

Every inch of the pipeline on land and every sealed joint were thoroughly checked, and we eventually finished at around 20.00. We had timed the work perfectly and I was pleased with the progress we had made in just one shift. I showered and went to the cookhouse for a late dinner at around 20.45, then slowly made my way across to the bar to watch the 1938 movie 'The Lady Vanishes.'

Coles Crane at Kelly's Garden

We are told that tomorrow a representative from the British government will lay a wreath at the grave of Lieutenant Colonel H Jones VC, and I wonder if the ceremony is to be filmed by the small outside broadcasting (OB) crew that arrived in Kelly's Garden earlier today. Sleep beckons and I am only too ready to answer its call. There is little else to do in the evenings other than go for a stroll down to Bonners Bay, watch a movie, read a book, write letters, or in my case I like to jog to the ridge of the Verde Hills that sit gracefully to the east. It is somewhat surprising that none of my colleagues miss the social life back in Tidworth.

This evening I decided to update my journal before climbing into my sleeping bag to listen to some of my favourite pieces of classical music over my headphones. The time is now fast approaching 22.15 and I am going to take a last look at the

Verde Hills for today, because high in the night sky above a beautiful silvery half-moon is shining down on the land and hills below, and along the flickering water of Bonners Bay. Out in the distance I can see the tiny lights coming from the houses over in San Carlos Settlement and it is all so very peaceful, and enchanting. The sheer beauty of this secluded location is quite simply staggering at times and to think that back home before we deployed, one slight concern my colleagues and I had was with regard to the notorious South Atlantic weather. We had heard stories of just how bad it can be but in truth and from what we have encountered so far, we have been quite lucky because the summer season is almost upon us. What a way to end the perfect day.

Saturday, 22 January to Monday, 24 January 1982

Today is Monday, 24 January and around 12.00 our troop staff sergeant arrived from Port Stanley and he brought with him the first delivery of mail from back home in almost a week, and for those who received letters it was time to grab a quiet moment alone to read their news from family and friends. The section assigned to Blue Beach Military Cemetery continued with their work and to their credit, they worked through the weekend and have now finally completed the foundation for the stone memorial wall.

Yesterday afternoon, I completed my check on the sewage pipeline and once satisfied that every joint was intact and there was no damage to the actual pipeline itself, I started to prepare footings for a 38,000-litre water storage tank which will be sited at the eastern edge of Kelly's Garden. John, a colleague who assisted me yesterday helped with the inspection of each and every single white PVC panel, and thankfully we found no issues of any kind and so our task progressed quickly, as did the work over at the helipad site and the fitting out of more new portakabins. All in all, 3 Troop has had a very productive weekend.

Pipeline at Kelly's Garden

The days here are certainly growing longer and the tasks are becoming more challenging, but at least during the evenings we had time to relax and take in a movie such as 'The Blues Brothers' and 'Convoy.' Today is Sunday, and a colleague came across an image he found inside a book which was of a young US casualty from the Vietnam War, which started on 1 November 1955 and ended on 30 April 1975. He passed it around for the rest of us to see and quite honestly, it was very upsetting to read the details of how he died and instantly it brought back memories of the training and preparation I had to go through before deploying to Northern Ireland in 1979.

The Medical Officer who gave the presentation on war injuries pulled no punches, and he spoke at length on what to do in certain combatant situations and outlined in detail the immediate actions to be taken when treating phosphorous burns, bullet wounds, severe bleeding, and other injuries. He ended his talk by showing a military medical training film called 'Army Medicine in Vietnam,' and to say it was brutally gruesome would be an understatement. We were first shown a black and white version of the film and then one which was in full colour, and while most of the squadron coped well with seeing such graphic images, others really struggled and I prayed that I never come across such incidents during my career. It really was the reality check that everyone needed before deploying to West Belfast, at that time.

Tuesday, 25th January 1983

With the weather constantly changing, I began work on assembling one of the three water storage tanks and there were hundreds of nuts, bolts, and washers involved but thankfully I was joined by three more of my colleagues including one who had worked over at Blue Beach Military Cemetery. Another team from 3 Troop undertook maintenance work on the Bulk Fuel Installation and Generator House and after my section finished putting together the first two water storage tanks, we checked the footings for a third tank and around 19.45 we returned all tools to the G1098 Store.

From there we headed back to the portakabin to read our mail which arrived earlier today. One letter I received was from my friend David Banahan who lives back in Llanelli, and attached to his letter was a copy of an article from a national newspaper that had been published after a soldier wrote to the editor while serving here in the Falkland Islands.

The letter had been sent anonymously and described the living conditions as 'terrible' and went on to say that there was a total lack of welfare for the military however, on reading out the article to my colleagues, we all disagreed with the claims being made. The soldier was certainly not speaking for any of us but he was either very brave, or naïve, because there were clues as to his location and unit.

Over in the bar, I sat with Kevin and others to watch the comedy musical 'Paint Your Wagon' which starred Clint Eastwood and Lee Marvin but halfway through the film, I headed back to my portakabin to write letters to my parents and David. We received word earlier that the remainder of 3 Troop will be joining us here at Kelly's Garden in the next few days, and our new troop commander. It is fast approaching midnight and as I write up today's events in my journal, I am still itching from the fibre glass I worked with today to seal the water storage tanks. The days must be passing quickly because already we are close to the end of our third week in Kelly's Garden and so far, it has been challenging, very different, yet very enjoyable. It is everything I expected it to be and I could not be happier, and as for the letter regarding living conditions, then I have to completely disagree with the soldier who wrote to the national newspaper.

Wednesday, 26 January 1983

This morning we only managed to work for one hour due to the heavy rainfall coming in from the west and when it stopped, I continued with my work on the water storage tanks and during the afternoon, the third tank was completed in record time.

To avoid further contact with fibre glass, I took to wearing a bright orange wet suit and it certainly did the trick because I no longer had any reaction on my skin. Amusingly, John who is a fellow lance corporal has written to several celebrities asking for signed photographs because he has heard that I wrote to my favourite comedians, namely Benny Hill and Eric Morecombe. For some reason though, he went one step further and wrote to the Governor of Her Majesty's Prison Holloway, requesting that inmates consider becoming penfriends with us bachelor Royal Engineers serving here in Kelly's Garden.

Gobsmacked at first by what he has written, I also found it hilarious and could not help but laugh at his reaction when I told him that HMP Holloway housed some of the most dangerous women prisoners in Britain. I explained that Myra Hindley for example, was once the accomplice of Ian Brady the Moors murderer and had been sent to Holloway on being found guilty in 1966 by Lord Elwyn Jones of Llanelli. Lord Elwyn Jones was an army officer in his early years and served on the British counsel during the 1948 Nuremburg Trials, and his brother Idris once captained the Welsh rugby team in the mid-1920s. Over lunch at the cookhouse, I just had to tell the rest of 3 Troop about the letter John had sent to the HMP Holloway and they just roared with laughter, so now we cannot wait to see if anyone replies.

Later in the day and with rain still falling heavily, I settled down to watch the movie 'Every Which Way But Loose' in 51 Squadron's bar when suddenly the door flew open, and in walked our troop commander who without any warning had decided to fly to Kelly's Garden earlier than expected. How the aircraft was allowed to fly in such torrential rain was beyond us but nevertheless, he has finally arrived and it is good to have him in charge of 3 Troop's Advance Party. Not to put too fine a point on it, ever since he took over from his predecessor last year, we have not really had time to get to know him properly and so we hope that he is approachable and listens to the views and opinions of our staff sergeant and senior corporals who between them, have amassed extensive experience and working knowledge of military engineering. I am confident he will.

Nothing much else happened today because unfortunately the rain literally stopped play, and it was all so very frustrating to think that no matter where we go on the Defence Base right now, the ground will be absolutely saturated and we have lost a full day's work. I guess this is what we will have to deal with in Kelly's Garden from time to time, and to that end we need to condition ourselves to remaining focussed and positive.

Before the rain

Thursday, 27 January 1983

Back in Port Stanley, the letter sent anonymously to the editor of a national newspaper regarding living conditions here in the Falkland Islands is now being investigated, while another newspaper has published an article in which it says that readers have donated to a large stock of canned beer and lager for the troops, and the newspaper will arrange for this to be delivered to the Falklands because of the high regard its readers hold for the Armed Forces. Everyone is keen to read this latest article but with regards to the anonymous letter, it is the general consensus in Kelly's Garden that we hope the soldier is never found out, and that he simply learns a lesson. We genuinely fail to understand what he expected when serving in a post-war military theatre such as the Falklands.

Everyone agreed that the best way he could have addressed his concerns was by bringing them to the attention of his troop commander, but certainly not by writing to the national press. This is where he has let himself and his unit down.

This morning was surprisingly warm and with the assembling of the water tanks almost complete, I had just one minor snagging to resolve. RAF helicopters flew in and out of Kelly's Garden all day and many were filmed by the two-man camera crew who we are told are here to make a television documentary about the war, and also about the subsequent recovery operation. The Officer Commanding 51 Field Squadron visited Kelly's Garden and throughout the duration of his stay he maintained a low profile, and allowed 3 Troop to get on with its work undisturbed. We all think that was extremely considerate of him and we are grateful.

A subject that arises from time to time is the anticipated Argentine air strikes that could potentially occur at any time here on East Falkland Island, and more specifically at Kelly's Garden given our distance from Port Stanley. To those who may be wondering back home if we are concerned or worried by this possibility, then our response is quite simply "not in the least." We know Prime Minister Thatcher's views on this subject through reading the newspaper reports we receive from back home, and we have also been informed that she has warned Argentina that Great Britain would have the full backing and support of every NATO member country and the United Nations if it ever attacked again.

Clearly her words have been noted because we have seen neither hide nor hair of the Argentine Air Force, and we are confident we never will. I completed the final snagging issue with the water tanks and then examined the short pipeline that runs from it, before inspecting the new portakabins that are now almost ready to be allocated to the troops we can expect at any time.

Additional engineering equipment and tools were airlifted to Kelly's Garden by RAF Chinooks, and these were taken straight to the G1098 Store. After finishing our work and after an evening meal over at the cookhouse, I watched the 1969 rock opera 'Tommy' with the rest of my colleagues. This is by far the finest album by The Who to date and written by lead guitarist Pete Townsend, it is an incredible soundtrack and a brilliant example of British rock music as its very best. I am ready for bed and have decided to finish my journal entry for the day by including an extract from an article I read earlier this evening.

"Since wars have occurred, this [the Falklands War] was probably the very best sort. Firstly, we won and that is an important consideration. Secondly, civilian casualties were low. Thirdly, it was contained within the area of dispute and no nuclear weapons were used. Finally, we could reasonably believe that we [the British Task Force] were taking military action against an armed aggressor. We could not expect a better war than this but in any further conflict, we are unlikely to be so fortunate!"

Friday, 28 January 2019

The work of signing off all three newly installed water tanks had to be postponed because of the need to start preparing an area of land for yet another project. The whole of 3 Troop signed out shovels and spades and reported to a large area of open area of virgin land at the western edge of Kelly's Garden. Although we heard something about this project when we first arrived, we have now received a more detailed report of the end product and its dimensions, the timeframe, and its purpose. What we are preparing is the site on which a large Rubb hangar will be constructed to house a RAF Boeing CH-47 Chinook helicopter, and in which maintenance and repair work will be carried out.

The site has already been surveyed so it is ready to be graded and levelled which will involve many tons of topsoil being removed by a D6 Digger, and then moved to another site using two Thwaites Dumper Trucks. Our work began at pace and 3 Troop managed to maintain this until 11.00 by which time, some started to look at their watches which was a sure sign that they were hoping for a tea break but we continued, because we needed to take full advantage of the fine weather. The backdrop of San Carlos Settlement on the northern bank of Bonners Bay and the Verde Hills to our east made a wonderful sight, and it still excites me more than I could ever describe.

In my section are four quality colleagues and the one thing you certainly need in the Armed Forces is humour, especially when you and your team are being pushed to its limit. At times, the physical and mental exhaustion will test your patience, while anxiety and pressure challenge your nerve and ability to remain calm and it is in times such as these, that some will see the funny side and make everyone laugh.

Such individuals are worth their weight in gold, and as my section worked hard on preparing the wooden shuttering for the hangar foundations, they came out with some hilarious anecdotes that had us laughing out loud. I am so fortunate to have the likes of Paul and Kevin in my team today.

Work continued and conversations varied from the ridiculous to the fascinating and all the while, the banter between colleagues was literally non-stop and I for one appreciate the amazing team spirit we have. Even in Canada last year, they were just incredible to work with. In the pleasant warmth of the midday sun, 3 Troop ploughed on with preparing the Rubb hangar site and as we began to assemble the timber sections of foundation shuttering, the progress made in just one day has exceeded everyone's expectation.

At one point during the morning, a rainbow suddenly appeared in the sky to the south as a Chinook helicopter arrived from Port Stanley. It made a wonderful photograph which I just had to capture. We were expecting another visit from our officer commanding this morning but for some reason it was cancelled, and so after a hearty lunch 3 Troop returned to the Rubb hangar site to continue with its work in glorious weather conditions.

Much sooner than expected it was time for us to pack away our tools and clean the Thwaites Dumper Trucks, and after I left the site I headed for the Ablution Block for a piping hot shower after which I went for dinner. At around 20.40, I took a stroll down to Bonners Bay where I sat alone while looking out to San Carlos Water to the west in complete silence, while totally mesmerised by the panoramic scenery that was all around.

This has become my favourite spot at Kelly's Garden and at dawn and dusk, the colours and beauty of the heavens change dramatically and often it turns into a biblical scene that takes my breath away, and it is at times such as this that I fully understand why artists, composers, and writers try to recapture such images on canvas, in music, and in words.

The Rubb site and rainbow

Later inside our portakabin, I wrote up my journal which I have now decided to cover with green transparent Fablon sticky-back plastic. At the other end, a card school has just started and next to the door loud snoring can be heard coming from deep inside a sleeping bag.

Someone else who is also inside his sleeping bag is Bob, and he must be dreaming about his wife judging by his random sighs of pleasure and the words he is speaking in his sleep. As agreed on our arrival at Kelly's Garden, nobody mentions the number of days we have left before we relocate to Port Stanley, or the weeks and months that are left before we return to Tidworth because quite simply, it will not make the time pass any quicker. I have decided to visit Morocco during my post-tour leave and I plan on spending three days trekking in the Atlas Mountains, as this is something I have wanted to do for some time. My other plans for Morocco are to visit the tax haven of Ceuta in the north, and the Cave of Hercules on the west coast from where they say you can look out to the Atlantic where the Battle of Trafalgar was fought on 21 November 1805.

I may also visit Gibraltar for a second time to see St Michael's Cave again, and the famous Barbary Apes.

Sunday, 30 January 1983

Today is the fourth Sunday of our tour and it is also our first half-day so the team is happy. Morale remains high and I hope this continues. During the afternoon a colleague and I dug a trench network and installed three French drains next to the water tanks. Around 11.30 a bag of mail arrived courtesy of the RAF and someone received news that their wife is expecting their second child. I received several delayed letters from my parents and was given the bad news that my Cousin Graham had been admitted to the Intensive Care Unit at Morriston Hospital, as he is suffering with a very serious chest infection. Graham is related to me on my father's side and is a 41-year-old sworn bachelor who is the most private person I have ever known.

I have often thought of him as being a recluse as he never ventures out except to go to work at Llanelli Railway Station. His mother, my Aunt Evelyn is sister-in-law to my father Alcwyn and was widowed at a young age when my Uncle Ernest died suddenly in 1945.

It is 19.40 and Kelly's Garden is as silent as the grave. Earlier, colleagues and I went for dinner at 18.30 after which some read books while others wrote letters or grabbed a quick nap but for me, I updated my journal. Before going to help in the bar, I went across to check the French drain and it seems to be working fine. Even now I know I am going to grieve over Kelly's Garden when I leave and this concerns me more than I dare to admit.

Monday, 31 January 1983

Today is the last day of January. It began with a briefing after which 3 Troop went about its continued business of installing additional French drains around the Defence Base, landscaping completed work sites, rectifying minor snagging, fitting out additional portakabins, and preparing both the helipad and Rubb hangar sites. With all this taking place, Kelly's Garden is certainly growing in size. Our work keeps everyone occupied until 19.30 most days and sometimes even longer, so I was glad to be given this morning off for helping out in the bar last night.

I woke around 07.15 and after having breakfast with my colleagues I spent some time in the Laundry Block doing my dhobi, or clothes washing as it is known in the army. Back inside the portakabin I decided to write a letter to my Cousin Cynthia who lives in Carmarthen, as she is planning to visit our first Cousin Roger and his family in Vancouver later in the year. After lunch, four of our colleagues returned to Kelly's Garden from Port Stanley and told us that the remainder of 3 Troop will be arriving any day and in truth, we need every available member now because we desperately need help with levelling and preparing the Rubb hangar site, and the foundation runs.

As we have already seen the plans and scale of the hangar frame, we are fully aware of the size of the structure and it is going to be enormous. Nobody on the team has any previous experience of working with Rubb equipment but that does not concern us, and we are all looking forward to start assembling the frame just to see how big it really is. We know it will be some 20 metres high when freestanding.

We also hear that food rations are starting to run low and that our chefs only have enough supplies to feed 35 personnel each day until replenishments arrive, and already the number of personnel here at Kelly's Garden has increased to just under 100. We are confident these supplies will arrive soon, as will the engineering tools and equipment I have requested from CRE Works in Port Stanley. Today has been long and very busy but everyone is smiling and morale remains high.

After our evening meal, I watched the blockbuster movie 'Zulu Dawn' with others from my troop. The film is based on the humiliating defeat by some 12,000 Zulus over part of Lord Chelmsford's column at the Battle of Isandlwana on 22 January 1879. Although 1,800 in strength, the British were armed with two field guns and a new state of the art breach-loading rifle called the Martini-Henry, but with poor military intelligence reports and a degree of brashness, Chelmsford's battle plan was certain to fail.

Firstly, he made the fatal mistake of splitting his column into two which overstretched his men and secondly, the ammunition supplies were sited too far behind his lines of defence. For the Zulu army that had an approximate strength of nearly 20,000 warriors, the Battle of Isandlwana was an easy victory and news of the defeat shocked the British government in London. 'Zulu Dawn' hardly veered from the true events of the day and the Irish born actor Peter O'Toole gave a sterling portrayal of Chelmsford, a man who history tells us was arrogant and stubborn as a Commander-in-Chief, and extremely economic with the truth when presenting his account of the defeat to Queen Victoria.

After the film finished, I decided to go and help in the bar as 51 Field Squadron were having a social evening and as I walked back to my portakabin at around 23.45, the temperature dropped considerably. I glanced across Bonners Bay to San Carlos Settlement and contemplated taking a midnight stroll to the old jetty which is a 30-minute walk, but it was dark and getting very late. I decided to play safe and went straight to my portakabin and climbed into my sleeping bag.

Tuesday, 1 February 1983

Now into the second month of our Falklands' tour, today began with backfilling trenches and stripping out an old water tank, and anyone unlucky enough not to be employed on either task was assigned to maintenance work in the Ablution Block. Everyone was kept busy the whole day and it was while I and others were working on high ground away from the Defence Base, that we suddenly realised just how much of a sitting target Kelly's Garden actually is.

For enemy aircraft approaching from the west, buildings such as the white portakabins and San Carlos Settlement make Kelly's Garden stand out like a sore thumb and what is even more apparent, is that San Carlos Water provides a natural attack flight path for enemy fighter aircraft and the Verde Hills and Bomb Ally are the perfect escape route.

Thankfully however, the Defence Base is protected from aerial attack by Royal Artillery Rapier ground-to-air missile sites that are strategically located all around, and each is manned by the best gunners you could ever wish to have on your side. And there are also our Gurkha colleagues who carry out daily foot patrols so all in all, we have no concerns when taking all of these factors into consideration. We carried on working until 19.15 and feeling tired and hungry, we returned our tools to the G1098 Store.

Terrible news has been received that a member of the Infantry stationed at Port Howard has died in unusual circumstances, however, we must await further updates to know what caused this tragedy and right now everyone feels for his family and friends. We do not know the soldier's rank or name but the news has saddened us all at Kelly's Garden because no matter who he was, soldiers are brothers in arms.

Today does not feel like a Tuesday and in truth, it has been quite surreal for obvious reasons but again it has ended with yet another magnificent sunset. Is it any wonder why people find sundown to be the most poignant time of day and after the sad news we heard earlier, it could not be more appropriate. Here in the Falklands you will see the most incredible sunsets ever, and the longer I am here and witness the magnificence of the southern hemisphere night sky, the more fond I become of this extraordinary location. Its sense of remoteness and isolation is hard to describe but I am so blessed to be a part of it.

A football match has been arranged between 3 Troop and the Gurkha Rifles. One of the Gurkha soldiers is named Bhan and earlier this evening he surprised me by visiting my portakabin to show me his personal kukri. He explained that he had heard about the journal I am writing and wanted to contribute to it by having a photograph of me taken with him, while holding the kukri. This was a real honour and privilege, and a wonderful gesture on his part but I was even more fascinated when he told me the history and purpose of this incredibly sharp weapon, which primarily is a working tool for the Gurkha.

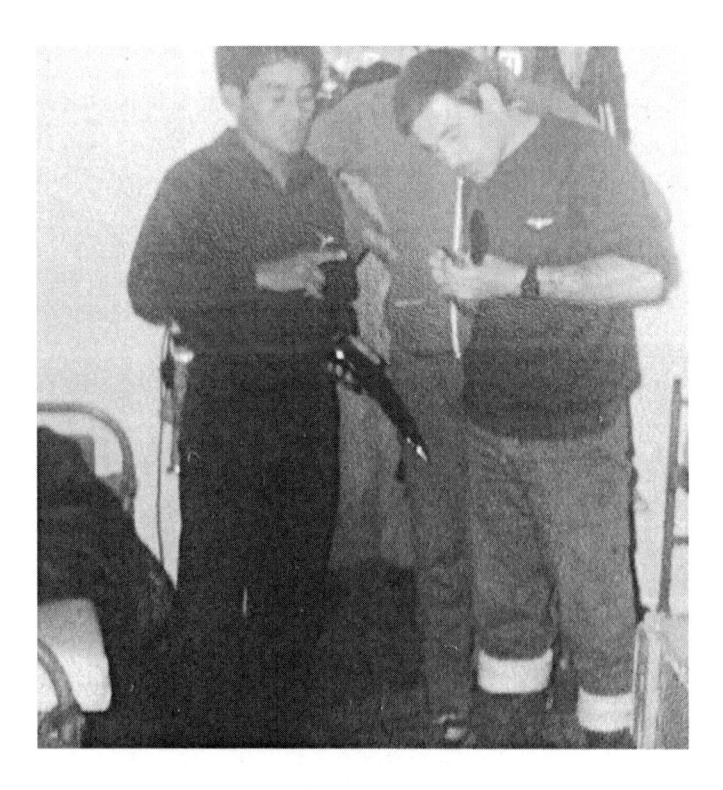

Bhan, me, and the kukri

Afternote

David Banahan and I were lifelong friends and we grew up just yards away from each other in Llanelli. Our parents were also good friends and we all attended Christ Church where my mother played the organ, while David and I were choirboys and I rang the bells while at Holy Communion, I also served as an altar boy to the Reverend Llewellyn Edwards. David was always older than his years and had what I would consider to be 'old fashioned' ways and outlooks. We often watched Llanelli RFC play at Stradey Park but then in 1976, I joined the local Territorial Army and my life changed overnight. David played bowls with my father for Havelock Park Bowling Club and between 1986 and 1989, he served as Secretary for Carmarthen County Bowling Association.

Not long after I retired from the British Army, I heard that David was seriously ill and the prognosis was not good. Just a few weeks later he passed away and during his funeral service at Saint David's Church in Llanelli, I struggled to come to terms that he had died so young. Tragically, David was not the only childhood friend I lost well before their time because there was also Janet Protheroe, Nigel Mears, Adrian Edwards, and Lillian Mylott.

During my time with the British Army, I served with the Gurkhas in a number of operational theatres including the Falkland Islands and Bosnia, and also on exercises in Canada and on army bases around the United Kingdom. Many became good friends and I learned much about their culture, heritage, and homeland, and I have nothing less than total admiration and respect for these remarkable soldiers who serve our country with such dedication and distinction. They are among the most humble and generous people I have ever served with, yet in battle their reputation for being fierce warriors is renowned, and rightly so.

Between 1995 and 1999, I served as Regimental Administration Office Warrant Officer with 36 Engineer Regiment at Invicta Barracks in Maidstone, and one of the sub-units under my administrative control was 69 Gurkha Field Squadron. My first actual experience of serving with Gurkhas was at Kelly's Garden in 1983, and I was instantly in awe of how professional and well trained they were and so much so, that I wrote an account of their history which is transcribed in Chapter Six.

Chapter Six
Falklanders and Gurkhas

Foreword

Following the 1982 conflict in the South Atlantic, the British Government needed to act fast in putting in place a programme of recovery and repairing the infrastructure of the Falkland Islands and more importantly, to establish a permanent British military presence. The chances of there being an Argentine reprisal were almost non-existent however, this could not be ruled out and so one crucial and immediate undertaking would be to select a suitable location for installing a Defence Base on the western aspect of East Falkland Island.

Another crucial requirement was to establish a RAF Station somewhere close to Port Stanley and to make urgent repairs to the war-damaged runway at Port Stanley Airport, following Operation Black Buck. Such an undertaking would be costly to Great Britain both in financial terms, military manpower, and equipment but that was the price that came with administering a British Overseas Territory and the work commenced almost immediately.

On the day I first arrived in the Falklands, I went ashore and as the Royal Naval Kiwi landing craft approached East Jetty in Port Stanley Harbour, a few soldiers standing behind me innocently muttered, "is this it?" Here was the archipelago's capital and largest community yet it was rudimentary if truth be told, and had I been a settler living on East Falkland Island in 1982 then that is exactly how I would have wanted it to be, because it was tranquil and somewhat idiosyncratic in its own way, and very homely.

I hardly saw any locals and the only traffic seemed to belong to the British military, and not even a barking dog could be heard which made it feel as though I had walked onto a film set. Houses along Ross Road on the harbour front all had a typical British look about them, while others further afield were basic both in their appearance and style. Another thing I recall quite vividly is that Port Stanley looked extremely colourful and fresh.

Christ Church Cathedral was no bigger than the average place of worship back home in Great Britain and Government House had a colonial look about it. Elegant in its own special kind of way, it was nevertheless modest considering its purpose and I guess that this was again how an island community would want to appear, irrespective of its location.

My respect for the people living in San Carlos Settlement grew the more I met with them, and I got to know one islander fairly well who often visited Kelly's Garden looking for work. It was he who gave some of my colleagues in 3 Troop horse riding lessons and from time to time, would take them out on horse trails across the Verde Hills. I asked him one day why he chose to live in such a remote part of the island and he simply replied, "because before the war, this was a safe place to raise my family."

On 3 February 1983, I resumed logging daily events in my journal and 3 Troop was completing its work at pace, especially as more of our colleagues who had been stationed at Port Stanley were now being relocated to Kelly's Garden. In late 1982 and not long before I arrived, Prime Minister Thatcher visited Kelly's Garden to speak with fellow Royal Engineers who were on site and one of them kindly gave me a photograph of that visit for my journal, and for that I remain extremely grateful.

San Carlos settler

Prime Minister Thatcher visiting Kelly's Garden, 1982

The Falklands and Islanders

(Transcribed from my journal written in 1983)

The official coordinates of the Falkland Islands are 51.75°S and 59.49°W. This British Overseas Territory is a remote archipelago made up of two main land masses called West Falkland Island and East Falkland Island and together, they have 740 much smaller islands dotted around their coastline. The territory sits approximately 300 miles east of Patagonia in South America, and the first language is English while 'God Save the Queen' is freely adopted as the national anthem. At the time of writing this account at Kelly's Garden in February 1983, the appointed Governor is Sir Rex Masterman Hunt CMG who also serves as Commander-in-Chief and Vice-Admiral.

Sir Rex first joined the British Colonial and Diplomatic Corps in 1952 and in January 1980, he was appointed Governor of the Falkland Islands shortly after serving as High Commissioner to Malaysia. The governor's residence is aptly named Government House which sits just off Ross Road in Port Stanley, and the building which dates back to 1845 has large pleasant gardens and grounds to the rear. In the distance and to the west are two prominent geographical features called Sapper Hill and Two Sisters.

Sapper Hill is approximately 455 feet in height and named after the Royal Engineers who once served at the nearby Moody Brook Barracks, while Two Sisters was taken by 45 Commando during the conflict on 11 June 1982, as part of the British Task Force's plan to establish an essential strategic control point for the final assault on Port Stanley. The tiny communities dotted around the Falkland Islands greatly appeal to me because of their uncomplicated lifestyle, rudimentary infrastructure, and strong sense of independence that promotes the excellent community spirit that settlers clearly enjoy and protect.

There is also a fervent determination to care for and safeguard their surrounding habitat, and the natural wildlife that thrives on the quiet and secluded beaches and in the waters around these islands, and for all of this, the Falkland Islands is a must visit for anyone who has a passion for the natural world.

Port Stanley sitting below Sapper Hill and Two Sisters

In 1983, approximately 2,500 settlers lived on these islands and the vast majority were of British descent, while others have varying European and South American ancestry. In 1884 and around the time that Argentina sought to have the matter of sovereignty resolved by having an Independent Board consider their case, the early settlers who remained at Port Louis included a small number of highly skilled Argentine horsemen called Gauchos, and people from Uruguay, France, Germany, Ireland, and Scotland.

Some descendants still live on these islands and those who live in San Carlos Settlement give the impression of being fiercely independent and self-sufficient. Their resilience in the face of such a tough lifestyle, harsh environment, and testing weather conditions is a clear demonstration of their absolute determination to continue living in this tiny community.

These people are born survivors and although there is no single large-scale industry on either of the two islands, those that seem to thrive are sheep farming and sea fishing. Children attend school in Port Stanley and because there is no facility for post-secondary education of any kind on either island, those who wish to study A levels are required to do so in the United Kingdom, or so I am informed. The West Store in Port Stanley is the only large general store on the island and provides a wide range of food products, as well as drink, tobacco, clothing, medical supplies, stationery, tools, household utensils, toiletries, and more.

Built between 1890 and 1892, Christ Church Cathedral is the most southern cathedral in the world and its whalebone arch is made from the jaws of two adult blue whales. These were erected in the grounds of the cathedral in 1933 to mark the first centenary of British protection and like Government House, it stands along Ross Road. Inside the cathedral are numerous historical artefacts including Sir Ernest Shackleton's flag that once hung in Saint George's Chapel at Windsor Castle. Christ Church Cathedral stands on the former site of the Holy Trinity Church which was destroyed by a landslide in 1886.

The Falklands currency is the pound and coins have the head of Her Majesty Queen Elizabeth II on the front, while on the reverse are animals and wildfowl such as the black-browed albatross which is on the five pence coin, the South American sea lion on the 10 pence coin, and the Warrah on the 50 pence coin. The Falkland £1 banknote is considerably larger in size than the British and the reverse has a Celtic design that is rather intricate, and all notes appear to be void of any visible security feature of any kind.

The islands also have an intriguing maritime history with remnants and wreckages from the past, such as the mizzen mast from the first ever propeller driven ocean ship *SS Great Britain*, designed and built by Isambard Kingdom Brunel. In 1886 and whilst out at sea, the *SS Great Britain* caught fire but on reaching the safety of Port Stanley Harbour she was deemed to be beyond economic repair and thankfully she was saved and floated back to Bristol Docks in 1970. Shipwrecks are dotted around both East and West Falkland Island and in Whalebone Cove you will find the most famous and photographed of all, namely the ghostly *'Lady Elizabeth.'*

This was a former three masted trading ship that was severely damaged by a storm in 1912 while bound for Mozambique. In 1936, she broke loose from her moorings and drifted across Port Stanley Harbour to where she remains to this day. The Falkland Islands continue to trade with other countries and owns its own freight ship that exports fleeces and other products around the world.

Life on the Falklands Islands is somewhat different to that on other islands such as the Orkneys and Outer Hebrides which sit north off the coast of Scotland, and it is certainly not the kind of existence that most people would choose to lead unless they were raised in a similar environment, or are determined to begin a new lifestyle which removes them from the hustle and bustle of busy towns and cities. Rudimentary, challenging, demanding, and unforgiving are just some of the terms that best describe the conditions you can expect to find in remote communities such as Port Howard and Johnson's Harbour, and each is off-grid.

Last week, I walked through San Carlos Settlement on my way to visit Blue Beach Military Cemetery, and I happened to come across the carcass of a slaughtered cow hanging upside down from a timber frame. It was not a pleasant sight but obviously this is how settlers survive in such a remote community as this, and I would not be exaggerating when I say that at times San Carlos Settlement can be like an outdoor abattoir yet the people have to work tirelessly in order to survive, and that is why I believe it takes a very special kind of person to live in such a location.

The Falklands £1 note that I still have

A major source of protein is kelp which is a type of seaweed found in abundance in the shallow nutrient-rich salt smelling sea that surrounds these islands. Kelp is similar in appearance, texture, and taste to the famous Laver Bread that we have back home in Wales and is still popular with locals and visitors. Life in the Falkland Islands has proven to be far more rudimentary than I had imagined before deployment, and for some of us who arrived one month ago it has already proved to be an interesting, mesmerising, and most memorable experience while for others, it has been quite a culture shock and not really their cup of tea.

Vast expanses of wild open ground are covered with the hardy Tussock grass that is to be found almost everywhere outside of Port Stanley, and the desire to want to settle down and live in such a remote location as the Falklands must obviously appeal to many. Indeed, I must confess that it attracts me far more than I ever thought it would because its charm is quite literally beyond words.

One thing I immediately noticed of on my arrival at Port Stanley was the total lack of everyday services and facilities that we in Great Britain take for granted, such as public transport, public houses, restaurants, cafés, an outdoor market, pedestrianised shopping centre, sporting facilities, a cinema, and so the list goes on. Whilst I fully appreciate and accept that such amenities cannot realistically be expected on such a sparsely populated island as East Falkland, they are nevertheless run-of-the-mill facilities in most countries around the world irrespective of size or population, yet this is what gives the Falkland Islands its unique character and wonderful charm, and I hope that nothing ever changes this.

The two main islands and 740 smaller islands that make up the Falkland Islands cover an area of approximately 4,650 square miles, which is almost half the size of Wales. Many of the smaller islands are completely uninhabited which allows for the rich diversity of wildlife to flourish, such as the several breeds of penguins that include the Gentoo, Rockhopper, Marconi, and King, and the Southern Elephant and South American fur seals, the black-browed albatross, and over 200 other species of bird.

There are no reptiles of any kind and the islands are the absolute haven for wildlife enthusiasts and indeed, their popularity is such that they are fast becoming a favourite for many thousands of tourists each year from all around the world. Through well-controlled and sensitively-managed tour operators, they get to visit and observe these incredible creatures that live in their own natural environment which in itself, is something that is to be celebrated and cherished.

As I sit here on the edge of Bonners Bay writing this account of the Falklands, it feels as though my family and friends are a million miles away and yet for some reason, I am so very much at home in this far-flung location that thrives on its remoteness and isolation. The vast expanses of untamed open ground are not hostile but instead they relax the body and soul, as do the views of the sea and the constantly changing weather patterns, and all of this makes you feel totally at peace with nature and yourself.

Many a time since I first arrived last month, I have felt as though I have rediscovered who I really am because back home it can be quite difficult at times to find true tranquillity and solitude. No matter how hard you try, before you realise it you find yourself smitten and overcome by the absolute sense of calm, peace, and serenity that exists in this part of East Falkland Island, and for those service personnel in Port Stanley who may never get to experience this place, they really have missed out.

Just six months ago, here in the South Atlantic two military powers fought on land, on sea, and in the air over sovereignty of this British Overseas Territory. Hundreds of troops paid the ultimate price for protecting what some people may have considered to be an archipelago of little or no significance to either Argentina or Great Britain, but how wrong they were. Such opinion was overwhelmingly rejected by many nations across the world because in their eyes, the Falkland Islanders had rightly shown a fierce and unwavering loyalty to Great Britain, and the defiance they showed in the face of Argentinian aggression was both admirable and highly courageous.

Wednesday, 2 February 1983

Today we have been notified that 51 Field Squadron will relocate to Fox Bay to commence engineering work on a new base tomorrow, and they will fly out of Kelly's Garden at 07.30. One of their electricians occupies the bunk next to mine and will stay behind to finish his tasks but no doubt, he too will leave Kelly's Garden in the coming days. Royal Engineers are accustomed to upheaval on operational tours because of the demand for sapper expertise and skills which very often, is called upon at short notice.

As such, you will often meet up with old colleagues in the most unlikely of places such as on a training or promotion course, on military exercises, and in theatres such as Northern Ireland, Gibraltar, and Cyprus. In front of 3 Troop's welding bay, some of my colleagues worked on laying a new path made from 600mm x 600mm concrete flagstones that are extremely heavy, and were delivered to the site using a Thwaites Dump Truck. Two electricians installed new wiring inside three newly anchored portakabins while another section worked inside the Generator Station.

Most of my day was spent sorting out keys for newly completed portakabins, servicing engineering equipment ahead of tomorrow's work on the Rubb hangar site, and before I finished for the day I gave a hand with the few remaining flagstones that completed the path near the welding bay. It has been a very productive day.

I received a second letter today from David Banahan who told me that Llanelli's David Pickering has been selected to play for Wales. I miss my rugby because as a player myself, I enjoy the physicality and intensity of the sport and David's letter reminded me of the atmosphere we used to enjoy on international match days, and the singing of the Welsh hymns and anthem. It is time for dinner and outside there is a cloud formation in the evening sky that looks like the wings of an angel, and so I grabbed my camera and took a photograph for my journal.

Wings of an Angel

A red empty ISO container has been placed at the northern edge of Kelly's Garden and this will serve as 3 Troop's G1098 Store which I have been informed, will now come under my charge. Peering out of the small portakabin window I can see the evening sky ablaze and splashed in shades of gold, red, and orange and it is a spectacular sight. I met two former colleagues who now serve with 8 Field Squadron and are here to construct part of the stone memorial wall at Blue Beach Military Cemetery. They showed me a scaled drawing and they will have performed nothing less than a miracle if they are to complete their work on time. They explained that they are required to erect a slate memorial measuring some six feet by eight feet which will weigh around two tons and on it, will be six cap badges and an inscription.

On either side will be five smaller plaques with all the names of those killed during the war. It looks mightily impressive and will no doubt be a fitting memorial to those who lost their lives.

Thursday, 3 February 1983

In glorious sunshine and under the bluest of skies, I and a team of four worked on the back-breaking task of laying more heavy concrete slabs to form footpaths between 10 newly installed portakabins that are numbered 94 to 103 on the site plan I drew last night in my journal. These units will be assigned to the RAF Technician

Team however, with the ground extremely uneven in parts the work took longer to complete and it proved very tiring.

Over lunch I chatted with a Lieutenant Wright, a Royal Engineer officer who informed me that he had been selected for promotion to captain and so I congratulated him. As he knew I am writing this journal, he kindly provided me with some interesting facts about San Carlos Settlement and its history, and also information on the ships that tragically now sit at the bottom of San Carlos Water.

The most recent is *HMS Antelope* which sunk during an Argentine air attack on 23 May 1982, and its wreck can be seen from the air on a calm day. Lieutenant Wright also confirmed that during the conflict, Kelly's Garden became known as 'Bomb Alley' because it was used as a flight path by Argentine fighter jet planes in attacks on British naval and merchant shipping. We both agreed that the threat we face of potential Argentine air strikes is still a reality and could happen at any time, especially as 15 February marks the 150th anniversary of Argentina's claim to the Islas Malvinas, the Spanish name for these islands.

Bomb Alley.

Before I finished my work for the day, I received word that the merchant cargo ship carrying 3 Troop's military engineering tools and equipment inside a red ISO container had finally arrived at Port Stanley Harbour, and that the container would be airlifted to Kelly's Garden before nightfall. This was very short notice to say the least and means I will need to check and sign for each individual item on arrival, then transfer the equipment across to a temporary store ready for the following day.

Thankfully the RAF Chinook helicopter arrived earlier than expected and as it approached Kelly Garden around 20.25, seeing the underslung red ISO container was truly a sight for sore eyes given what was inside it. These were the items we had packed back in Tidworth and are now desperately needed by everyone in 3 Troop. I quickly scrambled a six-man team and together we managed to check every single item before I could sign over the container to my charge. On board the Chinook was an old colleague of mine called Jed who took part on the portage expedition in Algonquin Provincial Park last year, but he was not allowed to disembark because the aircraft needed to return to Port Stanley without delay.

The RAF Chinook delivering 3 Troop's G1098

I returned to my portakabin to write an article on behalf of 3 Troop for the next edition of 52 Field Squadron's magazine, but I noticed that £15 was missing from my wallet and because theft in the British Army is not tolerated under any circumstances, I need to report the incident without delay. Such crimes are normally investigated by the Royal Military Police (RMP) or Special Investigations Branch (SIB) irrespective of the amount stolen, but because we have neither at Kelly's Garden, the matter was referred to my troop commander. Whoever the culprit is then that person will be in serious trouble if he is found out.

Morale thankfully was not affected by this isolated incident because trust and honesty are sacrosanct in the Armed Forces. I finished writing the article and then went across to the bar where the stock was beginning to run low. The movie 'Any Which Way But Lose' was being shown for a second time and again it had me laughing.

News of my stolen £15 has spread through Kelly's Garden but my gut instinct is shared by fellow colleagues, and we believe that whoever the culprit is, he is not a member of the Defence Base but rather, an individual opportunist who may have transited through Kelly's Garden on his way to another location. Before I retired for the night, I updated my journal and reflected on the day's work, and for me it has been yet again highly productive.

Friday, 4 February 1983

After morning parade, I went across to the G1098 Store to undertake a full audit of the engineering equipment that arrived yesterday, and I was assisted by three others. It did not take long to complete this work and in no time at all the store was organised, fitted out with shelves, and a counter installed. Shortly afterwards, I was issuing tools and equipment and my first customer was the ever-smiling Corporal Limbu of the Gurkha Rifles who is such an entertaining character, but frustratingly at times can be somewhat difficult to understand.

Lim as he is more affectionately known, signed out a total of 18 shovels which puzzled me at first because he had not been tasked with engineering work of any kind, but after he handed a shovel to each member of his section it all made sense. He shouted a short command in Nepalese and to my amazement, the Gurkhas immediately formed themselves into two teams of nine and then proceeded to play the most incredible game of hockey I have ever seen.

Gurkhas are natural warrior soldiers and justifiably feared in close combat however, they are also extremely talented in certain ball games such as volleyball and hockey, and they play at speed and with such power. The game lasted over 20 minutes but then suddenly and without warning, Lim shouted another command and they all politely returned their shovels by signing them back to the G1098 Store, then smiled and said 'thank you', and with that they were gone. They truly are remarkable and very charming soldiers who have a fascinating history, so I feel compelled to write an accoubnt about their heritage and culture in my journal.

Gurkha at Kelly's Garden

Afternote

In my entry dated Friday, 4 February I make mention that I felt compelled to write an account of the Gurkhas and their history and culture, and that is exactly what I did the very next day.

In 1996 and when serving as the Regimental Administrative Office Warrant Officer at 36 Engineer Regiment in Maidstone, the Chief Clerk of 69 Gurkha Field Squadron was a corporal who everyone simply knew as KP, and we became very good friends. I was honoured and privileged to be invited to KP's wedding and later that year, we both deployed to Bosnia on Operation Resolute which lasted six months and the Regimental Headquarters, 50 Headquarter Squadron, and 69 Gurkha Field Squadron were all stationed in a former industrial complex that was located on the edge of Gornji Vakuf. Corporal KP was without doubt my top squadron chief clerk and extremely thorough in his administrative duties, and his attention to detail and meeting deadlines were a credit to him. He was nothing less than exemplary.

Gurkha loyalty and devotion to Britain and the British Army is as absolute as it is unprecedented and still to this day, I feel ashamed and embarrassed that it took the British Government until 2004 to offer Gurkha officers and soldiers the right to reside in our country after completing their military career. I also considered it morally wrong that their case had to be taken to the Commons Home Affair Committee for a final decision to me made.

One leading campaigner who helped fight the Gurkha cause was the wonderful actress, author, and former model Joanna Lumley whose father had served with the 6th Gurkha Rifles as a commissioned officer. This talented and big-hearted British favourite showed her genuine awareness and concern for the welfare of our Gurkha friends, and eventually the case was won. Such political and completely cold-hearted displays by British governments bewilder and frustrate me at times, and especially when I consider those who illegally enter Britain yet are allowed to claim housing and financial benefits despite having been refused residency in other European countries.

The way in which the Gurkhas were denied similar rights before 2004 was totally wrong in the eyes of the British people and it was utterly shameful, and so the protests by those who supported the Gurkhas were absolutely justified in my view.

That was the situation shortly after I retired from the Army in 2000 and what follows, is a transcript of the account I wrote in my journal back in 1983 however, as this was 40 years ago, some facts and details may no longer apply or indeed, bear any relevance today but I have transcribed my account verbatim, as this is what I wrote at that time.

Gurkha Heritage and Culture

(Transcribed from the journal)

Of all the military troops I have served alongside, it is the Gurkha who has always impressed me the most.

Gurkhas originate from the Indian subcontinent of Nepal which is a Federal Democratic Republic that sits in the highest mountain range in the world, namely the Himalayas. At an altitude of 1,400 metres, Kathmandu is the country's capital and has a population of just fewer than 3 million people. Known also as the City of Temples, Kathmandu serves as the centre of Nepal's history, culture, and art, and it has a multi-ethnic population with Buddhist and Hindu being the two most prominent social groups.

We in the British Army are privileged to have such remarkable soldiers serve alongside us because their unprecedented military skills and remarkable physical ability, their mental strength and discipline, and their loyalty and steadfast commitment cannot be overstated or undervalued. And for the Gurkha himself, to serve in the British Army is considered to be both an individual and family honour and in many instances, it is the continuation of a family tradition that goes back many generations.

While serving in Germany back in 1980 with 31 Armoured Engineer Squadron, I was privileged to know a Gurkha by the name of Kep who was attached to my squadron, and in no time at all we became the very best of friends. I learned much about life in Nepal and about Gurkha culture and traditions, their history and beliefs, and from the very first moment I met Kep I saw and experienced for myself the humility, kindness, and true warmth that these people naturally possess, and from such an early age. They also display a courage and daring that makes them feared in military conflict and combat situations, so is it any wonder why these soldiers are respected and regarded so highly around the world?

Physically small yet immensely powerful and strong, their agility and capability just simply has to be seen to be believed, and Kep was a perfect example. Three years later and at Kelly's Garden, I have come across another Gurkha soldier who impresses me greatly and he is 2nd Lieutenant Ratha of the 1st Battalion, 7th Gurkha Rifles. Forever smiling and always immaculately dressed, he is incredibly polite and the most excellent ambassador for the Gurkhas, both as a fighting force and as a home and family-loving people.

During the Anglo-Nepalese War of 1814 to 1816, a series of ferocious battles was fought between the Kingdom of Gorkha as it was then known, and the East India Company which was essentially a powerful and mighty British trading company. Vicious skirmishes inflicted appalling casualties and significant loss of life on both sides and during one particular encounter, the British witnessed and recognised an unprecedented ruthlessness and bravery in their enemy that impressed them greatly, and so many were recruited into the East India Company to form its own powerful army.

This new fighting force was made up from three sub-armies or 'presidency' armies that were called Bombay, Bengal, and Madras, and by 1815 a large number of Gurkhas had moved across and joined the British Army. A religious and superstitious people, the Gurkha soldier traditionally wore a hook-shaped tuft of hair at the back of his head which they believed their God would use to pick up their body, and carry it across to the next life if killed in battle. If someone was to cut off this tuft, it would be considered a great insult and violation of a Ghurkha's belief, as it would deny him the opportunity to be united with his God. If the tuft was removed by an outsider, the Gurkha believed he could only save his soul and destiny by taking the perpetrator's life in an act of revenge.

As natural warrior soldiers in battle, the Gurkhas have always preferred close quarter fighting and in past conflicts they have displayed incredibly skill of pursuing and tracking down their enemy by working in small sections. On discovering an enemy's position, they would patiently wait until dark before drawing their kukri and silently cut the throats of all but one, and then quietly make their escape. On waking up the following morning, the sole survivor would be greeted by the gruesome sight of slaughtered comrades which would normally cause him to fly into a blind panic.

The traditional custom of drawing blood before replacing a kukri back in its sheath has over time become obsolete, but still this elaborate yet lethal accessory remains central to Ghurkha heritage and way of life. First and foremost the kukri is a working tool. An impressive looking knife that has a recurve in its blade, its primary use is for chopping and on formal and public ceremonial duties, the Gurkha carries a highly polished kukri which is only used on such occasions. On the kukri sheath are two smaller kukris called a 'Karda' which is used as a skinning knife, and a 'Chakmak' which is used as a sharpening tool.

The first language of the Gurkha is Gurkhali and also known as Nepali, while their second language is primarily English. There is a saying that when you befriend a Gurkha you make a friend for life. Most recruits are pledged to the British Army at a young age and nearly always by their father, and the selection process is considered one of the most difficult in the world. Army 'leave' or holidays can last between three to five months and during this time, the Gurkha is allowed to return to Nepal to visit his family and it is not uncommon for them to trek up to five days to reach their home.

Some will marry the girl chosen for them by their parents and in Nepalese villages, there are no established laws or rules yet crime and misdemeanours are rare because Gurkhas are taught to respect each other. Family life is at the very heart of Gurkha society and in remote villages, personal wealth and security is often measured by the quantity of livestock owned rather than materialistic and monetary possessions.

The Gurkha Rifles here at Kelly's Garden are from 'Demo Company' which is attached to the 1st Royal Hampshire Regiment, and comprises of officers and soldiers from different regiments within the Brigade of Gurkhas. There are 112 in total and they first arrived in the Falklands at Port Howard on 6 December 1982, as a relief force for the Queen's Own Highlanders. 'Demo Company' was due to move to Kelly's Garden on 15 February 1983 however, they arrived by helicopter on 4 February instead.

One of the fascinating stories that Bhan tells is that in the jungle, a Gurkha soldier could get so close to a foot patrol as it made its way through the undergrowth, that they could tell if it was a friendly or enemy force simply by running their fingers across the boot lace. A lace that was crossed would immediately raise suspicion that they were enemy, whereas laces tied horizontally would normally signify an ally.

A wonderful quote about the Gurkha soldier is attributed to Field Marshall Sam Manekshaw MC who served as Chief of the Army Staff of the Indian Army during the 1971 Indo-Pakistani War. Also known as 'Sam the Brave' he famously said, "if a man tells you he is not scared of dying then he is either a liar, or a Gurkha."

Chapter Seven
The Rubb Hangar

Foreword

By the last day of 3 Troop's first month at Kelly's Garden, our unrelenting 12 hour working days were acknowledged as being the new 'norm' and everyone accepted that this is what we could expect for the remaining five months of the tour. This was despite the fact that in all reality, there was very little else to do in such a remote location but to work and try to relax in the evenings in our overcrowded portakabins. Indeed, some saw this as a blessing in disguise because the time was passing by more quickly however, others including myself looked at this in a different light as we were thoroughly enjoying our time at Kelly's Garden and did not relish the thought of returning to Port Stanley or worse still, moving into the Coastel floating accommodation at Whalebone Cove.

If I were to be asked which two qualities I always associated with being a Royal Engineer, then my answer would always be the same and they are 'positivity' and 'determination'. In essence, I consider positivity to be another term for 'optimism' and as Walt Disney famously said, "if you believe it, you can do it" and as for determination, I have always advocated that if a person genuinely puts their mind to doing something then they will succeed.

With this in mind, I was always intrigued when 3 Troop undertook a new task because I enjoyed observing the methods some would use to achieve their end goal, and it reminded me of my Basic Military and Trade Training Courses at *1* and *3* Training Regiments in Southwood Camp. My training instructors frequently made references to old adages whenever they gave a lesson or presentation on various subjects, and the one I particularly liked was "the difficult we do immediately, the impossible takes a little longer." There are those who attribute this wonderful saying to the 18th century French statesman Charles Alexandre de Calonne however, others claim it was first used by the English civil engineer Isambard Kingdom Brunel.

What I do know for certain is that whilst at Kelly's Garden, most tasks were comparatively straight forward but there were moments when some proved problematic, and it was in such circumstances that other adages would spring to mind such as "fail to prepare, prepare to fail" or "plans are useful, planning is *essential", but everyone's favourite was "proper planning and preparation prevents piss-poor performance."*

From the very first moment that we in 3 Troop Advance Party arrived at Kelly's Garden, we heard whispers of a large-scale project that was going to be assigned to us however, we paid little attention because quite simply there was nothing we could do until our troop commander and staff sergeant joined us from Port Stanley, plus the remainder of our colleagues. When they did eventually arrive, a briefing was convened in the Troop Office for all JNCOs including myself and as we entered the portakabin, in the corner we could see a large board on which a photograph and detailed drawing of a Rubb Hangar were on display. Not only did these images instantly capture everyone's full attention, but it was the sheer size of the structure that took us all by surprise because everything about this project looked far bigger than anything we had anticipated. In truth it looked gigantic.

A Rubb shelter is basically a temporary industrial storage facility that is extremely robust and can be used for a multitude of purposes, such as an aircraft hangar or a vehicle workshop, a logistical warehouse or distribution centre, a field hospital and even an emergency processing centre, and so the list continues. They can be heated and ventilated and by their very nature, they provide the military with the perfect short-term solution in an operational theatre anywhere in the world. Rubb shelters vary in size and in 1983, the hangar that 3 Troop assembled and erected at Kelly's Garden was primarily to serve as a RAF Chinook Workshop, and we were told it would be the largest temporary structure on East Falkland Island at that time.

With powerful South Atlantic winds blowing through Kelly's Garden from the west, and with the constantly changing weather conditions, assembling and erecting the hangar proved to be far more challenging than first envisaged. Eventually, every member of 3 Troop was assigned to the project. Each of the 13 individual arch frames were made up of six large tubular alloy sections which when bolted together like a giant Meccano set, would be hoisted to a height of around 6 to 7 metres by a Coles Crane and then secured to a pair of supporting legs that were anchored to the foundation runs on either side.

This would increase the actual height of the Rubb structure to almost 20 metres and once free standing and fully secured to the anchor points, the whole frame would be covered using large sheets of green heavy-duty PVC that would be fastened to each alloy section. This would then be tensioned using strops that were attached to large rock-filled steel gabion baskets. A large motorised door would be fitted to the front of the hangar and the entire floor would be made from laying hundreds of interlocking metal corrugated PSP panels that were individually pinned to the ground. 3 Troop was given two months to complete this project and to lay an adjoining 150 metre long taxiway with three connecting helipads.

Having previously worked with RAF Chinooks helicopters, 3 Troop knew that the Rubb hangar was going to be big because the aircraft itself is 30 metres in length and 6 metres in height, and each has two sets of counter-rotating rotor blades that have a diameter of 18 metres. The Chinook at that time was one of the largest military helicopters in the world. Manned by a crew of four, the Boeing CH-47 can airlift 55 fully equipped soldiers or 10 tonnes of stores and as a matter of interest, although the aircraft cannot fly on a single set of rotor blades it can however, fly on just one engine. The Chinook is a true workhorse and just like the C-130 Hercules transporter airplane, it has a long and remarkable history of safety that is the envy of the military world.

3 Troop did not foresee problems or issues with the assembling of the Rubb hangar frame because the drawing and plans looked straight forward, plus we had all the necessary equipment, tools, and machinery to complete the project, however, the South Atlantic weather would certainly play its part in making this particular project a very memorable experience.

Saturday, 5 February 1983

Today's work began with the final survey of the Rubb hangar site, taxiway, and three adjoining helipads and responsibility for grading and levelling the ground was assigned to two of my colleagues namely Frazer and Randy. They will use a D6 Dozer and throughout the day they worked nonstop on grading an area measuring some 39 metres × 29 metres. This will be the site on which the Rubb hangar frame will eventually be assembled and erected with its front aspect facing east towards the Verde Hills, some 700 metres away.

The land to the front of the hangar will also be the site for the taxiway and three helipads and once this area of ground has been graded and levelled, it will be covered with a thick white polythene membrane. This will act as the underlay on which hundreds of interlocking metal PSP flooring panels will be laid, and ultimately pinned to the ground. As the work of grading began, the rest of 3 Troop worked on tidying the four edges of the hangar site which had been marked using white tape while above us, low clouds kept the air temperature cool. All the hard effort by 3 Troop has made this the perfect start to the project and by our reckoning, we are on schedule.

D6 Dozer

One of my other tasks during the morning was to inspect all newly arrived engineering tools and accessories that are needed to assemble and erect the Rubb frame, and I was assisted by Paul who gave me a hand up until lunchtime. He is a good and hardworking member of 3 Troop, and we are lucky to have him on the team. There were literally thousands of items such as nuts, bolts, washers, retaining straps, tubes of glue, socket sets, shackles and tensioners, heavy-duty PVC bundles, spools of twine and underlay, and never before have I seen such a quantity of fittings just for one task and this does not even include the actual Rubb frame panels.

As Paul and I studied our copy of the detailed drawing of the Rubb frame, we both considered the dimensions and weight of all individual Rubb alloy panels and it was at this point that we truly appreciated for the very first time, just how enormous the finished frame was going to be. For me, the scale of work that lies ahead of 3 Troop is going to take many of us by surprise. The morning passed quickly and as we walked across to the cookhouse, we could see the progress already being made on the grading, and it looks an excellent job.

During the afternoon 3 Troop worked tirelessly even though it rained quite heavily at times, but the RAF helicopters continued to fly in and out of Kelly's Garden and in the distance, I could see our Gurkha colleagues hard at work at the northern edge of the Defence Base. No matter where I looked, there was activity all around the Rubb hangar site and it is certainly starting to take shape. What sticks out the most is the floor area, because it looks much larger than we expected and around 19.40 and after a long 12-hour shift, 3 Troop finally called it a day and headed across to the cookhouse for a well-earned dinner.

After food I took my journal across to the Gurkha's accommodation because they have asked to see it, and in particular Bhan. I find it very encouraging to see such interest in my work and it helps motivate me to keep writing on a daily basis. I am always impressed by the professionalism and human qualities of the Gurkha that seem to be so very natural to them, and forms part of their true character such as caring for others, courtesy, respect and sharing, and never do they show any kind of resentment, envy, or self-centredness. It would be so refreshing if others followed their example and lived like these remarkable soldiers, because I genuinely believe society would be a much nicer place in which to live.

Rubb site during the levelling phase

I returned to my portakabin with a hot mug of tea and chatted away with colleagues on a number of different subjects, and it is wonderful to have such an array of characters in our troop. When the conversation finished, I updated my journal while others wrote messages to families and friends back home on 'blueys'. These are the blue coloured air-mail letters that are issued free to British military personnel and their families while serving on operational tours, or in military stations and on naval ships around the world.

I have written quite a number to date on tours such as this and in Germany, and they are a genuine lifeline with the outside world. Around 22.15 I climbed inside my sleeping bag and as I looked forward to a good night's sleep, word reached us that members of 51 Field Squadron had been called out to help tackle a peat fire which is spreading at the foot of the Verde Hills. Despite the heavy rain earlier today, the fire kept them out until 00.45 which was when they eventually returned to Kelly's Garden, sounding tired and with hands and faces blackened by the burning grass. They told us the fire was under control but their concern was the easterly breeze blowing in from across San Carlos Water and Bonners Bay, as this was constantly fanning the flames and with that, they went for a shower and a well-earned sleep. They have all done a grand job.

Sunday, 6 February 1983

Imagine the scene. A low thick grey cloud eerily drifts across the still water as it slowly floats like the veil of an angel, and begins to envelop the tiny sleeping community that is San Carlos Settlement. Nestled on the northern bank of Bonners Bay, the red rooftops peer through the sea mist while out in the distance of San Carlos Water, thousands of shrilling seabirds welcome a new dawn, while here in Kelly's Garden on East Falkland Island there is nothing but silence all around.

This was the picture that greeted me at 05.15 as I walked alone along the water's edge and the ice-cold breeze roused my senses. Had I stayed inside my sleeping bag, then I would have missed this magical moment in time with nature. These days, such sights and true feeling of solitude is what I have come to cherish so much because they all remind me of my childhood days playing in Machynys on the Llanelli coast. I knew that this was going to be another hard day for 3 Troop but the icy breeze I encountered first thing, made me feel alive and blessed, and that is why every time I stand next to Bonners Bay and welcome a new day, I say a prayer for being so privileged.

This place grows on me more and more with every passing day and even now, I know I will not want to leave when that day arrives because Kelly's Garden is in my blood. The thought of saying goodbye fills me with dread yet 3 Troop will have no option but to return to Port Stanley at some point, and rejoin our squadron for the final phase of the tour. I would be happy to remain here for the rest of my life.

The dawn that greeted me

Around 08.00, a Gurkha Rifle section assembled at our red G1098 Store ahead of their daily patrol, then walked across to the site of the temporary helipad but due to the deteriorating weather at Kelly's Garden, all helicopter flights were cancelled and as they approached our location, we greeted each other with the traditional Gurkha "namaste." Grading continued on the Rubb site while another section set about the task of anchoring down portakabins.

These units are not cheap and we cannot afford to damage any of them, because these have all been accounted for and are required to accommodate troops that will soon be arriving at Kelly's Garden. I have decided to draw a site plan of the Defence Base in my journal so that I can use this as a reference document, should the need arise. I was asked to help survey a section of land that has been chosen to be the site for a new Laundry Building and as Andrew and I began to mark out the site, we decided to our offer our individual explanation as to the difference between square metres and metres squared, just for fun.

I used the example that if a room has a length and breadth each of 2 metres, then its area would be 4 square metres, whereas 4 metres squared would mean that both the length and breadth were 4 metres which would equate to an area of 16 square metres. We then delved into a general knowledge quiz and the survey task took just under one hour to complete after which, I returned to the G1098 Store to carry out an audit of all engineering tools and equipment. Throughout the morning the peat fire near the foot of the Verde Hills continued to smoulder and in certain areas, flames could still be seen but these appeared small and posed no real threat. Around Kelly's Garden everyone got on with their work but for some reason, it was unusually quiet.

After our mid-afternoon break and with the weather finally improving, a Gazelle helicopter landed at Kelly's Garden and we were later informed that on board was the Adjutant General Sir George Cooper, a former Royal Engineer but after just a few minutes the aircraft took off and headed south, and presumably back to Port Stanley. Today was another productive 12-hour shift and most of the individual Rubb panels have now been fully accounted for and neatly stacked in their respective locations and also, grading of the Rubb site is almost complete. At 19.45 we all went to the cookhouse for a late evening meal while over in the bar, the movie 'Semi-Tough' starring Burt Reynolds, Kris Kristofferson, and Jill Clayburgh was being shown. After 10 minutes we decided it was so dreadful that we returned to our portakabin, and there I wrote up this journal while outside the evening sky was once again on fire and it looked so incredible.

I enjoyed a hot shower over at the Ablution Block and then had a conversation with my troop commander during which we exchanged views on the Falklands, how well we thought the work was progressing and also our own individual career and life ambitions. I am beginning to warm to him yet I still believe that when he first joined 52 Field Squadron, he may have underestimated our ability and experience as a team but that was then, and right now I can clearly see that his attitude and management skills have improved significantly, and for the better. It was an enjoyable discussion and I know we are going to get on well.

Afternote

When 3 Troop first arrived at Kelly's Garden, it was mentioned that the original site chosen for the Rubb hangar had been reviewed back at Port Stanley following concerns raised over its suitability. A preferred option was identified and suggested and after some consideration and consultation, this was agreed and although we never got to know the exact location of the original site, it was clear to everyone that the new site was absolutely perfect.

Being a keen hill and mountain walker back in 1983, I would often jog to the ridge that ran along the Verde Hills and once there, alone and feeling as though I was in seventh heaven, I would look out across to the distant features and open grasslands and to San Carlos Water. Still to this day and 40 years later, I can vividly remember those times when I genuinely did not want to come down and very often, it would be quite late before I eventually returned to the Defence Base.

Sometimes there would be no moon and it would be dark when I started my return trek, but I always made it safely back to camp. Between 1976 and 2014, I logged every trek I undertook regardless of mountain, region, or country, and I made it to the summit of Snowdon over 60 times and often, there too I would not come down until the early hours of the morning. I miss such walks so very much.

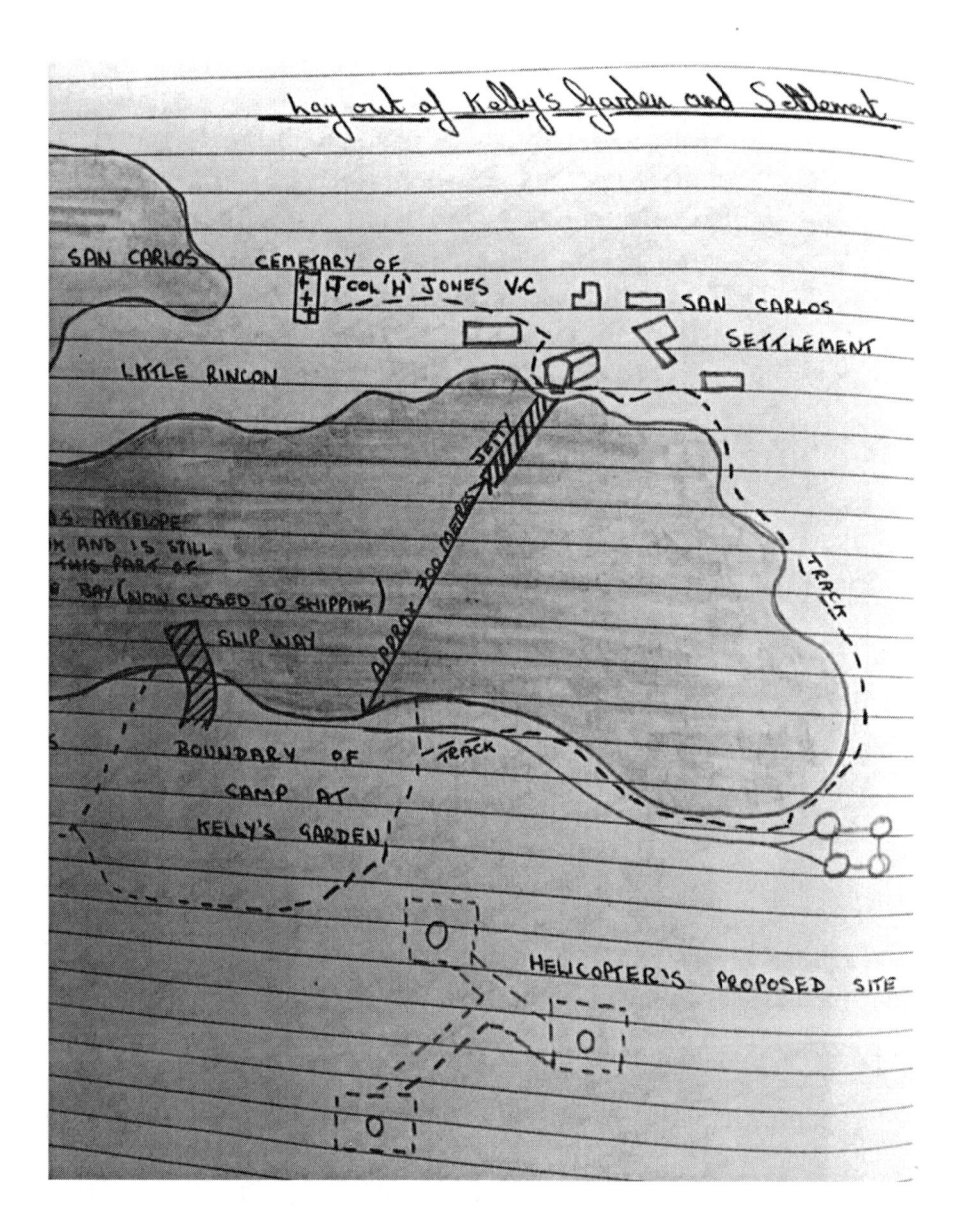

The plan I drew of Kelly's Garden

Monday, 7 February 1983

After one of the best breakfasts ever, 3 Troop Paraded at the Rubb hangar site and as we were being briefed we heard the unmistakable wokka-wokka sound of a CH-47 Chinook helicopter approaching Kelly's Garden, and it was coming from the east. As the aircraft hovered above the temporary helipad site, the powerful downdraft threw up dust and grass everywhere and after the rear ramp was lowered, out stepped a Gurkha Rifle patrol weighed down under their heavy backpacks and weapons.

Within minutes the Chinook took off and we continued our work of preparing the site for the hangar, taxiway, and three connecting helipads. Rarely do Royal Engineers miss a deadline as these can be critical and especially in an operational theatre such as this, and we are still on target to complete the Rubb project on time.

Around 15.00 however, we received word that concerned the whole of 3 Troop because it was being claimed that when 51 Field Squadron relocates to Fox Bay on 16 February which is just nine days away, they will be taking all engineering equipment here at Kelly's Garden with them, including the Coles Cranes, Thwaites Dumper Trucks, and D6 Dozer. A meeting was immediately arranged by our troop commander to address this matter and more importantly, to try and establish who had made this decision given many of the tools and vehicles had been signed to 3 Troop.

Wasting no time, he was booked onto a flight through the RAF and one hour later was on board a Gazelle helicopter bound for Port Stanley and a meeting with our officer commanding and CRE Works. We do not expect him to return until tomorrow evening at the earliest and so with the Rubb project now on hold, 3 Troop continued to work on alternative tasks and the one which I undertook was to check for damaged brackets on the Rubb frame sections. These were stacked immediately adjacent to the G1098 Store.

Two of my colleagues offered to help as each panel is a two-man lift and there were quite a number that needed checking. Thankfully it was dry but the air temperature dropped considerably as we started the work, and so we kept ourselves warm by drinking hot army tea. When the task was finished we spent time reminiscing on our tour to CFB Meaford in Ontario last year, and this brought back happy memories for all three of us. Meanwhile, another team was working on anchoring down portakabins while a third team focussed on landscaping, and a fourth team prepared more lengths of timber for use as foundation shuttering for the Rubb support leg foundations.

During the evening I helped in the bar and again the stock was starting to dwindle so a decision was made to close at 22.00, at which time I made my way back to the portakabin. I bumped into a colleague and we both stared up at the night sky which was so captivating and after braving the cold air for several minutes, we opened the door to our portakabin and once inside I wrote a letter to my parents.

Tuesday, 8 February 1983

Today, some of my colleagues were busy transporting the heavy Rubb sections that I had checked outside the G1098 Store to the hangar site, where they were neatly stacked in their allocated areas. Meanwhile, the welding team worked on backfilling a 50-foot-long trench in which electrical cabling had been laid, and this will be used to supply power to five portakabins that are due to arrive at any time. Neither of these tasks took long to complete and soon all equipment and tools were signed back to the G1098 Store.

The peat fire on the opposite bank of Bonners Bay continued to burn and with it, small clouds of smoke lazily drifted towards the Verde Hills but thankfully it stayed well away from Kelly's Garden, as this would prove a problem for the RAF and their helicopter flights, and also for those working on the site. There was talk that the fire in fact may have been accidently started by a local settler and had simply got out of control.

Checking Rubb panels with the Verde Hills behind me

It has been another long day and during the evening I had an interesting conversation with my staff sergeant about the Army Air Corps, and the various careers and opportunities it can offer to the right person. Ever since childhood I have had an interest in military aircraft and especially helicopters, so when I was asked why I had never applied to join the AAC, I gave my honest answer that there were no vacancies available when I attended my Army Selection Weekend in 1977. Furthermore, I mentioned that I was not aware that applications to transfer across to the ACC were allowed during operational tours but to my pleasant surprise, I was told that this was possible and that there were currently several vacancies.

I confirmed my interest in applying at the earliest opportunity and this was agreed in principle, but I must now wait for our troop commander to return from Port Stanley before I can proceed with processing my application. Around 17.30 the wind at Kelly's Garden started to pick up again, and soon several members of 51 Field Squadron were once again monitoring the peat fire at the foot of the Verde Hills. After dinner the air temperature dropped significantly and a few of us decided to go to the bar to watch the movie 'The Buddy Holly Story' after which, I went for a quiet stroll to Bonners Bay but after just a few minutes, I returned to my portakabin and wrote up this journal. The peace and quiet here is something I will never forget because it is unlike anything I have ever experienced before.

Wednesday, 9 February 1983

With no mail arriving today some in 3 Troop naturally felt despondent however, we are at the mercy of the RAF and I am sure there is good reason behind the interruptions we experience from time to time. To its credit the Army Postal and Courier Service Depot at Mill Hill in London provide an excellent service across the world and just maybe, the inevitable periodical cancellation of RAF flights play its part.

When it comes to the British military postal service, there is one thing that always amuses me and that is the BFPO Number allocated to the Falkland Islands. BFPO is the acronym for 'British Forces Post Office' and a BFPO Number is the military equivalent to the Royal Mail's postal code. Somebody within the Ministry of Defence obviously had a good sense of humour when they assigned the BFPO Number 666 to the Falkland Islands. How devilish was that?

Yet again, a South Atlantic wind blew hard from the west as dust and debris flew everywhere, making life and working conditions here at Kelly's Garden extremely difficult at times. We feel empathy for the Royal Artillery stationed around the Defence Base because these isolated Rapier ground-to-air missile sites can be absolutely freezing at times, however, they are our most effective defence system and our respect for their support and protection is unequivocal.

Throughout the day we endured hailstones, heavy rain, blustery winds, and not once did we have any respite from the elements. There is something else which I relish here in Kelly's Garden and that is the constant sweet aroma of fresh sea-air as this reminds me of my childhood days when I played on the sandy shores near my home in Llanelli, and the evening walks I often took near Machynys.

Paul and one of the welding team were given this morning off and it has been decided that members of 3 Troop will take it in turn to have one morning off on a rotating basis, and this news has gone down well with my colleagues. The electricity supply to the southern section of the Defence Base was completed and so the electrician team are now well and truly on top of their work, especially after forfeiting most of their free time yesterday to servicing the generators immediately next to the cookhouse. 3 Troop was visited this morning by 51 Field Squadron's pay sergeant who was extremely helpful, and it seemed that nothing was too much trouble for him as he resolved pay queries without fuss or bother.

The number of military personnel here at the Defence Base is increasing every day and we have troops from the Royal Artillery, Royal Electrical and Mechanical Engineers, Royal Pioneer Corps, Royal Signals, Army Catering Corps, Royal Air Force, and civilian stone masons who are contracted to work over in Blue Beach Military Cemetery. Our bar at night is getting busier and especially as the price of alcohol and cigarettes is so cheap.

Since leaving Tidworth, it has been my choice not to drink alcohol except for the single gin and tonic I had with a colleague and even then, I threw most of it away. Gin, whisky, vodka, and rum is sold for between 10 and 15 pence a shot, while a can of beer will set you back 20 pence, and a 20 packet of cigarettes is fixed at £1. Prices are incredibly low compared with back home and I am starting to save a small fortune.

A colleague and I began assembling a section of foundation shuttering on the Rubb hangar site and eventually, it will form part of four runs that will have steel wire reinforcement mesh placed inside them, then filled with concrete and finally each will have an anchor point inserted at precise positions to secure the arch support legs. While we were working on this task, the remainder of 3 Troop flew in from Port Stanley and thank goodness they have arrived because we now need every available member on site.

This was our last task of the day and we finished around 19.30 by which time, we were soaked to the skin. Once dry and back inside my portakabin, I updated my journal before going to watch the 1978 movie 'The Driver' starring Ryan O'Neal. I did not stay for long and returned to the portakabin for a good night's sleep. The welding team will have tomorrow morning off and outside the weather has again turned for the worse, but the portakabin is absolutely rock solid and does not move at all during high winds, and this is all down to the way it has been anchored to the concrete base. With my dhobi done and hung over my wardrobe to dry, and with colleagues inside their sleeping bags, I relaxed and began to read a book based on the British television series called 'The Professionals.'

Installing foundation shuttering

Thursday, 10 February 1983

3 Troop reported for morning parade at 07.30 and our troop sergeant was again the perfect example of how a British Army SNCO should be, immaculately dressed and clearly the person in charge. One rank below Warrant Officer Class Two, he is always meticulous in his turnout and you cannot help but admire and respect his authority and presence. One of my tasks today was to assemble wooden lockers and install these inside eight selected portakabins, and so with the help of two colleagues we began the work and aimed to have it completed by 18.00.

By lunchtime, we had already assembled and repaired more than a dozen units and we heard that other teams were achieving roughly the same number, and after we had eaten we headed straight back to the Rubb hangar site to carry on with our work because it was an indoor task, and the weather outside was deteriorating yet again. As we assembled the units, I was told that Wales had drawn with England at the Cardiff Arms Park on 5 February, and that David Pickering of Llanelli RFC had finally won his first senior cap. The final score was 13 points to 13.

Several of my colleagues were tasked with painting the new troop bar while a carpenter from 51 Field Squadron made six wooden cut-outs for the forthcoming horse racing Night. This will be a welcomed break for everyone and our troop commander has decided that the bar should be painted in a bright non-military colour for the event. To everyone's horror he picked green and flabbergasted by his choice of colour, 3 Troop playfully protested and expressed our light-hearted horror because the British Army lives, sleeps, and dresses in green. The cookhouse, Ablution Block, welding bay, and even the Generator House are all green, as indeed is the D6 Dozer and Thwaites Dumper Trucks, and even the grass outside.

Everything here is green except for the portakabins and we cannot escape it even if we try, but to his credit he listened to our appeal to have a different colour. "But green is the only colour we have," he explained, and so green it was. Eight civilian undertakers arrived at Kelly's Garden this afternoon and we were told that their gruesome responsibility is to recover recently discovered bodies of Argentine soldiers killed during the war, and to prepare them for repatriation. We have no idea as to where their bodies have been found but surely, this has to be one of the most distressing and upsetting aspects of post-war recovery. Clearly a matter of significant sensitivity and importance to the families involved, our hearts went out to each and every one of them.

This evening heavy rain poured down on Kelly's Garden but at least we were working inside warm portakabins, while next door a member of the welding team assembled more locker units. Without warning, we were visited by our staff sergeant who stood us down and so we headed to the bar which is now called the Ant Hill. We joined the rest of 3 Troop who were watching the comic movie 'Convoy' and around 22.00, I returned to my portakabin to read a newspaper that arrived earlier today and to my shock and great sadness, I learned of the passing away of American singer Karen Carpenter who died from a heart attack on Friday 4 February, at the young age of 32.

This news has upset me because she is only eight years older than I am. She and her brother Richard Carpenter were one of the world's most popular singing duos and during the 1970s, they wrote and performed great hits such as 'We've Only Just Begun,' 'Top of the World,' 'Yesterday Once More,' and the ever haunting 'Close to You.' In the article I read, it was reported that Karen Carpenter had died from complications associated with a long-term eating disorder and as I lay inside my sleeping bag, all I could feel was the deep sense of shock and disbelief that the world had lost such a young and talented singer.

Afternote

The preparation of the Rubb hangar site had got off to a great start but for me personally, the terrible news of Karen Carpenter's death had an impact that lasted several days. It reminded me that life is extremely fragile and it put the importance and value of it into perspective. Sadly, she was not the only celebrity who died in 1983 and below are just some of those who passed away.

David Niven (British film actor)
Carolyn Jones (American film actress)
Tennessee Williams (American playwright)
Muddy Waters (American musician)
Jack Demspey (American boxing champion)
King Leopold III of Belgium
Kenneth Clarke (British art historian)
Peter Farndon (British guitarist)
Buster Crabbe (American swimmer/film actor who played Flash Gordon)
Billy Fury (British singer)
John le Mesurier (British TV and film actor)
Richard Llewellyn (Welsh novelist)

Chapter Eight
A Letter from Eric Morecombe

Foreword

Mail would arrive from the United Kingdom on a regular basis to the Falkland Islands and this was down to the tremendous service provided by the Postal and Courier Depot which in 1983, was based at Inglis Barracks in Mill Hill, London. Unbeknown to many service personnel, the history of the British Army Postal Services is in fact quite extensive and very interesting and between 1945 and 1993, the corps that oversaw military mail operations was in fact the Royal Engineers before the service was formally handed over to the Royal Logistic Corps.

On one particular occasion whilst at Kelly's Garden, I received an official looking envelope that bore the stamp of the British Broadcasting Corporation (BBC) on the front while on the reverse, was the corporation's address and inside was a letter from the legendary British comedian Eric Morecombe OBE.

Born John Eric Bartholomew on 14 May 1926, he changed his surname at a young age to that of his hometown Morecombe in Lancashire and went on to become the other half of one of Britain's greatest comedy double acts of all time, namely Morecombe and Wise. Their first television performance was broadcast on 2 September 1968 and during their career, they performed on stage, screen, and television, and their Christmas Specials broke viewing figures year after year and still to this day, repeats are watched by tens of millions of adoring fans as part of the festive season.

As a young child growing up in the early 1960s, I would spend Christmas Nights watching their eagerly awaited television shows with my parents at 23 Cornish Place, and I fondly remember my mother laughing nonstop at Eric's antics with famous celebrities. Over the years they performed hilarious comedy skits which Ernie Wise would proudly introduce as being "the play wot I wrote," and the cast always included celebrated artists from the world of comedy, film, music, and television and indeed, many would literally beg Eric and Ernie to have the privilege of taking part in one of their shows. Peter Cushing, Eric Porter, André Previn, Dame Glenda Jackson, Dame Penelope Keith, Angela Ripon, Sir Tom Jones, and Dame Shirley Bassey are just some who were given that privilege.

Not long into my tour, I wrote to Eric Morecombe to say how much I had enjoyed the 1982 Christmas Special and I left it at that, but on 15 February 1983 and to my total surprise, I received a reply and a signed photograph. I could not believe that such a comedy genius had actually taken the time to write back to me but sadly, what I did not know at the time was that since 1967 Eric Morecombe had suffered with a heart condition. Almost one year after receiving Eric's letter, he was performing in a charity show at the Roses Theatre in Tewksbury with Welsh comedian and musician Stan Stennett, and the date was 27 May 1984.

After taking several curtain calls from a rapturous audience, Eric Morecombe suffered a third heart attack and collapsed at the side of the stage. He was rushed to Cheltenham General Hospital where tragically he died during the early hours of Monday 28 May.

On 21 March 1999, his lifelong comedy partner and friend Ernie Wise died at the Nuffield Hospital in Leeds, also from heart failure.

Friday, 11 February 1983

It is almost two weeks since I last had a morning off and it has come as a much-welcomed break, especially as it was on such a sunny day as today. Through my open window I looked up to the clear blue sky as the fresh scent of salt sea-air filled the portakabin when suddenly, my colleagues realised it was almost 07.30 and with that they stampeded through the door to report for morning parade. From inside the comfort of my sleeping bag I waved them off and felt no guilt whatsoever and in fact, I felt extremely content and thoroughly enjoyed the moment. On the bunk next to mine a colleague was fast asleep and within seconds of rolling onto my side, I too was back in the land of Nod. I woke at around 09.30 and got dressed before heading across to the Ablution Block for a shave and piping hot shower and on my return to the portakabin, I finished writing up yesterday's entry in my journal.

I wrote another letter to my Aunt Mair and Uncle Michael who have moved out of Hollington House in Beeches Drive, Tiddington which is near Stratford-upon-Avon and are now living in Roselea Crescent in Richmond, Vancouver. Letters were also written to my Cousin Roger and his wife Christine in Alberta, Canada and to my parents and friends back home in Llanelli. I often write to Aunt Mair because for as long as I can recall, we have enjoyed a very close relationship.

Stunningly beautiful and with long jet-black hair, she is the most elegant and stylish lady I know and many say she has something of Elizabeth Taylor about her. Her brother-in-law, my constantly cheerful Uncle Cliff, always reminds me that when she was young and lived with my grandparents Benjamin and Lena Williams at 3 Als Street in Llanelli, no matter where she went she could turn heads just by smiling at people. I know for a fact that she certainly turned my Uncle Eric's head because he became her first husband while serving with the RAF as a Squadron Leader.

Aunt Mair is my mother's youngest sister and during my childhood years, she always made me feel very special. I fondly remember the times when she would pay the family a surprise visit from her home in Morden, Surrey where she moved into a beautiful apartment block called The Sanctuary after Uncle Eric was tragically killed in a fighter jet training accident, while serving in Singapore in 1958. I also recall the times she would collect me from St Michael's School in her white Sunbeam Alpine sports car, and my hope is that one day soon, I will return to Canada to visit her and Uncle Michael at their new home in Victoria on Vancouver Island.

I am still cherishing Kelly's Garden but I wonder how the Falklanders will feel when the number of troops and tourists increase as they surely will, and especially when tourists get to know about the incredible wildlife that thrives here in abundance. I have no doubt in my mind that this will happen because I cannot begin to describe just how captivating these islands are unless you see them for yourself, and if like me they become overwhelmed by the natural ruggedness and charm, then visitors will surely want to return again and again.

After lunch I opened the G1098 Store and with the help of a colleague, I signed over all the newly arrived cooking equipment to 3 Troop's chef Private Hollings. His reputation grows with every passing day and I am confident that he will be in contention for promotion later this year, because it is his responsibility to keep us fed and he is doing a truly remarkable job. As Napoleon famously said, "an army marches on its stomach."

Throughout the day helicopters airlifted equipment, supplies, and personnel between Kelly's Garden and Port Stanley and one Chinook in particular, delivered an underslung Thwaites Dumper Truck which will be used to transport stone to Blue Beach Military Cemetery for the memorial wall, and then helped to move heavy alloy Rubb frames around the Defence Base. The military machine does not stop on operational tours and today a Gazelle helicopter arrived with the Commanding Officer 37 (Falkland Islands) Engineer Regiment on board. I met him during his walkabout and found him to be pleasant and easy to talk to, but what I liked most about him was his genuine attentiveness when asking colleagues about our welfare and living conditions, and the day-to-day work.

It was an absolute pleasure speaking with him and before he left, he expressed his genuine appreciation for what everyone had achieved to date, and the manner in which it was said was visibly heartfelt. It was clear to everyone that his visit had raised troop morale and during the afternoon, two of my colleagues worked on setting up 3 Troop's new bar, while four others continued with the work of assembling lockers inside portakabin number 76. This particular portakabin has been allocated to the Warrant Officers' and Senior Non Commissioned Officers' as part of their accommodation complex.

I received several letters today including one from my parents which informed me that my planned visit to Greece after this tour looks doubtful, due to a lack of accommodation on the island of Paxos. This news did not upset me and indeed, it has served as confirmation that Morocco is my best choice because I will get to trek part of the Atlas Mountains. Before finishing for the day I went across to the Ant Hill with colleagues to help set up the bar for tonight's horse racing and in no time at all it was ready.

The time passed quickly and the Rubb site is really beginning to take shape because the work of levelling the ground has been carried out to a high standard, and by 20.30 everyone was in the mood for a fun night of horse racing. My fellow Lance

Corporal John and I took charge of the betting while a member of the REME entertained the crowd with hilarious jokes and racing commentary and soon, he had the everyone roaring with laughter. Inside a small white portakabin in one of the most isolated parts of East Falkland Island, soldiers, airmen from the RAF ChinDet together, and two locals from San Carlos Settlement joined together for what surely was the best night of the tour to date.

This was our time for socialising and it did everyone the world of good to drop shoulders, and with eight races that had everyone cheering and for just a few hours, we had real fun and enjoyed each other's company while outside and some distance away from Kelly's Garden, our Gunner colleagues provided us with all-round protection as we toasted their good health.

After the bar closed at around 23.00, I walked back to my portakabin where some of my colleagues were already fast asleep inside their sleeping bags while others quietly chatted away, and so I collected my towel and washing kit and headed for the Ablution Block for a hot shower. Shortly after I returned, I too slid inside my sleeping bag and wondered if I will ever get used to sleeping under cotton sheets or a duvet again. Finally, I wrote up my journal and I am pleased with how it is progressing.

Afternote

In writing my memoir, I am reminded of family and relatives I have both past and present who at some point in their lives, served their country with the British Armed Forces and indeed, one of the research projects I undertook after I retired was to create a chronological family history that contains important documents such as Birth, Death, and Marriage certificates, school reports, ration books from the Second World War, newspaper cuttings, citations, and written correspondences.

Also incorporated are black and *white photographs and lots of colour prints and to date, my library comprises of ten volumes and my Falklands journal and collectively they have become priceless to me. My son David is a former Welsh Guardsman who served in Northern Ireland and Canada, and also on royal duties at Buckingham Palace and Windsor Castle. Today he serves as Chairman of the Welsh Guards Association (Llanelli Branch).*

David at Llanelli Armed Forces Day, 2022

During the Second World War my mother Enid served with the Auxiliary Territorial Service (ATS) as an Army Pay Sergeant at Phoenix Gardens in London. One day she and her friend Binnie had to take cover under an office desk during a daytime German air raid over Kensington. The bombs being dropped were classed as superweapons of their day and they included the German V-1 which was also called 'doodlebugs' and 'buzz bombs.' Both my mother and Binnie miraculously escaped unharmed.

An arrow points to Enid marching through London

My Great-Uncle Walter Cole also served as a Sergeant but with the Royal Welsh between 1914 and 1918. A prominent Welsh artist and close friend of the celebrated British artist James Dickson Innes, Walter was a fascinating and rather quirky character who I regularly visited on Saturday mornings as a young child. A devout bachelor and avid lover of boxing, we would sit together side by side on an old wooden bench in his kitchen and art studio at 1 Als Street in Llanelli. Forever adorning a flat cap, every now and then he would quietly mutter random pieces of advice such as "never pamper the whims of a woman," as he puffed away on his much beloved pipe. I didn't have the heart to tell him I was only 11 years of age and had no interest in girls and today, many of his treasured paintings hang in my home. The one story I still fondly remember him telling me was when he was fighting in the trenches during the First World War and during one particular battle, he suddenly felt something hit his head. He removed his steel helmet only to find a bullet had gone straight through it and survived the incident completely unscathed.

Walter Cole (left) and sister Lena wearing the dark hat

My mother's father Benjamin Williams, or 'Tadcu' as I used to call him which is Welsh for grandfather, was Walter's brother-in-law and he too served with the British Army. One of the most gentle and loving of men that I have ever had the privilege to know, not once did he ever mention his time as a soldier and I often think that just maybe, he may have experienced an incident or event that he simply wanted to leave in the past, as was his absolute right.

Benjamin and Lena

My Aunt Mair served in the RAF during the Second World War as did her first husband Squadron Leader Eric Pike from Pembrokeshire. In 1958 and while serving in Singapore as a fighter jet pilot instructor, he was involved in a fatal training accident at the age of just 36 and was killed instantly. I never got to meet Uncle Eric and Aunt Mair went on to marry for a second time to Colonel (Retired) Michael Kendall OBE formerly of the Royal Artillery, and they eventually emigrated to Canada.

Top Left: Aunt Mair and Uncle Eric
Top Right: Aunt Mair and Uncle Michael in Bermuda

Lieutenant John Cole RN was a once-removed cousin who served with the Royal Navy during the Second World War. Sadly, I never got to meet him and knew very little of his background.

Lieutenant John Cole RN

Last but not least was my wonderful and dearly missed Uncle Cliff who was genuinely the most entertaining storyteller I have ever known, and would always have me laughing out loud hearing about some of the antics he got up to in his day. Fondly known by friends as Cliff 'Ginge' because of the colour of his hair, he was a gifted rugby union player who played on the wing for New Dock Stars Rugby Football Club in Llanelli and one day, I asked him how he could run so fast with the ball in his hands. Being the joker that he was, he instantly replied "because I was bloody scared!" Uncle Cliff was another proud guardsman but not with the British Army I hasten to add, but with the Great Western Railway.

Cliff wearing Eric's fling suit

Saturday, 12 February 1983

Thank goodness I chose to be teetotal for the duration of this tour because on morning parade, several of my colleagues were reprimanded and sent packing by our staff sergeant for turning up "in rag order" as he eloquently put it. Clearly last night had taken its toll because two of my friends were a couple of seconds late and despite their amusing and entertaining explanation, they were ordered to run two laps of Kelly's Garden while carrying a shovel above their head.

Desperately trying not to laugh, my colleagues and I stood silent in three ranks as more were ordered to run two laps for one reason or another, until eventually there was only a handful of us left on parade. Watching our colleagues struggle as they made their way around the Defence Base was really entertaining and in times such as this, soldiers usually see the funny side and rarely show empathy. What did become clear from today's parade is that our staff sergeant's shouting is certainly improving and in his defence, he is a very fair SNCO and today's standard of turnout was truly awful.

3 Troop has genuinely worked nonstop since our arrival at Kelly's Garden and everyone deserved a good blow out. Without knowing it, he suddenly gave the show away because by chance I saw a wry smile on his face, and I heard him giggle as he dished out his punishment before dismissing the parade. We were all told to sort ourselves out and report back in ten minutes but this time, in immaculate order and when that happened, my colleagues looked almost human again and were standing perfectly to attention in the bitterly cold north-easterly wind.

One of the corporals and his section were tasked with separating the Rubb arch panels from the support legs, while I issued tools and engineering equipment to another section. I then went to help with a survey task on the southern side of the Rubb site and took with me several marker stakes, two tape measures, and a Theodolite. Others meanwhile continued to level the ground on which the taxiway and three helipads will be laid after which, they began the work of cutting into the far bank to provide an angle of repose with the help of the D6 Dozer. In simple terms, an angle of repose in respect of loose material is the angle at which the material stops collapsing and naturally settles.

During lunchtime, a team of Royal Navy divers flew into Kelly's Garden and were ferried out to San Carlos Water where they carried out undisclosed underwater tasks. Our pay sergeant also visited Kelly's Garden to cash cheques and deal with minor pay queries however, he did not stay long and his stand-offish attitude was observed by our troop commander who is now back from Port Stanley.

I continued to help with surveying the taxiway and helipad sites as the welding team carried out minor repairs to damaged lugs that had been noticed on several of the Rubb frames. Meanwhile, others worked inside newly installed portakabins and I was glad to see this evening arrive, because this is the time of day when I can sit down and write letters and update my journal. There was something else I needed to do this evening and that was to finalise and submit my transfer application to the Army Air Corps, because I am hoping to be called forward for an interview while I am here in the Falklands.

My troop commander has agreed to support my application after a 20-minute meeting during which time, he asked how my preparations were progressing for the interview, which questions I was going to ask, what my options were should I be accepted, and which career path I wanted to follow. Writing letters to my parents and friends took the best part of an hour and I was then back updating the journal, and today I have included a photograph which was gifted to me by a member of 51 Field Support Squadron. The photograph is of their bus leaving Claro Barracks in Ripon in October 1982, and I am extremely thankful for the contribution.

I was taken somewhat by surprise today by being given two pounds for working last night in the bar, which I was more than happy to accept because I am now on a saving spree to help pay for my trip to Morocco. The movie 'Yesterday's Heroes' was shown in the Ant Hill, but I decided to stay in my portakabin and retire early with a James Herriot novel, and within minutes of reading I could feel my eyes slowly start to grow heavier by the minute. I placed the book under my pillow and slipped inside my sleeping bag before rolling onto my side, and I must have been out like a light because I do not recall anything after that other than the beautiful evening sky which made me feel ever so content and blessed.

Sunday, 13 February 1983

Back home, Sundays are a day of rest and a time for families and friends to be together but here in the South Atlantic, it is just another working day and quite rightly so because we have a job to do, and that is to recover and repair the island's infrastructure and with winter only four months away, we cannot afford to lose any time. The names of the day mean very little to us right now because we have become fully accustomed to working 12 hour shifts, seven days a week, and furthermore we appreciate that our work routine here is very different to back home in Great Britain.

Earlier today, a Gurkha Rifle section deployed on foot patrol duty and as they left Kelly's Garden an icy cold sea-mist drifted in from Bonners Bay and in no time at all, engulfed San Carlos Settlement and the Verde Hills. It was a surreal moment and sight which I shall never forget because quite simply, it captured how life really is like here on East Falkland Island. It also served as a reminder that we are completely at the mercy of the elements, and it is in moments such this that we must keep our wits about us.

After morning parade, I was asked if I would be interested in attending a Basic Glider Pilot Course on my return to Tidworth, as this may prove useful in my potential transfer across to the Army Air Corps. Without hesitation I accepted and signed the application form. I can now look forward to the opportunity of flying solo and already I feel one step closer to achieving one of my ambitions, which is to own a glider.

The military excel at organising and running adventure training courses such as abseiling, paragliding, offshore sailing, orienteering, scuba-diving and so many more however, the cost of attending a civilian glider course is certainly not cheap. I would need to book time off to attend such a course and thankfully in this instance, the course will be fully sponsored by the British Army, including meals, travel, and accommodation.

For most of the day Kelly's Garden was immersed in a bitterly cold sea-mist which made working conditions quite difficult and unpleasant at times, and everyone was chilled to the bone. Working out in the open on the southern side of the Rubb site, one of the welding team looked like something out of a science fiction movie as he worked while dressed in black overalls and wearing a full-face welder's headshield, with blacked out visor. The team worked tirelessly and from time to time, Paul would lend a hand by holding the tubular frames as they welded new lugs that had broken off.

The task of levelling the Rubb taxiway and helipad site using the D6 Dozer continued but this time, a yellow BOMAG Heavy Roller was also used which was a sure sign that the work will soon be finished. The teams have done an excellent job and it will soon be time for us to start marking out the actual site on which the Rubb hangar will stand, and once this is done, we can begin to dig the trenches in which the foundation shuttering sections will be sunk, and where we will lay the PSP floor panels.

Suddenly and to everyone's relief, the low sea-mist broke for several hours during which time a single RAF Chinook flew into Kelly's Garden carrying the much-needed fuel to run the two generators that provide electrical power to the Defence Base. These generators were prepared for commissioning over a week ago and at present, we only have an estimated six-day supply of electricity yet for reasons unknown to us, we are only permitted to run each generator between 24.00 and 06.00 each day.

At 15.00 all members of 3 Troop vacated the portakabins that have been our home since we first arrived and moved into seven newly installed units which are numbered 98 to 104. These portakabins had originally been allocated to the RAF ChinDet however, as part of a major rethink it had been decided that all portakabins to the west of the Rubb site will now be assigned to the Infantry, Pioneers, and Royal Artillery.

We and the RAF will now occupy portakabins immediately adjacent to the Rubb site itself and quite frankly, this makes sense but during the afternoon, we discovered we were not the only occupants. Around 15.45 we were unexpectedly visited by a small herd of cattle that had roamed across from San Carlos Settlement, and were now enjoying their day out in Kelly's Garden.

I relocated to portakabin 104 along with three colleagues and because we are now the Troop Headquarter Section, we are more than happy with our new accommodation. Between us we made two tables and four benches out of old wooden pallets and storage boxes that once contained Rubb accessories and other miscellaneous items. Soldiers can make a home out of almost anything and here was the perfect example, but it was not without its moment.

Frazer and I decided to take the D6 Dozer across to an area which was approximately 150 metres away from the Defence Base. We were in search of more timber to make furniture however, it must have served as a death-pen at some time because as soon as the top soil was dozed away, we uncovered a mass of decomposing carcasses. In an instant, the air reeked of rotting flesh which made us both wretch, and we had no choice but run for cover with our mouths and nostrils covered as much as possible. Frazer eventually returned to the D6 Dozer to backfill the area and eventually, the unbearable stench disappeared. We managed to find one empty wooden box and this has now been converted into the table at which I am now writing this entry. Later this evening, I will write another letter to my parents before getting into my sleeping bag.

Monday, 14 February 1983

Today was not productive with regards to the Rubb hangar project because of an acute shortage of nails that are needed to construct wooden foundation shuttering sections, and as a result the day slowly dragged by. The angle of repose was completed as a Gurkha Rifle section returned from foot patrol duty at around 10.00, looking tired and ready for a shower and hot food.

General David Thorne, Commander British Forces Falkland Islands flew into Kelly's Garden by Scout helicopter around midday, and he spoke with practically everyone on site. He is a superb commander and I had the pleasure of speaking with him near the G1098 Store on a one-to-one basis. We chatted for several minutes and I was impressed by his interest in our welfare and tasks, and he shared his views on the progress of the Defence Base. I could have happily chatted with him for hours.

At 21.00 we received a replenishment of bar stock from Port Stanley courtesy of a RAF Chinook helicopter and soon our volunteer barman was busy restocking the Ant Hill. Other than this, nothing much happened today and just for once I decided not to do any writing of any kind, because the work we have been doing recently caught up with me and my colleagues, and we were all feeling tired.

Tuesday, 15 February 1983

Today is the day that the British troops serving in the Falkland Islands have been waiting for and quite understandably, some islanders must be feeling somewhat anxious because this is the day that Argentina could decide to launch its first air strike since surrendering to the Task Force last year. It is 150 years ago to the day that British sovereignty was first claimed over these islands but thankfully no action of any kind took place, and the day passed without incident. I received a number of letters from back home and among them was a wonderful surprise because I also had a reply from none other than Eric Morecombe himself, along with a signed photograph of him and Ernie Wise.

I was thrilled to read his letter and I could not believe he had taken time to write back and I decided there and then, to include his letter and photograph in my journal. I also received a letter from my parents and my godmother Aunt Dorothy, or Aunty Dolly as she is affectionately known, and she wrote to say she was keeping well and looking forward to seeing me when I next visit Llanelli.

Today the sun shone down on Kelly's Garden while out in the distance, San Carlos Water looked radiant as a mild breeze blew through the Defence Base. Our teams continued going about their work such as welding, installing foundation shuttering, preparing the ground for the Rubb hangar floor and helipads, and it was all carried out at pace. I was helping with the survey of a particular area of land when all of a sudden, my colleague and I were puzzled by our calculations which for some reason, was making no sense to either of us.

Despite checking and re-checking our figures, something was definitely not right even though the Theodolite was checked and it was precise. We double-checked each marker in turn and together we confirmed that they were in their correct place, yet one length of the floor area was still proving to be just slightly longer than its opposite length, and this baffled us. After carrying out a third check, there was still a discrepancy but thankfully we finally managed to resolve the problem and breathed a sigh of relief, but by now we needed a break and headed to the cookhouse for an early lunch. Such conundrums keep us on our toes and it is always satisfying when they are quickly fixed.

During the afternoon a Gazelle helicopter and a RAF Sea King landed at Kelly's Garden and on board the latter was General Thorne who had only visited us yesterday, but this time he was accompanied by a small group of British politicians who were on an official visit from London. Our section did not get to see or meet with any of these visitors however, over dinner we were told they had spoken with a number of personnel on the Defence Base and had asked questions about troop morale and living conditions, and other topics.

A consignment of stores and military equipment arrived around mid-afternoon courtesy of two Mexeflote landing rafts, and each was crewed by a team of six Royal Logistic Corps (RLC) operators wearing fluorescent life jackets. The Mexeflote is a large open sided military ferry used to transport large quantities of cargo and vehicles such as Bedford 4 Ton Trucks and armoured tracked vehicles, and it has the capability to carry up to 120,000 kilogrammes in weight.

Everything appeared to be running like clockwork until a low tide suddenly caused one of the rafts to run aground on the northern bank of Bonners Bay, close to the jetty near San Carlos Settlement. I was tasked with forming a standby section on the southern edge of the bay just in case the Mexeflote was re-floated, and so I sent for three of my colleagues to join me straight away.

I was becoming restless and frustrated by the whole incident because conditions out in the bay had been perfect, and the Mexeflote should have been with us by now. After working a 12-hour shift, all you want is a well-earned rest and not have to work additional hours because of another person's blunder or accident. I felt I just had to speak out and to my relief, our troop commander just happened to come down to the bay to see what was happening and fully understood my feelings.

At 22.35, a radio message was received from an embarrassed and apologetic Mexeflote commander telling me that he had finally managed to re-float his raft however, he considered it best to stay moored on the northern bank of Bonners Bay until 06.30 the following morning. I immediately agreed because tomorrow is thankfully my turn for another lay-in, and so I stood down my team and they headed back to their portakabins. I decided to remain on the shore of Bonners Bay, alone and to have time to myself because there is something special and relaxing about being next to the sea, and tonight I needed just that.

I recalled the times when as a teenager, I would often spend evenings standing on the edge of a narrow strip of water which was called The Chanel in Llanelli, and watch the dredgers sluggishly make their way back to dock while fully laden with sand, and their bulwarks almost level with the water. Around midnight I returned to my portakabin where I quickly revised for my Army Air Corps interview, and updated my journal before climbing inside my sleeping bag. Today has been a challenging and very long day.

Outside and in the darkness of the night, a section from the Gurkha Rifles was patrolling Kelly's Garden armed with 7.62mm self-loading rifles because of the possibility of an Argentine attack. Such confrontations are always possible but in truth, they are becoming extremely unlikely as time goes by and this is why we need the likes of the Gurkhas and the Royal Artillery to support and protect the Defence Base.

Just as General Thorne told us on the *Cunard Countess* as we approached the Falkland Islands, "we are here to fight; this is a real threat!" In the sound knowledge that we are well guarded by the surrounding Rapier ground-to-air missile sites, we feel extremely safe yet the thought of what could happen does come to mind from time to time however, as a military force that is now well established on East Falkland Island, we are more than ready for anything the Argentine could ever wish to throw at us.

The signed photo of Eric and Ernie

ERIC MORECAMBE O.B.E.

Thames Television Ltd.
Teddington Studios,
Teddington Lock,
MIDDLESEX.

6th. February, 1983.

Dear Philip,

Ernie and I were delighted to receive your letter and to hear that our video cheered you up a bit.

We can well imagine how hard it is on all the lads serving in the Falklands and very much hope that a lot more entertainment and recreation will soon be forthcoming. Nothing can fully make up for being such a distance away from your families.

Everyone is extremely proud of our men in the Falkla Don't think that now the fighting is over we've all forgotten you. Just wish to goodness you could all come home!

I've received one other letter from the Falklands ....so can boast that we have a fan club of two!

Hope you like the photograph.

All our best wishes.

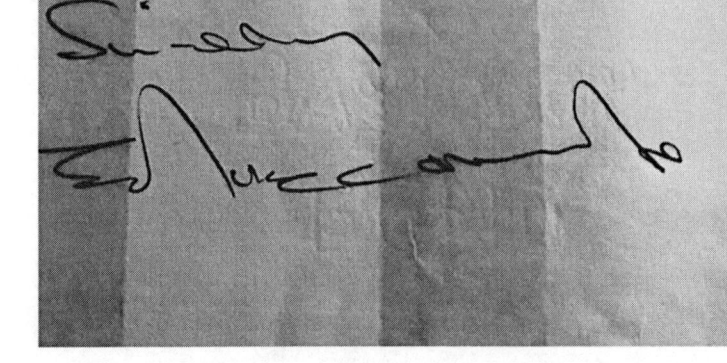

My letter from Eric Morecombe

Afternote

When 3 Troop first learned of the Rubb hangar project, we were naturally intrigued and keen to know more about the equipment and its capabilities, and also the work it would entail to have the structure assembled and erected. After a series of planning meetings with the CRE Works and senior RAF ChinDet officer, we had a far greater insight and understanding of the project and the complexities involved, but looking back at in now it was the actual timeframe allocated to completing the project that concerned 3 Troop the most, and understandably so.

The danger of working at height and in such an exposed and open environment as Kelly's Garden soon became apparent and a concern to us all, yet thankfully this soon gave way to a burning desire to get the project under way and as construction challenges go, this was the biggest that 3 Troop would encounter on our six-month tour. Furthermore, the Rubb hangar would not only test our combat engineering capability and project management skills to the full, but it would also prove that our measure of teamwork and teamplay was of the highest order. As we approached the start date, I could literally feel the troop's enthusiasm and excitement grow.

**Chapter Nine
Reach for the Sky**

Foreword

When I look back on my time with 52 Field (Construction) Squadron, it is always with mixed feelings because as much as I enjoyed my tours in Canada on Exercise Waterleap in 1982, and the Falkland Islands in 1983, combat engineering itself as a career was not proving to be as exciting or as satisfying as I had been led to believe, while at the Army Selection Centre in Sutton Coldfield in 1977.

Despite immersing myself into the different streams of military engineering such as armoured and combat, the simple truth is neither stimulated me and I have no idea why I was feeling this way but deep down inside, I just knew they were not the trades that I wanted to follow if I was going to serve a full career of 22 years. This naturally left me with a dilemma and the idea of transferring across to the Army Air Corps was becoming increasingly appealing because I was genuinely enjoying the military life far more than I could ever have imagined.

Furthermore I was thriving on the comradeship and teamplay that came with being a member of the British Armed Forces, and I valued the self-discipline and self-confidence it was instilling in me as well as the travel, adventure, sport, and outward-bound experiences which I was relishing. All of these were making me a better and more complete individual, and I wanted more. It was just the combat and armoured engineering that seemed to lack lustre yet for many of my colleagues, it was the complete opposite. Thankfully, my next posting after 52 Field Squadron brought with it an unexpected opportunity that completely changed the course of the rest of my time with the army, and I went on to secure a full and highly successful career but more about that later.

Through sound planning and preparation, 3 Troop entered the next phase of the Rubb project which was the installation and pouring of concrete into the hangar frame foundation runs, and laying the hangar floor using hundreds of PSP panels. We would need to mix huge quantities of cement and so it was time to make sure that each cement mixer was serviced and ready to go and at this point, the project site took on a completely new look and was much larger than we had expected.

New builds are normally problem-free and can progress at quite a pace and thankfully for 3 Troop, we already had one Coles Crane on site at Kelly's Garden but in reality we needed a second, despite the fact that we also had a Cherry Picker. One option of substituting the second crane was staring us in the face; why not borrow a RAF helicopter?

In 1983, British Health and Safety was still in its early days after first being introduced in July 1974 by Labour Secretary of State for Employment Michael Foot. When working in an open and potentially hostile environment such as Kelly's Garden, it was only to be expected that some sort of leeway would be needed in order to complete the task, and I for one have always advocated that taking a 'calculated' risk is far safer than 'running' a risk. Before taking a calculated risk, the normal procedure is to research or seek advice before weighing up your options, whereas with running a risk you simply keep your fingers crossed and hope for the best.

Irrespective of the varying circumstances that 3 Troop encountered at Kelly's Garden, not once did we ever contemplate 'running' a risk' yet there moments when we did encounter a scary moment, but full safety precautions were taken in each and every instance.

In September 2018 and whilst on holiday in Callao Salvaje in Tenerife, one sunny morning I stepped onto the balcony of my timeshare which is 35 feet above the ground, and there standing on top of the glass screen wearing no safety harness of any kind was a Spanish electrician taping the end of a bare electrical cable. He casually said "Ola" then stepped onto to my neighbour's balcony screen while holding onto nothing other than the awning frame. I could not believe the risks he was running with the electrical cable and working at height.

The following is a photograph I took from inside the Cherry Picker at Kelly's Garden and it gives some idea as to the height 3 Troop worked on assembling the Rubb hangar frame.

The Rubb frame

Wednesday, 16 February 1983

After yesterday's episode with the beached Mexeflote, I had my worst sleep of the tour because the air temperature dropped considerably during the night, and a bitterly cold portakabin kept everyone awake. As a well-seasoned hill and mountain walker, I am more than capable of tolerating cold temperatures for long periods of time and in all types of weather however, last night was just a little too fresh even for my liking. Today it was my turn for a lay-in and I happily remained in my sleeping bag while rubbing my hands and feet together, to stay warm.

Around 08.00, all peace and calm inside my portakabin was suddenly shattered by Sapper Kevin Diable who eagerly wanted me to listen to his favourite song by the mod revival band, The Jam and he played 'Town Called Malice' on my Walkman cassette player at maximum volume. As much as I like Paul Weller's music, this was far too loud for the time of day and so I politely gave him an ultimatum; either turn the music down or the cassette goes in the drink. Immediately he chose the latter. Kevin or 'Dibs' as he is better known is a real character and you cannot help but like him immensely. He switched off the music and after a quick chat headed back to work, and the peace inside my portakabin was eventually restored.

Around 08.15, I went across to the Laundry Building and on my return I got into my running kit and headed for the foot of the Verde Hills, from where I jogged to the high ridge. Getting my breath back while sitting on the grassed slope, I looked across to San Carlos Water in the distance and down on Kelly's Garden, Bonners Bay and San Carlos Settlement. Because of the low temperature, the air quality was excellent but it was certainly getting colder by the minute.

The panoramic view from this particular ridge always takes my breath away and one day, I will have my camera with me to take photographs for the journal. To my left was Bomb Alley and I could make out the level piece of land that is the Rubb hangar site, which sits at the southernmost edge of Kelly's Garden.

There was not a single sound to be heard other than the whoosh of the ice-cold wind that blew in from the west, and the thousands of seabirds flying over Bonners Bay and as I sat there alone and content, I felt as though I was the luckiest person alive. For as far as the eye could see there was nothing but wild open expanses of grassland and open water, and two tiny communities one of which is the Defence Base. I took in as much as I could and wished that my parents and friends back home could see this incredible view for themselves, and for as long as I live I will never forget the private moments.

On my return to the portakabin which was around 11.30, I sat at my desk and quickly updated my journal and once again I was immersed in my passion of writing while listening to music on my headphones. This time I was listening once again to 'Heat of the Moment' by progressive rock band Asia, and it brought back happy memories of my time at Owen Sound in Canada last year.

I appreciate and enjoy most types of music and I often listen to classical pieces written by Tchaikovsky, Verdi, Chopin, Mozart, and the four beautiful violin concertos composed by Italian composer Antonio Vivaldi that collectively are called the 'Four Seasons.' The weather outside had turned dull but gradually it is beginning to brighten up and this will raise 3 Troop's spirit. My colleagues continued to work on the Rubb hangar project which is now quickly developing into a large building site and its scale is starting to sink in.

Just before lunch the Mexeflote that ran aground last night eventually made it across Bonners Bay and was berthed close to the natural slipway at Kelly's Garden. Laden with more Rubb frame sections and two Land Rovers, it also had the most important cargo of all namely an entire replenishment of bar stock which was immediately transferred across to the Ant Hill.

Two generators and a Wolfe Plate Compacter were delivered to the G1098 Store by a Thwaites Dumper Truck and en route, the vehicle had a close shave with a newly installed portakabin. Luckily, I was standing inside the safety of the G1098 with Paul who could not believe what he was seeing, and it showed just how muddy and slippery the ground is at Kelly's Garden after heavy downpours of rain.

3 Troop had a surprise visit from our new officer commanding who arrived at Kelly's Garden in a Scout helicopter and spent most of his time in a meeting with our troop commander and staff sergeant, before taking a quick walk around the Defence Base with the senior RAF ChinDet officer. We did not get the opportunity to meet or to speak with him and as such, we know very little about him or indeed his expectations of us as a troop. This will no doubt be explained in a debrief we can expect to get from our troop commander later today.

We will also find out what plans he has for 3 Troop when we return to Port Stanley albeit we think we know what to expect. It was a shame we did not get to meeting our new officer commanding but it was perfectly understandable, and everyone appreciated that he was on a tight schedule and cannot be everywhere at the same time. He flew back to Port Stanley at around 13.00 and as soon as the Scout helicopter took off, our troop commander informed us that there would be another visit soon and the plan is for our OC to spend a whole day with us, to speak with everyone in turn.

By 13.30, I was back at work with colleagues and we continued working on preparing the ground for laying the PSP floor panels, checking the foundation shuttering, transferring newly arrived equipment to their respective work sites, and checking the repaired lugs on the Rubb alloy frames. Everything seemed to be in good order and the site was now a hub of activity. At 19.15 we finished for the day and a few of the team went across to the Laundry Building to do their dhobi while Kevin, Paul and Jock decided to go for a run around the edge of Bonners Bay, and over to San Carlos Settlement. I ran in the opposite direction and for the second time today, I headed for the open ground to the east and to my favourite place which is the Verde Hills that rise some 500 metres above sea level.

It was not long before I was well and truly into my stride and had found my second breath, and as I ran into the breeze my lungs started to burn because of the ice-cold air temperature. Managing to maintain a steady pace up the incline, I soon found myself once again on the top of the ridge where I stopped to give my legs a rest, and to catch my breath and take in the incredible view but when I looked down to the path that my colleagues had followed, they were nowhere to be seen. In the distance I could just make out a summit which I suspect was Mount Usborne, the highest point on East Falkland Island that rises 705 metres above sea level and is approximately two thirds the height of Mount Snowdon in North Wales.

While standing on the ridge and looking down again at the view that I have come to love so very much, out in the distance I unexpectedly caught sight of what appeared to be a small deserted ranch and I was surprised that I had not seen this on my previous walks and runs. When I get back to camp, I will look at my map to try and determine what it is. I could just see Falkland Sound out in the distance which is the stretch of water that separates East and West Falkland Islands and again, the air temperature dropped and I was looking at the most exciting and wild scenery I have ever seen.

Despite the cold, a golden ray of sunlight shone close to the site where *HMS Antelope* tragically sunk during the war and now rests at the bottom of the sea, and my heart went out to all those who served aboard her on that fateful day. As dusk drew closer, I was sat on the grassed covered ridge of the Verde Hills feeling pleased to be back on this most beautiful geographical feature, and I could have stayed there all night. Sadly time was not on my side and with daylight beginning to fade, and with mixed emotions, I decided to start my return jog back to Kelly's Garden.

As I scanned the track that skirts Bonners Bay, I suddenly noticed movement and realised it was my three colleagues Kevin, Paul, and Jock making their way back to Kelly's Garden. I decided to set myself a challenge of beating them even though I had almost double the distance to cover, plus I would by running on uneven ground for most of the way and so without them knowing I set off. The Verde Hills are ideal for fell running and very quickly I was back into my stride and running at 60 per cent effort, but with the cold breeze now behind me I was making good time and so I decided to pick up the pace.

Soon I was running at 70 per cent effort but right then, I lost sight of my colleagues and so I picked up the pace even further, just in case they were ahead of me and getting closer to the Defence Base. Running close to 80 per cent effort and with the ground starting to level off, my quad muscles started to burn but I was closing in fast on the stony path that would eventually lead me to the edge of camp.

With daylight almost gone and my lungs now burning, I maintained my pace and enjoying every second of the challenge. I finally began to close in on Kelly's Garden but my colleagues had spotted me and realised that I was racing against them. Sprinting towards the path, we almost merged into one group but to my delight I was just ahead and managed to beat them to the finish. Together we made our way to the cookhouse for dinner which we almost missed, because for some unknown reason the finish time had been brought forward by 30 minutes, but thankfully our chef made sure that we were fed.

After a hot shower I went to watch the John Wayne movie 'The Comancheros' starring Lee Marvin with a few friends, and we found the film to be quite enjoyable but soon I was ready for bed and I also needed to write up my journal. As the day approached its final hour, I climbed inside my sleeping bag and reflected on my time on the Verde Hills, the race back to Kelly's Garden, the scenery that surrounds us here on the western edge of East Falkland Island, and I could not be any happier than I am right now. I really do not want to say goodbye to Kelly's Garden.

Thursday, 17 February 1983

After rushing to the Ablution Block for a quick shower and shave, I met up with colleagues over at the cookhouse and together we enjoyed a full English breakfast however, in future I think we all need to pull up our socks if we are ever to beat the Ghurkhas to the first meal of the day. I have never come across troops who enjoy their food as much as they do and their appetite for good army food is simply incredible, and they are so entertaining in their own special way. When someone says a person shovels down their food, then spare a thought for Gurkhas because they can speed-eat like no other.

My main task today was to reorganise the G1098 Store which has turned into an organised mess but in all fairness, this is only to be expected given our working conditions and nature of work. After hours of hard work and with the help of two colleagues, progress was eventually made and the store was once again looking ship shape and Bristol fashion. It is my aim to keep it this way until the time comes for us to pack and leave for Port Stanley. No mail arrived today nor the sunshine that we had been expecting, and there were hardly any new arrivals or visitors to the Defence Base.

Indeed, it was unusually quiet and 51 Field Squadron were all packed and waiting at the temporary helipad to depart for Fox Bay however, the RAF Chinook that they had booked failed to turn up and their frustration was evident for all to see. With the G1098 Store neat and tidy and fully audited, all equipment was quickly checked one final time and then I headed across to the Rubb hangar site to help my colleagues until it was time for lunch.

At 13.30 precisely, 3 Troop Paraded outside portakabin number 100 and were briefed by our staff sergeant on the key safety regulations when working at height, and when operating construction site machinery. Such briefings are important because certain mishaps could prove serious, and as he went through the list of Dos and Don'ts, he informed us that a soldier back at Port Stanley had suffered a nasty hand injury while operating a cement mixer.

Such accidents act as a wake-up call and this particular incident reminded us never to become complacent or overconfident on any construction site, or indeed in any work situation. Still in my thoughts and some hours later, I prayed that the injured soldier makes a full and speedy recovery.

During the afternoon, our work on the Rubb site was suddenly brought to a halt due to a bizarre and unprecedented incident, namely a beret inspection of all things. Nobody could understand the reason for this inspection because we only wear safety helmets on the Rubb site, and as such our berets are kept in our portakabins.

It turned out that the inspection had had been summoned by an unknown visiting Gunner staff sergeant who without requesting permission or wearing safety equipment of any kind, just walked onto our site because his beret had gone missing. Our corporals quite rightly protested and asked him to leave on grounds of safety but he refused, and so two colleagues were immediately dispatched to have our troop commander and staff sergeant come and deal with the situation. Trying to explain to him that he was on a construction site proved a complete waste of time and within minutes, our troop commander arrived and demanded an explanation for the staff sergeant.

Confronting him in full view of 3 Troop, he rubbished the staff sergeant's reason for accessing the site and after receiving an apology, he was told to leave immediately so that a written report could be raised and sent to our officer commanding who was now back in Port Stanley. Later in the afternoon, we were informed that one of his own colleagues had picked up his beret by mistake, and that it had been returned to the staff sergeant who was no doubt feeling highly embarrassed by the whole affair. We also heard that he returned to Port Stanley around 15.45.

A small number of odd jobs cropped up from time to time around the Defence Base however, these only required two members of the team and the work was completed by 19.15. Everyone headed for the cookhouse with large appetites and among tonight's choices, was a Gurkha chicken curry which is always sensational and after enjoying a second helping we all returned to our portakabins. A few of my colleagues and I decided to go back to the Rubb site to double-check that everything was as it should be, and by the time we left it was 20.40 and still light.

As we stood near the southern edge we watched as four RAF Chinooks slowly approached Kelly's Garden from the south east, and each helicopter had a large underslung load including a crane for 3 Troop. The other three had engineering equipment and more Rubb shelter items and it was an impressive sight that gave me the ideal opportunity to take photographs for my journal. One Chinook in particular, created such a powerful downdraft that everyone was forced to turn away as it reduced altitude, then hovered just metres above the ground with its underslung container.

Without realising it, the pilot was the first to land a helicopter directly on the Rubb hangar site and when we informed him of this after he had shut down the engine, he smiled and gave us a thumbs-up. Some 10 minutes later he took off and headed back to Port Stanley. Over the course of the next hour more helicopters arrived and delivered underslung cargo at various sites around the Defence Base, and as they regained altitude the pilots flipped their aircraft from side to side to bid us farewell. Over at the Ant Hill, I enjoyed a soft drink while chatting with colleagues before deciding to call it a day, and as I walked back to my portakabin I gazed over Bonners Bay and across to San Carlos Settlement and felt so content at being stationed at here Kelly's Garden.

Delivering stores to Kelly's Garden

A trench from the Falklands War

Friday, 18 February 1983

I received a letter today from my parents which I read a couple of times before locking it away with the rest of their letters, and I pondered a while as to what they might be doing back home. I often think about them and the distance that separates us, and yet I am enjoying my time here in the Falkland Islands so much. To my pleasant surprise I also received a formal letter from 658 Squadron Army Air Corps inviting me to attend an initial interview at their Headquarters in Port Stanley, and so I will need to book a helicopter and the only person to organise that is my staff sergeant.

I am really excited and relieved to know that my transfer application is finally being processed, and that is because I have a very good reason for wanting to transfer to the Army Air Corps. As mentioned earlier, I have already started to lose interest in combat and armoured engineering as military career paths and I cannot hide this from my troop management because it would not be fair to them, or indeed to me. Furthermore, for some time I have wanted to become a pilot but more so after the experience I had 18 months ago when I flew in the navigator seat of a RAF Harrier T-Bird Jump Jet.

Since then, my wish to become a pilot has increased considerably and it is really exciting that I will be attending a Private Glider Pilot Course when I return to Tidworth. The experiences I have had of flying in a Scout, Chinook, Puma, and Gazelle helicopter have all added to my desire to take up flying as a career however, this now rests in the hands of the Army Air Corps, and I know that the selection course and training will be extremely demanding, very difficult, and highly technical.

Around lunchtime a Gurkha Rifle patrol returned to Kelly's Garden and as it approached our location, we went across to meet them for a chat and away from the hangar site. It was decided there and then to organise a BBQ for tomorrow evening. Our welding team offered to covert an old 50-gallon oil drum into a BBQ grill and our chef confirmed that he could provide beef burgers, sausages, chops, chicken wings and legs, onions, bread rolls, and a variety of sauces.

Our barman has also agreed to set up an outdoor bar and so all in all, we have a definite plan. I am looking forward to the event but I will probably go after I write up my journal which for me, is my top priority as I need to write my daily entries as regularly as I can. Everyone in 3 Troop and the Gurkhas are more than happy with the arrangements and I know it will be a most enjoyable evening, because our friends from Nepal are such great company. Meanwhile, one of our electricians was flown by RAF Sea King across to Fox Bay where 51 Field Squadron are now based, and he has been tasked with helping to install an electric supply over at their new location. He is one of the best at his trade and very well liked, and he is also an outstanding member of 3 Troop.

It was straight after lunch that I had the good fortune to meet up with yet another officer I served with during my six-month tour in West Belfast, between 4th October 1979 and 23 February 1980. We were both based at Woodbourne Camp and I thoroughly enjoyed our catch up during which, we updated each other on how our careers were progressing and in all honesty, he has not changed in any way.

We instantly recognised each other and it was so good to shake hands once again and to my pleasant surprise, he told me that he was now the adjutant of 37 Engineer Regiment which controls all roulement units including 52 Field (Construction) Squadron. He is a very interesting officer and very easy to speak with, and after we finished our conversation I accompanied him to the helipad where a RAF Chinook was waiting to fly him back to Port Stanley. We wished each other the very best of luck and with that he boarded the aircraft, and I made my way to the Rubb hangar site.

That's me in the navigator seat behind the pilot

Yet another bitterly cold breeze chilled everyone to the bone during the course of the afternoon, but it failed to hinder any of the team and work continued on the Rubb site, and also along the southern perimeter edge of Kelly's Garden. The time passed quickly and by 19.00, we had finished our work for the day and a lot had been accomplished so we are confident that the project is still well and truly on track.

Around 21.45 a delivery of essential supplies unexpectedly arrived by RAF Chinook and six of us went across to meet the aircraft, and as a small works party we off-loaded the entire payload and transferred it across to the G1098 Store.

Whenever I walk around Kelly's Garden under the increasing darkness of night, alone and unarmed, I often mull over how easily a surprise attack could take place because at times, it can be so dark it is almost impossible to see two yards in front of you. Without a torch or moonlight, the only thing you can see late at night are the stars and the dim light coming from inside portakabins. None of this bothers me or my colleagues but it does give food for thought that we are isolated and somewhat cut off in this location.

After I wrote up my journal I went for a shower and shave before climbing inside my sleeping bag to read James Herriot's novel 'Let Sleeping Vets Lie.' I was very fortunate to find this book because it was sitting amongst a pile of publications destined for incineration tomorrow.

I really enjoy reading Herriot's books because he has a wonderful style of writing and my favourite novel simply has to be 'All Creatures Great and Small,' which is the delightful story of his early years as a young veterinary assistant working in the Yorkshire Dales. His experiences are amusing, enchanting, and a delight to read simply because they are written in a manner that makes you feel you are there with him, and I love the characters such as his madcap employer Siegfried Farnon and his mischievous younger brother, Tristran.

Out of nowhere a beautiful half-moon suddenly appeared in the night sky and its silvery light shone down on Kelly's Garden, San Carlos Settlement, and Bonners Bay, and it is in moments such as this that I am at my happiest.

Saturday, 19 February 2019

A sunny clear morning welcomed me as I strolled across to the cookhouse around 07.30 with my colleagues, while wafting through the cold air was the mouth-watering smell of cooked sausages, bacon, and eggs which are just waiting to be eaten. Army tea is without doubt the best in the world and it is extremely moreish however, the one thing that surprises us here in the Falklands is that the traditional full English breakfast is apparently not popular with the locals who live in San Carlos Settlement and indeed, one who I chatted with quite recently said he would never touch it. I have to admit that there are times when I too consider it to be somewhat excessive for first thing in the morning, and so I can understand and appreciate where he is coming from.

During the morning parade, an easterly wind blew in from the west and increased in strength as we stood in three ranks and listened to the schedule of work that needs to be completed by the end of today. After issuing tools and engineering equipment, I returned to the Troop Office and signed out a Silva compass which I quickly checked before returning to my portakabin, and there I began revising on my map reading and navigational skills in preparation for the Army Air Corps transfer interview.

The Ordnance Survey map, or OS as it also called, has been loaned to me by my troop commander and so I used the red and green highlighters which I brought with me to identify the easting (x) and northing (y) coordinates. For those unfamiliar with using an OS map for navigation or orienteering, an easting and northing are the two principle sets of coordinates used to determine a position on the map, as well as on the ground. To determine the coordinates of a feature on a standard OS 1:25,000 map such as a church, hospital, or geographical feature such as a peak, you must first identify the grid in which that feature is located.

This is done by establishing the easting coordinate which runs vertically across the map from west to east (left to right), then do the same for the northing coordinate which runs horizontally from north to south (top to bottom). Once you have done this you will know exactly in which grid square on the map the feature is located, and this will also give you a four-figure grid reference.

All grid squares can be divided into 100 equal squares by using a Roma which is found on a Silva compass, and by using the Roma you can determine a six-figure grid reference which is the most common method used to pinpoint a fixed position on a map. This six-figure grid reference can also be used by others to determine the precise location to which you are referring. As complicated as this may all sound, orienteering and navigating using an OS map and compass is actually very easy to do, and extremely accurate. More importantly, it could prevent a person from becoming lost in adverse weather conditions such as thick fog or mist, or found if they are lost and so it a potential life-saving skill to have.

After an hour I rejoined 3 Troop over at the Rubb hangar site and when I got there, I was told that one of our colleagues had gone across to San Carlos Settlement to invite some locals to tonight's BBQ.

The remainder of 3 Troop were hard at work digging a trench which thankfully was made much easier with the help of a mechanical digger and at the same time, more surveying was being carried out on other sites around Kelly's Garden while another section of four were kept busy with landscaping the furthest edge of the taxiway. A RE Clerk of Works came over to check that all was well then left us to carry on with our tasks, happy and satisfied with what he had seen during his visit.

More Ghurkha patrols arrived and left Kelly's Garden throughout the day and as they walked past the Rubb site, they would stop and have a quick chat. These remarkable soldiers never speak ill of anyone and their discipline is exceptional. I genuinely believe they could teach us a thing or two about respect, reverence, and humility, and in particular I like Sergeant Bhan Gurung because he is such an amusing character, and also very interesting.

Throughout the afternoon we continued our work while close to the cookhouse, five more portakabins were being anchored to their concrete bases making the accommodation area even larger, and especially with the increased supporting facilities. The Defence Base is now expanding all the time and by 19.00, the only meal available in the cookhouse for 3 Troop and the Gurkhas was soup because of tonight's BBQ. It was then that I went for an early shower and shave.

Feeling refreshed and clean shaven, I returned to my portakabin to listen to Grieg's Piano Concerto in 'A' Minor, Elgar's haunting Nimrod, and a piece from Handel's Water Music. As I listened to all three, I logged today's entry in my journal which for me has now become a ritual at the end of a busy working day, and it provides me with a sense of peace and calm that now plays an even bigger part in my life here at Kelly's Garden. I have always had a liking for classical music ever since listening to my mother play the family upright piano in our parlour when I was young, and she taught me several such as Beethoven's 'Fur Elise' and 'Moonlight Sonata.'

Meanwhile, 3 Troop and our Gurkha friends went ahead with the BBQ and as I read and enjoyed the rest of James Herriot's novel, I was once again immersed in the somewhat unpredictable yet wonderful world of Siegfried Farnon and his brother Tristan, Joe Mulligan, James, and his wife Helen. Characters such as Mrs Donovan and Mr Crump keep me amused and there is one in particular, a Mr Pickersgill who hilariously mispronounces medical terms. The story gives me such pleasure and no doubt I will read it again before I return to Tidworth, and another book I take delight in reading is Gerald Durrell's wonderful story 'Rosy is my Relative.' After a while I was really hungry and went to join my colleagues over at the BBQ.

There was no mail again today and by 22.20, I was inside my sleeping bag and looking forward to a good night's sleep but around 23.15, I was called out by a visiting staff sergeant and four others who asked if they could be issued with five camp beds after being unexpectedly flown in from Port Stanley.

Afternote

James Herriot has always fascinated me both as a writer and a veterinary surgeon, and through reading his books and watching the television series based on his life and career, like many I genuinely felt as though I got to know the man personally. Sadly, Herriot passed away on 23 February 1995 and his ashes were scattered on Sutton Bank which is a beautiful hill in North Yorkshire. I would have so liked to have met the man but instead, I hope to visit Thirsk in Yorkshire one day to see the veterinary surgery where he worked at 23 Kirkgate.

As a veterinary surgeon and an acclaimed writer, he was not only gifted and skilled in his crafts but he was also a genuinely wonderful human being who cared passionately for the welfare of domestic and farm animals, and indeed the people of Yorkshire who he loved so much. James Herriot was actually born James Alfred Wight.

As mentioned previously, Gerald Durrell is another author whose books I thoroughly enjoyed as a child and when I was serving in the Falklands and although his bestselling novel was 'My Family and Other Animals,' it is the delightful and amusing novel 'Rosie is My Relative' that has always been my favourite. Sadly, like James Herriot he passed away in early 1995.

Chapter Ten
Falklands, South Georgia and Sir Ernest Shackleton

Foreword

While growing up in Llanelli in the 1960s, the one place I always enjoyed visiting was my local library because quite simply it was an Aladdin's cave packed with artefacts of old, old books and manuscripts, and information which was all freely accessible and fascinating. There were watercolours, oil paintings, newspapers, but best of all was the Reading Room on the first floor where I would sit for hours at a time in silence and do my homework, or research a particular subject, or rummage through monochrome images of the old town and surrounding communities. Llanelli Library was where I learned much about history and there was one item in particular that always captivated me from the very first moment I set eyes upon it, and it hung on the wall of the staircase that led to the Reading Room.

Mounted inside a huge elaborate hand-carved wooden frame was a three-dimensional map of Wales and every time I looked at it, my imagination would run wild because I could visualise explorers of old planning their expeditions on models similar to this. It was the polar explorers in particular who captured my interest and especially the likes of Captain Robert Falcon Scott who was better known as Scott of the Antarctic, and my favourite of them all was Sir Ernest Henry Shackleton who I researched at a very young age.

I produced page after page of hand-written notes and facts about his remarkable life and the perilous expeditions that he planned and led, and it was his tremendous courage that overwhelmed me and gained my utmost respect, and so when I actually deployed to the Falklands Islands I could not have been more excited.

As mentioned earlier, in 1982 not many people knew about the Falkland Islands or indeed where they were on the map, despite the archipelago being a British Overseas Territory and yet so many had heard of South Georgia and the main reason for this is quite genuinely because of Sir Ernest Shackleton. Of all the four expeditions that he led to the Antarctic, the most famous was the Trans-Antarctic Expedition of 1914–1916 which captured the attention of the whole world when it almost ended in disaster.

As history tells us, this became one of the most daring and incredible polar rescue missions of all time, and being so close to South Georgia in 1983, I would have given anything to have visited the island for myself. Regrettably, this was not possible because of the work 3 Troop needed to complete so instead, I chose to undertake another writing project while at Kelly's Garden and that was to write an account of Shackleton the man and his greatest expedition, through using my old research notes as references which thankfully, I had decided to take with me on the tour.

In 1983, the population of the Falkland Islands was just over 1,800 but by 2023, this figure has doubled to just less than 3,700. Compare this with South Georgia where there has never been a permanent population apart from the 30 or so personnel who work during the summer months only, and the 10 who remain throughout the winter. These people work for the British Antarctic Survey or BAS, which is an essential polar scientific research institute that monitors weather conditions and air quality, changes to our climate, and provide support to the management of the Marine Protected Area that comes under the Government of South Georgia and the South Sandwich Islands.

They also control the thousands of tourists who visit the frozen island each year and lead educational studies in the form of guided tours, as well as protecting the island from having foreign plants and animal species introduced. There is also a dedicated team of scientists and supporting staff who are based inside the futuristic looking Halley VI Research Station which sits on the Brunt ice shelf and comprises of eight inter-connecting giant pods, and a huge red laboratory. Each unit sits on four hydraulic legs that are fitted with large skiis and between 2016 and 2017, a remarkable television documentary was produced about the incredible project undertaken to relocate the station some 23 kilometres due to a newly discovered crack along part of the ice shelf. Halley VI is absolutely breathtaking.

As a key habitat for wildlife in the southern hemisphere, South Georgia is quite simply a jewel in Antarctica's crown and the world cannot sit back and do nothing about our changing climate, and of that there can be no doubt. Everyone in their own small way is a custodian of our beautiful yet fragile planet and while we have the privilege to be alive, we all have a duty to at least try and help minimise the causes and speed of what surely is becoming the greatest man-made catastrophe of all time. In protecting and preserving habitats, wildlife, and environments such as South Georgia, then the likes of the British Antarctic Survey Team is doing an incredible job.

Even though my memoir centres mainly on the journal I wrote in the Falklands in 1983, it also covers the whole of my military career and while I was at Kelly's

Garden, I also decided to write three further accounts which were the history of the Falklands and South Georgia, and the story of Sir Ernest Shackleton's famous Trans-Antarctic Expedition of 1914-1916.

Introduction

As I started to plan and compile my account of the Falkland Islands, the first thing that struck me was the comparatively short period of *'recorded history'* that exists in respect of this British Overseas Territory, and as I examined the chronology of key historical events, then all I was actually looking at was a period of approximately 500 years. In the eyes of historians this is a timeframe or period that would only just qualify it as being categorised 'early modern' because it covers a period in history that is between 1500, which is the end of the Late Middle Age and up to the start of the Industrial Revolution, which is around 1760 to 1763.

When I looked into the *'pre-history'* of this archipelago, the amount of information that was available was genuinely minimal yet for me, this made the Falkland Islands even more fascinating as a topic of research. When studying a period that falls into the timeframe of *'pre-history'* we need to try and work some of it out for ourselves rather than accept or make reference to another person's work and conclusions. In essence, this would be too easy to do but more importantly, it would not contribute any additional constructive research or suggestions of our own to that information already gathered. And neither would it challenge possible inaccurate data or support new evidence as being beyond any doubt.

To avoid misleading others who wish to learn the truth about the past, then all historical research must be accurate if it is to serve its true purpose, and that is why an historian's first duty is always be to keep an open mind.

To give just one example, most people will have been taught that it was the Italian explorer Christopher Columbus who first discovered the Americas in 1492, and that he was the first European explorer to visit the New World, however, new research and discoveries now proves this to be inaccurate on both accounts. I remember my history lesson in which I was taught the rhyme "In fourteen hundred and ninety two, Columbus sailed the sea of blue" and because this was also published in history books at that time, everyone took it to be correct.

Columbus may well have landed in the Americas in 1492 but it has been proven beyond doubt that it was the Viking chieftain Leif Eriksson who first discovered

North America, nearly 600 years earlier. The term New World was not assigned to the Americas until the mid-16th century after Europe recognised that this part of the western hemisphere was in fact a new continent yet the fact remains, that it was Eriksson who first landed in what is now Newfoundland around 1000 AD.

Researching the past involves numerous skills including archaeology, anthropology, geology, botany, forensics, medicine and dentistry, aerial imagery, facial reconstruction, carbon dating and many more. It is all incredibly complex work and an enormous undertaking by those involved, yet it is essential if we truly want to understand what happened so many hundreds of years ago, and already many aspects of history are now having to be re-thought and re-written through the discovery of new findings.

Recorded history is also known as *'written history'* and it relates to a period that has some form of documented record or narrative, and it is to such important proofs of evidences that experts and scientists often turn to in order to investigate and create an accurate picture and conception of the past. Such sources can be in the form of a written manuscript, a carving or painting, artefacts such as jewellery and clothing, weaponry, farming tools, and even human remains and for those who study such fields of interest, no matter how big or small their part may be, each is crucial to creating a tangible representation of times gone by.

All evidence is critical to determining and establishing how and where social groups lived, how they dressed and lived their daily lives, how they communicated and the languages they spoke, how they farmed their land, cooked and crafted tools and weapons, how they treated their dead, how they hunted, and how they worshipped their gods.

Pre-history on the other hand is defined as a period about which we have no written record or artefacts of any kind, and indeed it is like working with a carte blanche. Understandably, this is why researchers and experts in their field need to work closely together and keep an open mind when considering any new findings, because there is every chance that what could be a simple explanation and clear picture of the past, could easily become a jumble of ifs and buts.

The word *'history'* is derived from the ancient Greek *'historia'* meaning *'to understand'* or *'to know'* and institutes such as libraries, museums, art galleries, ancient places of worship, and universities are all excellent places to visit and spend time researching the past. Records of Births, Marriages, and Deaths, old books and manuscripts, coins, jewellery, and items of clothing and human remains all provide crucial information to help us understand and re-create how a person would have looked, and in many instances, sounded when they spoke. Through incredible advances made in specialised fields such as facial reconstruction, DNA, forensics, speech technology, computer graphics and modelling, the future of historical research is truly exciting.

The Falkland Islands

Sovereignty over the Falklands has been fiercely disputed ever since the islands were first sighted in the latter part of the 16th century, and countries such as Argentina, France, Spain, and Great Britain have each staked their claim. On more than one occasion, disagreements have resulted in military conflict on land, sea, and in the air and in 1982 the war against Argentina involved all three. One argument that Argentina still uses in its claim to having sovereignty over the Falkland Islands is considered by many countries around the world to be both fragile and unsubstantiated, because it is based on the country being granted full control of the islands by Spain in 1816. South American countries refer to the Falkland Islands by its Spanish name of *Islas Malvinas*, and up until the early part of the 19th century, Spain had full control over the islands, the cattle and settlements however, during the period leading up to 1833 she handed control over to Argentina.

But there is a second reason why Argentina believes it has rightful sovereignty over the Falkland Islands which is both convoluted and fanciful in the extreme. This is based purely on the geographical proximity of the islands to Argentina, and not only does this argument lack any legal merit but it has also been totally rejected by the international community at large. Understandably, Great Britain never has or ever would contest that the Falklands are much closer to Argentina because the margin of difference exceeds 7,000 miles nevertheless, proximity to a neighbouring country can never be used as a justification for determining who has rightful sovereignty over a territory.

Such an argument would be overwhelmingly rejected by the International Court of Justice (ICJ) which is also known as the World Court (WC), and forms part of the United Nations (UN). The history of the Falkland Islands is not exactly a complex subject but for my own personal reasons, when I first started to write this account the first thing I needed to establish was the date the archipelago was first discovered and more crucially, by who. As previously explained, accuracy of past events is always best determined through researching *'recorded history'* and in the case of the

Falkland Islands, historians widely accept that this was around the beginning of the early 16th century, somewhere between 1500 and 1520.

In 1504 the French navigator Binot de Gonneville was thought to have first sighted the islands albeit there is no actual record to support this, and so a case could be argued that this is pure speculation. Some also suggest that the archipelago may first have been sighted by a trading ship that drifted away from an expedition led by the Portuguese explorer Ferdinand Magellan, during his search for a new trading route for Spain around 1519.

If this is correct, then in doing so Magellan would not only have been the first explorer to circumnavigate the globe but also, that ship may very well have been the first to catch sight of the Falkland Islands but again, no record exists and so this too could be considered as conjecture. Other possible sightings include Spain's Pedro Vega in 1525, the Portuguese explorer and Governor Simon de Alcazaba in 1535, and England's Sir Francis Drake in 1580 however, the strongest case for who first discovered the Falkland Islands is generally attributed to the English navigator John Davis, whilst serving on board *Desire* in 1592. Davis was part of Thomas Cavendish's expedition to discover the Northwest Passage, and he continued that search after Cavendish returned to England.

The first recorded plotting of the Falkland Islands was by the Flemish Vice-Admiral Sebald de Weerdt around 1600, while serving as a navigator with the Dutch East India Company at the age of 23. In January 1690, the first recorded landing on the Falkland Islands was made by Captain John Strong, an Englishman who commanded the British naval ship *HMS Welfare* after first sailing through the strait that separates the two main islands the previous year.

Captain Strong named this stretch of water Falkland Sound after Anthony Cary, 5th Viscount Falkland who was a Scottish nobleman and politician who jointly owned *HMS Welfare*. Years later, the name Falkland was given to the archipelago and in 1764 the first settlement was established on East Island by the French explorer and scholar Louis-Antoine de Bougainville. Bougainville would become the first Frenchman to circumnavigate the globe and he named his settlement Port Louis, but three years later in 1767 he was ordered to hand over the outpost to France's ally at that time, which was Spain.

In 1765 and without knowledge of the existence of Port Louis, the British Royal Naval officer John Byron was appointed captain of *HMS Dolphin*. Supported by the naval ship *HMS Tamar*, Captain Byron was charged with leading an expedition to the South Atlantic to establish a permanent settlement for the replenishment of British naval vessels. Known as 'Foul Weather Jack,' Captain John Byron landed on a tiny island just off West Falkland Island and it was there that he established his colony which coincidentally, was also the first to be established on the island.

The harbour settlement was named Port Egmont but in claiming the Falklands Islands for Great Britain, Captain Byron's action was fiercely contested by Spain and as a result five gunships and 1,500 soldiers were deployed to reclaim the islands under the command of General Madariaga. Spain and Great Britain almost went to war but this was avoided and over the course of the next 60 years. Spain worked on reinforcing its claim of sovereignty over the Falklands by establishing additional garrisons and settlements on both East and West Island, and appointing a governor to the archipelago. During the 1790s and in an attempt to avert war between the two countries, Spain and Great Britain signed three agreements which collectively became known as the Nookta Sound Conventions.

By December 1832, relations between Great Britain and the former United Provinces of South America deteriorated considerably after the Argentine region of River Plate disputed British fishing rights. As a result, Britain's objection to Luis Vernet being appointed Governor of the Falkland Islands was ignored. Vernet was a merchant trader born in Hamburg, Germany and he established a settlement on East Island where he planned to profit personally by hunting all wild cattle that roamed certain parts of the island. He applied to Buenos Aires for permission to proceed with his hunting and to the anger and outrage of the British government, not only was Vernet granted permission but furthermore, he also allowed to hunt every head of cattle across East Island and to add further insult, he was no longer required to pay taxes to Argentina.

Great Britain protested to Buenos Aires in the strongest of terms however, the political division that now existed between the two countries served only to rekindle Britain's determination to re-establish sovereignty over the Falkland Islands. Over time Luis Vernet's blatant abuse of privileges and poor behaviour escalated out of control and in 1831, he ordered the capture of three American whaling ships in the station of Puerto Louis on East Falkland Island.

Outraged by Vernet's actions, the American consul in Buenos Aires reacted with fury and dispatched the American warship *USS Lexington* to recapture all three whaling ships. The operation was a success and a number of settlers were captured and taken prisoner, and charged with piracy. As evidence was gathered that proved Luis Vernet's part in seizing the American whaling ships, a powder store was destroyed.

In 1832 the Argentine government approved a commission to establish a penal colony on the Falkland Islands, but this was never completed due to the death of the Argentine Major Esteban Mestivier during a rebellion involving his own troops. In its determination to regain sovereignty over the Falkland Islands, Great Britain deployed the British naval ship *HMS Clio* which was commanded by Captain James Onslow and the vessel arrived at Port Louis on 3 January 1833.

Captain Onslow ordered the British flag to be flown and demanded the Argentine administration stand down immediately, and that it return to Buenos Aires. Port Louis was retained as a military outpost by Great Britain, and Argentina's claim to sovereignty was neither appropriate nor acknowledged by the British government.

On 1 October 1841, the former Royal Engineer Major General Richard Clement Moody was appointed first British Governor of the Falkland Islands and he remained in post until 1848. Moody was subsequently appointed Lieutenant Governor of British Columbia on 25 December 1858 and remained in post until July 1863, then in 1842 he was tasked by the British Secretary of State for War namely Lord Stanley to establish a new capital on the Falkland Islands, at Port William. Work started the following year and in 1845, Moody renamed the capital Port Stanley.

Argentina has never laid to rest her claims to sovereignty over the Falkland Islands but through diplomacy and peaceful gesture, the relationship between Argentina and Falkland Islanders improved during the twentieth century and in particular, between the 1960s and 1970s. The islanders insisted that before any agreement was reached between Great Britain and Buenos Aires over sovereignty being transferred to Argentina, it would first need their full consent. In 1971 however, a secret meeting was arranged and convened between the two governments which did not involve any dialogue whatsoever with the islanders.

Over the following decade, the political tension between Great Britain and Argentina once again deteriorated until in 1976 and amid social and economic upheaval and internal crisis across the whole of Argentina, a military junta seized total control. On 22 December 1981, the junta leaders elected General Leopoldo Galtieri to be the new President of Argentina however, he would remain in power for only six months.

General Mario Menendez surrendered to British Commander Major General Jeremy Moore at Governor's House in Stanley on 14 June 1982, and when the news reached Buenos Aires, the people took to the streets in their tens of thousands in open protest against President General Galtieri. Argentinians placed all blame for the humiliating defeat firmly at his feet and on 17 June 1982, he was forced out of office in disgrace. Retreating to his private villa, Galtieri went into hiding but in 1983 both he and his military commanders were detained, and prosecuted by a military court for Human Rights violations.

General Galtieri was further accused of mismanaging the war for which he was sentenced to 12 years in prison, and even more humiliating he was stripped of his rank upon losing an appeal. In 1998 he was granted a presidential pardon by Carlos Menem and released from prison, but he died of a heart attack whilst in hospital on 16 August 2002. His body was interred in Argentina's largest cemetery namely the Cementerio de la Chacarita in Buenos Aries.

Over 740 small islands make up the Falkland Islands while the two largest are separated by a strait called Falkland Sound, which is some 50 miles in length and seven miles wide at its narrowest point. These two islands are worlds apart in terms of population, yet both are captivating in their own special way and one thing I did pick up on during my time there, is that the islanders favoured being self-administered.

West Falkland Island is the smaller of the two and the closest to the eastern coast of Argentina. With a land mass of 1,750 square miles, its population is incredibly small with just under 200. The largest settlement is Port Howard which forms part of an extensive sheep farm, and the road connecting it to the neighbouring Fox Bay passes along the foot of Muffler Jack Mountain, which is a feature of the Hornby Mountains and overlooks the beautiful, rugged inlet located on the east coast of the island. The main industries on West Falkland Island are commercial fishing, sheep farming, and tourism. For some years there has been speculation over the possibility that mineral deposits may exist in and around these islands, with some energy companies believing that there could be up to 60 billion barrels of oil waiting to be tapped.

West Falkland Island also played its part in the 1982 war with Argentina. There was an Argentine presence in the form of the 5th Motorised Infantry Regiment and today, there is a small museum established at Port Howard for visitors. Geographically West Falkland Island is surprisingly hilly and especially the further east you venture, and wildlife is found in abundance with elephant seals predominantly found on the southern beaches while other places worthy of visiting include Port Stephens, and Roy Cove. What truly makes West Falkland Island so special is the solitude and harmony with nature but sadly, the last ever sighting of the Falkland Island wolf otherwise known as the Warrah was back in 1875.

East Falkland Island on the other hand covers 2,550 square miles and accounts for over half of the entire land mass of all 740 smaller islands. With a much larger population than West Falkland Island, the geography of East Falkland Island is both dramatic and spectacular. The island is almost split in half by two stretches of water called Choiseul Sound to the east, and Brenton Loch to the west. Between these is a narrow isthmus on which the settlements of Goose Green and Darwin are to be found. To the north of Choiseul Sound which flows into the South Atlantic is Mount Pleasant Airbase, while Port Stanley sits some 40 kilometres to the north-east.

Port Stanley not only serves as the capital but also as the seat of power for the entire archipelago, and the post of Governor is a highly prestigious appointment because the incumbent acts as 'de facto' head of state on behalf of the British monarchy. This means that the office exists in reality and practice, however not necessarily by legal right because the Governor of the Falkland Islands is an appointment approved only by royal decree. The purpose of this historical office is to govern the Overseas Territory in the absence of the British monarch, to appoint political positions, and to carry out all ceremonial duties. The official title is Governor of the Falkland Islands and Commissioner of the South Georgia and South Sandwich Islands.

East Falkland is the economic heart of the archipelago and recently, it was announced that the island is at long last free of Argentine mines that were planted during the 1982 war. On 1 March 1833, the naturalist and author of the theory of evolution Charles Darwin visited the island whilst taking part on a global survey expedition aboard *HMS Beagle*. A permanent British military presence in the Falklands today serves two crucial purposes. The first is to provide security and protection from RAF Mount Pleasant.

The second is to boost the islands' economy through generating employment and increasing spending on local products, supporting local communities, and providing essential medical services. The future of these islands is not only exciting but it is also visionary. They enjoy remarkable growth and economic development and are one of the United Kingdom's most thriving Overseas Territories.

South Georgia

You only have to look at the flag of South Georgia and South Sandwich Islands to realise that these are no ordinary islands but instead, a cold and remote location deep in the southern hemisphere and close to the southernmost continent of all, namely Antarctica. To clear three misconceptions about South Georgia:

1. It is not technically classed as a polar island but does have a polar climate.
2. The penguin is a bird and not a mammal, and only found in Antarctica.
3. There are no polar bears in Antarctica. They live only in the Arctic and therefore are not a natural predator of the penguin.

Sitting on a blue background with a British Union Jack in the top left-hand corner, the flag of South Georgia and South Sandwich Islands bears a coat of arms which has a reindeer standing on a knight's helmet, and on top of a blue and white chequered shield. Also on the coat of arms are a fur seal to the left of the shield and a Macaroni penguin to the right. The shield stands on top of the motto '*Leo Terram propriam protegat*' which translates from Latin as '*Let the lion protect its own land.*'

South Georgia and South Sandwich Islands are a relatively young British Overseas Territory and was first formed in 1985, after being part of the Falkland Islands Dependencies that existed from 1843 until 1985. Located 800 miles east-southeast of the Falkland Islands, the island of South Georgia is 103 miles in length and just 22 miles wide. It is among the most isolated and desolate of islands anywhere on earth and with the vast majority of its craggy mountains covered in ice and snow all year round, and it has no native human population whatsoever. The only people who occupy the island are 30 seasonal residents all of whom work for the British Antarctic Survey (BAS) Team. During winter months this number reduces to ten.

First sighted by the London merchant Antoine de la Roche in 1675, South Georgia was claimed exactly 100 years later in 1775 by the British naval explorer and navigator Captain James Cook. In 1927, Argentina staked its claim and still to this day it maintains that the island rightfully belongs to her. South Georgia's capital is King Edward Point named after King Edward VII and it is situated on the northeast of the island, close to where the permanent BAS station is established.

South Georgia covers approximately 1,500 square miles and the summit of its highest feature namely Mount Paget is 2,935 metres high, making it twice the height of Ben Nevis in Scotland. It is the highest mountain in any British Overseas Territory and was first climbed by a Combined Services Expedition led by British Royal Naval Commander Malcolm Burley in 1964. In 1904, the Norwegian Antarctic explorer Carl Anton Larsen established a commercial outpost at Grytviken which over time, went on to become the largest whaling station on the island and at its height employed approximately 300 workers and the Larsen Ice Shelf is named after him.

Larsen died in 1924 and in 1965, all whaling came to an end. Located on King Edward Cove this tiny and remote settlement is today deserted except for the ghostly relic of the former whaling station and yet it is visited by thousands of tourists each year, who wish to see the island's most famous landmarks. These include the beautiful white painted Lutheran church built in 1913 and the grave of British Antarctic explorer Sir Ernest Henry Shackleton who with Tom Crean and Frank Worsley in May 1916, became the first people to walk across South Georgia during one of the most daring and perilous polar rescue missions of all time.

What follows is my account of Britain's greatest polar explorer and the Trans-Antarctic Expedition of 1914-1916 which I wrote in 1983 at Kelly's Garden.

Sir Ernest Henry Shackleton

(Incorporating the Trans-Antarctic Expedition of 1914-1916)

Sir Ernest Henry Shackleton was born at Kilkea in County Kildare, Ireland on 15 February 1874 and he went on to become one of the greatest polar explorers of his day. A distinguished and celebrated member of Victorian and Edwardian society, at the age of 25 he served under Captain Robert Falcon Scott as a third officer on the 1901-1903 *Discovery Expedition* from which he returned prematurely, due to illness. On 9 April 1904, Shackleton married Emily Mary Dorman with whom he went on to have three children namely Raymond, Cecily, and Edward who later became the Labour Party politician Baron Shackleton of Burley. Between 1907 and 1909, Ernest Shackleton served on the *Nimrod Expedition* during which he got to within 95 miles of the South Pole and climbed Mount Erebus, the second highest volcano in Antarctica.

For these achievements alone he was awarded a knighthood on his return to Great Britain by King Edward VII. The expedition leader was Captain Robert Falcon Scott and this was the first of three that Shackleton made to the Antarctic.

Captain Robert Scott tragically died on 29 March 1912 whilst trapped on the Ross Ice Shelf during the *Terra-Nova Expedition*, an ill-fated race to become the first person to reach the South Pole. Scott was beaten by the Norwegian Roald Amundsen and the challenge was eagerly followed by the world's media but tragically, Scott, Edward Adrian Wilson, and Henry Robertson Bowers died inside their tent.

It was not until 12 November 1912 that their frozen bodies were discovered by a search party that included the Norwegian explorer Tryggve Gran. The most famous yet heart-breaking story of the expedition was that of the British Army officer Captain Lawrence 'Titus' Oates. Realising that he had become a burden to his colleagues due to severe frostbite and failing health, he took it upon himself to walk to his death during a severe blizzard and as he left the tent, his last words to his companions were "I am just going outside, and may be some time."

Following the events of the *Terra-Nova Expedition*, Sir Ernest Shackleton decided upon a new challenge and that was to become the first person to lead an expedition across the Antarctic, from the Ross Sea to the Weddell Sea via the South Pole, a distance of 1,800 miles. Emily his wife, being the wealthy and highly important lady that she was in her own right, used her status and influence to help raise the £90,000 that Shackleton needed to fund his expedition, and this sum of money in 2023 monetary terms would be the equivalent of £10,350,000. Named the *Imperial Trans-Antarctic Expedition of 1914–1917*, the venture almost claimed the lives of Sir Ernest Shackleton and his team, and it culminated in one of the most courageous and daring of polar expedition rescue missions of all time.

Shackleton's expedition involved two ships namely *Endurance* and *Aurora*. *Endurance* was a three-masted schooner some 145 feet in length and she would take Shackleton and his hand-picked team from South Georgia, across the Weddell Sea, and to a pre-determined landing point at Vahsel Bay on the continent of Antarctica. Meanwhile, the *Aurora* which was a 165-foot steam yacht would act as the expedition's support ship, and she would make her approach from the southern side after setting sail from Hobart in Tasmania.

Once she reached her destination, the *Aurora* would establish three supply depots along the Great Ice Barrier with the furthest being at Beardmore Glacier. This would be the first supply depot that Sir Ernest Shackleton and his team would encounter after crossing the South Pole, but on 5 December 1914 the weather conditions out in the Weddell Sea deteriorated rapidly and on 15 January 1915, *Endurance* eventually became trapped in the frozen ice and could venture no further. Completely cut off and out of action, the ship was doomed.

Meanwhile, the *Aurora* had also become ice-locked but fortunately for her she managed to break free and sailed on to Discovery Bay in March 1915, and it was there that her supplies were offloaded and the three feeding depots established. For an incredible 10 months, *Endurance* remained trapped and imprisoned in the slow drifting ice pack until 24 October 1915, the day on which her fate was sealed. With her wooden hull weakening with every passing hour from the mounting pressure of the ice pack, *Endurance* started to take on sea water.

With the ship now listing heavily and dying like a fatally wounded animal, she was slowly devoured by the frozen Weddell Sea and with no other option available to him, Sir Ernest Shackleton reluctantly gave the order to abandon ship and in a race against time, the crew evacuated onto the ice floe. There was nothing more Shackleton's team could do but try and recover as many of the food supplies and stores as possible, and over the course of the next 28 days they watched as *Endurance* slowly broke apart. *Endurance* slowly inched her way beneath the frozen Weddell

Sea until finally, on 21 November 1915, the ship sank to its watery grave. The expedition's Australian photographer Frank Hurley captured some of the most evocative and unforgettable black and white images ever seen in the history of polar exploration, as he followed the tragic demise of *Endurance*.

Stranded on the ice floe for a further two months, Sir Ernest Shackleton hoped that the expedition party would gradually drift towards Paulet Island where he knew there would be supplies and provisions for his men. Paulet Island was some 250 miles away however, with the ice floe now beginning to break and with no other option available to him, Shackleton finally ordered his men to board the three lifeboats. On 9 April 1915, the tiny flotilla headed for land and on 14 April, they eventually reached Elephant Island. All too quickly both Shackleton and his men realised they stood very little chance of being spotted by a passing ship, but at least the expedition was back on dry land and for the first time in almost 500 days.

Frostbite soon became a serious concern for many including Sir Ernest Shackleton himself, and recognising that his men were now in great danger, he decided the only realistic chance of survival would be to try and reach the nearest place of safety from which he could plan and execute a rescue mission, to recover those members of his expedition who would be selected to remain on Elephant Island. With weather conditions in the Antarctic now beginning to worsen with every passing day, and with concerns over diminishing food supplies, increasing cases of frost bite, and a flagging morale among some of the team, the situation was fast becoming dire for Shackleton and his options were fast running out.

He eventually decided that there was just one possibly place he could reach by open boat, even though the odds in all probability were heavily stacked against him, and that was to head for the whaling station on the frozen island of South Georgia, some 800 miles to the north-east. Shackleton himself was now suffering badly with frost bite so without further delay, he selected a crew of five and instructed his men to have the lifeboat *James Caird* prepared for the perilous sea voyage that would hopefully save the expedition. The whole mission was literally in the last chance saloon and when the *James Caird* left Elephant Island, it would be Frank Wild who was given command of those who stayed behind.

Sir Ernest Shackleton's crew in the *James Caird* were fellow explorer and captain of *Endurance* namely New Zealand born Frank Worsley, the Irish explorer and seaman Tom Crean, Englishman John Vincent who did not receive the Polar Medal, Irish seaman Timothy McCarthy, and finally the Scottish born ship's carpenter Harry 'Chippy' McNish, who knowingly had no liking for Shackleton after he had the ship's cat *Mrs Chippy* shot when *Endurance* was lost. Shackleton had no trust in McNish either, following a failed mutiny attempt earlier in the expedition and as such he wanted McNish as close to him as possible, because he was considered a genuine liability to the success of the rescue mission.

The *James Caird* set out on its hazardous journey to South Georgia on 24 April 1916 with enough provisions to last just one month, however, after 14 days sailing through some of the most terrifying seas that Shackleton later admitted he had ever seen, and with the extraordinary navigational skill of Frank Worsley, the *James Caird* eventually landed safely on the southern shore of South Georgia at Cave Cove on 8 May 1916.

During the voyage, the *James Caird* endured and survived a powerful South Atlantic storm that sunk a 500-ton merchant steam ship. Once ashore and not wishing to tempt fate again out at sea, Sir Ernest Shackleton took the decision that he, Frank Worsley, and Tom Crean would trek across the snow-capped mountains of South Georgia in their attempt to reach the whaling station that was located some 30 miles away on the north-eastern side of South Georgia. On 20 May 1916 and with hope fast running out, Shackleton and his two colleagues eventually reached the Stromness Whaling Station.

Sir Ernest Shackleton was determined to return and rescue the three remaining crew that had been left on the south side of South Georgia namely Harry McNish, Timothy McCarthy, and John Vincent and also the 22 expedition members he had left behind on Elephant Island. After three failed attempts and pleading for assistance from the Chilean government, a rescue mission was finally agreed and organised. On 30 August 1916, the Chilean naval vessel *Yelcho* and the British whaling ship *Southern Sky* eventually reached Elephant Island, four months after Shackleton had set off on his rescue mission but tragically, three had died by the time Shackleton returned.

Although making a comfortable and easier living through giving lectures and publishing a book based on the *Imperial Trans-Antarctic Expedition*, Sir Ernest Shackleton was again ready to return to organising and leading more daring polar explorations, and so he approached his old school friend John Quiller Rowett who reluctantly agreed to fund a new expedition to circumnavigate the Antarctic. On 5 January 1922 and once again back on the island of South Georgia, and just minutes after having been examined by the expedition's doctor in the early hours of the morning, Sir Ernest Shackleton died from a heart attack. At the request of his wife Lady Emily Shackleton, her husband's body was laid to rest in a simple grave at Grytviken Cemetery and still to this day it is visited by thousands of tourists each year, who pay their respect to one of Britain's greatest ever polar explorers.

Chapter Eleven
Patience and Progress

Foreword

*H*aving spent an incredible sun-soaked three month tour of duty at CFB Meaford in Canada only five months prior to deploying to the Falklands, the reality of serving in a remote and secluded part of East Island such as Kelly's Garden proved quite a shock for some members of 3 Troop, and quite rightly so. The two locations were quite simply worlds apart because Canada was absolutely huge, modern, and unbelievably picturesque, plus Ontario was having its hottest summer in over 30 years. The towns and people were a delight and so 52 Field Squadron's tour was truly memorable, and I got to spend time in wonderful places such as Wasaga Beach, Thornbury, and Clarksburg the tiny yet quirky village near The Blue Mountains, Beaver Valley, and of course my favourite of place of all, Owen Sound.

The hospitality we received was completely unexpected and we met some of the most wonderful people ever, but what really stood out was the huge difference between Canadian and British standards of living and quality of life. The general day-to-day level of happiness and contentment which we experienced in Canada was genuinely unprecedented, and I still miss it to this day. The country is literally light years ahead of Great Britain and it is one of the reasons why in 1981, I applied to transfer across to the Canadian Armed Forces on a Military Exchange Programme which was being run at that time but unfortunately, the programme was cancelled some three weeks before my selection process was due to begin, which disappointed both me and my Canadian counterpart.

West Falkland Island was and still is a complete stranger to me, because sadly there was neither the time or opportunity to visit despite my burning desire to see Saunders Island, Pebble Island, Roy Cove, Keppel Island, and Hill Cove that overlooks Byron Sound. I also wanted to visit the many secluded beaches to observe colonies of elephant seals, sea lions, Gentoo and Macaroni penguins, and other species of wildlife. To think that only 200 years earlier, West Falkland Island was home to the now extinct Falkland Wolf which was called the Warrah and as incredible as this might sound, the one thing that I never saw in all my time in the Falklands was a tree.

Although Canada and the Falklands are literally worlds apart, I still cherish both so very much and maybe one day I will visit them again, but under very different circumstances.

Niagara Falls, 1982

Southern edge of Kelly's Garden, 1983

By the third week of February 1983, everyone in 3 Troop was eager to start the work of assembling and erecting the Rubb hangar frame in order to finish the project on time. As sappers, our combined artisan and military engineering skills and experience was extensive and we were determined to deliver the highest standard of work that we could, before we returned to Port Stanley. That said, there was a suspicion that lost time could become an issue for a number of reasons that were outside of our control, such as the continuous changing weather conditions we had to deal with, the delays in delivery of engineering equipment and resources from Port Stanley, queries and issues that necessitated answers or advice before we could continue with the project, and the unplanned tasks that seemed to crop up in areas around the Defence Base on a regular basis.

All of this proved time consuming and very frustrating nevertheless, we remained resolute in our belief that we would not be beaten and so everyone ploughed on regardless. Maintaining a focus on what needed to be achieved while working as a team, came into a league all of its own and was clearly being observed by the RAF ChinDet, others at Kelly's Garden, the CRE Works Team, and visitors to the Defence Base. Troop confidence was also growing as was the standard of our teamwork, and I genuinely do not recall a single disagreement or dispute between any of my colleagues despite the considerable pressure and difficult conditions we were working under.

3 Troop had become much more than just another team of sappers, and during the whole of my three-year posting with 22 Engineer Regiment I could not have served with a better group of colleagues who clearly enjoyed each other's company. In its own strange way, it genuinely felt surreal and extraordinary at times and the comradeship truly did continue right up until the day I was posted to my next unit.

Sunday, 20 February 2019

At 05.30 and with a magnificent sunrise appearing slowly from behind the Verde Hills to the east, the early morning silence inside my portakabin was suddenly shattered by the unexpected cacophony of ear-piercing alarm clocks that exploded into life, and all at precisely the same time. Some of my colleagues yelled blue murder while others jumped out of their sleeping bags still half asleep, desperately trying to switch off every alarm clock, and those that could not be silenced were instantly thrown out of the nearest open window. Who the hell had set them all to go off at the same time and so early in the morning? Everyone pleaded their innocence and the only person who remained fast asleep throughout the whole charade was none other than our new military chef who had flown in from Port Stanley late last night.

It just had to be him because this guy could sleep through a nuclear war, and everyone agreed that he must have set our alarms while we were fast asleep. After a quick discussion it was accepted that just maybe, he did not want to wake us up when he arrived but still needed to report for his first shift in the cookhouse by 06.30.

With peace and quiet finally restored and in a hilarious act of sweet revenge, one of our corporals picked up his highly polished army boots and after quietly opening the portakabin door, hurled them as far as he could out into the darkness of Kelly's Garden like an Olympic discus thrower. We heard the boots hit a neighbouring portakabin before landing heavily in the mud and after he quietly closed the door, Bob jumped back inside his sleeping bag and remarked "well, that was fun!"

At around 07.20 we all woke again but this time in a more composed and relaxed environment and after a quick shave and shower, we strolled across to the cookhouse for breakfast and as we approached the hot plates filled with bacon, sausages, beans and eggs, standing behind the counter dressed in his whites and with a huge welcoming smile across his face, was our new chef Graham.

"Sleep well?" he asked before bursting into laughter and with that, we shook his hand and introduced ourselves. A genuinely nice guy and with a great sense of humour, Graham had quickly fitted in and already we were enjoying his company.

Every morning I follow the same routine and on my way back to the portakabin today, once again I looked out over Bonners Bay and across to San Carlos Settlement. For me, this is the best way to start a new day here in Kelly's Garden because it truly is a magical location, and the natural calm and serenity is something I now cherish more than ever. This morning was sunny and warm and with a beautiful clear blue sky above the Verde Hills in the background, the scene that was before me resembled an oil painting with rich earthy colours.

I breathed in the fresh sea-air and tried to absorb as much as I could while inside the portakabin and snoring loudly, was a colleague who last night consumed several large tots of whisky. Today was his turn for a lay-in and so we left him to it because he had the most content expression on his face, and whatever he was dreaming about, it was obviously making him extremely happy.

Inside the G1098 Store, I reorganised the Rubb tools and equipment and with the help of two of my colleagues we examined the large green bulky bundles of Rubb PVC that will eventually be draped over the entire frame, and all the while we chatted away with Sergeant Gurung of the Gurkha Rifles who had decided to pay us a visit. To my surprise, he handed me a can of Coke and I thanked him. Gurkha generosity knows no limits and we have become good friends.

As we exchanged stories about our homeland and shared childhood memories, he suddenly mentioned his wife and children who are back in Nepal and instantly, there was a melancholy in his voice, and yet he showed true strength of character. He handed me a photograph of them all together in their mountain village back home, and I could see the joy on their smiling faces. Our conversation continued for some time while outside in the morning sunshine, the remainder of 3 Troop continued their work on digging the foundations, and the trenches are now almost ready to install the foundation shuttering panels.

These have been prepared by colleagues some of whom who are carpenters by trade, and they were assisted by others including myself from time to time. Martin and Steve between them make an excellent team and even though today is Sunday, we knew we would be working right up until 19.45, despite some of my colleagues having made plans to spend their late afternoon visiting Blue Beach Cemetery and San Carlos Settlement.

I had been hoping to do more revision for my interview with the Army Air Corps however, this will now be postponed to another day. With the whole of 3 Troop working on the Rubb site, progress was again being made at pace and we tried visualising how tall the completed structure will be when it is finally free standing, and secured to the anchor footings which will be buried into the foundation runs. It is certainly going to be mightily impressive. After lunch, I was asked by a fellow lance corporal if I could spare time to tell him about the history of Kelly's Garden and point out the location of *HMS Antelope* which was sunk during the war. I was more than happy to oblige and I informed him that all diving in close proximity of the wreck had now been cancelled by the military authorities.

Word is spreading around the Defence Base that a Combined Services Entertainment (CSE) concert is to visit Kelly's Garden and among the line-up of artists will be a female duo called Lips, who apparently perform cover versions of

ABBA songs. Back at the Rubb site, a section from 3 Troop had been tasked with working on the three planned helipads and connecting taxiway to ensure the ground is perfectly level.

With our surveyor on site and with the support of the D6 Dozer and two operators, this task was completed inside two hours while others were assigned to checking one more time the repaired hangar frame panels. These are extremely heavy and the effort it takes to lift just one requires four pairs of hands. Thankfully they were all found to be in excellent condition and so another important job has been completed, and we are now even closer to filling the foundation shuttering with concrete.

During the course of the evening, two colleagues and I decided to take a walk across to the Gurkha bar after dinner and on our arrival, we could see that they were deeply engrossed in a movie from back home in Nepal. As we entered the portakabin, not a single sound could be heard which was most unusual as was the fact that nobody turned to greet us but instead, they all stared at the screen with eyes and mouths wide open as if in total disbelief at what they were seeing.

Bewildered by this, we watched part of a movie in which a young Nepalese actor and actress embraced each other and with soft traditional music playing in the background, and then passionately kissed in the pouring rain before singing to each other. They then they danced and our friends gasped and clapped enthusiastically. It was all quite tame to us and not at all raunchy or erotic, yet the Gurkhas thought it was seriously hot action and sighed as the light was switched on for the interval. During the break one of them explained that the man and woman were big stars back in Nepal.

One of my colleagues asked me what I thought of the film and the Gurkhas' reaction to which I replied, "well it's obvious they haven't seen Deep Throat." We could see that they were eager to watch the second half of the movie and it was not long before the film resumed and within minutes, many of them had tears in their eyes once again, so we thought that it must have reminded them of their wives or girlfriends back home and so out of respect, we decided to leave and let them enjoy their movie.

We popped into the next portakabin where some of 3 Troop were watching a movie called 'Bloodline' which is based on the novel of the same name, and written by Sidney Sheldon. It carried a 'Restricted' rating which meant that it was only suitable for persons under the age of 17 if accompanied by an adult and later, I discovered this was the only restricted rated movie that British actress Audrey Hepburn ever starred in. I returned to my portakabin where I am now sat writing this entry in my journal.

Signed photo of 'Lips'

Monday, 21 February 1983

A former recruit from Training Party 77/8 flew into Kelly's Garden today who is sat to my right in the photograph in chapter one. It was wonderful to see him again and to catch up on the five and a half years since we last met, and he brought news of when 52 Field Squadron will depart the Falkland Islands and return to Tidworth. He also shared the dates of our post-tour leave but I had mixed emotions because as much as I want to visit to Morocco, my affection for Kelly's Garden grows stronger with every passing day.

He told me that 52 Field Squadron will set sail for Ascension Island on Sunday 12 June, and that our post-tour leave dates have been confirmed as After Duties (AD) Friday 12 July to First Parade (FP) Monday 8 August. We could not believe how much leave we have been granted and so my visit to Morocco and Gibraltar is now a reality, as indeed are my plans to trek parts of the Atlas Mountains and visit Ceuta, as well as the Cave of Hercules.

In a breezy yet sunny Kelly's Garden, the Rubb hangar foundation trenches are almost ready yet still more stores and equipment arrived by helicopter from Port Stanley. A friend of mine who serves with 3 Troop and is from Cardiff, mentioned to me that one of the helicopters which landed at Kelly's Garden earlier had no British markings, and so he asked if I would take a look at the aircraft because it was still on the Defence Base. I agreed and we walked to the western edge and close to Bonners Bay and as soon as I saw the helicopter from a distance, I recognised it as being a Puma and very possibly a SA-300, as these were used during the Falklands War by the Argentine Forces. I did not have time to watch it depart as I had two more tasks waiting to be finished, but some 20 minutes later it took off and headed south-east and so I presumed it was heading for Port Stanley.

The sky started to cloud over at around mid-afternoon and then all of a sudden, it started to rain and quickly turned into one almighty downpour which brought all work on the Defence Base to a temporary halt. Everyone ran for cover and at the same time, a radio message was received from CRE Works in Port Stanley with an instruction that the Rubb hangar project was being put on hold with immediate effect, because of a suspected miscalculation over the precise coordinates for the hangar itself. This would prove a major setback if it turned out to be correct as it is these coordinates that will determine the exact location of each Rubb anchor pad which in turn, will ensure the stability of the assembled frame.

We must now await CRE Works' final decision before we are allowed to do anything else on the site. Somewhat surprised by this, 3 Troop decided it would make sense to finish for the day given there was nothing else we could do in such deteriorating weather conditions and also, there were no indoor tasks of any kind that needed to be completed anywhere on site. Yet again, it was a case of "rain stopped play."

I am writing up my journal as a Gurkha Rifles section departs Kelly's Garden on its night patrol and thankfully for them, the weather has changed for the better. Out in Bonners Bay the British *RFA Sir Percivale* is moored not too far from shore and so I will stop writing shortly, and go to see the ship with colleagues. RFA stands for Royal Fleet Auxiliary and *Sir Percivale* was quite a ghostly sight as she silently lay anchored all alone in the eerie darkness of the night, and with just a few dim lights showing from her starboard side. Inside portakabin Number 104, I am finishing this entry and I feel ready for a good night's sleep as a light wind blows through the Defence Base, and as always, I revel in the comfort and safety of Kelly's Garden.

There is something about military barracks and camps that I find appealing and safe and yet it is difficult to pin down exactly the reasons why, but this is something that I have always felt. Today has been long and challenging and I wonder if the Rubb hangar project will be given the go ahead soon.

Tuesday, 22 February 1983

Following a quick morning parade and kit inspection, 3 Troop was dismissed and told to report to the Rubb hangar site. Today was special for our married colleagues because 52 Field Squadron's Rear Party back in Tidworth had made a one-hour video in which wives and families had recorded messages. The video was shown to anyone who wished to see it during today's mid-morning break inside the Ant Hill, and all single soldiers were invited. Most of us saw little point in watching it as none of our parents or friends are involved, which was understandable given they do not live near Tidworth.

The word is however, that a separate video had been sent especially for us bachelors and that it is by no means a family video. It is called 'Let's Get Laid' which stars the British sex symbol and nude model Fiona Richmond and British actor Robin Askwith. Both are renowned for appearing in cheap sex romps and unsurprisingly, we single soldiers felt somewhat branded and demeaned when we heard that this had been sent to Kelly's Garden and especially for us. This did not go down well at all and after a mug of hot tea and a few rounds of toast in the cookhouse, some of us took a stroll to Bonners Bay.

What did make my morning worthwhile however was the arrival of a large package from Bonus Print which contained five sets of photographs, and five free rolls of film. Even though it is 14 days late, I was absolutely thrilled to have finally received these and then to my complete surprise, I was asked along with fellow bachelors from 3 Troop if we would like to record a video just for our parents and friends back home in the United Kingdom.

It was suggested that the filming take place at the Rubb hangar site with us sitting on an army bed and then take it in turn to say a few words on camera. It was a nice gesture even though we knew most of our parents realistically will never get to see it, and as for the video 'Let's Get Laid,' we were later informed that somebody managed to get hold of it and took it down to Bonners Bay, where it was hurled as far as possible into the sea. That raised a smile on all our faces.

We received an update around mid-afternoon on the forthcoming Combined Services Entertainment concert and were told that stars from both stage and television will be performing. The names mentioned are the female comedienne and impressionist Faith Brown, Ken Goodwin from the ITV series 'The Comedians,' and Bob Carolgees with his puppet Spit the Dog, but the best news we received today was from CRE Works who confirmed that the Rubb coordinates had been checked and were correct. This means that the project can proceed and that the concreting can go ahead as planned.

Out of the blue at around 15.45, I received word that a situation was quickly developing at the southern edge of Bonners Bay and involved one of the two Thwaites Dumper Trucks. I and others immediately headed off to investigate and when we arrived just a few minutes later, it was plain to see what the problem was. The tide was on the turn and the vehicle had broken down and with that, both front wheels were almost half submerged and so word was sent for the second Thwaites Truck, which was Number 88, to come to our location as a priority.

To our horror and disbelief, we were told that this truck had crashed into portakabin Number 98 as it was being driven to our location and so with the situation now deteriorating and the tide rising quickly, assistance was desperately needed to recover the Thwaites from Bonners Bay. Just then, the D6 Dozer turned up to save the day. By now some of us were almost up to our waists in seawater as we managed to secure a towing strop to the rear of the vehicle, and soon it was recovered by the D6 Dozer.

From the edge of Bonners Bay it was towed to the REME Workshop where a corporal mechanic carried out a quick inspection of the vehicle and engine, and thankfully diagnosed that apart from some minor work it would be working by the following morning.

On leaving the REME Workshop a few of us heard the news that someone had been medevacked to Port Stanley during the afternoon by the RAF, but nobody knew the reason why, then over our evening meal we learned that the individual concerned had suffered a nasty laceration when he fell over at far southern edge of the Defence Base.

Apart from these two isolated incidents our day passed went really well and at 21.00, a few of us strolled across to the Ant Hill to watch the movie 'The Mountain Men' starring Charlton Heston. To my surprise it was enjoyable and after it finished, we discussed the events of the day and appreciated just how easily things can go wrong on a project work site, and how important it is not to panic.

Thwaites Dumper Truck 88

For some reason I have been given tomorrow morning off, and so I have decided to leave writing up my journal until then as I will have peace and quiet and the entire portakabin to myself. Since childhood, my writing has been very important to me because not only is it something I passionately enjoy as it allows me to express my myself, release creative energy, and also record historical accounts which I enjoy producing.

For me, sharing my experiences and imagination through the written word is a gift I believe I have been blessed with, and one I know I will continue for as long as I live. There are different types of written work including articles, poetry, scripts, novels, and journalism and there are many different styles of writing such as creative, narrative, and reflective but for me personally, I like to write about anything and everything.

I have just checked my calendar and I cannot believe that as of today, there are only 15 weeks remaining of this six-month operational tour of the Falkland Islands. My emotions are mixed and at times this unsettles me, because as much as I miss my family and friends back home, I still want to travel and visit Morocco and return once again to Gibraltar, and yet I feel such a powerful sense of true belonging here each time I gaze out across Bonners Bay and across to San Carlos Settlement.

There are times when I look out to San Carlos Water and try to imagine how those members of the British Task Force must have felt when they first landed here on Operation Corporate, in April 1982. Their adrenalin would surely have been pumping hard as they first stepped ashore and my respect for them is beyond measure, because as I mentioned in an earlier chapter, war is a deadly business. Very often I look around at the expanses of open land and sea that surrounds Kelly's Garden, and also to the rugged Verde Hills and the thick grassland that brave the elements every day, and it in times such as this that I close my eyes and listen, and then try to imagine in my mind what the sound of war must be like, and the mixed emotions that must race through the minds of those involved.

Conflicts and wars are not a game and neither are they like the scenes we watch in a film. Furthermore, I try from time to time to imagine how I would feel in such a combatant situation where I came face to face with my enemy and at close quarter, or hear the sound of fighter jet aircraft flying low towards me and explosions going off all around.

As I opened my eyes and returned to the present day, I was genuinely grateful to hear only the wonderful sound of silence and sense the harmony that once again exists here in the Falklands. Even though the threat of an air strike is still very real, they do not frighten any of us in the slightest and why should they? We are now more than prepared for anything the Argentine Forces decide to throw at us.

Wednesday, 23 February 1983

This morning was warm and sunny and one of the four-man sections that include Kevin and Paul hope to have some of the foundation shuttering filled with concrete by lunchtime, while in the background I could hear the sound of plant machinery and the constant rumbling of the concrete mixer.

Earlier and over at the Ablution Block, I enjoyed a piping-hot shower and when I returned to my portakabin, I wrote a letter to my parents to inform them that I am due to leave the Falkland Islands on Sunday 12 June and will be at sea for 12 days, before arriving back at Ascension Island on 24 June. I also gave them my post-tour leave dates and my plans to visit Morocco and Gibraltar.

After writing the letter, I quickly updated yesterday's events in my journal while listening to one of my favourite pieces of classical music, which is Grieg's mesmerising piano concerto in 'A' minor. I am always fascinated by how similar the Norwegian composer looks to the brilliant German theoretical physicist Albert Einstein. Their resemblance is nothing short of remarkable.

With time on my hands, I popped across to 3 Troop's Office and posted six packs of negatives to Bonus Print for enlarging together with two rolls of colour film for developing as part of my journal project. With the weather again rapidly changing for the worse, I decided against doing my dhobi and instead, I remained inside the warmth of my portakabin to read three chapters of James Herriot's novel 'It Shouldn't Happen to a Vet'. For some reason today is not a busy one for me.

Within minutes, I was again immersed in the delightful characters and amusing situations the young veterinary assistant writes about, as he innocently goes about his daily chores in the fictional village of Darrowby which is set in the North Riding of Yorkshire. This morning passed quickly and soon I was ready to go back to work but first, there was lunch to be had and so I joined my colleagues over at the cookhouse for chips, beans, and steak and ale pie. The meal was stunning and our military chefs play such an important part in keeping morale high, and as such everyone appreciates their hard effort far more than they may realise.

My afternoon was spent chatting with colleagues as we sheltered from the strong winds and heavy rain, and the weather eventually turned out to be so bad that no aircraft was permitted to fly either in or out of Kelly's Garden. As such there would be no mail or delivery of stores, nor equipment or newspapers and definitely no chance of our troop commander visiting CRE Works Team in Port Stanley.

With rain now pouring down heavily and delaying the concreting phase of the hangar project, frustration was understandably beginning to creep in because we cannot afford to lose a single day's work. Every day that is lost burdens us with an additional 12 hours which we need to make up, and this is in addition to the jobs we already have scheduled for completion before we leave. If we are ever to finish the Rubb hangar project on time and judging by the way our work has been disrupted recently, meeting our deadline is already beginning to slip away and maintaining morale and positivity could become a concern to troop management, as well as the team at large.

With the Rubb frame sections prepared for assembling and crushed rocks piled ready for packing into the steel gabion baskets, all we need now is the delivery of cement from Port Stanley but with the rain still pouring down, there was no realistic possibility of that happening today. How many more days can we afford to lose? By mid-afternoon we had no alternative but to throw in the towel in and pack away our tools and equipment, while feeling somewhat hopeless as we walked off the site to return to our portakabins.

The weather here knows no restrictions and at times it can be horrendous and then sunny, overcast and then bright, and in all honesty I have never come across such high winds as here on East Falkland Island. After enjoying a mug of good hot army tea inside our portakabin, we were soon laughing and back to our normal happy selves while outside, the wind continued to howl through Kelly's Garden as our portakabin remained rock solid thanks to the anchoring we have installed. This is exactly how life is here in the South Atlantic, yet I absolutely love it.

Someone decided to show a movie called 'The Exterminators' and some cracked open a can of beer and then later at around 19.30, we defied the elements as we made our way across to the cookhouse for our evening meal. Back inside my portakabin the team for once decided on an early night and it was a good call, because when a storm is raging outside there is nothing more enjoyable than to lay inside a warm sleeping bag while chatting away with colleagues.

In the soft glow of a dim light, I let my mind wander and thought to myself that this was how it must have been for those early polar explorers and their expedition members, when they were holed up for days on end. This is comradeship at its very best and there is none better than in 3 Troop, 52 Filed (Construction) Squadron. Suddenly, the portakabin door blew open and in walked our newly arrived corporal chef Graham who was soaked through to the skin, and as he got his things ready for a shower, he cheerfully remarked, "lovely weather for penguins!" I really like his humour.

Thursday, 24 February 1983

We were accompanied to breakfast by yet another bracing and powerful easterly breeze that blew in from San Carlos Water and straight through Kelly's Garden, and then towards the Verde Hills. I looked across to the peaks in the distance and pictured in my mind's eye the incredible views I see whenever I walk along the ridge. They are absolutely breathtaking. As a passionate hill and mountain walker with experience in Snowdonia, the Peak District, the Harz Mountains of Germany, and soon hopefully the Atlas Mountains in Morocco, I was recently asked by a colleague why some geographical features are prefixed 'Mount' while others are suffixed 'Mountains.'

It was a very good question. I explained that the term 'Mount' is assigned to a high isolated aspect that normally has only a single prominent peak, such as Mount Baker which is the volcano I watched erupt in 1978 whilst visiting the US state of Washington. Other examples are Mount Everest in the Himalayas, Mount Etna in Italy, Mount Olympia in Greece, and Mount Kilimanjaro in Tanzania, East Africa.

The term 'Mountains' however refers to a range or group of bulky peaks that collectively cover an extensive expanse of land such as the Rocky Mountains in Canada, the Appalachian Mountains in North America, the Caraballo Mountains in the Philippines, and the Black Mountains in Wales. Ironically, another passion of mine is space travel and astronomy and so I went further and explained that an excellent example of a mountain on a planet in our own solar system is Olympus Mons, or Mount Olympus which is found on Mars. This remarkable volcano's lava flowed over a vast area before it cooled and created a saucer-like appearance which in turn, led to the expression 'shield-volcano'. Olympus Mons is the highest volcano on Mars at 72,000 feet and it is almost two and a half times the height of Mount Everest.

What else was there to do on a wet and windy morning in Kelly's Garden but go across to the cookhouse for a mug of good old army tea, and so with colleagues in tow I braved the lashing rain. We have lost a lot of time to poor weather conditions these past few days and it is not going unnoticed back in Port Stanley, yet it is completely out of our control and quite worrying at times. On morning parade, our troop commander informed us that we could expect a visit from a member of the House of Lords albeit he could not confirm who the person is, or why he or she is coming to our location.

Surely it would be cancelled given the weather was not ideal for flying and so putting it to the back of our minds, we went to work with the rain still pouring down on the Rubb hangar site. We started to secure the corner sections of the foundation shuttering while other sections worked on final odd jobs, and there was absolutely no chance of the cement arriving today and even if it did, the weather would put certainly pay to 3 Troop making a mix. Furthermore, there was now no way the VIP would fly in from Port Stanley.

Just then and quite hilariously, we lost our section commander. There was no sign of him anywhere until someone reported that they could hear shouting and banging coming from inside a nearby ISO container. This had everyone laughing as one of the team desperately tried to open the heavy metal door, but what was even more hysterical was watching him fly backwards with both feet off the ground, as the container door suddenly flew open with the full weight of our section commander behind it. Walking past Paul who was now lying on his back totally spread-eagled, Bob nonchalantly brushed himself down and said, "bloody dark in there." It was entertainment at its very best.

Around 15.30, 3 Troop was given the go ahead to start preparing a cement mix using the limited quantity we had available inside the G1098. This would barely be sufficient for the first foundation run but at least the Rubb hangar project would again be up and running, or so we thought. Sections of steel reinforcement mesh had been laid inside the shuttering together with the first pair of anchor bases for the hangar legs, but again all work was postponed after a radio message was received from Port Stanley to say that due to the ongoing weather conditions, the supply of cement that was due to arrive would now be delayed until 6 March, a whole two weeks away.

Frustrated and understandably close to losing patience, our troop commander spoke with the RAF who reluctantly agreed to fly him to Port Stanley by Gazelle helicopter, to try and resolve this latest delay. 3 Troop's concern was that its primary task of constructing a Rubb hangar on East Falkland Island was yet again being hampered by delays in the supply of critical logistical resources from Port Stanley.

Furthermore, without the Rubb hangar project then 3 Troop would be more or less redundant because there was hardly any other work to do, apart from lay the PSP flooring for the helipads and taxiway. This latest delay of 14 days would inevitably lead to boredom and in turn, had potential to impact significantly on troop morale which is a situation no Royal Engineer troop commander wishes to have, especially in an isolated location such as Kelly's Garden. Everyone genuinely empathised because he was now dealing with so many issues that were not of his making but to his credit, he was holding his own.

Inside the G1098 Store and with the rain still falling heavily and with hardly any work to do, there was nothing for it but to return to our portakabins. I finished reading 'Let Sleeping Vets Lie' and as I had anticipated and hoped for, James finally married Helen which made me happy because I now have something special to look forward to now when the television series is shown back home later this year. Suddenly the sound of a low flying RAF Chinook helicopter could be heard approaching Kelly's Garden.

Somebody shouted, "it's the cement!" but they were wrong. Instead, it was the VIP from the House of Lords who was accompanied by a very small entourage but within less than half an hour of arriving, they left and headed back to Port Stanley. This really was the last straw because if the RAF could dispatch a Chinook helicopter for a visiting dignitary, then why could they not deliver crucial building supplies to a priority military project that was working to a very tight schedule?

Everyone just stood silent and in disbelief and frustration, and our corporals stormed over to the troop office. They soon returned and said that neither our staff sergeant nor the RAF had got to meet the VIP even though it was confirmed that she was indeed a member of the second chamber at Westminster. Everyone agreed such fleeting visits are becoming a complete farce and totally unnecessary but this latest incident was completely inexcusable, given we could not get supplies for the Rubb hangar. Others at Kelly's Garden are also starting to voice frustration and anger over VIP visits which appear to be nothing other than a busman's holiday, and all at the expense of the British taxpayer. Is it any wonder why troops on the ground are disillusioned and infuriated over such wastage of public money, and non-productive visits? We still do not know who today's VIP was and quite frankly, nobody cares.

Foundation shuttering being assembled

Strong wind hitting Kelly's Garden

Afternote

When I was serving in the Falkland Islands and throughout the whole of my 24-year military career, British soldiers rarely spoke negatively or critically about government or civilian officials who visited military bases and operational theatres. Contrary to a common misconception by many that members of the British Armed Forces are not permitted to vote, they do in fact have the option of registering themselves every five years either as an ordinary or overseas voter, and this was passed through the Representation of the People Act 1918 after royal approval was granted in February 1918.

Section 5 of this Act was at first somewhat imbalanced and allowed all officers and men who were aged 19 or over on the 15 April 1918, the right to vote by completing an Army Form W.3940. At home these forms were readily available, and for anyone serving in France or Italy they could be obtained from their Commanding Officer, or any Field Post Office and British Military Hospital. For women who were serving however, the minimum age to register was 30 and for members of the nursing corps primarily, and those serving with voluntary organisations such as the Territorial Service and Voluntary Aid Detachment. Over the years, both the terms and conditions were revised to bring them into line with the rest of British society.

Speaking for myself, I have always used my vote yet I have not always agreed with governments on certain policies relating to national security such as defence spending, and one decision in particular will forever be wrong in my eyes. In 2003, British troops were deployed to Iraq to fight a war alongside the US that still to this day, is branded as illegal and unjust by many and in 2016, the findings of the Chilcot Inquiry were released and highly critical of Tony Blair's decision to go to war.

Sir John Chilcot outlined several valid concerns that were based on deception, exaggeration, and inaccurate intelligence yet Blair rejected them all while across the United Kingdom, the general public had already made up its mind and indeed many called for Blair to be prosecuted. Was he right to take the country to war? Personally, I have always disagreed.

Chapter Twelve
A Show Comes to Town

Foreword

The Combined Services Entertainment (CSE) took over from the Entertainments National Service Association (ENSA) in 1946 and has continued to provide live entertainment to members of the British Armed Forces around the world, both in operational theatres, on permanent bases outside the United Kingdom, and on Royal Naval ships. Its part in supporting and promoting the wellbeing of our Armed Services is significant and the history of the CSE as a live entertainment organisation is remarkable. Famous stars from the past who are sadly no longer with us yet performed and visited troops include Dame Vera Lynn, Frankie Howerd, Gracie Fields, Sir Harry Secombe, Peter Sellers, Benny Hill, Kenneth Williams, and Stanley Baxter and those who are still with include Jim Davidson, Fish of Marillion, Geri Halliwell, Al Murray, David Beckham and Peter Andre.

In 1939 and around the beginning of the Second World War, the British actor and theatre director Basil Dean and comedian Leslie Henson between them formed an entertainment organisation which they called the Entertainments National Service Association, or ENSA. Household names from the world of dance, screen, song and stage visited military personnel to entertain and inspire them and such was ENSA's success that in the 1970s, it gave the British comedy script writers Jimmy Perry and David Croft an idea for a new television comedy series that would run for seven years up until 1981. The series was called 'It Ain't Half Hot Mum' and it went on to become one of Britain's national television treasures.

As already mentioned, in 1946 ENSA was disbanded and taken over by the CSE which in turn was revamped in 2020 and became BFBS Live Events. The British Forces Broadcasting Service itself was first formed in 1943 and it has provided radio and television services to the British Armed Forces around the world, and past presenters include Adrian Juste, Tommy Vance, Tony Blackburn, Cliff Michelmore, David Hamilton, John Peel and the wonderful Alan Freeman who was affectionately nicknamed 'Fluff.' David Jacobs went on to present the long running television music panel show 'Juke Box Jury' and he also hosted BBC Radio 4's 'Any Questions.'

Whilst serving with 32 Armoured Engineer Regiment in Munsterlager in 1985, I received an unexpected phone call early one Saturday morning from the duty guard commander to say that a Welsh rock band had turned up at the main gate, and were asking to speak with me in person. Intrigued and wondering who on earth these people could be, I drove to Dennis Barracks only to find two of my childhood friends namely Stephen 'Steph' Williams and Clive 'Buddy' Edwards standing by the main gate with huge smiles on their face. I could not believe my eyes!

Steph was an exceptional drummer and Clive was a great guitarist and together, they had formed a four-man band called Santiago and were on a tour of West Germany to perform at British Army of the Rhine bases and RAF stations. That night they had a concert at Dennis Barracks and after spending the day together and helping them set up their equipment, I watched as they them went through their playlist which included superb cover versions of songs by Dire Straits, David Bowie, Deep Purple, Queen, and the Electric Light Orchestra.

The audience absolutely loved them and after the show, we drove to a quiet local bar and then went back to my apartment where we drank and chatted away into the very early hours. I next met up with the band some two years later at the Crown and Cushion public house on Minley Road, Hawley and I was invited to be their full-time manager, however, as wonderful as their offer sounded it was completely out of the question because my military career was progressing well, and I had my pension to think about.

In May 1990 and whilst serving with 26 Engineer Regiment at Iserlohn in Germany, I phoned the Tommy Vance Morning Show on BFBS Radio because he was giving away a pair of tickets for the Rolling Stones' Urban Jungle concert at the Müngersdorfer Stadion in Cologne. To my surprise, I got through and as we were chatting away live on air Tommy explained that to win the tickets, all I needed to do was answer correctly one question about my homeland.

The question he asked was could I name Wales' most famous railway station. Knowing exactly which one he was referring to, which is pronounced Llan-vire-pooll-guin-gill-go-ger-u-queern-drorb-ooll-llandus-ilio-gogo-goch as displayed on the platform, the joker in me replied 'Cardiff Central' and Tommy Vance burst out laughing, and I got to see one of the best live concerts ever.

In 1996 and whilst serving on a six-month Implementation Force (IFOR) tour of duty with 36 Engineer Regiment at Gornji Vakuf in Bosnia-Herzegovina, I met the British rock star Fish when he was the main performer of a CSE concert. Fish was the former frontman of Marillion who's two biggest hits were 'Lavender' and 'Kayleigh' and he was the nicest and most genuine person you could ever wish to meet.

Me and Fish, Bosnia 1996

My interest in music goes back to my childhood when my mother Enid taught me to play the piano in the parlour at 23 Cornish Place and during my teenage years, I would travel literally anywhere to watch a rock concert or orchestra perform live. In Llanelli's once famous Glen Ballroom in the 1970s, I saw bands such as Mungo Jerry, Quicksand, Man, Mott the Hoople, Cozy Powell, Budgie, and Fusion Orchestra, and another passion of mine was musicals on London's Kings Road and at the Shaftesbury Theatre in the West End. Such was my fondness of music that in 2004, I taught myself to play the acoustic guitar and in 2015 and 2016, I presented two weekly radio programmes with the West Wales station Radio Tircoed. On Wednesday afternoons I presented a three-hour show called 'Drive Time' and 'Prime Time' on Sunday evenings, which was a two-hour rock programme.

Friday, 25 February 1983

Weather conditions today were again a concern to 3 Troop and it now appears as though the Falklands' summer is already drawing to an early end, given the conditions we are encountering here at Kelly' Garden and this could potentially result in the premature start to a South Atlantic winter. This does not bode well for the Rubb hangar as any realistic hope of completing the project on time could be significantly hampered, or in the worst-case scenario, missed completely and that would be devastating for CRE Works back at Port Stanley.

And still the heavy rain continued and showed no sign of stopping as Kelly's Garden once again turned into one huge mud bath, with almost every path and dirt track submerged under water. The daily working conditions have become more challenging and difficult to deal with and practically every task now seems to bring with it more unanticipated issues and at times, it can be too risky to go on site.

After all the work and hard effort that 3 Troop has put into the Rubb project to date, we are now truly desperate for good weather and parts of the Defence Base are a sorry sight. It was genuinely heartbreaking but then suddenly as if by some kind of magic, a miracle happened in front of our very eyes when the wind and rain stopped in an instant, and sunshine broke through the clouds. The change in weather was quite extraordinary and all we had to contend with was a cold breeze which would actually work in our favour. I just simply could not believe what happened in the space of just a few minutes.

Most empty portakabins on the base are now ready for new arrivals and the Ablution Block, Generator House, Medical Centre, Ration Store, Cookhouse and the REME Workshop have all passed their final inspection and so the decision was made to bring forward the handover of the Defence Base to the RAF ChinDet, and at the earliest opportunity. Around 14.00 a small team of Royal Engineer Clerks of Works flew in from Port Stanley and after conducting a thorough inspection of the camp, a two-hour meeting was convened and Kelly's Garden Defence Base was officially signed over to the RAF senior officer.

For the first time since our arrival, the camp was now under the full control and management of the Royal Air Force and all incoming troops will have a comfortable camp in which to serve their six-month operational tours of duty. Despite the weather and other obstacles that we have had to deal with over the recent days, we now have a lot to catch up on and there is no time for complacency or back-slapping but instead, we must hit the ground running and finish the foundation runs before we can even begin to think about assembling the Rubb frame. During the afternoon and despite the improved weather, the ground at Kelly's Garden was still drenched and there was no possibility whatsoever of filling the foundation shuttering with concrete at this moment in time.

Two four-man teams began the work of laying steel reinforcement mesh inside the shuttering while the welding team inspected all steel gabion baskets and where necessary, they carried out minor repairs which took no time at all. It was decided to make three additional baskets to be on the safe side, as these could be used on other sites around the Defence Base and with everyone busy at work again, I visited 3 Troop Office to complete an item of personal administration and update the G1098 Ledger with the equipment that arrived recently from Port Stanley.

At around 18.45 the decision was made to call it a day which took several of my colleagues completely by surprise, and reason was because the steel reinforcement mesh had now finally been laid inside the shuttering that will form the northern side of the Rubb hangar. This section has a length of some 45 metres and was covered using large sheets of tarpaulin until it is ready to be filled with concrete.

At 19.30, a RAF Sea King helicopter flew in from Port Stanley with several personnel on board who have been assigned to the Defence Base, and they brought with them a sack of official and personal mail, and I had another wonderful surprise waiting for me. The British comedian and actor Benny Hill had obviously received my letter because among my mail was a large brown envelope which had inside it, a signed letter and photograph of Benny Hill himself and his dancing troupe Hill's Angels, which includes Sue Upton and Louise English.

It is surprising how one tiny gesture such as this can raise a person's morale, and especially when it comes from such a famous and much-loved British comedy icon. I have always enjoyed watching his hilarious programmes on television and once again, the kindness of certain celebrities is a reminder that we are not forgotten by the folk back home, or indeed by national treasures. Even while serving in West Belfast back in 1980, such gestures meant the world to the troops, and they still do.

Benny Hill's signed photograph

I went across to the Ant Hill with colleagues to watch the 1978 comedy movie 'Who Is Killing the Chefs of Europe' which starred Robert Morley, George Segal, and Jacqueline Bisset and what an odd title it was for a film. I had hoped to show Frazer the photograph I received today but he was acting as Dining Room Orderly over in the cookhouse, so I returned to my portakabin and wrote a long letter to my parents back home in Llanelli.

For some reason I am missing them today more than ever, and although my love for them is beyond measure and they are forever in my thoughts, I know deep down inside that it is my intention never to return to live again in my hometown. I still do not really know why I feel this way, but from the very moment the train pulled out of Llanelli Rail Station in July 1977, I instinctively knew there and then that my life had changed forever and that my mother's advice to move away was the best.

By transferring across to the Regular Army I have discovered a far more exciting and interesting life that makes me extremely happy and extremely fulfilled, and I want to see more of this wonderful world and meet lots of new people along my journey. I know none of this would ever have happened had I remained in Llanelli because the career opportunities and extensive travel, and the adventures and outdoor activities that the British Army has to offer are all so incredible, and I am thoroughly enjoying every single minute. The camaraderie and friendship which I have discovered is also very different to that which I had back home, and my colleagues have become like a second family and everything is all so very wonderful, and to think that this is just the beginning.

As I was writing to my parents, I received a report that there was a leak in one of the water tanks which I installed just a few weeks ago, and so I went across to investigate and when I arrived with my toolbox, I immediately identified the problem. For some reason and to my bewilderment an outlet pipe had split and water was escaping however, something did not look right and although I had no idea as to what could have caused the rupture, and especially so close to the ground, I wanted to get to the bottom of the problem.

I made a temporary repair and went to find a plumber to get their opinion and after Bob examined the damaged pipe, he looked at me and said that the leak had been caused by a sharp object such as a knife, or quite possibly a screwdriver. We agreed that this could have been a simple accident but whoever had caused the damage, he was probably too embarrassed to admit to it. I replaced the pipe and then headed back to our portakabin where I finished writing my letter.

After dinner, I was handed a Nepalese 10-rupee banknote by Frazer who asked for it to be included in my journal and I readily agreed. Another colleague by the name of Steve has also become a good friend and he is an interesting individual who like Kevin, has a natural ability to make people laugh and later this evening we both went across to the Gurkha accommodation to visit Sak and together, he and Steve enjoyed a few whiskies and so I headed back to my portakabin.

Some two hours later Steve returned a little worse for wear, and entertained us all by struggling to climb into his sleeping bag and at one point he danced and hopped his way around the portakabin with one foot stuck inside his trouser pocket. He did not utter a single word but instead just tried to get his foot free and it was like watching a slapstick comedy which was absolutely hilarious.

To his credit and always the perfect gentleman, Steve behaved impeccably before crashing out on top of his mattress and then began to loudly snore. There was nothing we could do to stop him and after a quick discussion, four of us carried his bed out of the portakabin and took it some 20 metres away with Steve still fast asleep, and that is where he will stay for the rest of the night. Back inside the portakabin and in perfect silence, I finished writing up this entry in my journal.

Saturday, 26 February 1983

The weather here is certainly testing 3 Troop because yet again the rain poured down and the ground at Kelly's Garden is saturated. The mud clings to almost everything it comes in contact with including our boots and clothing, tools and equipment, furniture, and no matter how hard we try nobody can avoid dragging it wherever they go on site. It is all over the floor in the Ablution Block and cookhouse, the Laundry Building and especially our portakabin, and it is becoming quite annoying.

The Defence Base has taken on the appearance of an Alaskan mining town from the 1890s gold rush period, and our daily conservancy tasks are no joke so we are going to address the problem with the troop management. Portakabin Number 27 is being converted into a temporary theatre for the Combined Services Entertainment concert that is planned for tomorrow afternoon, and chairs and staging have already been flown in from Port Stanley and an awning fitted to the side of an adjoining portakabin which will be used as a changing room for the performers. CSE shows are usually presented by well-known celebrities from the world of show business but on this particular occasion, nobody has any idea as to the line-up or indeed who will act as compere.

For no known reason, everything about this concert is being kept a secret which quite understandably has led to some on the Defence Base believing that this is not in fact a CSE concert as such, but instead another cabaret comprising of military performers who are serving in the Falkland Islands, and similar to the type of show that we in 3 Troop organised on board *Cunard Countess* during the voyage south in January.

When I see such shows, I am reminded of the 1970s British television comedy series 'It Ain't Half Hot, Mum.' Based on a Royal Artillery concert party stationed at Deolali in India during the latter months of the Second World War, the cast includes wonderful characters such as Gunner 'Lofty' Sugden played by Don Estelle, 'La-de-da' Gunner Graham played by John Clegg, the ever so posh but imbecilic Captain 'Tippy' Ashwood played by Michael Knowles, and the unforgettably Welsh homophobic Battery Sergeant Major Williams played by Windsor Davies.

Today, the welding team supported by Steve and Paul continued the work of grinding down and shortening metal pickets that will be used to anchor the gabions baskets to the ground, and although their work is somewhat monotonous, they worked tirelessly to have the job completed as quickly as possible. Inside the G1098 Store, I chatted with colleagues about the Rubb hangar project as we serviced items of engineering equipment and masonry tools ahead of the concreting task, and we froze as the temperature yet again dropped significantly.

With morale sky high, we chatted about our individual plans for post-tour leave and reminisced on last year's tour in Canada, and it would seem that we all hope 52 Field Squadron will return to CFB Meaford next year for another three-month tour. This is not as crazy as it sounds because there is still much to be done on the Canadian Forces Base. Our Regimental Sergeant Major visited Kelly's Garden today and he is extremely pleased with what he has seen.

We like him because as a senior Warrant Officer he is fair, firm, and friendly and in the British Army these qualities are better known as the 'Three Fs' and together, they are considered the difference between a good and bad manager. To his credit, our Regimental Sergeant Major is highly respected by 3 Troop and considered to be among the best in the corps and throughout his visit, RAF helicopters flew in and out of the Defence Base but sadly none carried mail or parcels from back home.

The RSM flew back to Port Stanley at around 17.45 after which all tasks planned for today were completed by 19.30, and we were pleased that we had managed to make up for some of the time lost to bad weather, and delays in delivery of supplies. Steve decided to go for another drink with Sak who for some reason failed to turn up, and so it was not long before he rejoined us in the Ant Hill where we watched the 1980 movie 'Urban Cowboy' starring John Travolta.

Watching a movie is one way to pass away the evenings here at Kelly's Garden as it allows us all to relax as a team and to meet soldiers from other units. The weather can impact hugely on our physical fitness programme which is primarily circuit training because in all honesty, the ground here is not exactly suitable for squad runs and we have to be extra careful when jogging across to San Carlos Settlement, or up to the ridge of the Verde Hills.

We will certainly have plenty of demanding fitness training sessions when we return to Tidworth but in all fairness, our physical fitness is being kept extremely high just by the day-to-day work we are undertaking. I stayed a short while after the movie and chatted with colleagues before heading across to the Ablution Block for a shave and hot shower, after which I returned to my portakabin which proved quite a challenge because there were no outside lights working, and the only source of light was coming from inside the portakabins.

Tired yet content, I climbed into my sleeping bag and read the last few pages of Peter Benchley's novel 'Jaws' and I must admit I personally found the ending to be quite different to Steven Spielberg's film. Through an open window and out in the distance, I could hear the faint sound of singing coming from the Ant Hill as the stars in the night sky above sparkled in their tens of thousands and I reflected on my first few days here in the Falklands and in particular, the time I briefly spent with colleagues visiting Port Stanley and photographing deserted Argentine equipment near the meteorological centre, and seeing *Sir Tristram* so close. Right now, it feels like ages since that all happened and yet it was only seven weeks ago.

Sunday, 27 February 1983

"This will be a memorable day" Frazer remarked to me as our portakabin slowly came to life and in its own sweet way, it would be the same for everyone at Kelly's Garden. The day began as usual with a hearty breakfast over in the cookhouse at around 07.00 and as always, the food was plentiful and very well prepared. Our two military chefs between them continue to feed us with such a high standard of catering, and both are the best colleagues you could wish for.

We consider ourselves to be extremely fortunate to have them in our troop because neither complains or moans about anything at all, and they always join in troop activities and so for me personally, they are an absolute credit to their corps. After we had eaten, it was straight back to the portakabin to collect our equipment before heading across to the Rubb hangar site and this time we had smiles on our faces, because the weather was once again pleasant and dry. It was nevertheless quite gusty as we examined the condition of the foundation shuttering which thankfully was intact and in excellent condition, and ready to be filled with concrete.

Some of 3 Troop made a sweep of the helipad and taxiway sites while others cleaned and brushed out our portakabins, then checked the two concrete mixers and oiled the trowels. At midday, the decision was made to have an early lunch in readiness for this afternoon's CSE show and still, nobody had any idea as to who would be performing but at least we do know that a show is definitely coming to town. The CSE concert party arrived at Kelly's Garden courtesy of a RAF Sea King helicopter at around 13.00, and the aircraft landed at the southern edge of the Defence Camp and close to the Rubb hangar site, on one of the windiest afternoons in a long time.

Inspecting the foundation shuttering

Their arrival did surprise us because helicopter flights are strictly controlled by the weather and in particular strong winds, poor visibility, fog, and low cloud but nevertheless, the Sea King flew in. After a wait of around three minutes, we gave a thumbs-up to the pilot that all was well and that he could shut down his Rolls Royce engine. The concert party was accompanied by half a dozen military personnel who were greeted by the senior RAF ChinDet officer at Kelly's Garden, plus a small contingent of RAF technicians and a photographer.

As our visitors were escorted across to their portakabins, we made our way back to the Rubb hangar site where we stood around and chatted in an attempt to pass away the time yet still, the question that had not been answered is who the hell is performing? As the artists made their way through the Defence Base, apparently not one was recognised by anyone who managed to catch a glimpse of them.

With a small number of engineering stores still unavailable, and with the arrival of the cement delayed yet again, the Rubb project was placed on hold and by now it is becoming rather tedious and extremely frustrating, so to focus our minds on something else I asked Paul and Frazer if they would meet me over at the Ablution Block. A faulty shower had been reported by members of the Royal Artillery and by the time I reached the building, the floor was completely under water but thankfully I could see the problem straight away and it looked like a quick fix.

After briefing my colleagues, we cleared the blocked drain and cleaned the entire building and within one hour, the floor was like new again and the time was now around 13.45. We walked back to the Rubb hangar site and could hear the CSE concert party rehearsing in portakabin number 27. The weather started to break and it was turning out to be quite a nice afternoon apart from high wind that was still blowing in from San Carlos Water, and in an easterly direction towards the Verde Hills.

Being the dedicated powerlifter that he is, my colleague and good friend has made himself a bench on which to do his bench-presses and exercises, using barbells and dumbbells. Because of the weight of these items of equipment, he was not allowed to bring his own from Tidworth but as soon as we arrived at Kelly's Garden, his top priority was to make himself a set by using an old crowbar, and various sized empty tin cans from the cookhouse which he filled with concrete and chippings. I am convinced that because of his passion for powerlifting, following the stock market, charging colleagues for haircuts, and eloquent speaking, he is the most fascinating member of 3 Troop.

Back in our portakabin and while I was chatting with Frazer and Paul, suddenly Bhan from the Gurkhas knocked on the door and asked if he could catch up on my journal. When I showed him the 10-rupee note that had been donated to it, he asked for a pen and with that he proceeded to write the name of the King of Nepal immediately next to the banknote in both English and Nepalese.

Completely taken by surprise, I could not thank him enough and this is exactly how considerate Gurkhas are as a people. They freely show affection and are incredibly thoughtful, big-hearted, and extremely friendly. After this tour Bhan will be posted back to Hong Kong while in Nepal, his wife will have to wait another two years before they have their next reunion.

15.00 arrived and I walked with Paul, Frazer, and Bhan across to the CSE concert which we have now been informed is organised by the RAF, and as we approached the door we were greeted by more Gurkha friends. The remainder of 3 Troop soon joined us and as we queued for what seemed like an eternity, I chatted with a Gurkha sergeant who showed me a letter he had received from his wife which was written in Nepalese.

Eventually we were allowed inside the portakabin to take our seats and for reasons I did not understand at the time, I ended up sitting between Jock and the man-mountain that is Pabs. He has to be one of the largest men I have ever known but all eyes were now glued to the stage door, and we were told the show would start in three minutes. Suddenly and with a loud crash, the stage door flew open with tremendous force, and onto the stage walked a perplexed and nervous looking performer who was carrying a guitar.

He introduced himself and mumbled an explanation that the comedian who was due to act as compere was unwell and as such, could not take part. Thinking that this was a prank and part of his act, everyone laughed and clapped but he was not joking and could not have been any more apologetic. With the audience somewhat bemused by what was happening, we sat in silence as the guitarist who had not sung a single song sheepishly started to walk off stage, but then turned and gave us all a pitiful smile before closing the door behind him.

Some of the Gurkhas clearly had no idea what was going on but thought it was absolutely hilarious, and so they gave a big round of applause and cheered. Thinking that this just had to be a set-up, the stage door once again flew open with the help of a strong gust of wind, and onto the stage stepped a very attractive female singer who instead of bursting into song, spent several minutes battling and struggling to close the door behind her. I am sure I heard the odd expletive as she cursed the weather conditions that was now ruining her act.

Here on a windy Sunday afternoon in possibly the most remote locations on East Falkland Island, where not a single female served on the Defence Base and inside a portakabin packed to the brim with red hot-blooded testosterone filled male soldiers, stood the first woman we had seen in two months ago, and she was dressed in a low cut body-hugging dress with a slit running all the way to the top of her thigh.

Sat in front of her and drooling away were several rows of open-mouthed gaping soldiers who just stared in disbelief at this vision of beauty standing before them, and without blinking an eyelid not a single word was uttered. Almost crushing me against Jock, Pabs exhaled a long sigh and muttered, "wow, I'd give her one!" I turned to look at him and I swear he was having a seizure by the expression on his face, and as she finished her introductory song she made the fatal mistake of asking the audience "any request boys?"

With eyes shut and cupping my face in my hands, I said to myself "oh dear God no!" and with that I waited for the inevitable, and it wasn't long in coming. Pabs who was now breathing like a deranged Rottweiler shouted something that clearly the singer clearly thought had come from me, because I was given the coldest glare ever, and to make matters even worse, someone directly behind me hollered another comment that I dare not repeat.

Sitting to my left, Jock decided to join in. "Can ye nee seeng a Scoottish toon hen?"

This was quickly followed with, "awe you're a wee brammer so ye are!" and as I cowered as much as I could, and while wishing I was sat with Frazer, Paul, and Bhan, the audience roared with laughter and looked across to where I was sitting and pointed at me. They then gave an almighty cheer and to cap it all Jock, elbowed me in the ribs and with a big grin across his face he said, "awe she's brilliant mun!"

The next performer stood in for the comedian who had failed to turn up, and he received a huge applause after his act because he came out with some of the best come-back lines I have ever heard, and genuinely had the whole audience in stitches with jokes, stories, and observations. The banter between audience and performer continued, and boy he could stand his ground because no matter what the audience threw at him, he came back with some incredibly retorts. I do not remember his name for the life of me, but he is certainly one to look out for in the future. Three more acts followed and it was all such a welcomed change to everyday life here at Kelly's Garden, but no sooner had the show started when suddenly, it was all over and the time was only 17.15.

I wonder where his eyes are

Within minutes of the show ending, the portakabin emptied and everyone including the performers and their entourage were in the cookhouse enjoying an early meal during which, I kept my distance from the female singer. At around 18.00, the concert party boarded the RAF Sea King and after the pilot carried out his pre-flight checks the aircraft took off and headed back to Port Stanley.

The concert party had done an amazing job and they had given us all such a memorable time however, life at Kelly's Garden immediately returned to normal and within less than an hour, I was once again enjoying the peace and freezing-cold breeze at the edge of Bonners Bay. It was an indescribable feeling of happiness and for me, it is never a concern being so far away from a town or large society such as Port Stanley which is 55 miles to the southeast. I do not consider it being lonely here but instead, I feel completely free from the pressures of everyday modern day life and it is all wonderful, so very perfect.

With no more tasks assigned to 3 Troop for the remainder of the day, everyone relaxed and I began to write up my journal and also this account of the CSE show. Some opted to return to portakabin number 27 to watch the movie 'The Prince and the Pauper', and I rejoined my colleagues about half an hour into the film. I left at around 22.15 and headed back to my portakabin to read another novel which is 'Jaws 2' and written by Hank Searls. I was told that rather than going to watch the CSE concert, a few colleagues had trekked to Bodie Peak which is some five miles south-southeast of Kelly's Garden, and it is my intention to do the same if I ever get the chance to do so.

The evening sky tonight is at its most beautiful and with a clear moon shining down on of Bonners Bay, I want to put on my boots and warm clothing, and venture back out into the night and walk across to the foot of the Verde Hills. It would only take me 40 minutes at the most to reach my favourite spot where I often sit alone and absorb the sheer splendour of this beautiful landscape, but sadly time is not on my side and being much wiser from past experiences, I decided to stay inside my sleeping bag and quickly finish writing up my journal.

Our world is without doubt a most beautiful and finely balanced planet and we humans, as custodians, have a care of duty to look after it as best we can and not only for the next generation, but for the many generations to follow. The increasing damage I see each year is becoming a concern for me, and if it is allowed to continue then I see no end to the long-term harm it will all bring.

I always remember Vaughan Evans who was my head-teacher at St Michael's School telling my class one day, that nature is such an incredible force and it will always fight back and win. I have no doubt that nature will indeed have the final say, and we cannot simply allow the damage that we are inflicting on the likes of the Amazon forest and oceans to continue. I also remember my geography teacher Mister Withey saying something profound at Saint Michael's and it was this, "plastic is man's worst invention and it will become the scourge of our planet." How right he was.

Bad conditions at Kelly's Garden

Afternote

The much-loved British comedian and actor Alfred Hawthorne Hill was born in Southampton on 21 January 1924, and went on to become one of the greatest masters of slapstick comedy that Britain has ever produced. Surrounded by his troupe of young, beautiful, and scantily dressed dancers called Hill's Angels, the man was a genius and adored by millions from across all age groups because they loved his unique brand of comedy. Was it risqué? Well yes of course it was, and that is exactly how he and the public wanted it to be.

I accept that sometimes it was very close to the knuckle but it was all nevertheless hilarious and very tongue in cheek humour, especially when the sketches were speeded up. Even the head slapping on Irish comedian Jackie Wright was so funny to watch as was the portrayal of female celebrities such as Fanny Craddock, who was played by Benny Hill himself. For me, the man oozed hilarity and fun yet in his private life he was a troubled man. A lifelong bachelor, private, and extremely insecure financially even though he was a multi-millionaire, he lived a very basic lifestyle and only rented rooms. He never owned a car or a house but one passion was visiting France where he could freely move without being noticed.

In October 1992, I was posted to Southampton in Hampshire as the first Regimental Chief Clerk of a new unit called 78 (Fortress) Engineer Regiment (Volunteers). The Regimental Headquarters was established at Blighmont TA Centre on Millbrook Road and the start-up team included a new Commanding Officer, Training Major, Adjutant, Regimental Sergeant Major, three Permanent Staff Instructors, a REME Workshops Sergeant and me.

My role was to plan, setup, equip, and organise regimental and squadron administrative offices in Southampton, Brighton, Aldershot, and Royal Tunbridge Wells. Not too far from Blighmont TA Centre was a tower block in an area called Upper Shirley. This I was told was where Benny Hill grew up as a child.

On 20 April 1992, Benny Hill died at the age of 68 at Teddington in London, and his body was discovered slumped in a chair in front of a television that was still switched on. Buried at Hollybrook Cemetery in Southampton on 26 April, rumour *quickly spread that Benny Hill's coffin contained valuable items such as cash and jewellery and on 4 October 1992, his grave was vandalised and robbed. Following a police investigation into what was truly a very shocking crime, Benny Hill was again laid to rest but this time his grave was sealed under a large heavy memorial stone.*

Chapter Thirteen
Daffodils and Dilemmas

Foreword

Britain's Armed Forces are exceptional.

In times of national and international crisis and emergency, they can be relied upon to deliver the very highest standard of military disaster relief to civil communities and one perfect example was in December 2015, when unprecedented rainfall and high winds during Storm Desmond devastated much of the United Kingdom. The programme of building and repairing flood barriers, rescuing thousands of stranded victims, and strengthening breached dam walls in order to avoid catastrophic disaster was exceptional. Four years earlier in 2010, almost 200,000 stranded British nationals across Western Europe were repatriated after the Icelandic volcano Eyjafjallajökull erupted over six days.

In 2020 an outstanding military success story unfolded when seven temporary Nightingale Hospitals were established across the United Kingdom, in support of the British government's response to the Covid-19 pandemic and in 2021, Operation Iron Viper was launched to help the NHS administer Covid-19 vaccines which in itself was a mammoth undertaking. Both of the life-saving operations were headed by a senior staff officer from Llanelli who commanded 101 Logistic Brigade in Aldershot at the time.

These critical Nightingale Care Hospitals were set up, furnished, and fully operational within unprecedented timeframes and to give just one example of how quickly the British Armed Forces can react in a crisis, then just consider this. London Dockland's ExCel Exhibition Centre in the Royal Victoria Dock was transformed into a fully equipped 500 bed Nightingale Hospital in just nine working days, and what was even more remarkable, was that it had the capacity to deal with 4,000 patients.

Further afield there is a non-combatant talent that makes our Armed Forces celebrated and greatly appreciated by the public at large and around the world, and that is its precision and meticulous pageantry at ceremonial events, and on public, and royal duties such as Changing of the Guard at Buckingham Palace, Trooping the Colour at Horse Guards Parade, Air Shows, and large-scale displays such as military tattoos.

The RAF's Red Arrows, the Royal Navy's field-gun competitions, the Army's Red Devils Parachute Display Team, and the military massed bands are just some of the many exhibitions that take place each year, and not just within the United Kingdom. As a nation we should be extremely proud of our Armed Forces for the brilliant part they play in helping our country define its true character, and I for one will always remember the huge sense of pride I felt when as a serving Warrant Officer, I visited my son David while he was on royal duties with the Welsh Guards at Windsor Castle in 2000.

It is a fact that where a positive exists, so will a negative and for the British Armed Forces the biggest negative of all must surely be Defence Spending Reviews by incumbent governments. Serving through the whole of Margaret Thatcher's tenure as Prime Minister between 1979 and 1990, not once did I have cause or reason to worry about job security or pension rights, however, in 1995 I was appointed Regimental Administrative Office Warrant Officer of 36 Engineer Regiment in Maidstone and things were starting to change drastically for our Armed Forces.

The very next year, a programme of redundancies was announced by the Ministry of Defence which naturally concerned many who had no wish or intention of leaving the British Army. Some however did apply for voluntary redundancy, as was their right but on the day the bundle of brown envelopes landed on my desk in the Regimental Headquarters, I read the list of names of those to be made redundant and to my surprise, quite a number were not volunteers. As the RAOWO, it was my duty to inform my commanding officer. A date and time was set by the Ministry of Defence for chosen individuals to be notified and when those who had not volunteered were informed, I recorded their appeals for re-consideration and I took it upon myself to ensure that each was passed up the chain of command but sadly, most proved unsuccessful. This was an extremely difficult time both for my clerical and administrative team and the individuals, and every help and support was provided during their transition back into civilian life.

On 22 March 2021, Ben Wallace the British Secretary of State for Defence announced in Westminster that the size of the Regular Army would be reduced from 82,000 to 72,500 by 2025, which in real terms accounts for a loss of almost 10,000 professionally trained personnel. When I enlisted in 1977, the strength of the British Army was approximately 167,000 and while I fully appreciate that this was during the Cold War, this is precisely where President Putin is taking Russia and NATO back to given his illegal invasion of Ukraine in February 2022.

With geopolitical tension growing between Russia and the West, I cannot support any reduction to Britain's Armed Forces but instead would argue that there is now an even greater need to increase numbers, and also defence spending in order to safeguard our nation. Is it any wonder why British taxpayers despair at such announcements when highly contentious government spending continues on vanity projects such as the HS2 railway which is not a priority, and Foreign Aid continues to be given to nuclear countries including India? None of it makes any sense.

The term that governments use when cutting back drastically on public spending is austerity, but what exactly is austerity? The word originates from the Greek 'austeros' meaning 'harsh' and 'severe' and refers specifically to the way life is lived, so in other words it defines the most basic standard of living. It is the British government that spends our money and not we the taxpayers, so is there an argument that austerity is a suffering inflicted upon the less well-off by the overly privileged, and without the people having a say? I think there is.

Protecting its people and land is the responsibility of all governments and the last thing Britain needs is a weakening of its national defences. Every day the country lives under a constant threat from cyber-attacks, hacking, espionage on an industrial scale, breaches of British waters and airspace, terrorism, sponsored anti-social activity, and many other forms of attack. Yet all the while, Britain and other NATO member countries appear to spend far less percentages of GDP annually on defence than the likes of China, Russia, and North Korea.

As modern warfare becomes increasingly advanced and more cutting-edge, it is only right that old ships, aircraft, weapons, and other vital military equipment are replaced but this is not cheap, nor can it happen overnight. For example, the cost of replacing Britain's aging fleet of Vanguard class submarines with four Dreadnought class submarines is around £35 billion, yet the first unit is not expected to be in service until 2030. Compare this with the spiralling cost of HS2 which some analysts believe has increased from its original budget of £30.9 billion to over £100 billion. I genuinely do worry over government spending priorities at times and ask myself if we are being somewhat naïve and off the mark?

Monday, 28 February 1983

Today was another extremely cold start to a working week at Kelly's Garden, and it began with the usual morning parade and was then followed by an inspection. As expected, some of my colleagues were pulled up by our troop commander for having 'unkempt hair' as the military call it, and if truth be told he was absolutely right. I could not help but smile as I watched Paul and a few others sneakily tilt their heads back into their neck, as if on guard duty outside a royal palace, in their amusing attempt to make their hair look shorter than it actually was. It is an old trick that rarely works as Paul soon found out. Lance Corporal Bell left us today to return Port Stanley after we wished him good luck because in a few weeks, he will leave the British Army and return to civvy street.

He has decided that the military life is not for him and so he applied for discharge through Purchase Voluntary Release, otherwise known as PVR, which is the process by which a soldier can purchase their early release provided he or she meets the qualifying criteria. He is a good soldier and will be missed.

Over at the G1098 Store another consignment of army catering equipment arrived and was checked before being delivered to the new cookhouse, which is building number 23 and located immediately adjacent to the present canteen. This will be a the second restaurant for when Kelly's Garden's established strength is fully reached, and this will include officers and soldiers from the Royal Engineers, Gurkha Rifles, Royal Army Ordnance Corps, Royal Artillery, Royal Signals, Royal Electrical and Mechanical Engineers, Royal Army Medical Corps and civilian visitors. The Defence Base is already close to capacity which leaves very limited accommodation for those requiring an overnight stay.

3 Troop continued its work on the Rubb hangar site and also on the floor of Numbers One and Two helipads however, some PSP panels were found to be slightly twisted after the recent high winds and so the job of straightening these was immediately assigned to the welding team. I am told that PSP panels are known by the US Army as 'Marston Mat' and it is used all around the world. The remainder of 3 Troop began the work of pinning down large sections of white polyester underlay which was not an easy task, given the wind that was blowing through the Defence Base but eventually we were making good headway and the task progressed well.

I received a letter from my parents this morning who informed me that Wales beat Scotland in the Five Nations at Murrayfield on 19 February. The final score was 15 points to 19. I am thrilled because as a rugby player, I miss watching Llanelli RFC play at Stradey Park which is one of the most famous rugby grounds in the world, because of its history and the likes of living legends such as Phil Bennett, Ray

Gravell, Barry Llewelyn, Roy Bergiers, Derek Quinnell, JJ Williams, and of course the great Carwyn James.

Before leaving Llanelli in 1977, my father and I were regular season ticket holders and together we went to watch matches with our Post Office Master friend and neighbour Glyn Sherlock. I can also proudly say that "I was there" on 31 October 1972, the day that Llanelli beat New Zealand by 9 points to 3. It was my 18th birthday and yes, the pubs really did run dry as Welsh comedian Max Boyce tells us in his song 9-3. I could not get a birthday beer anywhere in Llanelli that day.

With everyone wearing their cold weather clothing, we worked throughout the morning on the PSP flooring and the helipads are now truly taking shape. It was a bitterly cold morning and although there are hundreds of panels still to be laid, there were only so many men we could safely have on site at any one time, and so it was decided to rotate the four-man sections to allow everyone the opportunity to stay warm and enjoy a hot beverage.

What surprised us all was the low volume of aircraft that flew in and out of Kelly's Garden and before we knew it, our morning shift was almost over. Eventually, the temperature dropped below zero and as we made our way across to the cookhouse for lunch, I covered my face with a military neck scarf to try and stop the sting of a freezing cold easterly wind.

3 Troop returned to continue its work at around 13.30 and for the rest of the afternoon, each section took it in turn to work a 90-minute shift before taking a short break and by 19.30, we had made considerable progress and were now close to the task of pinning down the end sections. After dinner Frazer and I again visited the Gurkha Engineers where I purchased a tie as a gift for my father. It is dark green in colour and bears the sapper exploding grenade above a pair of crossed kukris with the motto 'Ubique' embroidered in gold. This motto was presented to the Royal Engineers in 1832 by King William IV who died at Windsor Castle on 20 June 1837, and was succeeded by his 18-year-old niece who went on to reign as Queen Victoria for 63 years. She was coronated at Westminster Abbey on 28 June 1838.

Preparing the helipad site

Afternote

Each British Army corps and regiment is unique, and most will have their own standard or colours, and in the US Army such flags are also known as a guidon and signifies the unit or company. Normally awarded by a head of state, standards and colours are the most symbolic item in the British Army because they display the history of a corps or regiment by listing such details as their official emblem and names of battles fought, which are known as 'battle honours.' As such, these flags are highly prized and guarded at all times. Many corps and regiments gift old colours to a church or cathedral as part of its military heritage, and many will also have their own museum and band. The history of British Army standards and colours date back to the High Middle Ages which is the period between the 12th and 14th century, and kings who ruled England included William I, Henry I, Henry II, Richard I, and John.

The purpose of an army cap badge is to distinguish the corps or regiment in which an officer or soldier serves and for non-commissioned ranks, these are made from a material called anodised aluminium or 'stay-brite' which gives the badge its glossy appearance. Commissioned officers on the other hand wear either a metal or cloth cap badge. On military Service Dress, a second emblem is usually worn on both lapels and certain corps will also wear a lanyard as part of their uniform. Royal Engineers for example wear a navy blue lanyard on the right shoulder but never on Mess Dress uniform.

Medals awarded to an officer and soldier are always worn on the left side of their Service Dress and immediately and above the breast pocket, whereas medals awarded to deceased relatives may be worn on the right as a mark of respect, and to show that the bearer is not the recipient. Under the terms of Section 197 of the Army Act 1955, it is illegal for anyone to wear a medal that has not been awarded to them in the pretence that they are a member of the British Armed Forces. Service Dress medals are of the normal size whereas miniature medals are worn on Mess Dress uniform.

The origin of the Royal Engineer exploding grenade dates back to 1824 when it was worn on the tail of an officer's short tunic, and in 1825 a brass version was instituted for non-commissioned ranks. The Royal Engineer grenade has nine flames whereas the Royal Artillery grenade has seven.

As mentioned, each corps and regiment will have its own unique motto and usually describes in just a few words an objective or value that is relevant only to it. The most famous British Army motto is that of the Special Air Service which is 'Who Dares Wins'. Other mottos include:

The Royal Lancers:	Death or Glory
Parachute Regiment:	Ready for Anything
The Rifles:	Swift and Bold
Royal Tank Regiment:	Fear Nought
Infantry:	Follow Me
Royal Logistic Corps:	We Sustain
Adjutant General's Corps:	With Resolution and Fidelity

Tuesday, 1 March 1983

Back in my homeland of Wales the people will be celebrating our national patron Saint David. The story of Saint David, or Dewi Sant is quite remarkable insomuch that historians know a lot about his life through historical research and records. Born around AD 500 his mother Non is also a saint, and he was a true native of Wales. He and made Bishop of Mynyw, the ancient Pembrokeshire village of Meneva which today is better known as St David's and home to the famous ancient cathedral that sits in the smallest city in the United Kingdom.

David was the grandson of Ceredig ap Cunedda, a King of Ceredigion who died in AD 453 and people across the country will be wearing the traditional flower of Wales which is the daffodil, and many school children will be wearing their national costume and singing songs, telling stories, and reciting poetry.

Wales is known as the 'Castle Capital of the World' and 'The Land of Song' and each year, tens of thousands of people visit the National Eisteddfod and the Llangollen International Musical Eisteddfod that takes place in North Wales. Everyone will be enjoying Welsh cakes and Bara Brith which is a rich tea and fruit loaf, and also our much-loved traditional soup called 'cawl'.

Wales is a nation steeped in Celtic culture and history and there is no better example of the deep-rooted passion we share of our heritage than when friends and families sing the Welsh national anthem 'Hen Wlad fy Nhadau', which translated is Land of my fathers. Other famous songs will also be sung with gusto and fervour such as Cwm Rhondda (Bread of Heaven), We'll Keep a Welcome in the Hillside, Calon Lan, and Myfanwy but for me here in Kelly's Garden, today is just another working day in the Falkland Islands.

The much-awaited delivery of 95 bags of cement finally arrived and within minutes of the Chinook helicopter landing nine of us reported to the southern edge of Kelly's Garden, and very quickly we had every bag delivered to the Rub site using the Thwaites Dump Truck. I lost count of the number of trips the truck made but very quickly all 95 bags were stacked in neat piles around the site and covered with tarpaulin, along with the tons of sand and chippings.

As the Chinook took off and headed back to Port Stanley, work began on moving the project forward at a much quicker pace than planned, to make up for lost time. If there is one thing 3 Troop needs to achieve right now is to have the Rubb project back on track as quickly as possible, and to that end everyone was fully committed to the task in hand. We reminded ourselves of the original completion date for the project and that the taxiway and three helipads, and we know that the expectation is for us to finish the project before we return to Port Stanley.

Strange as this may sound, the heavens suddenly smiled down on Kelly's Garden and the camp basked in sunshine for the remainder of the day. It was the most perfect weather we could ask for and as I walked across to the G1098 Store to collect my toolbox, I suddenly came across a piece of waste timber that caught my eye, because it had a character all of its own and a colour and grain that was quite remarkable.

I picked it up and brushed it down with both hands, then took it across to the G1098 Store where I very quickly sanded it and within minutes, I could see that this simple piece of weathered timber could be transformed into something quite beautiful and pleasing to the eye. I already had an idea in my mind as to how it will look and so I shall see if this comes to fruition however, I am confident that it will look magnificent by the time it is finished. Around 11.30, one of the surveyors and I walked across to the new laundry site which we had recently marked out but on our arrival, we noticed that each wooden marker that we had placed in precise places had either been pulled out of the ground, or taken.

Andrew and I were furious and we knew this was the work of somebody outside of 3 Troop. Whoever the person or persons are, they have shown no consideration to the effort we had taken to place these markers in specific locations, because each had white tape attached to them and was marked with a number, but clearly they had decided their need was greater. No Royal Engineer would have removed these and instantly my colleague went to report the incident to our troop commander. On visiting the site for himself, he assured us that he would make every effort to find out who was responsible.

With thoughts drifting back to Wales and in quiet contemplation, I wished everyone back home a 'Happy Saint David's Day' or as the Welsh say 'Dydd Gwyl Dewi Hapus'. I took my dhobi across to the Laundry Block around 18.30 as we had finished our work earlier than expected, because by now my pile of washing was seriously starting to stack up. Inside the Ant Hill and while chatting with my staff sergeant and troop commander, we were joined by Frazer and the conversation quickly turned to the idea of trekking back to Port Stanley at the end of our time here at Kelly's Garden.

It certainly sounded like a challenge and the distance we would be covering is 55 miles but more importantly, it would serve as 3 Troop's tribute to those British troops who took part in the famous 'yomp' across East Falkland Island during the 1982 conflict. This remarkable feat started on 21 May 1982 and took three days to complete. Frazer who had four cans of McEwan's beer cradled in his arms, left the Ant Hill and I continued my conversation with the troop management and Sid who was acting as barman for the evening. Soon I was back inside my portakabin and after climbing into my sleeping bag, I caught up with *Jaws 2* and after reading several pages, I decided it was time to write up my journal. By 23.15, I thought enough was enough and so I looked back on what had been a very different kind of Saint David's Day and wondered how the celebrations were enjoyed back home.

Wednesday, 2 March 1983

I spent part of my morning working on the plaque which I have decided to make out of the piece of timber I found yesterday. If my idea works, the plaque will make a nice keepsake of my time here at Kelly's Garden and my plan is to draw a map of the Falklands on the front, secure a Royal Engineer's cap badge to the top right-hand corner, and in the top left-hand corner I will mount four polished Falkland coins. These will be a 1p, 2p, 5p, and 10p and each will be glued to the plaque.

After sanding the timber several times and applying two coats of clear varnish, it is already starting to take shape and several colleagues have asked to sign the reverse. Just like my journal, in the years to come this plaque will remind me of this isolated location and all the peace and happiness it has brought me. Reflecting on life back home, I can now truly understand why some folk opt out of society at some point during their life, relocate to a solitary island, or move into a tiny community to live a quiet life.

At around 11.30 our new officer commanding flew into Kelly's Garden by Gazelle helicopter from Port Stanley for a second visit, and he was shown around the Defence Base and Rubb site. Our respect for him has grown considerably because in Port Stanley, he often defends our concerns over issues such as shortages of stores, delays in delivery of materials, and other engineering matters. We also like his personality and style of management, and he seems extremely approachable. It is also reassuring to know that he listens to our views and those of other troops.

As he inspected the Rubb site, one of our senior corporals explained to him how the delay of cement and recent bad weather had impacted on 3 Troop's morale, and very cleverly he emphasised how well we had coped and with that, he assured officer commanding that morale was again high and the response was nothing other than positive. He genuinely did seem empathetic and understanding of how testing these past few weeks have been for us, and he expressed gratitude for what we had achieved. After several words of encouragement over lunch he flew back to Stanley at around 13.45.

During our lunch break, I wrote up my journal and looked out of a portakabin window and across to the Rubb site where I could see the teams hard at work mixing and pouring concrete into the foundation shuttering section, along the northern side. In a few minutes I will be re-joining them.

A Gurkha Rifle section left Kelly's Garden today for a three-day patrol and they have literally taken every piece of personal equipment with them. They looked dwarfed as they made their way heavily weighed down under backpacks, 7.62mm rifles, and 84mm Carl Gustav recoilless anti-tank rifles. Such weapons are used in operational theatres around the world by the British Army, because of their accuracy and portability. After a quick wave, our friends from Nepal started to make their way towards the Verde Hills and away from the safety of Kelly's Garden, and each had a big smile.

Gurkha Rifles ready to go on patrol

Mail from back home arrived this afternoon and I also received a payslip so I went across to the Ant Hill inside portakabin number 26, where our pay sergeant was dealing with pay matters and cashing cheques. I decided to withdraw £10 and around 14.00, I joined the rest of 3 Troop and was soon covered in dry cement powder. With morale high and progress quickly being made on filling the foundation shuttering with concrete and chippings, everything was going exactly to plan and even the PSP floor panels were being laid at a much faster pace than we had anticipated.

At times, the speed at which the concrete was poured into the shuttering, tamped down, and then finally trowelled to create the perfect finish increased significantly, and it was looking quite impressive. Very soon the concreting was completed and everyone agreed that it was a job well done and with that, we all made our way across to the cookhouse for a mug of hot army tea while feeling extremely pleased with ourselves.

Our post-tour leave dates have again been confirmed and morale throughout 3 Troop was high but right then, the sky clouded over very quickly and down came the rain which quickly turned into hail, and as the air temperature plummeted further, I could not believe how heavy the downpour had become. Everyone was caught off-guard as high winds lashed against the buildings and portakabins in Kelly's Garden, and we all rushed back to the hangar site to place canvas sheets over the newly mixed concrete and then ran for cover inside our portakabins.

Again, the southern hemisphere weather had played its tricks on us and we decided to finish for the day when suddenly, the rain stopped and within seconds we had blue skies looking down on Kelly's Garden and with a bright sun shining. This weather is just crazy! As we made our way to the hangar site, a colleague asked if he could see the plaque I was making when we return to our portakabin, and if I would consider making one for his parents who live in Porth in South Wales.

3 Troop worked right through the afternoon and we were extremely pleased with what we achieved and around 19.30, we closed the site and returned our tools to the G1098 Store before heading across to the cookhouse for dinner. Along with a few fellow lance corporals, I stayed behind in the cookhouse for a meeting with our staff sergeant during which he updated us on the feedback he had received earlier today from our new officer commanding.

He then talked about promotions and career courses, and finally the squadron's future tour which sounds very interesting. From time to time in the British Army, you come across certain officers and senior ranks that stand head and shoulders above others, and I have a hunch that our officer commanding is destined to go far. After the meeting, I headed for the Ablution Block and a well-earned shower and with music playing on my Sony Walkman cassette player, I listened to Supertramp's amazing new album 'Breakfast in America' as the building quickly filled with steam.

On returning to my portakabin, our junior chef was saying goodbye to fellow colleagues and then came across to shake my hand. Nobody had any idea of why he was returning to Port Stanley, but we all wished him well and told him that we hope he returns to 3 Troop soon. The RAF Chinook took off and the distinctive wokka-wokka sound of the double rotor blades soon faded into the distance. I decided to visit the Ant Hill and join the rest of 3 Troop who were reading books while some lounged on an old chesterfield sofa that had kindly been donated by the RAF.

We discussed what our staff sergeant had mentioned earlier and I stayed for about 30 minutes, during which time I enjoyed a cold glass of Coke but soon my eyes began to feel heavy from all the hard work and fresh air, and soon I was back inside my portakabin. I listened to Frazer incessantly talk about his beloved Scotland

and so I asked him if he knew which two famous actors starred in the black-and-white 1935 movie 'Bonnie Scotland.'

Racking his brain and clearly not knowing the answer, we chuckled as he tried to bluff his way by claiming that he was suffering from a momentary lapse of memory. To try and help him, I gave two dead giveaway clues as to their identity yet still he failed to come up with the answer. The two clues were they both wore a bowler hat, and one was thought to be Clint Eastwood's father but still he kept on pretending that his mind had gone blank. With everyone now teasing poor Frazer, I decided to put him out of his misery and told him that the answer was Stan Laurel and Oliver Hardy. "Aw mun, I was just going to say Laurel and Hardy," he replied and with that, everyone in the room laughed as he protested that he knew the answer all along.

I am now inside my sleeping bag and writing up this entry before I close my eyes. I feel shattered.

Thursday, 3 March 1983

Everyone rose early this morning because today is 3 Troop's turn to have an officer commanding's inspection and according to our staff sergeant, it needs to be a good result and nothing less. Inspections play an important part in British Army life whether they are held in barracks, on operational tours of duty, or on military exercises, and they normally take place first thing on a Monday morning and a Friday straight lunch. In truth, these inspections serve a number of purposes such as maintaining high standards of hygiene and good order, instilling pride in appearance and bearing, ensuring sound discipline and good team-play, and they are also considered a right pain in the arse by the vast majority of troops.

There was a wonderful saying I heard during my Basic Military Training which was, "If it moves, salute! If it doesn't, paint it!" I genuinely do not mind preparing for inspections these days, because I consider them to be nothing less than a challenge thrown down by the person who is going to carry out the inspection. Be it personal equipment, accommodation, vehicle, or even your uniform before a military parade, they will only bring out the very best in you and your colleagues, and your overall level of readiness.

By the time you have finished preparing, you will be determined to come out on top and today was no exception because 3 Troop had prepared well and more importantly, we knew that our officer commanding had already inspected the rest of 52 Field (Construction) Squadron and was generally pleased with what he had seen so far. Our troop commander and staff sergeant took the morning parade then handed over to the officer commanding and as predicted, we passed our inspection without a hitch.

We eventually started our work but again the rain was falling heavily and as it drenched the Rubb site, we checked the concrete we had poured into the shuttering panels yesterday which thankfully we had covered with large sheets of tarpaulin. Our two senior section commanders slowly uncovered the front section and it had not suffered any visible damage whatsoever, from both the overnight rain and severe drop in air temperature.

With our primary checks completed and the foundation concrete intact, there was no immediate cause for concern yet the work of getting the foundations finished before we can begin to lay the PSP floor and start assembling the Rubb frame is still proving more challenging than anticipated, and all because of the weather here at Kelly's Garden. It is genuinely starting to test our patience and especially as we have heard that the hanger will be the largest ever built by the British Army anywhere on East Falkland Island. With that in mind we are even more determined that our project will be a total success and that nothing, absolutely nothing is going to beat us.

Working under temporary covers and after mixing and pouring more concrete into the second shuttering section, the cement mixers were cleaned and oiled because we would not be mixing anymore concrete today. With the rain still falling, I returned to the G1098 Store to work on my wooden plaque and I applied a final coat of clear varnish and I must say, I am very pleased with the finished product.

A little tender loving care has completely transformed what was once a discarded piece of waste timber into something that is now quite lovely and pleasing to the eye, and so I began to work on another plaque which I have promised to make for my colleague's parents back home in Wales. The welding team erected two large interlocking army green marquees to make one long welding bay, and thankfully it has freed up some badly needed storage space inside the G1098.

The morning passed quicker than expected but the afternoon presented us with a problem of a very different kind, courtesy of a colleague who is a first-rate Plant Operator Mechanic. Unfortunately, he unknowingly drove his Muir-Hill digger across a heavily saturated piece of ground and as a result, the front wheels sank into the mud and so two recovery sections were quickly formed and both worked for over two hours in recovering the vehicle.

We first tried using the digger's own bucket and hydraulic arms to pull itself out however, this did not work and as rain continued to fall the front end of the digger sank a little deeper. Concerns increased when to our horror the vehicle visibly listed to the right, which naturally caused the operator to panic and jump clear of the vehicle. We tried explaining that towing the digger was no longer an option because of the ground conditions and deteriorating weather. It was also becoming dangerous for anyone to stand too close to the vehicle so we roped together the entire team as a precautionary measure.

Thankfully, we managed to lay a couple of wooden pallets close to the front wheels and cover them with PSP panels, and after a lot of perseverance and determination we eventually managed to lay more PSP until they touched the front wheels. The operator then climbed back into his cabin and carefully put it into gear and slowly but surely the digger inched its way out of the mud, and to everyone's relief it was eventually recovered.

With the rain still pouring down, we all dropped to the ground and sat in silence as the rainwater washed away much of the mud off the vehicle, and also our saturated clothes. The silence was quickly broken when someone called out for Paul to get the beers in, and fair play to him that is exactly what he did several hours later in the Ant Hill. I chatted with a few colleagues and after the banter had finally died down, everyone was laughing and we had forgotten about the incident. Camaraderie between soldiers is priceless. We all have each other's back and around 22.00, I retreated to the peace and quiet of my portakabin where I am now writing these events.

The double-marquee welding bay

Earlier this evening we heard that there is work that desperately needs to be carried out at Wreck House which is on the other side of Ajax Bay, and a couple of miles west of Kelly's Garden and so we may be assigned to this task but only after the Rubb project is completed, and signed over to the RAF. Not everybody looks forward to returning to Port Stanley because we are enjoying the challenges here at Kelly's Garden, and also the sense of calm that comes with being deployed to a remote and secluded location such as this. In its own strange way, being so far away from a large community such as Port Stanley with its noise, traffic, and lifestyle, makes us feel less stressed and it is so therapeutic. I chatted with colleagues for about half-an-hour and discussed individual career opportunities and ambitions, and the conversation was both enjoyable and eye-opening especially when I said that mine was either to begin a completely new career with the Army Air Corps, or failing that, anything other than combat or armoured engineering. At around 22.50 I was ready for bed and I wondered if indeed 3 Troop could ever be deployed to Wreck House because personally, I cannot even begin to see how we would find the time. We shall have to wait and see.

Afternote

To celebrate my retirement from the Regular Army after 23 years' service, 9 Supply Regiment RLC Rear Party organised a Top Table Silver-Service Lunch in the Warrant Officers' and *Sergeants' Mess at Hullavington Barracks, in Wiltshire. The date was Thursday, 24 August 2000, and it took place just a few days after I returned from a three-day visit to my commanding officer in Bosnia-Herzegovina, where I had my final interview and discharge papers signed.*

After several speeches and toasts were made, I was presented with a black panther figurine mounted on an engraved wooden plinth. The Black Panther was 9 Supply Regiment's emblem and as this was a lunchtime event, and with the Main Party still in Bosnia-Herzegovina, it was decided by me and my fellow Warrant Officers that we stay in the mess and continue the celebrations. At around 18.30 we walked to a local pub called the Star Inn, in the quaint Wiltshire country village of Hullavington which was immediately behind the barracks and carry on the party. It was a wonderful way to say goodbye to my British Army career.

My retirement presentation

As a person who does not display military memorabilia of any kind at home, I have nevertheless retained a small number of items that will forever be very special and important to me as a former soldier and warrant officer, and they total six in number. The first is my Royal Engineers Mess Dress followed by my No 2 Service Dress uniform, my three medals and miniatures, an engraved Blenheim Lead Crystal Square Spirit Decanter, a wooden plaque carved by an old carpenter in Bosnia, and my Harrow Rugby Head Coach Training Top. Sadly, because of the extensive travel and numerous postings, the wooden plaque I made in Kelly's Garden became mislaid over the years.

The wooden plaque from Bosnia

Chapter Fourteen
Times Gone By

Foreword

More often than I admit, I reflect on my time with the British Army and wish I could turn back the clock if only for a few minutes, to re-live and savour some of those experiences that remain very special to me and to speak once again with former colleagues and folk who I met along the way. Some of the barracks in which I served and places I visited were truly fascinating, and I genuinely consider it a blessing that I am still able to recall with such clarity the sound of my colleagues' voices, the layout of old military camps, the cars I owned, and the colour and style of clothes that were in fashion at that time.

Yes, I admit there were some experiences that I did not particularly enjoy such as spending whole weekends on guard duty in the old REME Workshop in Munsterlager, Nuclear, Biological and Chemical (NBC) Tests inside gas chambers, and worst of all the deploying on Active Edge exercises in the former West Germany.

The one experience I really enjoyed was taking part in Exercise Medicine Man 4. Ever since 1972, a series of four to seven large-scale battlegroup exercises take place each year on a vast prairie in Alberta, Canada at the British Army Training Unit Suffield which is better known as BATUS. Each 'Med Man' as these manoeuvres are also known by troops is in essence a 25-day armoured battlefield exercise during which live-firing and Tactical Effect Simulation (or TES) take place, and an Advance Party normally deploys three weeks ahead of the Main Party.

The role of the Advance Party is to help BATUS Permanent Staff prepare vehicles and equipment ahead of the actual exercise and on 9 July 1981, I flew to Calgary as part of the Med Man 4 Advance Party with colleagues from 26 Armoured Engineer Squadron. I was even more excited when I was selected to stay behind as part of the Rear Party, because as soon as all the vehicles and equipment had been signed back to the Permanent Staff, I would have 14 days to myself in Canada before returning to Germany.

Another time I also enjoyed was my second visit to Berlin which took place in 1984, and as a serious road runner at that time I was regularly competing in 10km and 20km road races that made up the annual Lower-Saxony Volkslauf series. When

I competed in the Berlin City Race, the last section was extremely tough because it was a four kilometre long incline that led to the finish which was inside the historic Berlin Olympiastadion, and as I ran around the track and crossed the line, the surge of energy and emotion that swept through my body is impossible to describe.

After the race I met up with my three running colleagues and had photographs taken, and then we headed back to Edinburgh House on Theodor-Heuss-Platz which catered only for British troops at that time. We went sightseeing and visited the Brandenburg Gate and also the Victory Column which was erected to celebrate the Prussian victory during the Second Schleswig War, and has Austrian, Danish, and French canons attached to its tall column. My time in Berlin also increased my fondness for the German people, the country and its heritage and architecture, its culture, cuisine, and superb hospitality.

The experiences I did not particularly enjoy as I doubt not many others did, were the annual Military Readiness Tests which every officer and soldier had to pass regardless of age, rank, or gender. The purpose of these were to assess the physical fitness and military battle skills of each individual, to ensure they met the required standard to remain in service. Such tests included Nuclear, Biological and Chemical, Battle and Combat Fitness, Swimming, Personal Weapon Handling which involved a minimum of two Live Range Days, First Aid, and Law of Armed Conflict.

There was also a test that was not carried out annually but randomly, and without any warning and this was the Compulsory Drug Test. These were conducted by visiting teams who would turn up unannounced and on arrival at a military establishment, the Duty Officer would be instructed to immediately close the camp and not allow anyone to leave.

The testing team would have a nominal roll of all officers and soldiers serving with the unit and they would be required to report to a central location such as a gymnasium where under strict supervision, they would provide a urine sample. When the results were received some 10 to 14 days later, those who tested positive would be summoned to the Regimental Headquarters and notified by the commanding officer, then discharged from the service.

Of these annual readiness tests, it was NBC that I dreaded the most, and for good reason. Officers and soldiers would report in groups of around 10 to the test chamber dressed in full NBC clothing, which comprised of a charcoal-lined hooded smock, trousers, rubber boots, inner and outer gloves, and the S10 Respirator. They would also have a full water-bottle, several packs of Fuller's Earth, one pack of Number 1 Chemical Agent Detector Paper, and three pouches attached to their webbing belt.

When the command was given, each group would enter the chamber in single file and line up in front of two masked instructors who would give a short briefing on how the test would be conducted. For those taking part in NBC training for the very first time, the experience can be extremely unsettling because it is dark, claustrophobic, distressing, and in many instances panic would set in which often results in individual trying to exit the chamber. Everyone would be reminded that in a real warfare situation, remaining calm is critical to having any chance of surviving.

After each item of NBC equipment was checked, the instructors would light two or three Chlorobenzylidene Malononitrile (CS) gas pellets and thick white smoke would quickly fill the chamber. You would then be told to walk in single file around the inside of the chamber with your hand resting on the right shoulder of the person in front and when told to stop, you would check that your respirator was not leaking. The slightest inhalation of CS gas will make your eyes burn beyond belief and create a severe tightness in the chest, which would lead to uncontrollable coughing and possible vomiting. Trying not to inhale more gas, it was the symptoms of choking and eyes burning that would cause individuals to panic.

When the instructors were satisfied that everyone's respirator was working correctly, the next test would begin. This involved taking and holding a deep breath while keeping your eyes closed and then unscrew and remove your respirator canister, and hold it at arm's length for three seconds before re-fitting it. You would then exhale as hard and long as possible to expel all fumes from inside the respirator. This was quite difficult to get right the first time, because you would be holding your breath for dear life with your eyes shut, and you would be wearing two pairs of gloves. Anyone who inhaled CS gas would be told to exit the chamber immediately to re-fit their canister and then re-enter when ready.

Next was the eating and drinking test which was followed by demonstrating to the instructors that you could self-inject a nerve agent antidote into your thigh using a Test Combi-Pen, while adopting the correct injecting position. The final test would be to remove your respirator fully while keeping your eyes closed and tell the instructor your number, rank, name, where you were born, your favourite sporting team, and all of this without inhaling CS gas. When you passed all tests, you would be allowed to exit the chamber.

To neutralise CS gas, you had to 'Tap-Pat-Blot' both hands and your respirator, and all clothing with pads of grey powder called Fullers Earth, and finally your NBC boots. The smell of CS gas is quite similar to chlorine and every time I use a bathroom cleaning product, I am often reminded of my time inside NBC test chambers.

For days afterwards, you would see NBC suits hanging from open windows and on clothes' lines in gardens, as fresh air helped neutralise the fumes. The one thing that everyone would avoid at all cost after being exposed to CS gas was contact with water because this would spread the powder and make your skin feel as it is was on fire.

Friday, 4 March 1983

The early morning scene that greeted me today was yet another ground-hugging ice-cold sea mist that eerily drifted in from the west, and completely covered San Carlos Settlement. Luckily for 3 Troop it made its way towards the Verde Hills to the east and missed Kelly's Garden by almost 300 metres. The time was 06.35 and for me it is the time of day I love so very much and after quickly getting dressed into my military works dress, I walked down to the edge of Bonners Bay and stood there all alone and completely mesmerised by the incredible beauty and stillness that was before me.

Surely, this is the most magical place that I know of and feeling chilled to the bone, I listened to the lonely and beautiful shrill of thousands of seabirds that broke the silence of the dawn but again, the heavens opened and rain began to fall. Near the Rubb hangar site I could just make out the profile of two RAF Chinook helicopters with their double-rotor blades hanging limp as they stood parked and grounded by the poor weather conditions. After breakfast and a bitterly cold morning parade, 3 Troop returned to our portakabins to collect our wet-weather clothing and then headed across to the site with the rain still pouring down. I have genuinely not encountered rain like this before, and it often arrives without warning.

We finished putting the final touches to the second run of foundation shuttering which will form the southern side of the Rubb hangar frame, and after removing the large heavy tarpaulin sheets in turn, my section began to pour several loads of concrete mix into the wooden frame and then worked it into the steel reinforcement mesh. This in fact was a job we had planned to do tomorrow and everyone on site was now soaked to the skin, and yet there was something refreshing and invigorating about working in such inclement weather and it is becoming something I really enjoy.

Another section was kept busy preparing the first concrete mixer for another load while others carried out maintenance work on a second mixer. Just then word reached us that the Mexeflote we had been expecting had finally arrived and was berthed west of the POL Point but by now, the rain was literally lashing down. For the rest of the morning our work continued on filling the second shuttering with concrete, smoothing the surface, and then finally covering it with the protective tarpaulin sheets as quickly as we could.

Around 14.40 one of our sections made the most of a break in the weather by offloading stores from the Mexeflote which included numerous crates of canned food for the Ration Store, a significant quantity of urgently needed engineering and catering equipment, and several crates containing electrical fittings. The head chef was more than happy that his stores had finally arrived, and I took three colleagues down to the Mexeflote to give the team a hand because the work of offloading stores was taking much longer than expected, due to the wet and ice-cold conditions.

Eventually we managed to get the Thwaites Dumper Truck down to the edge of Bonners Bay, despite the ground being heavily saturated and within an hour, most of the crates were delivered to their allocated sites. As we finished this task the Gurkha Rifle section returned to Kelly's Garden because they had cut short their three-day patrol, and despite it being early afternoon, the low clouds gave the appearance of late evening but at least it was not raining.

The Gurkhas stayed for us to take photographs and then headed for the cookhouse in the hope of getting fed, even though we told them it was now 15.25. As ever they gave us a warm smile. 3 Troop decided to stagger its lunch breaks in order to allow everyone to have a hot meal because of the terrible conditions, and this proved a good call. By 15.45 and although the rain had now stopped, it was still freezing cold and most unusual for me, this drop in temperature became so unbearable that I finally resorted to wearing a pair of thick army woollen gloves.

The welding team received the stores they needed to complete their work, while we on the Rubb site had three generators delivered which will power the pneumatic concrete vibrator pokers for the foundation concreting work, which is now rescheduled for tomorrow.

Gurkha patrol just returned to Kelly's Garden

3 Troop also had a supply of additional bags of cement delivered by the Mexeflote which was taken across to a spare ISO container by one section using a

Muir-Hill Tractor, and the Eager-Beaver Forklift. Today's work kept everyone busy right up until 21.30 by which time, we were almost working in darkness and because our tasks had taken much longer than anticipated, we missed dinner but thankfully the chefs saved our day by cooking a beef curry.

With the heavy rain and today's thick sea mist, Kelly's Garden was once again ankle-deep in mud and as such, we have heavy plant machinery and military vehicles beginning to slide precariously in certain parts of the Defence Base. Something needs to be done soon if we are to avoid an incident, and so one of the corporals produced a Situation Report (SITREP) which was signed off by our staff sergeant and within minutes, it was transmitted to CRE Works at Port Stanley.

After all the hard work we had completed today and with no mail delivered due to bad weather, everyone felt so tired that nobody cared. Halfway through offloading the cement earlier, today the REME reported that their workshop was starting to flood and a section of four including myself was sent to investigate and resolve the problem. We hurried across Kelly's Garden only to find another section hard at work digging a temporary French drain outside the building but when we stepped inside the workshop, it was clear that the problem was far worse than expected.

Given this is the only REME Workshop we have at Kelly's Garden, it is crucial that we have this facility fully operational at all times. A leaking pipe was discovered and repaired which was a relief to everyone concerned. After an hour of sweeping water out through a side door and into the new French drain, the workshop was again working as normal, but our main concern is how did the leak occur? I spoke with my fellow section commander and we agreed that it would be best to mention this to the REME Workshop Team Leader and recommend that he keeps his officer commanding fully updated on the situation, even though he is back in Port Stanley.

Covered in cement, some of 3 Troop headed across to the Ant Hill at around 22.30 to dry out in the warmth of the portakabin, but I and a few others made our way to the Ablution Block for a well-earned hot shower. I returned to the Ant Hill at around 23.15 and chatted with colleagues and a local settler who often lends a hand at Kelly's Garden with his tractor. I did not stay long and neither did my colleagues because we were all feeling tired however, the ever-hilarious Kevin and stayed behind while fully dressed in a white toga.

In one of the most remote parts of East Falkland Island he sat looking like a Roman senator while drinking and laughing the night away. Kevin is the most outrageous character we have in 3 Troop and he is worth his weight in gold, even if only because his humour and antics at times are priceless and so good for morale. He was exactly the same in Canada last year.

Inside the comfort of my portakabin, I finished reading Hank Searls' novel '*Jaws 2*' which turned out to be a good read and far more exciting than Peter Benchley's ground breaking '*Jaws*' but right now, I have another book I want to read. It landed on my sleeping bag just a few minutes after mentioning it to one of my roommates and it is called '*Polly Wants a Zebra, The memoirs of Michael Aspel.*' Michael Aspel is a British TV presenter of many popular programmes such as 'Give Us a Clue,' 'Crackerjack,' and 'This is Your Life.'

I am already enjoying his autobiography because it is very well written and contains lots of humour, and he tells wonderful anecdotes. I finished reading '*Jaws 2*' inside my sleeping bag and it only took a few minutes which was perfect, as I could barely stay awake. Tomorrow will be a more demanding and challenging day given today's arrival of cement, which means we can at long last begin mixing the concrete for the final sections of foundation shuttering which will form the front and rear base for the Rubb frame. We have estimated this task will require 30 tons of concrete and eight hours work if we can operate two sections of eight, who are supported by heavy plant machinery and two cement mixers. We are confident we can meet this deadline and hope that the weather will be kind to us, but nobody can bank on that in Kelley's Garden.

Spot the homemade dumbbells

Saturday, 5 March 1983

Today was the day we had eagerly been waiting for, yet again the heavens opened and heavy rain fell down on Kelly's Garden. Immediately after morning parade we divided ourselves into two teams, with eight in the first and nine in the second and while both were allocated separate tasks, they would nevertheless work together. The first section would be responsible for preparing, mixing, and delivering concrete to the Rubb hangar site while the second of which I was a member, would be responsible for pouring the mix into the foundation shuttering, and packing it down into the steel strengthening mesh using pneumatic vibrator pokers before screening the surface and covering each run with tarpaulin sheets. Both sections worked well and although the rain kept falling, it had no negative impact whatsoever on the task and troop morale remained incredibly high throughout the day.

It was around 08.30 and straight after three of my section had finished lining the wooden shuttering with white polythene sheets, that the first concrete mix arrived. Both Thwaites Dumper Trucks were used to transport the concrete and in most instances, they were able to tip the mix directly into the wooden frame which saved quite a lot of shovelling.

The team managed to stay ahead of each delivery and with everyone hard at work packing the concrete into the strengthening mesh, we had the easy job of Vi-Poking each mix for several minutes at a time which ensured there were no air pockets inside the concrete, and that every square inch of foundation was filled. Screening the surface with dampened trowels and sponges was the final touch and at first, the pace at which we worked was neither frantic or rushed given we had a good system in place and by lunchtime, the pace had picked up and we quickly realised that the task had the potential to be completed well ahead of time.

As the work progressed, some members of 3 Troop needed to visit the Ablution Block to rinse cement powder from their eyes, after a sudden gust of high wind blew through the base however after just a few minutes, they were all back on-site busy mixing more concrete. With the rain still falling, the protective glasses that some of the teams were now wearing proved more of a hindrance and so it was decided to carry on working without these.

Our colleague Pabs bid us farewell before he flew out of Kelly's Garden in a RAF Chinook to return to Port Stanley. He will remain there for the remainder of the tour and in his place, we have Sapper Newman from Support Troop who brought with him a delivery of mail, and this included two IQ test books which I have purchased through my parents as part of my preparation for the forthcoming Army Air Corps selection test. After taking a number of IQ tests recently, I am averaging a score of 147 which exceeds my own expectation and I am pleased with these results. I am unsure as to whether sitting an IQ test is an actual requirement for the interview nevertheless, I have found it intriguing testing my intelligence quotient from time to time.

We also received pay slips today yet frustratingly it would appear we are still waiting to receive our first payment of Living Overseas Allowance (LOA), and so everyone in 3 Troop including our troop commander and staff sergeant is owed two months' allowance which is not good.

Meanwhile, the work of mixing and pouring concrete into the foundation shuttering continued and just for fun, we ran a sweepstake with the winner being the person who was closest to the time the last load of concrete would be shovelled into the shuttering, to the nearest minute. The entry fee was 10p with as many goes as you want, and it would be a case of 'winner takes all.'

I lost by 8 minutes and Stevie claimed the prize. Soon, he was regretting it because it was decided at the eleventh hour that the winner would buy everyone in 3 Troop a beer in the Ant Hill later this evening. The winning time was 18.09 but by now everyone on site was covered from head to food in concrete, and looking as pale as ghosts as well as aching all over but because we had completed our work ahead of schedule, yet troop morale was high. After we cleaned the Rubb hangar site we returned all engineering equipment and tools to the G1098 Store where they were greased and prepared for tomorrow, which took us up to 19.15.

We all showered in the Ablution Block before going for our evening meal which did not take long to devour, because everyone was understandably famished and it was the finest roast dinner ever. There is something very dreamlike and perfect about the evenings here at Kelly's Garden and I put this down to the peace and tranquillity that is all around us, and the complete lack of heavy traffic, streets filled with people, parks, shops, and urban life in general.

Even the complete lack of light pollution makes the night sky look so very different and far more captivating, and nobody ever needs to dress up to go to the Ant Hill because quite simply, this is a completely different life and I am much more relaxed and happy being here in Kelly's Garden. I know I have no wish to ever leave this place when that time comes, and the thought of returning to Port Stanley fills me with dread. I accept it will be tough to deal with at first but I also realise that nothing stays the same forever, no matter how much I wish it could.

After another of chef's mouth-watering hot dinners, my colleagues and I made our way to the Ant Hill and this evening, they deservedly got a little merry. Poor Stevie! He now totally regrets winning the prize for coming closest to guessing the actual finishing time of the concreting task, because he is well and truly out of pocket after buying everyone in 3 Troop a drink. Tiredness and aching muscles got the better of me and I decided to remain inside my portakabin and listen to classical music, while writing up this journal and also a long letter to my parents back home.

I miss them and tell them so in my letters however, I also tell them that I could not be happier than where I am right now, sitting in the most basic of accommodation over 8,000 miles from home in the South Atlantic. I know they will totally understand because they too searched for excitement when they were my age, and I also know that they will be extremely happy for me in the knowledge that I am enjoying my time with the British Army.

There is something quite exhilarating about the whole experience of being here in the South Atlantic because for me, it offers some kind of perception of how early polar expedition teams must have spent their evenings, even though we do not have the -40° temperatures and frozen ice packs of Antarctica to deal with. Sir Ernest Henry Shackleton was indeed a truly incredible adventurer and explorer in his day.

We wonder if we will be permitted a half-day tomorrow given all the work we have accomplished today, so our hope remains high but there is no confirmation as yet. I continued to write up today's events in my journal and I thought about my grandmother Lena because like her, my handwriting leans heavily to the left and is very small. It is her style of writing that I have copied ever since childhood and I have created my own special signature for formal letters, and a shortened version for notes.

My father Alcwyn also has a wonderful style of handwriting which for some reason I find difficult to replica, because the way he writes the letters *H, G, R,* and *T* is always curled and extremely regal in appearance, and very similar to the style of handwriting used by Recorders on certificates of births, marriages and deaths. I find it so very pleasant to look at but at times it is also somewhat hard to decipher. It is a style I very rarely see today except when visiting museums and looking at correspondences dating back to the 18th and 19th centuries.

Afternote

For many years after my time in the Falkland Islands, I had an overwhelming urge to give up smoking and as strange as it might sound, even when I did smoke it was a habit I genuinely did not enjoy because I considered the smell of cigarette tobacco to be acrid and unpleasant. Also, my smoking pattern was somewhat erratic as there were days when I would not smoke a single cigarette, and especially when in the presence of other smokers. I considered it a very expensive habit and would often say to others that spending money on tobacco was "watching money go up in smoke." What I wanted more than anything was my dignity and self-respect, and also good health and eventually, I decided to stop and feel proud of the fact that I was no longer a smoker. The year was 1993.

While serving at the Army Apprentice College in Chepstow as Chief Clerk, part of my sporting profile was that of College Rugby Head Coach and I was also an active Class 1 Rugby Referee for the Army Rugby Union (ARU), the Rugby Football Union (RFU), and the Welsh Rugby Union (WRU). I took the Army Apprentice College through to the semi-finals of the Fern Cup and covered South Wales and the South East of England as a referee, but during an evening training session I developed a tickly cough that irritated me, and there and then I made the decision to stop smoking immediately. While walking back to the Warrant Officers' and Sergeants' Mess where I had rooms, I came up with a plan on how best to quit smoking.

Still in my training kit and sitting on my bed I realised that for me to stop smoking I would also need to give up alcohol, because for me the two habits complimented each other, and it worked. Within six months I became an ex-smoker and 30 years later, I can say in all honesty that not once have I ever had an urge to have a cigarette. It was the easiest thing I had ever undertaken and accomplished, and it boosted my self-respect and self-worth.

Munsterlager, 1981

Sunday, 6 March 1983

In the opinion of both our troop commander and staff sergeant, 3 Troop have done a remarkable job on completing the hangar foundations on time, and especially in such awful weather conditions. As a reward for our hard work, it was decided we would be allowed an extra half-hour lay-in but because today is a Sunday, we thought such a gesture was somewhat empty yet we recognised that there is still much to be done, especially before we can even think about assembling the Rubb frame. I took full advantage of my 30 minutes by sorting out my personal clothing and equipment which was still stained from yesterday's concreting.

At precisely 08.30, the whole of 3 Troop Paraded at the Rubb site for a briefing and our first task today was to have all tools and equipment used yesterday re-cleaned and re-greased, even though this had already been done last night. We also carried out a total clean-up of the Rubb site and G1098 Store and we worked flat out in the hope of an early finish but this never happened. Sapper Newman from Support Troop requested a Fitter's toolbox which he checked and signed over to his personal charge and for a pleasant change, the weather improved and so we revelled in glorious sunshine as the ground slowly began to dry across the whole of the Defence Base. Up until now it had been like a giant mud bath, and quite understandably everyone was grateful but the one question everyone asked was "why couldn't this have happened yesterday?"

I received a letter from my parents today with the worrying news that my Cousin Graham is now seriously ill in hospital, but all they said is that his health had deteriorated following a recent accident. For reasons unknown to me, all details are being withheld and I wonder if it is work related. I pray he makes a full and speedy recovery because he is naturally a weak person, and his mother who is my Aunt Evelyn would be devastated by his loss.

Graham is reclusive unlike his elder brother, my Cousin Desmond who enjoys a party and goes on as many rugby tours as he can every year with friends, and he also likes to travel to countries such as Russia, France, and Italy. I do not recall Graham ever having been in a relationship of any kind and yet he is such a kind and gentle person.

3 Troop cleaned every single weapon in the armoury today, and some of us chose to do this inside the welding marquee where it was warm and dry. As much as I enjoy live-firing range days, it is the weapon cleaning that I dislike if truth be known. We stripped down, cleaned, oiled, and reassembled every 7.62mm Self Loading Rifle, 9mm Browning Pistol, Sterling L2A3 9mm Sub Machine Gun, and L7 7.62mm General Purpose Machine Gun inside one hour. Kelly's Garden would make an ideal

firing range because of the vast expanse of open ground and also, the Verde Hills would serve as the perfect target bank.

I am surprised we do not have live-firing days here in the Falklands but I guess the most obvious reason for this, is because we are here to carry out a full and busy schedule of critical military engineering tasks and projects in repairing and enhancing the island's infrastructure. I have no doubt we will be making up for lost time when we return to Tidworth.

As we left the welding marquee to return the weapons to the armoury, a pair of low-flying RAF Phantom fighter jets screamed above San Carlos Water and performed tactical flying manoeuvres. They repeatedly approached our location at incredible speed from Ajax Bay which is to the west, and as they flew over Kelly's Garden they banked sharply to the right before heading south along Bomb Alley, then re-gained altitude on their way towards the direction of Sussex Mountain. Is it any wonder British RAF jet fighter pilots are considered among the finest in the world for their incredible agility, skill, and pinpoint accuracy?

Something happened today that took some by surprise and especially our Royal Artillery Rapier missile teams that are dotted around Kelly's Garden. Out in the distant San Carlos Water, I observed with colleagues a British Type 42 Destroyer slowly making her way south and at first, nobody could identify which naval ship she was. To us in Kelly's Garden, it appeared as though she had made her approach south from Ajax Bay where tragically *HMS Antelope* rests on the seabed. Then suddenly it dawned on me that the two RAF Phantoms we had seen earlier, may have been acting as the ship's escort, or were using her as target practice however, we had no idea why she was so close to Kelly's Garden.

Maybe she was on patrol duty or taking part in a joint service exercise and we will probably never know, but I did take the opportunity to photograph her for my journal. I then hurried across to the G1098 Store and signed out a pair of binoculars but as I zoomed in on her pennant number, she turned a full 180° and started to head north towards the open sea. To me she looked like *HMS Cardiff* and within a very short space of time, she was almost completely out of sight.

Looking west from Kelly's Garden

Inside my portakabin I am now writing up today's entry in my journal, including the sighting of the British Naval Type 42 Destroyer and then I will do some more work on a plaque I am making for Frazer. I have etched the Welsh feathers on the front and will pen the inscription *'To Frazer, wishing you every success in your future.'* The reason I have decided to make this plaque is because he has applied to join 59 Independent Commando Squadron Royal Engineers, which is also known as 59 Indep Cdo Sqn RE.

This is an elite unit made up entirely of Royal Engineer volunteers who go through full commando training, and such a course will surely test both his mental and physical abilities to the absolute limit. Ahead of him will be nine weeks of gruelling endurance and survival exercises, extreme physical training, day and night patrols, and all of these in extremely harsh and hostile environments such as rivers and frozen lakes, and under the most challenging of conditions. The pre-training phases he will need to go through before attending the All-Arms Commando Course will take over two months alone and for that, I genuinely admire and respect his decision to volunteer and I hope he gets to wear the much-coveted Green Beret.

After varnishing the plaque, I gave it a thorough inspection and I am pleased with the finished product, because it has turned out exactly how I want it to look. For now, I need to let it dry whilst completely out of sight of Frazer, and so I have concealed it under my bunk bed. Standing at the edge of Bonners Bay and looking across to San Carlos Settlement, a silvery half-moon sits low in the sky and it is the most beautiful sight I have seen in a long time. The stars are also out in abundance and so I will remain here alone in the quiet of the night and listen to the lapping of the water on the shore, while absorbing the splendour and magnificence of this magical location.

Sat alone in my works clothes and wearing my green heavy-duty army jumper, I slowly breathed in the cold sea-air at the edge of the bay. This for me is paradise and nothing troubles me because by being here, I am as far away from modern day life as I could ever wish to be and as I looked up to the sky, I said a quiet prayer for my Cousin Graham. I do hope God heard my words.

Afternote

If there is one thing the military thrive on then it is camaraderie. The word is derived from the French 'camarade' meaning companion and surprisingly, it only entered the English vocabulary during the late 19th century.

Between April and October 1996, I served in Bosnia for six months on Operation RESOLUTE with 36 Engineer Regiment, as part of an Implementation Force (IFOR) following the end of the Bosnian War in December 1995. The country and its people were still suffering the effects of years of bitter fighting which literally tore families and communities apart, and many of the atrocities that were committed in the name of war were horrific, and very difficult to comprehend.

Towns such as Gornji Vakuf where I was stationed and the once beautiful city of Sarajevo, and the many mountain villages were literally bombarded with shelling and some even razed to the ground and on top of all this, there was house to house fighting involving extensive gunfire. As Regimental Administrative Office Warrant Officer (RAOWO), I had clerical teams deployed in four separate locations including Vitez and Tomislavgrad which I needed to visit regularly, and often I would support important post-war tasks such as witnessing the clearance of a minefield and photographing a suspected war-crime scene.

On one occasion, I was invited to make up a 12-man section comprising of three British soldiers and nine serving members of the Army of the Republic of Bosnia-Herzegovina, and my role was to photograph the clearance of a minefield. We were accompanied by a local female interpreter who worked for IFOR and together we trekked several miles through dangerous countryside, and en route to the marked minefield we passed several former Bosnian-Serb battle trenches and bunkers.

The minefield itself contained unexploded anti-tank and anti-personnel mines and my first job was to photograph these as they were being prepared for detonation and then post detonation, as evidence that they had been successfully destroyed. The sound of the explosion could be heard for miles and the shockwave that rumbled through the heavily wooded valley actually knocked one of the Bosnian soldiers off his feet. Working on such a task as this and with people I had never met before, required not only solidarity and teamwork but also complete trust in the person in charge.

Another experience I vividly recall was driving through a remote mountain village on my way to Vitez, where every single house and outbuilding had been destroyed during the war and the only people who lived there were a large group of young children. It was obvious that all adults both male and female had either been killed or taken prisoner, and driving through this village was like being in a scene from William Golding's novel 'Lord of the Flies.' It broke my heart to see these children fight over the handful of sweets we threw out of the back of the Land Rover, because they were dressed in rags and were having to fend for themselves.

Visiting my clerical teams required me to travel hundreds of miles through hilly deserted regions and very often with an armed escort, but one day a fellow Warrant Officer from 50 HQ Squadron and I were driving back to Gornji Vakuf alone in our Land Rover. We were both armed and during the journey, we decided to visit a famous monument that was then called Tito's Fist which was at Makljen, some 1,123 metres up in the mountains. This monument was later destroyed in November 2000 by an unknown group using dynamite, and what remains can apparently still be seen to this day. As we approached the monument, we found ourselves driving through thick cloud and soon we could barely see the road in front of us.

Eventually, we parked on a slight incline but there was no hope of taking photographs unless the cloud disappeared and having heard reports that former Bosnian-Serb troops were still in the area, we kept our wits about us. Suddenly out from the thick mist we heard voices which my colleague and I could tell were a military patrol. Whoever these soldiers were, we strongly suspected they had heard our vehicle and were trying to track us down and so there was only one thing we could do, and that was to get away as quickly as possible.

Quietly we made our way back to the Land Rover but by now all visibility was getting worse and with my colleague sitting in the driver's seat, I looked into my side mirror and could make out the silhouette of soldiers dressed in black approaching from our rear. After releasing the hand brake, the Land Rover slowly started to freewheel down the track with the engine off and as I kept an eye on the soldiers in my side mirror, all we could hear was the sound of the tyres travelling over loose stones.

It was an anxious moment and as the vehicle picked up speed, my colleague fired the engine into life and pressed his foot hard on the accelerator. Soon we were flying down the mountain track and heading towards the safety of the main road. That was teamwork and camaraderie at its best.

Trekking to the minefield

Inside the minefield (HVO soldiers in background)

Preparing mines for detonation

The shockwave knocking a soldier to the ground

Chapter Fifteen
Football's Coming Home

Foreword

Many friendships established during the course of a British army career continue long after officers and soldiers leave the service, and there are a number of organisations and associations through which former military personnel can stay in touch with each other such as the Royal British Legion, Veteran Associations, Regimental Associations, Reunion Clubs, websites, and journals which can be subscribed to.

From my own experience, it would appear that friendships formed between troops who have served together within a with regiment such as the Royal Irish, Royal Welsh, or 1st Battalion of the Yorkshire Regiment are more inclined to last longer than those personnel who served within the same corps, such as the Royal Engineers and Royal Logistics, and I would suggest that this is partially due to two key reasons. But before I go into these, let me first explain the structure of the British Army and the two principal differences between a corps and a regiment.

The head of the army is the Chief of the General Staff or CGS for short, and they hold the rank of a 4-star General which is also the most senior rank, yet up until 1994, the highest in the British Army was Field Marshal albeit this is now an honorary rank only.

The tenure of a Chief of the General Staff is usually between two and three years although there is no actual fixed term and while in post, they will also sit as a member on the Chiefs of Staff Committee as well as the Army Board. Nominated by the Secretary of State for Defence and appointed by the Prime Minister, the CGS's ultimately responsibility is to maintain and develop the fighting effectiveness of the service as a whole.

The British Army is made up of three deployable divisions and they are:

- *1 (UK) Division which is multifaceted.*
- *3 (UK) Division which is always on operational standby, and*
- *6 (UK) Division which provides Specialised Operations.*

Each division has up to four brigades and each will normally have three infantry battalions, plus three calvary or armoured regiments supported by members of a corps such as the Royal Engineers, Royal Artillery, Royal Signals, and Royal Logistics.

At the time of writing my memoir the British Regular Army has 81,500 trained regular officers and soldiers and these are supported by 27,000 trained reservists who in effect, are salaried part-time voluntary combatant troops. Many reservists are highly qualified specialists in their own chosen civilian career and highly experienced such as medical consultants and surgeons, dentists, pilots, civil engineers, and many are former members of the Regular Army.

There are two key differences between a corps and a regiment and both are central to reason why I believe that friendships formed between members of a regiment quite often continue long after leaving the service, unlike those who served in a corps.

The first difference between a corps and a regiment is 'size.' A corps is much larger in number and personnel are posted between units on an individual basis, and usually every three to five years whereas officers and soldiers serving in a regiment such as the Parachute Regiment, are normally posted as a whole unit.

The second difference is that unlike a corps which recruits officers and soldiers from all over the United Kingdom and Commonwealth, most regiments will normally only recruit from specific geographical areas such as Wales in the case of the Welsh Guards, Scotland in the case of the Scots Guards, and so on, and there are many other examples.

A 'posting' is the military term used for the official transfer or movement of an officer and soldier between units, countries, and theatres. 'Posting Orders' for soldiers are issued by their respective Manning and Records Office (MRO) and these documents are official notices that outline important information such as the unit to which the soldier is being transferred to, the soldier's personal details such as name, ran, and number. Also within the Posting Order will be the reporting date and rank which he or she will hold as well as Established Post they will fill, plus any other additional information the MRO wishes to issue. As well as the individual soldier, the Posting Order will also be sent to the current Holding Unit, the new Receiving Unit, and in some cases to a Training Establishment or Divisional Headquarter, for administrative purposes. The Posting Order will also outline the reason for the posting such as promotion, attending a trade training course', or just simply on posting.

With regards to promotions, these play an integral part in an individual's career and progression and also enables the British Army to maintain and protect the junior and senior management structure. Furthermore, a posting on promotion allows an individual the opportunity to settle into their new rank and role without possible envy or indifference from peers, such as a colleague in the same unit who may not be selected despite having the same skills, qualifications, and experience and the officer or soldier who gains promotion. Posting on promotion also provides an officer or soldier to begin their new role in a different unit which helps them gain the confidence, experience, further skills to potentially climb further up the promotion ladder. The average timeframe between promotion to the next higher rank is usually between two and four years, with each rank having a set timeframe in which promotion can be authorised which is normally seven years however, once this ceiling has been reached without being selected then officers and soldiers have their names permanently removed.

Officer careers and postings are manged and controlled by Personnel Branches (PB) within the Ministry of Defence and in 1994, I served at the MoD Stanmore which has since closed. One important role I undertook as PB2 Chief Clerk was to supervise a team of civil servants in their day to day work of processing and issuing Posting Orders and all documentation involved in promotion boards for British Infantry officers up the rank of lieutenant colonel, through liaising with units and divisional headquarters across the whole of the British Army, and it was an extremely taxing and challenging duty because you constantly had to be four steps ahead during the planning process.

As a Royal Engineer with 16 years' service before being transferred across to the newly formed Adjutant General's Corps in July 1993, I was posted to 10 different military establishments during my 23-year career with the Regular Army and of these, six were regiments, two were headquarters, one was the Ministry of Defence, and one was the Army Apprentice College at Chepstow.

With each posting and promotion came increasing challenges, new faces, far greater responsibility, and only on the rare occasion did I reunite or serve with a former colleague so realistically, the only time that friends could stay in touch was either through attending the same course, serving on the same exercise or in the same operational theatre or coming across each other purely by chance.

Throughout the whole of my military career, I can say with full confidence that I only served with a handful of Royal Engineers who I knew were from South West Wales, and there were even less in the Adjutant General's Corps and as such, I saw no reason for joining a branch of either association after I retired in August 2000.

In a regiment such as the Infantry, it is not uncommon for officers and soldiers to serve alongside each other for the vast majority of their career and as such, *friendships understandably continue long after they leave the service and especially in situations where they might live in the same town or county.*

3 October 1996 was my final night of a six-month operational tour in Bosnia with 36 Engineer Regiment, and I was booked into the Transit Accommodation Block close to Split Airport because I flying back to the United Kingdom the next day. As I walked through the grounds overlooking Kastela Bay, to my total disbelief yet great delight I happened to bump into my old friend and fellow Warrant Officer Jim Pridding who by chance, had just returned to theatre that very same day. It felt so surreal to suddenly come face to face with a friend and former colleague who I had first met on 15 February 1978, when I reported to the Guardroom at 26 Armoured Engineer Regiment in Munsterlager and we served together for three years, but we did briefly one day in 1981.

Individual postings and different career paths had kept us apart for almost 15 years and we had so much to catch up on, and so we arranged to meet up in the Warrant Officers' Mess that evening. Together we reminisced over old times and toasted absent friends and it was a wonderful and emotional reunion, mainly because we both knew we would never see each other again. As I shook Jim's hand and said goodbye at around 23.30, out of the blue he told me that he had been diagnosed with a brain tumour and would soon be returning to the United Kingdom to undergo further treatment, despite the prognosis not being too good.

Shocked and saddened by this news, my mind immediately froze and I did not know what to say, and still to this day I have never forgotten that moment and get emotional thinking about it. Together we shed a tear and had one final hug before we went our separate ways and for several months after, I could not stop thinking about his circumstances.

Two and a half years later and while serving as Staff Assistant to the Commander Royal Engineers at 3 Headquarters (UK) Division in Bulford, I was given the tragic news that Jim passed away on 3 April 1999 at the age of 41 and that his body was laid to rest in Tidworth Military Cemetery, which was just seven miles away. I promised myself that I would visit his grave at my earliest opportunity and exactly one week later and at sunset, I drove to Tidworth and spent time alone with my old friend and as I was walking back to my car, I made another vow that I would visit his grave one more time before I retired from the Army.

True to my word, I stopped off at Tidworth Military Cemetery on my way to Hullavington Barracks on 4 May 1999 and the following August I retired from the Regular Army. I went on to live in Abbeymead in Gloucester, Cumnor near Oxford and eventually in 2004, I returned to my hometown of Llanelli and every three years

I have made the journey to visit and lay flowers at Jim's grave. My last visit was on 17 July 2022 when I took this photograph.

In memory of Jim Pridding

Monday, 7 March 1983

Looking as smart as we could in our works dress, 3 Troop made a quick inspection of the engineering tools and concreting equipment.

With everything looking in good order, I began to make another wooden plaque for a friend back home because there is no shop here at Kelly's Garden or San Carlos Settlement, so gifts can only be purchased from the General Store back in Stanley.

During the course of this morning I recorded the serial numbers of each item of engineering equipment and during my lunch-break, I started to read a book that was given to me by Paul which is Gareth Edwards' autobiography. Considered one of rugby union's greatest players of all time, I have wanted to read his life story and I hope that at some point in the years to come, I too will be able to tell the story of my career and have it published, and I will include this journal in that memoir.

Even though this can only happen after I leave the British Army, such a project already excites me and it is an ambition I genuinely believe I can achieve given my passion for both history and writing. There are a number of hobbies and interests I share but the one I am totally committed to is my writing and even as a schoolchild, I regularly entered essay competitions with local newspapers such as the *Llanelly Star* and *South Wales Evening Post*.

In 1967, I won first prize for my written account of the *SS Nevasa* Educational School Cruise to Madeira, Tenerife, Lisbon, and Gibraltar but sadly, a few days after the award ceremony at Zion Chapel in Llanelli my beloved grandmother Lena passed away in the parlour of 3 Als Street. Only a few days earlier I had given her a colourful silk scarf that I had bought for her as a gift in Funchal, the capital of Madeira.

Over at the Rubb hangar site we checked the concrete we had poured into the foundation shuttering yesterday and to our relief, it was in excellent condition. It is curing precisely as we had wanted and so we carefully re-laid the tarpaulin sheets over the surface, and then proceeded to examine the other foundation run and again we were pleased.

Another task we undertook was to inspect every individual anchor base that will be bolted into the foundations when the concrete is set. These anchors will be used to secure the Rubb frame supporting legs once they are assembled and freestanding in their vertical position, and before being attached to their adjacent frame. There will be a total of 13 arches by the time the Rubb hangar is fully assembled and everyone in 3 Troop, and indeed on the Defence Base, is looking forward to seeing the finished structure, because its dimensions are impressive and when covered with the green PVC membrane, it will be quite a sight.

During my free time which is not often these days, in addition to writing my journal I am also making more plaques from pieces of waste timber and I find this very relaxing. By 18.45 everyone was feeling cold, hungry, and tired so 3 Troop cleaned the Rubb site as best we could and quickly checked the helipad and taxiway matting. Paul was working as Duty Storeman so I helped him clean and grease the engineering tools and equipment before returning them to the G1098 Store, and although it was bitterly cold the evening sky was awash with brilliant splashes of red, gold, and purple and again it took on the appearance of a biblical scene.

Sights such as this are not only spectacular but extremely inspiring, and what never ceases to amaze me is just how low in the sky the clouds hang here in the southern hemisphere. It is almost as if you are standing on the very edge of the world and the sky has literally nowhere else to go, and as odd and bizarre as this might sound it is exactly how it all looks when you see if with your own eyes.

I did not want to stop gazing across Bonners Bay but I was famished and needed a shower before joining my colleagues over in the cookhouse. After a piping hot shower and feeling totally refreshed, I changed into a clean pair of olive green army works trousers, woollen Heavy Duty (HD) jumper, thick parka coat and eventually made my way to the cookhouse. There, I was greeted by the wonderful smell of a roasted beef dinner and it was mouth-watering.

As we slowly walked back to our portakabin, I was once again drawn by the incredible gold, yellow, and purple that was splashed across the early evening sky. I told my colleagues that I was going to take a stroll down to Bonners Bay and with that, I followed the old rutted path for about 100 metres and soon I was alone and deep in my thoughts, while gazing across to San Carlos Settlement and San Carlos Water to the west. I sat on my favourite boulder and stayed there for at least half-an-hour listening to the glowing water of Bonners Bay rhythmically lap against the shore, and I felt so content and at peace with myself.

With another drop in air temperature, I headed back to 3 Troop Office where a colleague was giving Frazer a haircut, and so I continued to sand down the new wooden plaque as we chatted and discussed the proposed trek back to Port Stanley. I drew two inter-twining blood-red roses on the plaque I am making before applying a coat of clear varnish which by chance, has highlighted a beautiful grain running through it and it is starting to take shape. Just then my troop commander walked into the office and I could see that he likes what I have done so far. About an hour later, I was sat inside my portakabin with Paul, Frazer, and John, and between the four of us, we came up with several ideas for the video we have been invited to film for our parents and friends back home.

The camera and sound equipment is being provided by a staff sergeant from another troop and he has also very kindly offered to do the filming for us, and in no time at all we had decided which idea would make the best skit, and with that we wrote an amusing script. The video will conclude with a comical scene that we know our families back home will appreciate.

Over at the Ant Hill, certain members of 3 Troop were entertaining our Gurkha friends with their whacky antics but I decided to retire for the night and write up my journal. Thankfully, today did not turn out to be as quiet as we had expected because what we do not need in Kelly's Garden is boredom and idle hands, as both of these combined generally create low morale and we know that the pace of work will soon pick up and when that happens, I am sure 3 Troop will eagerly rise to the challenge of assembling the hangar frame. We genuinely cannot wait to start because our two corporals are among the finest in 52 Field Squadron and they will direct and manage the project through to a successful conclusion, and in their highly professional manner. I am so proud to be a part of this great team.

Afternote

Even back in 1983, I wrote in my journal that "one day I would very much like to write a memoir of my time with the British Army" and this was despite my not knowing what the future had in store for me, both as a writer and former member of the British Armed Forces.

In July 2016, I wrote a short book entitled 'The Story of Parc Howard' which was published in full compliance with the 'legal deposit' protocol when registering a new publication in the United Kingdom. This involves submitting gratis copies to the British Library and also to the national libraries of Wales, Scotland, and Trinity College in Dublin. The book sold well in and around Llanelli, and also with several expatriates who moved to the United States, and it tells the story of the land and earliest settlers who date back to 8,000 BC.

It also incorporates a history of the original residence which was built in 1800 and the subsequent build of a replacement grand Edwardian Italianate mansion constructed between 1882 and 1886 which was called Bryncaerau Castle. In September 1911, it was purchased on the marriage of Sir Edward Stafford Howard to Lady Catherine Meriel Cowell-Stepney who then gifted the estate to Llanelli Urban District Council on 21st September 1912, the day of their first wedding anniversary and for the benefit and wellbeing of local people. Sir Stafford Howard was a prominent Liberal politician and direct descendant of Edward Howard, 3rd Duke of Buckingham who on 17 May 1521, was executed at Tower Hill in London for treason against King Henry VIII. Sir Thomas Moore refused to support this trial on grounds that Henry VIII had witnesses tortured, statements fabricated, and evidence extracted from Edward Howard through prolonged torture.

Book signing at Llanelly House, 2016

Tuesday, 8 March 1983

Kelly's Garden and Bonners Bay is most certainly a sight to behold at 05.30, and especially when the early morning sun sparkles on the water. The assortment of rich earthy colours and varying shades of green, blue, and yellow are breathtaking and they lift the soul and already, for some reason I knew that this was going to a perfect day. After a hearty breakfast over at the cookhouse and a quick morning parade outside the G1098 Store, 3 Troop made its way across to the Rubb site and began to focus on the task of preparing the ground which will make up the hangar floor, by using hundreds of metal PSP panels. This work would also involve our Gurkha colleagues however, just as we were getting ready to start levelling the ground inside the foundation runs, we encountered a mishap when the Muir-Hill Digger refused to start.

As frustrating as this was, we wasted no time in requesting support from the REME who were on site within minutes and after a quick inspection, the mechanic identified the problem and informed us that it would take approximately one hour to repair which under the circumstances, was a huge relief. With work temporarily on hold, there was nothing else we could do but carry out minor maintenance repairs, inspect completed sites, check all engineering equipment, and look for anything else that could be done while we had the opportunity.

Around 11.30, our Petroleum Fitter surprised everyone by flying in from Port Stanley to change a fuel pump in the Generator House. We explained to Sid what had happened with the Muir-Hill and in a flash, he was over at the Rubb site speaking with the REME and then returned to say that they would have the vehicle working within 10 minutes. Sadly he brought no mail from Port Stanley but instead, gave us the news that morale on the Coastel at Whalebone Cove was apparently beginning to decline. He went on to add that this was being put down to troops continuously working around the clock, and many were now starting to show signs of fatigue.

He also informed us that the schedule planned for repairing the damaged runway at Stanley Airport was beginning to fall behind, due in part to an unexpected shortfall in manpower and delays in the delivery of essential resources and materials from back home. We looked at each other with bated breath because we sensed what was coming next however, he confirmed there were no plans for 3 Troop to be reduced.

We acknowledge that we will eventually have to leave Kelly's Garden and return to Port Stanley to support our colleagues on essential engineering tasks, such as repairing the runway, highway construction, building maintenance, and infrastructure upgrades. No doubt everything will come to light when our return date is confirmed however, back at the Rubb hangar site several tons of gravel was being delivered for the helipad site by our two Thwaites Dumper Trucks, and once dropped it would be compacted by a team operating the Bomag Roller.

The Muir-Hill was fixed and it has to be said that 3 Troop made excellent progress on the preparations for laying PSP panels, while the welding team continued their work of inspecting and repairing the steel gabion baskets. Once again our teams picked up the pace and hopefully the work of assembling the Rubb frame will commence soon. This is the phase everyone is now eager to start because after seeing the different shapes and sizes of the alloy panels being stacked neatly at all four corners of the site, they give the impression of a giant Meccano set and it is only now that we are finally forming a picture as to how big the finished structure will be.

The powerful downdraft from a Chinook helicopter created a huge dust cloud as it hovered close to the Rubb hangar site, and as two colleagues helped the loadmaster connect the four straps to a heavily-laden red ISO container. After checking all four were secure, the aircraft slowly climbed to an altitude of approximately 50 feet which provided the ideal opportunity to take excellent photographs, and after giving the pilot the all clear, he turned the aircraft through a full 360° and headed back to Port Stanley.

It did not take long for us to level the ground on which the Rubb hangar frame will stand and what a difference today has made to the project. Already we are ready to begin laying and pinning down the large sheets of white underlay, before proceeding to connect the PSP panels together to form the hangar floor which should be a very straightforward task. Time here really does fly and waits for no man and of that, you can be absolutely certain. Whenever an opportunity comes along to try something new, we grab it with both hands and that is part of the reason why I believe morale is as high as it is.

Without warning, our portakabin was mysteriously painted in military camouflage colours today while we were working on the Rubb site, and we have been informed that other buildings at Kelly's Garden are to be painted in a similar style. Apparently, this is a directive from Port Stanley. Our portakabin looks awful and not one single person believes for a moment that we are any safer from an air-attack because in all honesty, it has made Kelly's Garden stand out even more.

Given there are no trees or woods, or indeed any natural features that could genuinely blend fully with army camouflage colours, painting the portakabin has in all honesty achieved the opposite effect, as it now compromises the whole of the Defence Base. We discussed the rationale, or lack of rationale, with our troop management and they too consider the concept to be somewhat a waste of resources, time, and manpower. We will now have to wait and see what the feedback is to concerns expressed by almost everyone on the base. This has been another long and productive day, and we all feel pleased with what we have chieved and as always, the REME mechanics have been worth their weight in gold.

Over at the Laundry Building at around 20.15, it took a lot of scrubbing to remove the caked cement from my works dress but eventually and with a lot of determination and elbow grease, I finally managed to have it looking like new. I returned to the 'Green Alien' as our portakabin in now known by others on the base, and wrote two entries in this journal before quickly cleaning my bed space and heading across to portakabin number 26 with fellow colleagues.

We watched Mel Brooks' masterpiece 'Kentucky Fried Movie' and it had everyone laughing. I have always enjoyed Brooks' madcap humour and for me the man is a comedy genius, and I adore his other films such as 'Blazing Saddles' and 'Young Frankenstein' and after the film finished, some colleagues returned to our portakabin and I began to sand down another piece of waste timber which I have found. I shaped it into a rugby ball on which I have sketched a picture of a player being tackled.

At around 22.00, I collected my dhobi from the Laundry Building then gave the plaque a first coat of varnish as I have done with the others I am making, and I have decided that this particular plaque will be another gift for my parents. I know it will be appreciated by my father because as a child, I watched him work with wood and he is a natural at making items such as a lamp stand, pipe rack, stools and other furniture. He is also a very gifted all-round sportsman with tremendous ability.

Around 23.00, I climbed into my sleeping bag and I lay there thankful in the knowledge that tomorrow is my morning off, and I plan to spend it yet again on the ridge along the Verde Hills providing the weather stays dry. I enjoy running across uneven terrain because it exhilarates me, and makes me feel fulfilled and invigorated. It is a feeling like no other but then suddenly and for no known reason whatsoever, I tried to imagine how I will feel when I am no longer able to run or trek over hilly features as the Brecon Beacons or parts of Snowdonia. The thought has really scared me and I pray that day never comes.

Afternote

Up until the age of 55, road running and mountain trekking had always been activities at which I excelled and pursued relentlessly. Sadly, and only to be expected, 40 years of competitive sport such as playing, coaching, and refereeing rugby union while maintaining an intense daily fitness training regime eventually took its toll on my body, and parts began to break down. This was the payback I was always dreading and it literally came overnight when was on holiday in Lanzarote in 2014. During my sporting career, I sustained multiple injuries including strains and torn muscles, stress fractures, decompression surgery on both shoulders, three left knee arthroscopies due to a torn medial meniscus, lower back injury, cracked ribs, and a badly lacerated left shin. Over time I realised that some sports were not good for the body and so I gave these up.

Much sooner than expected, I had no option but to completely stop what I was doing and start looking after myself. The human body is no different to a car because both get us from A to B, at a speed and in a manner of our own choosing. Some people will sensibly take some activities easy while others such as myself, always felt the need to push hard and go as fast as possible but then suddenly in 1988, I badly tore my left medial meniscus during a somewhat heated rugby match. Fortunately, I made a quick recovery from my first arthroscopy at the Cambridge Military Hospital in Aldershot and I was soon back playing at scrum-half, but nevertheless it was the start of a series of surgery and I still live with the pain to this day.

To celebrate my 50th birthday on 31 October 2004, I raced the Snowdon Mountain Train to the and my chosen starting point was Pen-y-Pass car park. I checked my watch and set off at the same time that the train pulled out of Llanberis Mountain Rail Station, and I jogged along the Miner's Track which I knew blindfolded at a pace I could easily maintain. I had run this route so many times and I was confident that age would not hinder me. The final section of the Miners' Track leads to a mountain lake called Llyn Glas and at the far northern side, the track ends and you encounter a very steep incline covered with large loose slabs of rock.

If you try and jog up this section as I often did, it is incredibly exhausting and an absolute power drain on the quadriceps femoris or quad muscles as most athletes know them, but eventually I made it to the steep section called the Zig-Zags, and from there I power trekked as hard as I could to the prominent marker that is the 'Gate Post.' This large upright slab of Welsh slate sits on the top of a ridge that looks directly across to Anglesey in the far distance, and is just above the railway track.

Suddenly, I heard the Snowdon Mountain Train chugga-chugga choo-choo its way up the track but because I could not see it because of the cloud, and by now I was extremely tired and thought it was slightly ahead of me. Believing I had lost the race and with a final burst of energy, with lungs and muscles screaming I finally made it to the old station and remarkably, I had beaten the train.

My last road run was on a windy day in 2010 and it started from my house and followed the Llanelli Millennium Coastal Path around Machynys Championship Golf Course. I tried to beat my personal best which was around one hour but due to the weather conditions, potholes, fading light, and drop in temperature I genuinely struggled. My physical strength and mental willpower finally let me down, even though I could always depend on them in previous years and my left knee was in agony. I had just tuned 56 years of age.

While serving with 32 Armoured Engineer Regiment in Munsterlager between July 1984 and June 1986, I regularly competed in local German Volkslauf 10km, 15km, and 20km races, and competed every year with colleagues from the Regimental Headquarters Troop in the Munsterlager Tank Road Race. I also played regimental rugby and in 1985, took part in the 25km Berlin City Road Race.

Sport has always played a huge part in my life but the human body can only take so much, and the more I pushed myself the more things started to break down until eventually, I had to call it a day. Would I do things differently if I had my time all over again? You bet I would, even though nothing lasts forever.

In my running kit, 1985 in Greece

Wednesday, 9 March 1983

With my colleagues still inside the portakabin and rushing to get ready for morning parade, I lay in the warmth of my sleeping bag and enjoyed every single second as I watched them barge their way through the door. It was just like a scene an old black-and-white 'Keystone Cops' movie. I felt content and relaxed, and went back to sleep until around 08.30 which was when I was awoken by heavy rainfall hammering on the roof. Outside, I could see colleagues running for cover and I realised there was no way I was going to run to the ridge on the Verde Hills today.

With the sky darkening further and signs of a thunderstorm heading our way, I grabbed my dhobi and made a dash to the Laundry Building where I put my washing into a spare machine, before running across to the Ablution Block. After a shave and welcomed shower, I changed into my works dress and went for a late breakfast. Returning to the portakabin, I wrote a letter to my parents and I gave their plaque one final coat of clear varnish while outside the ground was again turning into a mud bath, and I felt sorry for my colleagues working on the PSP matting.

3 Troop helping Gurkhas lay PSP

Around 11.00 the rain finally stopped and the sun tried to shine through the low cloud but all the while, the wind continued to howl as it blew along Bomb Alley and south towards Sussex Mountain. I prepared my personal equipment for an afternoon of work and decided on making an early start to help my colleagues over at the Rubb site. The reason for this decision was because later today, 3 Troop will play a football match against our Gurkha friends after hearing that they apparently are not as good at soccer as they are at volleyball. We accepted their challenge and felt confident they would not stand any chance of winning.

Over at the G1098 Store, I collected the stores needed to mark out the football pitch and then walked across to the site with Stevie, who was asking lots of questions about my possible transfer across to the Army Air Corps. At the Rubb hangar site, 3 Troop was helping our Gurkha colleagues to lay PSP panels on top of the white polyester underlay that was now pinned to the ground, and we could see that they were making good time despite the continuing high wind.

A few of them saw me point towards the site that I had chosen for the football match and with that, Gareth and Paul gave a thumbs up and started to make their way across to help me mark out the pitch. The goals were marked using bundles of camouflage nets while white tape was pinned to the ground to act as the half-way and touch lines, and because of the strong wind the referee would need a foghorn instead of a whistle. In no time at all, the pitch was looking good except for the odd clump of earth and potholes which we filled-in as best we could, and there were also scattered patches of mud but by now, the wind was blowing even harder but it was decided to go ahead, no matter what. Below is the match report I produced:

3 Troop, 52 Field Squadron v Gurkha Engineers
Venue: Kelly's Garden, East Falkland Island
Date: Wednesday, 9 March 1983
Kick Off: 17.00
Reporter: Lance Corporal Thomas 809

By winning the toss 3 Troop, 52 Field Squadron had first choice of team colour and which goal to attack in the first half, while the Gurkhas would take the kick-off. 3 Troop chose white PT vests and the Gurkhas being the true gentlemen they are, opted to wear their much-loved green military tops. Even though conditions were dreadful with high winds blowing in from San Carlos Water to the west and ice-cold temperatures, it was agreed no gloves would be worn by either side and the number of substitutions would be five maximum.

Two halves of 30 minutes each would be played on a relatively flat piece of land at the western end of Kelly's Garden which is so close to Bonners Bay, that even the seals could throw back any ball that landed in the water. A 10-minute half-time period was agreed but it would be up to both teams to decide if they wanted to carry on with the game.

3 Troop opted to play with the wind in their favour and chose the half that was furthest from the Defence Base but seconds before kick-off, there was a technical

problem that held up the kick-off. The football was leaking badly and making vulgar sound as air inside was slowly expelled which made the Gurkhas roar with laughter. The referee deducted one point from their score by the impartial referee who by chance, happened to be 3 Troop's chef.

Pre kick-off Score
Royal Engineers 1 v Gurkhas 0

With no substitution ball available, the leak was eventually repaired by a REME mechanic and once again, both sides were ready to play. A group of Gurkha supporters were gathered along the northern touch line and making a lot of noise, but despite the fact that there were only three of them and all were Gurkhas, another point was deducted. The south touch line supporters however, were extremely well behaved and comprised of six Royal Engineers who were busy chatting away with their backs to the wind.

Pre kick-off Score
Royal Engineers 2 v Gurkhas 0

Just as the game was about to start, another technical problem came to light over the number of players the Gurkhas had on the pitch. A quick headcount was made by the referee who counted 21 and after explaining to the team captain that they were only allowed 11 players at any one time, a protest was formally submitted. Eventually the Gurkhas agreed to remove 10 players and placed them all on the touchline, which now meant the Gurkhas had 15 available replacements as opposed to five, unlike the highly cooperative and very sporting sappers.

For a team who claimed they were no good at soccer, the Gurkhas had 3 Troop fooled because they turned out to be naturally gifted players, and gave the sappers a run for their money. One in particular had spectators howling with laughter during the first half. Lance Corporal Gurung was clearly a talented gymnast but was almost wiped out by a beautiful yet illegal sliding tackle by a sapper.

Quick as a flash, Lance Corporal Gurung launched himself into the air and performed the most perfect back somersault, and after landing and standing motionless with arms outstretched, he held this victorious pose for several seconds, and then bowed to both touchlines.

He was awarded nine points by the Gurkha supporters on the north touchline, while the sapper supporters on the south awarded only six. Lance Corporal Gurung went on to score a brilliant goal and this was football and gymnastics combined, and at its best.

With wind gusting harder in the second half the sappers laughed as they watched the opposition chase long kicks blown off the field like excited cocker spaniels, and then dribble the ball back to the field of play while performing other dazzling and amazing footballing skill. This was true entertainment and even though conditions remained horrendous throughout the match, spectacular dives to save penalty kicks were made and the referee used his loudspeaker well. With the light beginning to fade and despite numerous amusing 'off the ball' incidents, hilarious fouls and shirt pulling, both teams played some very exciting football.

At around 18.45 the match ended with a final blast of the foghorn which startled everyone and then in customary fashion, cans of beer were handed to each player instead of a trophy over at the far western end of the pitch. After plenty of congratulations and stories exchanged over how good the match was, everyone headed across to the Ant Hill for more celebratory drinks and a post-match buffet.

Final Score
Royal Engineers 6 v Gurkhas 4 (plus 9 for the somersault)

Wednesday, 9 March 1983 (cont'd)

Over at the Ant Hill, we were joined by the welding team who had carried on working during the football match and also Sid our Petroleum Fitter, who flew in yesterday from Port Stanley. He asked to see my journal and so we both walked across to my portakabin where he read several pages, and then mentioned that it was being talked about by other members of 52 Field Squadron back in Stanley. I received a letter from my old friend Lance Corporal Shaw who for some reason has been admitted to Queen Elizabeth Military Hospital in Woolwich, but he did not mention the reason why.

Within minutes of reading his letter, I received a visit from a former colleague from Cardiff who is now serving with 51 Field Construction Squadron, and he too asked to see the journal. I read out the letter I had received from Lance Corporal Shaw as they too are friends of old, and we reminisced on past times. I later wrote a reply to Bob and suggested that we meet up when I return to Tidworth. I am now updating today's entry in my journal before I polish my boots ready for tomorrow, and I am beginning to feel tired but so looking forward to working again on the Rubb hangar tomorrow. The project is progressing well and we are almost close to starting the next phase which is to assemble the frame itself. We are getting there slowly.

Afternote

When it comes to football, Royal Engineers can lay claim to an impressive list of honours with regards to FA Cup Finals played at the Kennington Oval in London, which today is simply known as The Oval.

1871–1872 Lost 1-0 to Wanderers.
1873–1874 Lost 2-0 to Oxford University.
1874–1875 Drew 1-1 against Old Etonians.
1874–1875 Won 2-0 over Old Etonians (Replay.)
1877–1878 Lost 3-1 to Wanderers.

Chapter Sixteen
Work Hard and Play Hard

Foreword

Whenever I am asked which three aspects I enjoyed and appreciated the most while serving with the British Army, my answer would always the same because I can say with full confidence that they were career opportunities, personal development, and job satisfaction.

Recruitment is crucial in maintaining correct manning levels in today's British Army yet it is the actual fulfilment of promises made to newly enlisted service personnel that safeguard retention. The most appealing promise for me was the guarantee of a worthwhile career through such attending trade training and promotion courses, taking part on outward bound and adventure training activities, and further education to name just some.

As mentioned in the previous chapter, competition for promotion within the British Army is fierce and quite rightly so because as with Maslow's Hierarchy of Needs which is a pyramid-style model of understanding human needs in ascending order of priority, the British Army rank structure is also based on a pyramid. In the case of non-commissioned ranks, Privates are shown at the bottom with all subsequent ranks listed in ascending order to Warrant Officer Class One which sits at the very top. Each level has established numbers required to meet the needs of the service and these naturally reduce with the next higher rank, and this is why military cutbacks in personnel is referred to as "slicing off the side of the pyramid."

Competition brings out the very best in people but rivalry should always be healthy and respectful, and especially in the case of those who may be overly ambitious eager to rise to the top. Throughout my Basic Military Training, the instructors constantly hammered home the point that although Training Party 77/8 was made up of 14 individuals, we all needed to work as a team despite being in competition with each other for prizes such as 'Best at Drill' and 'Best at Sport' and the most coveted of all, 'Top Recruit'.

Controlled competition helps enhance personal development as well as teamwork, and although they say there is "No I in Team", in certain instances such as promotion, this rule tends to be overlooked from time to time yet nevertheless, you still work as a team.

After I changed my trade while with the Royal Engineers and transferred across to the clerical roster, my sense of job satisfaction literally crashed through the ceiling overnight because each day brought with it new challenges, and I was always learning something new. This in turn was having a positive influence on my career and performance, and also on my professional development because the British Army is second to none at bringing out the very best in people through top quality instructors, and excellent training facilities. Even the resettlement courses and seminars I attended before retiring, the standard of tutors, speakers, and presentations was unprecedented and unlike anything I have come across since.

In addition to my military and trade qualifications, I was fortunate enough to attend numerous outward bound and sport courses such as Joint Service Mountain Expedition Leader (JSMEL) at the British Mountain Training Centre (BMTC) in Norway, sailing and competent crewman at Kiel in Germany, sports injury and rugby referee in both Germany and the United Kingdom, parascending and canoeing during my Basic Military Training, and so many more. These incredible opportunities all helped enrich my personal development and job satisfaction.

Thursday, 10 March 1983

The G1098 Store opened around 07.30 on a bright and sunny morning and everyone in 3 Troop was smiling. Some of us had started to believe that summer may already be over despite the fact that here in the Falkland Islands, the summer season officially begins on 21 December and ends on 20 March. Technically, this means we still have 10 days remaining but we have every reason not to believe this judging by the recent weather we have had to endure, but at least today started dry and with a blue sky and no clouds.

The arrival of 30 Battery Royal Artillery at Kelly's Garden has sadly brought with it the departure of 14 Air Defence Battery, who will soon set sail for Ascension Island on board the same luxury cruise liner that brought us to these islands, namely the *Cunard Countess*. We are told that this is to be the ship's final voyage as a requisitioned British Troop Carrier before she undergoes a complete refit, and then returned to her parent Cunard fleet.

However, there is also worrying news that *Cunard Countess* is to be replaced by *St Edmund*. This is a much smaller ship and former Sealink English Channel car ferry, and it is this ship which we spent our first two nights on when we first arrived in the Falkland Islands back in January and even then, we heard others express alarm that the ship had been allowed to sail across the South Atlantic. What we are hearing is that she has been purchased by the Ministry of Defence and will be signed over to the Royal Navy as *HMS Keren*, after being repainted and fitted with a helipad, and re-classed as a troopship.

With a crew of just 35, she will take over transporting British troops between Port Stanley and Ascension Island and to say that such news is unnerving colleagues is a complete understatement, because we also hear that the ship has no stabilisers. If this is true, then it would mean that sailing across the South Atlantic during a storm would be extremely unpleasant.

HMS Keren formerly Sealink Ferry *St Edmund*

3 Troop said farewell to 14 Air Defence Battery before we made our way across to the Rubb site where we continued to assist the Gurkhas with laying the many heavy PSP floor. These panels will be interlinked with each other which can prove difficult at times and especially when wearing thermal gloves, plus they are made of perforated steel which makes them horrible to work with in inclement weather. There are mixed emotions running through Kelly's Garden today because on the one hand, there is melancholy at seeing our Gunner colleagues leave for Port Stanley while on the other, there is genuine relief that 3 Troop is to remain here until the Rubb hangar project is finished. All of this means that we will not be moving into the Coastel accommodation for quite some time.

With the increasing number of new arrivals and departure of troops to and from the Falkland Islands, we foresee Port Stanley becoming much busier with regards to shipping and air traffic over the next few months, and that makes me wonder if the islanders will be happy at seeing their homeland slowly turn into a permanent British military garrison. I suspect that in time, many will be stationed outside Port Stanley as there is now clear justification to have a permanent military presence, and my personal view is that the only logical solution would be to establish a RAF station some distance away from the capital, but certainly not at Port Stanley Airport.

This should revert to being an international airport and used only for civilian and commercial flights such as tourists and trade, whereas a RAF station would cater for troops and military air freight, and with a wider and much longer runway. Such a base would need to accommodate a squadron of fighter jets and transporter aircraft as well as supporting military personnel, and replicate RAF stations such as those back in the United Kingdom that also have shops, sporting facilities, cinemas, churches, accommodation and medical facilities. This would significantly enhance the military presence here in the Falkland Islands and deter any future Argentine threat of attack.

Taxiway and helipads

The Gurkhas carried on working regardless of the departure of 14 Air Defence Battery and the arrival of replacement troops, and the three RAF helipads are now laid and connected to the 150-metre-long taxiway that runs directly towards the Verde Hills to the east. Helipad Number One sits at the far eastern end while helipad Number Two is located at the northern, and Number Three is connected to the southern aspect which is furthest away from the Defence Base.

Around 15.55 the sky suddenly turned grey and rain began to fall but within minutes, it was pouring down and this caused everyone including the Gurkhas to down tools immediately and make a hasty retreat to our portakabins. After an hour of persistent rain, everyone was back on site and 3 Troop worked on pinning down the last of the PSP panels and repairing damaged sections that had been identified during their final inspection.

Ensuring that the ground around the helipad site was as level as possible, four teams of two took it in turn to run the heavy yellow Bomag Roller over the ground and within two hours, the entire site was completely transformed into a neat and tidy helicopter holding area with a well-defined boundary. Just then and to nobody's surprise, we had a second deluge of rain. The constant change in weather conditions here at Kelly's Garden is starting to test the patience of 3 Troop's management team and after a meeting with our senior corporals, the only sensible option was to call it a day. It is the same story time and time again yet we manage to work eleven hours every day.

As evening approached I lay on top of my sleeping bag, and listened to the exciting new album *Love over Gold* by the British rock band Dire Straits on my Walkman cassette player. I have borrowed the cassette from John who is one of our corporals, and it is one of the finest albums I have heard in years and quite sentimental to me personally. Mark Knopfler's style of guitar playing and the lyrics he writes remind me of my time at CFB Meaford in Canada last year, and there is one track in particular that I have come to love so very much.

The song is called *Telegraph Road* and even now I realise that for as long as I have air in my lungs, this song will forever bring back wonderful memories of the five-mile-long dusty track that ran from the military base and down to Highway 26. A solitary road lined with old wooden telegraph poles that leaned like those in a scene from an old cowboy movie, it had a character and charm that I can still visualise to this day. Terry Williams the Swansea born drummer plays with Dire Straits, and his contribution to the band and its success is yet another great advert for Welsh rock musicians.

Around 21.00, I was making a wooden stand for the plaque I am making for my parents when another air-strike alarm sounded and with it everyone at Kelly's Garden reported to their dedicated rendezvous points, or RV as they are known. In 3 Troop's case, this was our G1098 Store and as soon as everyone was accounted for, we were briefed by our staff sergeant that reports were coming in thick and fast of a potential attack from the west.

It was highly likely that it could be heading for our location and with that, we immediately went to our assigned shelter areas dotted around the Defence Base. The faith and confidence we have in our Royal Artillery Rapier Missile teams is absolute, even though this latest incident proved yet again to be a false alarm however, we cannot afford to take such threats lightly.

Making my way across to the Ablution Block, I tried to avoid as many puddles and muddy patches as I possibly could and when I eventually arrived, I enjoyed one of the best hot showers in weeks, and on the way back to my portakabin I called into the cookhouse for a mug of tea. I logged today's entry in my journal and then for some unknown reason, I was reminiscing on the many memorable moments I shared with my friend Lance Corporal Shaw and others, whil we were all serving in Munsterlager with 26 Armoured Engineer Squadron between February 1978 and December 1981.

These were indeed fun times and a good example of what working and playing hard was all about, because a British troops stationed in West Germany during the Cold War, we socialised with local people and it was only right that every now and again we would let our hair down, to some extent. Everyone went out of their way to enjoy each other's company and in most instances, our socialising took place within the confines of the Squadron Bar and NAAFI at Dennis Barracks, or the neighbouring towns.

Afternote

Even 44 years after first arriving at Dennis Barracks in Munsterlager in 1978, I can still vividly recall my time and experiences. The town of Munsterlager or Munster-Örtze to give it its correct name, sits on the edge of an extensive military training area between the towns of Soltau and Uelzen, and not far from the beautiful Lüneberg Heide or Lüneberg Heath which is a large rural region in the north-eastern part of Lower Saxony. Munsterlager had two military camps with one being occupied by a German Panzer Division, while the other was home to 26 Armoured Engineer Squadron and 2 Squadron Royal Corps of Transport.

The former Dennis Barracks had a fascinating World War Two history and one day in 1979, I was shown inside a small bunker which had once served as a sulphur mustard gas test chamber, and the emotions I felt when I entered are difficult to describe because they were a muddled mixture of melancholy and disbelief, and my head was swirling with so many questions I wanted to ask.

Today there is no barracks because the buildings have all been converted into private houses, an industrial business park, and where officers and soldiers including myself once lived and worked on maintaining a fleet of armoured engineering vehicles such as the Centurion AVRE and Chieftain AVLB, they are now commercial units and offices.

Even the Officers' Mess has been turned into a hotel and I have seen a short film on YouTube of a motorbike ride through the former barracks which I presume, was filmed by a British serviceman who once served at Dennis Barracks given his knowledge of the old camp. He knew each building including the former Accommodation Block 42 and 108 in which I myself was billeted between 1978 and 1981, the former cinema and cookhouse, the RHQ and post office, and the Officers' Mess and old medical centre. The film is a wonderful trip down memory lane and I hope to re-visit Munsterlager sometime in the future.

Around early 1981, I recall reading a controversial British newspaper article written by a journalist who had nothing good to say about the British Armed Forces who were serving in West Germany at that time.

Whoever wrote the article, he or she was highly critical and clearly ill-informed on what life was like serving with the British Army of the Rhine. In the report the journalist rather cynically wrote that BAOR stood for 'Boozy Army of the Rhine' and this rightly caused outrage both at home and in Germany.

Obviously the reporter failed to appreciate that troops serving in BAOR at that time were permanently on standby and at a constant state of readiness to deploy to the border with the east, or to military other regions across West Germany either in response to an act of Soviet aggression, or as a show of military strength and presence. As such, all NATO troops worked long days training and maintaining military equipment, practicing regular battle manoeuvres on training areas such as Soltau, Bergen-Hohne, and Sennelager, and often during ice-cold German winters. There were military exercises of unprecedented scale that involved fellow NATO member countries such as LIONHEART and CRUSDAER, and although these were no doubt considered by the Soviet Union to be politically and militarily aggressive, in the eyes of NATO they were paramount to western security.

The one manoeuvre most BAOR personnel disliked was Exercise ACTIVE EDGE which was nearly always instigated during the early hours, and could continue for up to seven days at a time, but in the main they would only last for one to two days. Nevertheless, every time Exercise ACTIVE EDGE was called, it would require a full deployment of BAOR personnel, equipment, and vehicles, and you never knew where you would be deployed to.

The one thing you cannot have is an army that is unfit and as such, robust physical training sessions regularly took place to ensure that the highest standard of physical and mental fitness was maintained at all time. In addition, there were the regimental sport afternoons, the commanding officer's run on Friday afternoons, and at the weekends personnel would participate in regimental or local civilian sporting events, whilst at Iserlohn I was also coaching TVD Hagen Rugby Club and competing in German Volkslauf races. And if this was not enough, there were also the mandatory annual Basic Fitness Tests (BFT), a Combat Fitness Test (CFT), Swimming Test, and all of these had to be passed to avoid discharge on medical grounds.

In short, BAOR was most certainly not the 'Boozy Army of the Rhine' as the journalist claimed because no army could ever possibly survive such a strict and harsh fitness regime, and still do their job as professionally and as effectively as we did.

Friday, 11 March 1983

Today, everyone in 3 Troop felt extremely motivated and the day quickly passed. The weather was again good which boosted morale and so with our spirits high, and with a real eagerness to get started, the time to assemble and erect the Rubb hangar frame was fast approaching. We all wish that every working day could be like this and around 15.00, we began to lay the actual hangar floor by working in teams of four, and in no time at all the PSP panels were ready to be laid on top of the pinned white membrane. This is the very same material that made our task so difficult during recent high winds however, it is an essential part of the work because it serves as the underlay.

The PSP sections will be interlocked and pinned to the ground to provide maximum strength and stability and between the hangar floor and the three helipads and helicopter taxiway, several thousand metal pins will be used for this part of the project. Fortunately, a slight oversight was identified when we began to lay the first row of PSP panels for the hangar floor, and very quickly each panel was disconnected, stripped out, and then re-laid while ensuring the northern edge ran flush with the concrete foundation runs.

Had this not been spotted and rectified when it was, the amount of time that could have been wasted in recovering the situation at a later stage is considerable. Two teams worked on delivering the panels and pins to the two other teams who focussed purely on connecting the panels together, and pinning them to the ground by using sledge hammers.

One member of 3 Troop had a lucky escape thanks to the white safety helmet he was wearing at the time, and could have easily resulted in a nasty laceration to his face. For some reason, a corner of one particular PSP panel was slightly bent and protruding some two inches as it lay amongst of a pile of panels, and at a height of around five feet.

As he walked past, his right cheek brushed against the metal edge which caused a facial wound that bled a lot at first, but thankfully he was immediately seen by a medic and the cut was cleaned and dressed. All he needed was three butterfly stitches. Five colleagues worked with a troop of Gurkhas and helped lay three additional rows of PSP panels at the eastern end of the taxiway, in order to provide more length just as a precautionary measure and the helipad is now looking impressive, and so we have booked a RAF Chinook to test its stability.

Along with two fellow lance corporals, I was informed that I have been nominated to attend an Education Promotion Certificate (EPC) course when I return to Tidworth. The EPC course runs for four weeks at an Army Education Centre and involves intense periods of instruction and written exams covering five key subjects, and every Junior Non-Commissioned Officer (JNCO) is required to pass the EPC course to qualify for promotion to Sergeant. The Education Promotion Certificate (Advanced) or EPC (A) is needed to qualify sergeants for promotion to Warrant Officer Class Two and both EPC courses are held at nominated Army Education Centres worldwide. The five modules are:

1. Communication Skills.
2. Communication Skills (Oral)
3. Military Calculations.
4. Army in the Contemporary World.
5. Military Management.

Another course I must attend and pass in order to promote beyond the rank of Sergeant is the Royal Engineer Senior Non-Commissioned Officer Course (RE SNCO) which I am told, is intense and highly demanding, and runs for three weeks. This course however can only be taken at the Royal Military School of Engineering (RSME) Wing at Chatham in Kent, and I have heard from those who have attended this course that it is the one that most SNCOs dread.

Work on laying the Rubb hangar floor proved especially hard on the hands today but by 19.00, we had completed the entire site and we all felt extremely pleased with the end result. After cleaning and returning our tools and equipment to the G1098 Store, I cleaned my boots and gave them a good polishing after which I worked on updating my journal. I plan on going across to the Ant Hill later to watch a 1976 movie called 'The Duchess and the Dirtwater Fox' starring Goldie Hawn and George Segal, but it was ruined by expletives used throughout, and many of my colleagues stopped watching it.

After a hot beef dinner over at the cookhouse, I headed for Bonners Bay to spend some time on my own and I wondered if I will pass my interview with the Army Air Corps. It will be a new career for me and one I know I will relish were I to be successful. I am more than prepared for the interview but the time seems to be dragging, and so I wonder if indeed it is going to go ahead. Returning to my portakabin, I climbed inside my sleeping bag and listened to Asia's record 'Heat of the Moment' and again, it brought back memories of my time in Ontario last year. There is no moon to gaze at this evening however, the stars in the night sky sparkled like diamonds and I felt so happy because it is truly a most wondrous sight. I am now ready for a good night's sleep.

Chinook being used to test PSP panels

Saturday, 12 March 1983

I often think about what the folk back home are doing from to time, and especially on Saturdays because for most people it is the main social day of the week. Sporting fixtures, meeting with friends, afternoons in beer gardens, and concerts nearly always happen on a Saturday however, that is not the case here in Kelly's Garden. Work carried on regardless and no matter what day of the week it is, each has no real significance or relevance of any kind unless we have a visiting concert party or senior officer visiting the Defence Base. I have now become fully accustomed to this new way of life and I prefer it to the daily routine we had before deployment.

Today we straightened the remainder of unused PSP matting sections as a light shower started to fall, and I helped several colleagues up until tea break. Around 10.45, I made my way down to Bonners Bay and helped Sapper Diable and Richards offload a further delivery of PSP panels. These were stockpiled into two separate groups marked 'Damaged' and 'Approved.' Two more colleagues gave a helping hand and we completed the task inside two hours. Bonners Bay looked exceptionally calm today, and the backdrop was magnificent as I looked across to Ajax Bay where the cobalt-coloured water sparkled as the sun shone down upon the waves.

Back at the Rubb site, Stevie and Paul joined me and together we discussed how quick we thought assembling the hangar frame will take. Just then, word was received that 3 Troop could stand down for an early lunch because there was no essential work that needed to be done. After a meal of sausages, eggs, baked beans and chips, we looked to see if there was anything else we could do to pass away the time however, for some reason the site was unusually quiet and at 15.30, everyone agreed that it was time to go across to the Ant Hill to watch the horror movie 'Happy Birthday to Me.'

Curiously, nobody can understand why the work on the Rubb hangar project had suddenly stopped, and so we waited to be called back on site but the call never came. Frazer and I went to the G1098 Store to test a Hilti Power Drill which had reportedly failed to work, and yet it immediately kicked into life as soon as we tried it. Soon we were back inside the Ant Hill watching the movie which quickly bored everyone, and so we all went for an early dinner at around 18.55. Yet again, it started to rain.

British merchant ship in San Carlos Water

On my return to the portakabin, I chatted with another visitor from Port Stanley who greeted me with a very warm smile because he too is a former Armoured Engineer colleague and is from Wales. Steve and I shook hands before reminiscing on the good times we shared at Munsterlager and then completely out of the blue, he offered to take me out in his Combat Support Boat (CSB) on Bonners Bay and towards San Carlos Water. He mentioned that he had heard about my journal back in Port Stanley, and asked if he could have a quick look because he would like me to write about the CSB experience.

I jumped at the chance and showed him the book, and then went to get my camera from the Troop Office before walking down to the edge of Bonners Bay to board the CSB. We headed west and out in the distance, we could see the merchant shipping vessel that Steve had radioed to request permission to approach from its port side, for me to take photographs. With permission granted and almost at full speed, we soon came to within 100 metres and from there, the CSB engine was put on idle and I took five shots for my journal. Dwarfed by this huge container ship, we waved to the bridge and headed towards *HMS Grange* which again was approached from her port side.

    I took more photographs and then we headed back to Bonners Bay and eventually Kelly's Garden, but at a more leisurely speed and I revelled in the sunshine and smell of the salt sea air. This had been an incredible experience and one which I will always fondly remember, and after we secured the CSB, we walked back to my portakabin where I wrote up this entry before heading across to the Ablution Block for a hot shower. When I returned, Steve went for a mug of tea over at the cookhouse and I climbed on top of my sleeping bag to listen to Queen's album 'Flash Gordon' on my headphones. Today has truly been exciting and very memorable.

Afternote

When I joined the British Regular Army in 1977 my life changed completely and for the better, and far more than I could ever have imagined, however, if I were ever to be asked to summarise what the 23 years meant to me, I would say that it was without doubt the most wonderful and rewarding period of my life. Indeed, I would describe it as the adventure I was hoping for, and I am so blessed that it all happened.

There are justified reasons for me saying this because first and foremost, I pursued a number of exciting opportunities and interesting trade paths during my time and I am so glad that I did. Having always been a firm advocate that things happen for a reason, the challenges and careers I followed were not only calculated, but they were also gut feelings that I felt at the time, and I have always listened to these because they have never let me down. Volunteering to serve in West Belfast on a six-month operational tour of duty and witness the clearing of a live minefield in Bosnia-Herzegovina did not scare me in the slightest, simply because something deep inside me made me feel confident that I would be totally safe in undertaking these opportunities.

At no time did I ever consider these would be a risk or a danger, but instead they were safe and pre-planned undertakings on my part, and even sailing in the Baltic whilst scared of water and coming face to face with an adult black bear in the wilds of Canada were choices of my own doing. Because I listened to my own instinct, not once did anything go wrong and each proved to be an amazing life experience that served a purpose, and helped me discover more about who I really am. It was through experiences and moments such as these that I also came to truly understand the importance of true fellowship, and what it brings to a group of people who have only themselves to rely upon.

Between 27 June and 2nd July 1991, I attended an Army Expedition Leader's Course at the British Mountain Training Centre (BMTC) near Kristiansand in Norway, and it was demanding and surprisingly tough both mentally and physically. The instructor was a Royal Marine Sergeant by the name of Steve who undoubtedly was the fittest man I have ever known and I gained my certificate, and two months later I returned to the BMTC with a four-man team from 26 Engineer Regiment in Germany. After co-leading a seven-day expedition, my qualification was upgraded to Joint Service Mountain Expedition Leader (Summer) on 19 September, 1991.

BMTC Kristiansand, Norway

Ice climbing in Norway, 1991

JSMEL Course, Norway 1991

Norway 1991

Afternote

During my time with Central Volunteers Headquarters Royal Engineers in May 1987, I participated in a seven-day recruiting campaign in the Channel Islands and the Ministry of Defence was promoting an advert that read 'Join the Army and see the world.' Another popular slogan was 'Join the Professionals' and both worked well because they were extremely attention-grabbing, powerful, and tempting to those who had an interest in joining the British Army.

Then in 1994, a new catchphrase was adopted which said, 'Be the Best' and this for me hit the nail on the head. It was absolutely perfect and pitched at the right level because not only did it attract attention, more importantly it threw down a challenge because below 'Be the Best' were the words, 'or perhaps you find a night in the front of the telly more exciting'.

Chapter Seventeen
High Hopes

Foreword

I am being completely honest when I say that every time I met or spoke with a senior British officer during my 23-year career, I was both inspired and enthused and especially when the occasion took place within an operational theatre such as Northern Ireland, Bosnia-Herzegovina, or the Falkland Islands. Even when working in a Divisional Headquarters and with the Ministry of Defence, every time I spoke with a staff officer it was such a privilege because of the immediate sense of presence, authority, power and command experience they had, and their warmth and kindness was infectious and they always made you feel at ease. My admiration and respect for them was absolute.

This is why such moments remain important to me, because I knew they were genuinely interested in hearing what I and others had to say, and always without putting you on the spot or under pressure of any kind. Each had a personality all of their own and one in particular, had a wonderful habit of giving you an encouraging slap on the back whenever he spoke, while another always crossed his arms which just oozed self-belief and confidence. But the one thing they always did was to shake you firmly by the hand and smile, and for me that was priceless because it was almost showing their respect back to others.

Between 19 April and 4 October 1996, I was serving in Bosnia with 36 Engineer Regiment and our role was to provide engineer support to the NATO led Implementation Force, which was more commonly known by the acronym IFOR. One day we received a visit from the Commander 3 Division who was a high profile two-star major general, and he was accompanied by his military entourage. I was lucky enough to be in attendance during a briefing at Gorjni Vakuf and it was an experience I will never forget.

Firm and with a no-nonsense approach, he outlined his objectives and how our regiment fitted in with his plan and throughout his visit, he exuded nothing less than total authority and command of the situation on the ground, and an inspirational strength of character and dogged determination to succeed.

Anti-IFOR graffiti, Gornji Vakuf 1996

If you were to ask most military personnel which group of people they tend to avoid in operational theatres, I am quietly confident they would say it is the media. While serving with 26 Engineer Regiment at Iserlohn in Germany during late 1990, I knew an infantry sergeant who was stationed at Hemer and before he deployed to Iraq on Operation DESERT STORM, which was the First Gulf War, he was a bubbly character yet on his return in February 1991, his personality has completely changed and he was constantly anxious and unsettled and it displayed the typical hallmarks of someone suffering with Post Traumatic Stress Disorder, or PTSD.

We were having a conversation when quite unexpectedly, he told me that whilst in the desert one day, he became disorientated while riding his motorbike through a sandstorm between two safe locations. He did not go into detail but whatever happened, it must have left a psychological scar because it was so upsetting to see the sudden change in character. He then spoke disparagingly about one television war correspondent in particular, and the length to which that individual would go to sensationalise her report.

I stopped buying newspapers after that conversation and even today, I try and avoid watching the news because it has become excessively alarmist, political, and unbearable because of the huge decline in overall standard of reporting. A more worrying trend is the increasing insensitivity by some when interviewing victims of crime or conflict, and I genuinely gasped in disbelief when I recently watched a

British news reporter interview a distraught mother in Ukraine who had just lost her child to the war, and asked her how she felt. This for me was heartless news reporting of the very worst kind!

Back in the Falkland Islands and by mid-March 1983, the Defence Base at Kelly's Garden was progressing well and 3 Troop was almost ready to start assembling the Rubb hangar frame.

Sunday, 13 March 1983

No rain and no wind? Surely not, but there it was and the weather conditions this morning were perfect as we paraded outside the G1098 Store at 07.30, and everyone felt the warmth of the sun on their face as it shone down on Kelly's Garden on the 10th Sunday of our tour. For me there is one thing that I will always remember about this extraordinary location and it is the unpredictability of the weather, and speed at which it changes from one extreme to the other which can literally be as little as just a few minutes.

I have never come across such inconsistent weather patterns in my entire life and when the sun does shine, it completely transforms this western part of East Falkland Island into the most captivating and enchanting of places. At no time whatsoever have I ever felt lonely or isolated and we are quite literally surrounded by the most barren yet striking backdrop you could ever wish to see. I am always speechless when I look out across to Ajax Bay and the distant San Carlos Water, and every time I smell the salt sea-air it warms my heart and makes me feel so very happy.

Quite often I will sit alone and listen to the total silence while on the ridge of the Verde Hills, and I feel as if I am in heaven and so very far away from the hustle and bustle of modern-day life which thankfully, I no longer miss. How could I ever want to leave Kelly's Garden but one day I will, and that thought is beginning to worry me because lurking in the back of my mind is the question of how will I cope with having to re-adapt to everyday life when I return to Great Britain? I am no longer a lover of the manic hustle and bustle of busy towns and noisy traffic, the fast lifestyle, and hectic shopping centres. None of these are important anymore and they most certainly do not appeal to me.

All preparations for assembling the Rubb frame are now complete and the heavy alloy tubular sections have been inspected for a second time, and are stockpiled at all four corners of the Rubb site. We are still on target to complete the project on time however, the frequent changes in weather conditions could have an impact and so we will need to remain fully focussed on our work and remain positive. We all have a good idea of just how large the finished frame will be, and it is certainly going to be a spectacular sight when it is assembled and free-standing at a height of some 20 metres.

We plan on having all 13 arch frames fully assembled, erected, and firmly secured to their foundation footings inside two weeks and with that in mind, my fellow team leaders and I met with our troop commander and staff sergeant for a project update in 3 Troop's office. The meeting was kept short even though several important issues were raised and thankfully, each was discussed and resolved with the minimum of discussion and fuss, and so all in all it was a constructive and very important 45 minutes. After the meeting concluded we grabbed a short tea break over at the G1098 Store where some colleagues were reading letters that arrived in today's mail run from Port Stanley.

I received two from my parents and one from a friend back home in Llanelli. The mail arrived by RAF Chinook at around 11.30, and I also received a financial statement from the Midland Bank. The account is starting to look healthy and so my plans of improving my finances during this six-month tour are already starting to work, and to my pleasant surprise it is proving far easier than expected to cut back on personal spending. A four-man section helped the Gurkhas with their work of laying more PSP panels but sadly, we have learned that our colleagues from Nepal are due to leave Kelly's Garden tomorrow morning, and return to Port Stanley to support those safeguarding the war-damaged runway at Port Stanley Airport.

Their departure will be a huge loss to 3 Troop because they are so hard-working and totally committed to their role and also, they have become very good friends. They are quite extraordinary and each individual will be sorely missed however, this again just goes to show how versatile and adaptable British troops need to be, and how quickly they can be re-deployed and assigned to new roles at short notice. This is one of the reasons why we easily acclimatise to new environments without fuss or bother of any kind and in short, it is all part of military life.

I also received confirmation today that my Private Glider Pilot Course will take place at the Army Gliding Club Upavon in Wiltshire, and will commence on Monday 5 September and finish on Friday 16 September. I am determined to gain my glider pilot's licence and the instructions that I have received are comprehensive. I will need to pass a written exam and log 10 hours flying whilst under instruction and then complete two hours solo, and all this must take place before an assessment can be made as to whether or not I am to be awarded my private licence. The experience will be so very different to the time I flew in the RAF T-Bird Harrier Jump Jet over the Ruhr Dams of North Rhine-Westphalia in 1979. Being handed the controls of the aircraft at a speed of around 400 miles per hour really boosted my determination to follow my dream, and I am confident that it will help me to possibly become a helicopter pilot one day, but who knows what lies ahead? Fixed wings and helicopters are two completely different types of aircraft.

Work continued on the Rubb site and during my lunch break, I took time to make a sign for our new bar which is to be named the 'Blue Lanyard,' after the much-coveted lanyard we sappers proudly wear as part of our military uniform. The sign has a red background with two vertical rows painted in dark blue as these are our corps colours. For the remainder of the day, we worked on assembling several large steel gabion baskets which when filled with heavy rocks, will act as anchorage points for the Rubb PVC covering tension straps. Some colleagues from 3 Troop examined the nine heavy green PVC bundles over at the G1098 Store and around 18.00, a walk-through of the whole site was undertaken to ensure that there were no discarded pieces of steel or underlay anywhere.

By the time we finished the inspection the site was looking as tidy as we could make it, and everyone returned their tools and equipment to the G1098 Store.

At 20.00 Paul and Frazer went to watch the movie 'Jaws 2' over in the Ant Hill and I decided to go along with them. After the film finished I returned to my portakabin and drew a French village scene on another new plaque I am making, and I am now receiving requests to make more plaques either as mementos or gifts of our tour. My plan tonight was to write to friends back home and to my parents however, tiredness got the better of me and so I decided to climb inside my sleeping bag.

I have now totally forgotten what it is like to sleep between cotton sheets and under the warmth of a duvet, because living in such basic accommodation while packed into a portakabin that barely has any home comforts such as a carpet, has been something of a shock to the system. And yet everyone is happy with our new home and the organised chaos it provides. A good night's sleep inside a warm green army sleeping bag is now the new normal and it is comfortable. The welding team are working outside on a task that could take until 05.00 to complete, however, as a reward for their hard effort they will both be given tomorrow morning off.

The long days spent working outdoors in all types of weather for 12 hours each day is now starting to take its toll on 3 Troop, and it came as no surprise when I calculated that as a troop we have collectively worked over 13,860 hours over the past six weeks, which is considerable given we only have one morning off every eight days. After I finish writing this entry in my journal, I will close my eyes and imagine myself trekking the Verde Hills while looking down on Bonners Bay and Kelly's Garden. I am now very tired yet so very content. The sky outside looks beautiful but I cannot see any stars at the moment.

Monday, 14 March 1983

At precisely 08.00, 3 Troop Paraded next to the northern edge of the newly laid PSP taxiway for a personal kit inspection, and for some reason our troop commander did not seem pleased with our standard of turnout. Everyone's works dress had been washed and ironed and we were looking as smart as we could be in such conditions, plus our boots were highly polished despite the mud that sits everywhere here at

Kelly's Garden. Some of our troop commander's recent remarks and random ideas have puzzled us at times, and we believe they could be the effect of all the pressure he is being put under by CRE Works back in Port Stanley and in particular, to have the Rubb project progress at a much quicker pace.

We all fully appreciate his concerns and frustration and we are all fully behind him. It is not good to see a young officer's confidence deflated by pressure from above, or be expected to pull a rabbit out of a hat on such a large military engineering project as this. We all agree that we should say nothing but be seen to support him and go along with whatever he believes is the right way forward and try to recover any oversights, as discreetly as we can and without bringing them to anyone's attention.

Ironically the CRE Works and RAF Advisory Team flew into Kelly's Garden this morning to inspect our work and for a short while, there were only a handful of us from 3 Troop on site because our visitors decided to assess their findings in 3 Troop's office. This will serve as the final inspection before a decision is made as to whether or not we are to proceed with assembling the Rubb hangar frame, and so we waited for their verdict with bated breath.

The welding team worked through the night on their tasks and quite deservedly, they have been given the day off. Meanwhile, the lead welder carried on checking the Rubb base beam sections that will be secured to the foundation but suddenly, he mentioned to me and my colleagues that he suspected the Project Planning Team had miscalculated the lengths of two beams, and that if he continued to work on their figures, it could prove disastrous to the project.

Some miscalculations were described as being 'significant' and thank goodness we have him as our senior welder. As the saying goes "measure twice, cut once" and his attention to detail has done him credit. With remarkable tact and diplomacy, he informed the CRE Works before leaving them to consider his findings. In our eyes he has handled this sensitive issue extremely well and with that, we all walked across to the cookhouse for an early tea-break.

I happened to meet Lance Corporal Mann who is a former colleague and now serves with 7 Field Squadron at Nienberg in Germany. He flew into Kelly's Garden just a few hours ago and we spent half an hour catching up on what we have done since we last met, and it was so good to see him again. Over at the Rubb hangar site the Gurkhas continued with their work on finishing the taxiway before they depart for Port Stanley later today.

We were extremely lucky with the weather because the sun shone the whole time we were on site, and it was nice to feel the warmth of the sun after the dreadful weather conditions we have had to deal with recently, such as heavy rainfall, hailstones, high winds, and sudden drops in temperature which at times fell below zero. I had my first conversation with our new troop sergeant today. We know very little about him other than that he once served, or so we are informed, as engineer support to 22 Regiment Special Air Service at Hereford.

If this is correct then obviously he is a SNCO with impressive military skills and experience, and is it any wonder why he is so highly rated by both the Royal Engineers Manning and Records Office, and also by 22 Special Air Service. My first impression is that he a little reserved but approachable, highly intelligent, confident, and a good judge of character, and I hope to learn much from his extensive expertise, guidance, and advice.

Our day's work finished at around 19.35 and over at the portakabin Lance Corporal Mann, Frazer, and I discussed our individual post-tour vacation plans, personal posting preferences and career ambitions. Royal Engineers will often spend time discussing options with colleagues because they are crucial to our individual development and progression, and to its credit our Manning and Records Office goes out of its way to make sure that all ranks have a genuine grasp and understanding of what they require to climb further up the ladder. On operational tours and on military manoeuvres, sappers are often required to think on their feet and act quickly to resolve situations while at the same time, remain calm and see each task through to a successful conclusion. They are also quick at assessing and analysing problematic situations and identify workable solutions, and to implement working practices and processes to the benefit of all.

As I lay inside my sleeping bag after another full day's work, and with no word on whether we can proceed with erecting the Rubb hangar frame, I listened to 'Pyramids' which is an incredible album written and performed by a musician who I have always considered to be among the finest in his industry, namely Alan Parsons. He and Eric Woolfson form one of the most successful song-writing partnerships in the world of rock music, and there is no doubt in my mind that 'The Alan Parsons Project' is among the top 10 live bands of all time. Outside, the welding team is again working through the night on another task, while here inside my portakabin all is warm and I am now writing this entry in my journal.

Rubb alloy frames being repaired

Tuesday, 15 March 1983

Kelly's Garden was immersed in a cold sea-mist this morning as we continued our work on making additional steel gabion baskets, which will now also act as anchor points for certain Rubb hangar leg sections, as well as the PVC tensioning straps. These are being sited along all sides of the hangar apart from the front aspect, and on ground that has been levelled and reinforced with newly compacted shingle. Their purpose quite simply is to help stabilise the completed hangar frame and will be filled with rocks that will need to be airlifted in from the quarry near Whalebone Cove, just outside Port Stanley.

The RAF ChinDet at Kelly's Garden have for reasons known only to them, hinted at possibly changing the location of the three helipads and taxiway which understandably puzzles and confounds 3 Troop. We have expended considerable amounts of time on preparatory work and put a lot of hard effort into laying hundreds of PSP panels, and often during awful weather conditions. The decision has taken us by surprise yet strangely, not a single word of frustration has been uttered by our troop commander or staff sergeant who have called for a meeting with the RAF senior officer to discuss the matter further. They have also tasked our corporals with finding a workable solution that can be presented to the RAF at the meeting, and so hopefully they will have an agreeable alternative should we be asked to dismantle the many PSP sections that have already been pinned to the ground.

My troop commander took me by complete surprise today during my appraisal interview, by suggesting that I give consideration to applying for a commission as a course of action which he described as being 'nothing short of sound common sense.' It was a very positive and interesting interview and I thanked him for having such confidence in me, and I agreed to give the matter a lot of consideration before we return to Tidworth.

Sir Rex Hunt the Governor of the Falkland Islands flew over Kelly's Garden today to see for himself the progress that is being made, and we hear that he was impressed by what he saw from the air but sadly, the helicopter did not land and so we never got the chance to meet or speak with the man himself. He is the one person we would all like to meet because of the way he stood up to the invading Argentine troops last year, and the true grit he showed in the face of such hostile aggression.

It now only remains for the first series of base beams to be bolted together and then 3 Troop will be in a position to commence assembling and erecting the first hangar arch frame. This of course is provided we receive the go-ahead from CRE Works and the RAF Advisory Group Team which I must say, we are confident we will get.

Receiving the go-ahead finally came and it was a huge relief because it has given 3 Troop a massive boost of renewed enthusiasm to complete the frame, and have it assembled and free-standing inside two weeks. A fellow lance corporal and his section finished work on minor snagging over on the helipads after working non-stop until 20.35, and with everyone on site happy that they had fully completed their tasks we packed away our tools and equipment and returned them to the G1098 Store. We also heard that the RAF have reconsidered and reversed their suggestion of re-siting the three helipads.

By now another thick sea-mist had silently crept in from across Bonners Bay and was making its way towards the Verde Hills as night slowly approached. No mail arrived today and so 3 Troop understandably felt a little disappointed however, that quickly passed and laughter soon filled our warm and dimly lit portakabin where inside, Sapper Diable was once again making everyone laugh with his hilarious anecdotes.

Frazer handed me a postcard of Mount Everest which had been given to him by one of our Gurkha colleagues, and he kindly donated it to my journal because on the reverse was a message written in Nepalese. I then wrote up today's entry and reviewed what I had produced over the past seven days and so far, I am pleased with how the journal is coming along.

Frazer, Paul, and I went to watch two movies that arrived from Port Stanley just a few days earlier. The first was 'McQ' while the second was 'The Shootist' and both starred the legendary American actor John Wayne. Born Marion Robert Morrison and nicknamed 'Duke,' I am told that 'The Shootist' was the last film that John Wayne starred in before his death at Los Angeles, in 1979. They were both entertaining but halfway through 'The Shootist,' we decided to return to our portakabin to wash the floor ahead of tomorrow morning's accommodation inspection.

Once satisfied that the portakabin was as clean as we could get it, Paul headed across to the Ant Hill to try his luck at cards while I decided to remain in the portakabin to write up today's entry in my journal, while listening to Asia's 'Heat of the Moment' and some classical pieces by Grieg and Handel. For some reason I feel drained of energy and to think that it is only 12 weeks before our six-month operational tour in the Falklands comes to an end, yet there is still so much that needs to be completed in addition to the Rubb hangar project. Right now the days are passing even quicker, and we often wonder if we will have enough time in which to complete all our tasks. Outside it is dark and all I can hear out in the distance is the shrill of seabirds flying over Bonners Bay and again, there are no stars and the air is chilled by the sea-mist that envelops San Carlos Settlement. I am so very happy to be here.

Wednesday, 16 March 1983

For the vast majority of today the wind blew and howled as it whipped Bonners Bay into an expanse of frothy sea water, and for as far as the eye could see, there were white waves crashing out in the distance. Back home in Wales we call such waves 'White Horses' and they are incredibly spectacular to watch, especially when walking along Llanelli beach during a storm. In fact, the waves today looked quite perilous in certain areas and it was clear that this is not a day for working outdoors, and especially at height in an exposed location such as Kelley's Garden.

It is my turn for a lay-in but with the wind howling, and the constant clattering of debris being blown throughout the Defence Base and outside our portakabin, there was no peace or quiet of any kind and so I decided to write a letter to my parents instead. It was while writing at my desk that I heard the news of an accident involving a good friend of mine, but the details were sketchy at first and I just hope that he is safe and well. I have also heard that a Combat Support Boat had been involved in an accident and the craft requires repairs but again, the details are pretty vague and I have no idea as to what has actually occurred, or indeed who was involved.

Work on the Rubb site could only begin during the early afternoon when the weather improved, and after a RAF Chinook was made available to airlift the damaged Command Support Boat to Port Stanley for assessment and repairs. On seeing the CSB for myself, I do not think the damage is as bad as first envisaged and the only repairs needed seem to be to the cabin, and a damaged steering wheel mechanism. There are also minor scrapes along the bow and stern which can easily be made good by applying a couple of coats of paint, and all this would take no time at all and the craft would soon look as good as new.

By 18.00 we had completed the task of assembling Arch Frame One which will form the east face of the Rubb hangar and to which the main door will be fitted. After an inspection by our section corporal, it was prepared for hoisting and bolting to a pair of tall alloy supporting legs. This was not going to be an easy task and more importantly, nobody on the team had any previous experience of working with, or assembling a Rubb frame. Thankfully, the sun came out and the wind calmed and so working in teams of six, one continued working on the first arch while the other two began to lay out the alloy sections that would make up Arch Frames Two and Three.

These were laid on the ground adjacent to the southern foundation run. At around 19.00 we had finished for the day and I packed up my personal equipment in readiness for moving to another part of camp. It is becoming clear for all to see that Kelly's Garden is starting to look more like a military Defence Base with every passing day, and although we do not like being moved from pillar to post, it is nevertheless accepted as being a necessary part of the camp's development programme. Incoming troops must be accommodated first and foremost, because it is they who will be posted here for six months at a time and this will continue for as long as the British Government deems it necessary to have a military presence here at Kelly's Garden.

Arch Frame One being assembled

Over at the cookhouse we enjoyed a hot beef dinner with the best roasted potatoes and fresh vegetables ever. Suddenly, in walked 15 Gurkhas who waved across to us after having played a one-hour game of football. What had been a lovely sunny afternoon quickly turned into one of the most beautiful evening skies I have seen in a long time, and I stood at the side of my portakabin totally mesmerised by this incredible sight before me, and then I made a dash to get my camera. For some reason I felt extremely overcome with emotion at seeing this beautiful sunset, and I sensed a presence which I cannot describe but I believe that moment happened for a reason.

At around 20.00 I joined my colleagues in the Ant Hill where a Billy Connolly video called 'Hand Picked by Billy' was being shown. I did not stay for long and went back to my portakabin but by 21.00, I was again back in the Ant Hill watching the movie 'The Boys in Company C.' The film tells the true story of three American Marine recruits who before they enlisted were a drug dealer, a draft dodger, and a journalist, and after Boot Camp they are posted to Vietnam. I am told that this was one of the first films ever to be made after the Vietnam War ended in April 1975, and that it had to be watched. Tomorrow, one of our colleagues will fly to Port

Stanley to undertake a task that will take a few days to complete, so it will be a pleasant break for him because he has often mentioned he does not like the remoteness of Kelly's Garden.

I find it fascinating the different likes and dislikes that soldiers have, the varying outlooks and opinions they hold, and the wide-ranging principles by which they live their lives. Today I am writing this entry with a completely frozen right hand which I had assessed earlier by an Army Medic and strongly suspects that I am showing early symptoms of carpal tunnel syndrome, a medical condition about which I know very little. All I can say is that when it occurs, my hand hurts and indeed these past few entries have been very painful to write.

The numbness and sense of swelling in my right hand can at times be unbearable and as a consequence, my handwriting has unfortunately suffered however, as my grandmother Lena always used to say, "by hook or by crook". I am totally committed to finishing my journal at all cost because one day in years to come, I will use it as the core content when writing my military memoir. Outside the portakabin, a colleague is puffing and panting heavily as he goes through his daily routine of body-building exercises.

The training sessions or 'pumping iron' as he calls them sound demanding and tiring, yet he has a physique and shape to be proud of. I will listen to my favourite pieces of classical music next, and then I plan on getting into my sleeping bag. Today has been surreal and for so many reasons. Hopefully the Combat Support Boat will be repaired quickly while on land, we have assembled and erected Arch Frame One and at long last, we can see just how tall the Rubb hangar frame is, and it is mightily impressive but yet again, we must move into a different portakabin.

Arch Frame One about to be hoisted

Arch Frame One almost completed

Afternote

Ironically, it was while working on my memoir that my carpal tunnel syndrome finally flared to the stage that both hands were suffering intense discomfort, and I was left no option other than to seek medical attention and to their credit NHS Wales were wonderful. Within weeks of having both hands tested and diagnosed in February 2021, I was seen by a consultant who arranged for my left hand to be operated on at Prince Philip Hospital in Llanelli on 7 May 2021. The surgeon and his team completed the procedure in just under eight minutes and it was an instant success, with full recovery and the healing process taking only six weeks but due to Covid-19 restrictions, and the mounting backlog of surgical procedures, NHS Wales paid for me to have my right hand operated on at St Joseph's Private Healthcare Hospital in Newport, on 8 January 2022. Again it was an instant relief.

In January 2006 and after an absence of almost of 30 years and the vow never again to live in my hometown of Llanelli, my gut instinct was telling me to come home and I finally returned in February 2006. Ever since 1983 I have safeguarded my hand-written journal and by the time I started to write my memoir, it was almost 36 years old and the green sticky-back plastic was still looking as good as new.

Understandably this journal means everything to me because I can still physically touch something that was with me throughout the whole time I was in the Falklands, and each time I hold it and close my eyes, I can see myself writing the daily entries while listening to classical and rock music on my headphones. I find it very hard to believe it is 40 years since I first arrived in the Falkland Islands, and still my heart yearns to re-visit Kelly's Garden and San Carlos Settlement.

Because I live very close to the sea, whenever I walk along Llanelli Beach and look across to North Gower I am reminded of Kelly's Garden and my old colleagues who were like a second family, but sadly some have passed on. My journal has travelled everywhere with me and has become a dear friend, and to think that it only came about when by chance one day in 1982, I decided to tell just part of the story of my life with the British Army.

Since returning to Llanelli, I have from time to time re-read the introduction I wrote in the style of handwriting that I inherited from my grandmother Lena, and there were times when I genuinely worried that I might never fulfil my ambition of writing my military memoir. My business interests and voluntary commitments all got in the way then one day in 2019 it all came together purely by chance, and as the saying goes "the rest is history".

Always have high hopes.

Chapter Eighteen
What Goes Up

Foreword

Throughout this memoir I make reference to four military terms that are specific to combatant scenarios, and these are outlined below:

Term	Definition	Example
Theatre	An area in which military action takes place and can be on land, sea, or in the air.	A theatre of conflict.
Operation	Military action(s) planned to seek resolution to an ongoing situation and is usually given a codename	Operation Overlord (The Normandy Landings of 1944)
Conflict	Armed fighting between two or more forces where no open declaration of war exists.	The Suez Crisis (1956 to 1957)
War	Open and declared fighting between two or more states where extreme hostility is involved.	World War One (1914 to 1918)

Britain's history of war and armed conflict is extensive and you only need to consider the numbers fought since the beginning of the 18th century to understand this. Interestingly, if there was a league of countries that have fought the most wars then Spain would come out on top with a staggering 300 plus, while France would be ranked second with over 250, followed by Hungary with 190 and in fourth place, the United Kingdom with 180.

The causes of war and armed conflict vary and categories they come under include Economic, Expansionism, Ideological, Political, Religious, Territorial, Civil and National Defence however, some will have more than just one reason alone.

By their very nature, where an alliance exists then some wars will involve more than one country and this in turn can result in finding a peaceful resolution becoming extremely complex. As a historian, I often find myself having to refresh my *understanding of the circumstances behind certain wars that are of particular interest to me, such as the War of the Roses which was fought between May 1455 and June 1487, the English Civil War which was fought between August 1642 and September 1651, and the one I have studied more than any other which is the Anglo-Zulu War. This started on 11 January 1879 and ended on 4 July 1879.*

It is my belief that peace and war cannot exist without each other and as convoluted as this might sound, it is a philosophy I have always held. When I consider Britain's past, it is undeniably plagued with armed conflicts and wars fought with countries across the globe and from my own understanding, two core reasons have been Expansionism and Political.

There have been others but a prime example of Expansionism was the building of a British Empire, while an example of Political was Britain entering World War One. Sadly, wars will continue to be fought for as long as humans inhabit this world because of the wide-ranging diversity of international agenda, the mindset of single state leaders, and the draconian ideology held by dictators who do not tolerate non-conformity with the state, and it is in the name of National Defence that alliances such as NATO was formed on 4 April 1949.

The biggest concern with regards to 21st century warfare has to be the threat of a rogue nation threatening to use nuclear weapons, but this is being controlled to some extent by enforcing the Treaty on the Non-Proliferation of Nuclear Weapons or NPT, which was first created in 1968 which has 190 member states and countries signed up.

China, France, Russia, the United States, and the United Kingdom are recognised by the NPT as being openly declared nuclear-power states and as such, are governed by the terms of this treaty. In 2003, North Korea withdrew its membership and continues its irrational and irresponsible programme of developing and testing of nuclear weapons, and nearly always close to Japan's border yet no international objection or outcry seems to stop this from happening.

The vast majority of the world's population openly object to war because of the senseless loss of human life and the sheer brutality that conflicts inflict on innocent civilians, and the damage it does to world stability and to our planet. Tragically however, it seems as though this is the status quo that we and future generations will have to learn to accept as being a part of life, and all because of narcissistic dictators who believe it is their right to have power and control over others.

This is why I hold the philosophy that peace and war cannot exist without each other, because peace is always destroyed by war, and war is the only means to bring about peace.

During my time with the British Army, I believe not everyone truly understood the background to certain wars and I say this with all sincerity, because some were very complicated. On one occasion and just before I deployed to Bosnia with 36 Engineer Regiment in 1996, I was asked by a junior member of my administrative team why was the Bosnian War was fought between 1992 and 1995. This was an intelligent question and I sensed that others were also uncertain, or too embarrassed to ask.

Yugoslavia was created in 1918 after the end of World War One, and it was originally called the Kingdom of Serbs, Croat, and Slovenes. In 1923 the country was renamed Kingdom of Yugoslavia and during World War Two, it was invaded by Nazi Germany which was part of the Axis Powers along with Italy and Japan.

Two years later in 1943 a Democratic Federation of Yugoslavia was officially declared by the National Liberation Army, a communist partisan group that was led by an insurgent named Josip Tito who bitterly opposed the Nazis. In 1945, the country was renamed the Socialist Federal Republic of Yugoslavia or SFRY, and it comprised of six republics namely Croatia, Macedonia, Serbia, Montenegro, Slovenia and Bosnia-Herzegovina. Within the geopolitical boundary of Serbia was a region called Kosovo.

This newly formed Socialist Federal Republic of Yugoslavia was led by its architect President Josip Tito, and in return for his support and opposition to Nazi Germany during World War Two, both he and the SFRY were formally recognised by the Soviet Union, even though they were outside its influence. As a country, the Socialist Federal Republic of Yugoslavia was destined to fail because of the deep divisions in religion, politics, and multi-ethnicity. Josip Tito died in 1980 and in 1991, both Slovenia and Croatia withdrew from the republic.

The Republic of Bosnia-Herzegovina had three main political and religious groups namely Muslim Bosniaks, Orthodox Serbs who were fundamentally of Christian denomination, and Croat Catholics. In 1992, Bosnia-Herzegovina held and won a referendum for independence from the Socialist Republic of Yugoslavia however, the referendum was opposed and vetoed by every Bosnian Serb politician, and the result was rejected. Nevertheless, independence went ahead and the constitution was changed and this angered the Bosnian Serb leader President Radovan Karadzic.

Supported by Slobodan Milosevic and his government, President Karadzic took the decision to deploy the Bosnian Serb Army which was under the command of General Ratko Mladic, and the purpose was to safeguard Bosnian Serb territory within Bosnia-Herzegovina. Fierce fighting soon broke out between the Bosnian Serb Army who were known as the VRS, and the Army of the Republic of Bosnia-

Herzegovina which had Muslim Bosniaks and Croats in its ranks, and these were known as the HVO.

The three-year Bosnian War claimed the lives of an estimated 100,000 people. Heavy shelling of towns and villages was broadcast across the world and when I drove through Sarajevo in 1996, I hardly saw a soul out on the streets. Heinous acts of genocide, ethnic cleansing, and mass rape were reported to the International Criminal Court (ICC) at the Hague, but what truly shocked the world was the genocide committed at Srebrenica in 1995 when 8,000 Bosnian Muslim men and boys were slaughtered by Bosnian Serb soldiers. General Mladic was eventually hunted down in 2011 and tried by the ICC for genocide and crimes against humanity, and was sentenced to life imprisonment.

Shelled village in Bosnia, 1996

Bosnia, 1996

Thursday, 17 March 1983

Today had all the ingredients to make it an eventful day. At precisely 08.00, the whole of 3 Troop reported for morning parade before beginning the work of hoisting arch frames Number Two and Three, and securing them to their respective supporting legs which would need to be anchored to the two side foundation runs. This would require the Coles Crane to lift each frame in turn, some 20 feet into the air, and then have teams working in pairs to bolt them to their supporting legs.

However, we were concerned when several hairline cracks were discovered in certain parts of the foundation concrete, and especially around the masonry bolts. A report was immediately dispatched to CRE Works at Port Stanley however, because of the time that that had already been lost to inclement weather conditions, delays in delivery of essential supplies, and the time it would take for us to drill out and refit each anchor base, an instruction was issued back in Port Stanley for us to go ahead with erecting the Rubb frame. As confusing as this sounded, it did actually make sense and so quick minor repairs were made to the hairline cracks, and everyone felt confident and comfortable with the action we had taken to resolve this particular issue.

Around 10.45 a single RAF Chinook helicopter arrived at Kelly's Garden and was marshalled to a landing site close to Helipad Number One. This was the second aircraft that would be used to test the stability of the PSP floor which we and our Gurkha colleagues have installed to date, and more importantly it would also be used to check that we had laid enough panels for the RAF pilots to manoeuvre their aircraft. With the Chinook helicopter attached to a small truck, a thumbs up was given by the pilot for the aircraft to be towed through a full 360° and after a somewhat lengthy discussion with our troop commander, it was agreed that the PSP floor was both rigid and sufficient in size.

With the pilot more than happy with what we had laid, 3 Troop could now continue the work of erecting arch frames Number Two and Three, and after the Chinook took off and headed back to Port Stanley, every available pair of hands was called to site to begin the work of checking the second arch frame. Each nut and bolt was fully tightened and suddenly the alloy frame began to look much larger than we had expected, and eventually it was hoisted by the Coles Crane and bolted to the two individual supporting legs on each side of the foundation runs.

The teams worked well and in no time at all, we were ready to fit the axial panels which would pull the structure together and strengthen the frame considerably, and with that, the first two arch frames were now freestanding. In total silence, 3 Troop walked to the southern edge of the Rubb hangar site and looked up to fully appreciate the height and stability of the structure, and to take photographs as others looked on. It was indeed very tall and impressive. With arch frame Number Three also assembled, the panel was again hoisted and secured to its supporting legs and secured to arch frame Number Two, as two teams of six worked together on the ground and stabilised the hangar frame by pulling on 40-foot lengths of rope.

As the teams continued to tighten the nuts and bolts, a small crowd of observers gathered with their cameras and they too began to take photographs. It was a nervous moment yet everyone felt proud of what we had achieved, and because at long last the frame was beginning to take shape and progressing at a pace that even impressed us in 3 Troop.

We had now assembled three individual sets of arch frames and supporting leg sections, and secured them to the foundation runs and also to each other. This meant that realistically we had constructed the first two complete sets of arches, given that each arch must have two sides to which the PSP cover sheets can be attached. Two teams worked tirelessly on assembling and securing more arch frames and as the wind began to pick up, it was decided not to use safety harnesses because as bizarre as this might sound, they were actually proving to be a hindrance to the teams, and so it was agreed after some discussion that it would be easier and quicker to work without them but only until we were working at height.

At that stage of the project, the safety of everyone on site would be 3 Troop's number one priority, and every precaution and safety procedure would be strictly observed and complied with. What we did wear however, were our safety gloves and helmets because of the significant drop in air temperature which by now, was just above zero, despite the sun shining down on Kelly's Garden.

Everyone's happy

No mail arrived today and for once, not a single member of 3 Troop felt disappointed because nobody wanted to stop working and so in our sections, we carried on regardless for the remainder of the day and with many opting to forfeit their tea and smoke break. This for me was a clear demonstration of the dogged determination we all had to complete as much of the frame as possible, and while weather conditions remained dry.

To say that today passed quickly would be an understatement, and eventually at 19.00 and with a low cloud starting to hang over Kelly's Garden, we finished our work. As a group we walked back to our portakabins to pack away our personal belongings, because yet again we have been asked to relocate to another portakabin. This time we must also take our bunk beds with us. Army bunk beds are made of cast iron and they can prove somewhat difficult to dismantle and re-assemble. The portakabin we have been allocated is number 26 and to his credit, one of our corporals felt it was only right to know the reason behind this latest change of accommodation. Our troop commander explained that the RAF needed an Operational Control Room that was close to the Rubb hangar, and we all agreed and appreciated this however, as correctly pointed out, the RAF could have easily occupied the newly fitted portakabin which was immediately next to ours. This was not only vacant and ideal for their needs but also, it would have saved us having to relocate just 20 metres. At around 19.30, Paul and I went back to our old portakabin to give it a quick clean which was completed in less than 20 minutes, but we still could not understand why we had moved in the first instance. It was all so very unnecessary.

Preparing to hoist Arch Frame Three

As night closed in, I walked across to the Rubb site to look once again at the tall arch frames that we had assembled and erected today, and still it makes quite an impressive sight and I cannot wait to see the finished structure. Hopefully this should not be too long given the speed at which we have been working these past couple of days, and as I headed back towards my new portakabin, I took my usual detour to visit Bonners Bay where I sat alone in silence and enjoyed the view out across the water to San Carlos Settlement.

In the distance, I could make out several tiny lights shining inside the dwellings that make up the tiny community, and still I remain completely captivated by this location and its remoteness, and its stark contrast to Port Stanley. I really will miss Kelly's Garden when the time comes for us to leave and return to the Coastel at Whalebone Cove. I slowly made my way back to the Ant Hill where I watched the movie 'Kramer v Kramer' starring the American actor Dustin Hoffman, and I enjoyed every minute.

Around 22.00 I walked across to Block 45 which is the Ablution and there I enjoyed a hot shower, and as I opened the door to return to my portakabin, the steam followed me and quickly faded into the darkness of the night. Thank goodness I had my torch with me because the lighting outside portakabin number 24 is not good, and so I will mention this to the team. A colleague asked if I would critique an article he has written for 52 Field Squadron's magazine which I did while others either slept, played cards, or wrote letters to loved ones back home, and then I decided to write up today's events in my journal.

We have heard good news that the damaged Command Support Boat has been repaired and is fully operational again however, a fellow lance corporal today received the bad news that his application to become an instructor at 1 and 3 Training Regiments in Farnborough had been unsuccessful. Everyone fully empathised with him because he would have made an excellent instructor and we know that he had his heart set on becoming a Senior Drill Instructor (SDI) for quite some time. Had he been successful and completed his two years as a Royal Engineer Military Training Instructor, it would have guaranteed immediate promotion to corporal and a posting of his own choosing, anywhere in the world.

Hoisting Arch Frame Five

Friday, 18 March 1983

Strolling across to the cookhouse for breakfast with colleagues at 07.00, I mentioned the need for improved lighting outside our portakabin and everyone agreed, but then someone suggested we also fit a cover over the footpath so that when it rains, troops can stay dry and especially as winter is due to begin in June. The idea has gone down well but who can we spare to do this work? At 08.00 we paraded at the Rubb hangar site and after a quick inspection, we began our second day of assembling the arch frames which needs to be seen to be believed.

Today's weather was at first dull, damp, and overcast, and a cold wind chilled us to the bone because the air temperature must have dropped close to freezing. As we approached the site, clouds quickly disappeared to reveal a brilliant blue sky and without exaggeration, everyone shivered throughout the day and nobody seemed to warm up. Paul and I took it in turns to work as a pair in the Cherry Picker basket to secure the axial poles to arch frame Number Three, and it was then that we realised just how high the Rubb frame actually is. It looked a long way down to the ground and with the wind blowing at some 25 feet, it became touch-and-go as to whether or not we should be working this high in the Cherry Picker.

With the wind showing no sign of easing, the decision was made to return to the safety of terra firma and change vehicles. It was a good call and after attaching a basket to the Coles Crane's beam, Paul and I went back up to continue our work feeling more safe and far more confident, even though we still kept a close eye on the wind speed.

For reasons we could not understand, it was discovered that incorrect supporting legs had been fitted to the foundation anchor points for arch frames Number Two and Three, which in turn required us to completely disassemble the supporting legs and replace them with the correct pair. But what was even more confusing to the team was the fact that no markings of any kind could be found anywhere on the alloy panels. This would have prevented such inconvenience and saved everyone a lot of time, but very quickly the problem was resolved. Two pairs climbed the correct leg sections on either side of the hangar, and waited for the Coles Crane driver to start hoisting the arch frames.

As they slowly reached the correct height, others troop members climbed the supporting legs and quickly bolted and secured these to the frame, and then fitted new axial beams to help strengthen the stability and rigidity of the Rubb hangar. We all worked nonstop until 12.45 at which point, it was time to go over to the cookhouse for a welcomed lunch of fish fingers, beans, and hand cut chips. Outside it was bitterly cold and low cloud was beginning to gather out to the west, plus the wind was beginning to pick up and we still had arch frame Number Four to assemble and attach to the hangar frame. Thankfully we have already broken the back of today's work schedule.

Fitting Arch Frame Three to its supporting leg

Over lunch we discussed our concerns over the weather and our earlier dilemma with the leg sections on arch frames Number Two and Three, and after we had eaten we returned to the Rubb site and continued to assemble the supporting legs for arch frame Number Four. When this had been completed, the legs were bolted to the anchor footings and it was at this point that the other two sections were almost completing the arch frame.

Visitors to Kelly's Garden visited the site from time to time and they were clearly impressed by what they saw. Indeed, one officer told us that as he flew into Kelly's Garden earlier this morning, he was told by the Chinook sergeant loadmaster to look out of the window to see the Rubb hangar site. He described what he saw as spectacular and that it made a great photograph. Our troop commander and staff sergeant joined us and we all felt that yet again, that we had made good progress during the course of the day. We were then suddenly offered an incentive by our troop commander. If we erected all 13 arches within the next four days, 3 Troop would be rewarded with a whole day off which would be our first since arriving in the Falklands back in January, and alsowe would have a BBQ outside the Ant Hill.

At around 19.10 we packed away our tools and equipment and returned them to the G1098 Store and at 19.40, we went for dinner. Back inside my portakabin I changed into a clean set of clothing after enjoying a piping hot shower over at the Ablution Block, and I started to sketch the face of BBC TV's popular antique dealer Arthur Negus on an old piece of waste wood, that had once formed part of the foundation shuttering.

It is quite strange that here in the Falkland Islands, I find myself making souvenirs of my tour from waste pieces of timber as this is something I have never done before, and yet it makes quite a pleasant side-hobby. I watched the movie 'Midnight Express' over at the Ant Hill with others from 3 Troop, and it had my undivided attention from the very beginning.

The movie tells the harrowing true story of Billy Hayes, an American who was sentenced to four years in a brutal Turkish prison for smuggling cannabis out of the country in October 1970. His life sentence was reduced to 30 years but his time in prison remained traumatic nevertheless, due to the treatment he received from prison wardens.

Driven to the edge of despair, during one visit his horrified girlfriend warned that unless he escape then his life would end in prison. Eventually he did escape and fled to Greece in 1975. It is a remarkable story that fills me with horror to know that such brutal detention centres operate in certain countries in this day and age.

Over in our portakabin a card school was taking place and after a team meeting, it was agreed to introduce a house rule immediately that no music, card school, or any other type of disturbance be permitted after 22.30. Outside, Kelly's Garden was in total darkness and we now have to use torches at night to find our way to facilities such as the Ablutions, Laundry Block, Ant Hill, and REME Workshops.

The nights are already starting to draw in because here in the southern hemisphere, it is fast approaching winter and after I logged today's entry in my journal, I chatted with my fellow lance corporal about his body building regime and the movie 'Midnight Express' and also, his plans for post-tour leave.

After some 40 minutes had passed, I climbed inside my sleeping bag and reflected on how the tour is progressing. I am now really looking forward to visiting Morocco and Gibraltar, and for once I contemplated on what else I could expect to see and do while I am there.

Saturday, 19 March 1983

Life in the Royal Engineers is as exciting as it is rewarding, and rarely are two projects ever the same. Here at Kelly's Garden our military engineering and artisan skills are being tested to the full, and working in our sections we are bonding stronger than ever and I feel so proud to be a part of it all. Despite the varying tasks that 3 Troop has been assigned, we tackle each with an absolute determination to produce nothing but the very best results, even though some tasks do fall into the category of 'hazardous' but every care is taken to ensure the safety of all team members on site.

Today we were faced yet again with inclement weather, and just before lunchtime the wind started to blow hard when suddenly, disaster struck. As part of a four man section, I was working on arch frame Number Four when out of the blue a freak gust of powerful wind blew in from the west and literally spun its way through Kelly's Garden like a mini tornado. Just then, something did not feel right with me or my colleagues and someone to our rear suddenly yelled for everyone to run because some of the free-standing arches were starting to collapse, and this all happened within just a couple of seconds.

As we reacted to the warning, all that could be heard was the ear-piercing and sickening sound of metal scraping against metal as arch frame Number Two began to buckle, and then crash to the ground. Some ran for cover and managed to get off site but others including myself, were left stranded and standing close to the frame. All we could do was not panic but instead, walk as quickly as we could towards the nearest edge of the hangar site while covering our heads with our arms crossed.

With partially closed eyes because of the dust that was still flying through the air, and amid all the noise and chaos, we held our breath and thankfully not a single team member was injured, and not even our crane operator who was still inside his cab. We gathered ourselves into a group to make sure that everyone was accounted for, but then to make matters worse, arch frame Number Three also started to buckle and in total disbelief and with hearts in our throats, we watched as this frame also crashed to the ground.

With arch frame Number One still standing and looking stable, we cautiously walked back onto the Rubb site to inspect the collapsed sections, and to our surprise and huge relief many of the panels showed hardly any sign of long-term or real damage and in fact, some only had damage to the bolts. After a quick meeting it was agreed that arch frames Number Two and Three should be dismantled without delay, then examined by our welding team and repairs immediately carried out, and the frames reassembled and re-erected before we finish for the day. We were absolutely confident that this could be done.

Both arches required some minor welding repairs but the hardest task was to remove the bent bolts, however this only took the team about an hour to complete and after each panel was laid out for inspection, we sent a member of the team to go and fetch our troop management. It had been a very lucky escape because it could have ended with a number of casualties but we put that thought completely out of our minds, and what frustrated us the most was the fact that we had spent hours out in the freezing cold assembling and securing both arch frames to their supporting legs. It had all been going so well until that gust of wind blew in from the west with such force.

But what truly confused everyone on the team was that despite being rigid and stable, the sheer power of the wind had caused two sections to collapse, so it could not possibly have been just a 'high' wind. When we explained to our troop commander and staff sergeant what had happened, they immediately gave us their full support and told us that other parts of the Defence Base had incurred structural damage as well.

Morale was not affected and they both went across to the cookhouse to organise an urn of tea for the team. After a short break and out in the freezing cold, we began the process of re-inspecting each alloy frame for signs of damage and marked each part that required repairs with red paint. The welding team did a superb job of repairing the damage and although the wind still blew, we knew we could recover this situation quickly.

The Gurkhas having heard of our dilemma immediately rushed across to help, and they were worth their weight in gold. Reassembling the arches and leg sections progressed far quicker than we anticipated, and we reminded each other of the need to be extra vigilant given the continuing wind speed. Personal safety was now of paramount importance and especially as the first team began the work of re-bolting both arches to the supporting legs, and at height. By 19.00 we had both arches fully repaired and reassembled, and as I headed back to my portakabin I heard even more bad news. Wales had lost to France by 16 points to 9 in the Five Nations in Paris. Jeff Squire the blind-side flanker had scored the only try for Wales. Could this day get any worse?

At around 19.10, everyone strolled across to the cookhouse and just wanted to put today's minor setback behind us. We chatted about Canada and everyone enjoyed their meal after which, I went over to the Ablution Block for a shower. Over at the Gurkha Bar they were showing a replay of 'Midnight Express' and so Frazer and I went to see it for the second time. As the film finished, a Gurkha who I seemed to recognise but could not recall his name, walked over and smiled the biggest smile ever, and I instantly remembered him from two months ago when we both chatted in Port Stanley. He said he had heard about my journal and was eager to have a copy when it is finished and with that he gave me his address in the United Kingdom, and also in Nepal. The two of us chatted for some time about our homelands and we learned quite a lot from each other. On returning to my portakabin, I decided to head back to the Ablution Block for a shave but by the time I returned to my accommodation block the daylight was almost gone.

The portakabin was unusually quiet when I eventually returned and in truth, it looked and felt extremely basic however, we had only just settled in after being relocated yet again. In its own unique way, military life can at times feel nomadic to those who frequently deploy on exercises or on tours such 3 Troop, and so having to make comfortable shelters through using the most basic of materials becomes normal. Old wooden pallets and storage boxes can be converted into everyday items of household furniture such as cupboards, shelves, tables, chairs, and in my case even a desk.

Sunday, 20 March 1983

With sunshine, a cloudless sky, and finally warm air we thankfully had the perfect day in which to recover yesterday's minor disaster on the Rubb site. Although it is Sunday we have no church here at Kelly's Garden and 3 Troop was desperate to get started. As we arrived at the Rubb site we could see that the welding team had already started to check the re-assembled arch frames Number Two and Three, and in no time at all they had finished their work. Four two-man teams worked on re-securing the supporting leg sections to their anchor points, and very soon both frames were free-standing once again and checked to make sure that they were perfectly vertical. We were now able to begin the work of reconnecting both arches to the main frame and strengthening the structure using axial beams.

Andy and Frazer began working from inside the safety of the Coles Crane basket that was fitted to the main boom, and soon they were tightening bolts that held together the cross sections to arch frame Number One. Some of the team had no alternative but to climb the 15 feet on each supporting leg to retighten the bolts, and by wearing their harnesses they were safe and eventually the task of getting the project back on track was finally complete. We were now in the prefect position to carry on assembling more arch frames and at one point, it appeared that we had more workers on site than we actually needed and so it was decided to operate a rotating shift system, and this went down well with everyone. The speed at which arch frames number two and three were hoisted and re-secured was nothing less than remarkable, and the recovery we had achieved from what could had been a total disaster was nothing less than commendable. 3 Troop had excelled and it boosted morale further.

There was a strong feeling throughout the team that all was going well, and it was such a huge relief that we had recovered so quickly from yesterday's dilemma. Hopefully nothing else will now stop us from completing the assembling phase of the Rubb hangar project, and within the deadline we have been given by CRE Works. The shift system was working well and it continued without a break until 19.00 by which time, most of 3 Troop had finished for the day.

Much later and as the daylight slowly faded, two mobile lighting towers were towed to the edge of the hangar site where they were placed in their assigned positions and when both were switched on, the light they generated created one of the most remarkable and haunting scenes I have ever witnessed in my entire life. Immediately, I was reminded of the mesmerising black and white photograph taken of the ill-fated *Endurance* as she sat ice-locked and a prisoner of the Weddell Sea, before she sank on 21 November 1915.

Collapsed Arch Frames Two and Three

Back in portakabin number 24, a few of the team were getting ready to go and watch another CSE Show that had flown in from Port Stanley earlier today, and would take place in portakabin number 26 which is immediately next door to ours. Due to the work that some of us had decided to carry on with, we decided to give the concert a miss even though there was word that an extremely attractive female singer would be performing. We finally completed assembling more arches of which the last was Number 7, and so we packed away our tools around 21.05 and I headed back to the portakabin for an overdue haircut.

It was then off to the cookhouse for a very late evening meal followed by a visit to the Ablution Block, and again it proved quite a problem finding the unit in the dark. Even with our torches shining, getting around camp at night is becoming a real issue and so something will need to be organised soon, however, this is one for the electricians in the troop to sort out and we have already discussed this. After enjoying a long hot shower, Steve and I headed back to our portakabin via the CSE Show. The audience was surprisingly small considering the number of military personnel that are now stationed here at Kelly's Garden but nevertheless, it looked like a good show and comprised of a comedy duo and the female singer. Sadly, there was only 10 minutes left.

After the show finished Steve and I returned to our portakabin, where I sat for a while reading anything I could lay my hands on before writing a letter to my parents. After writing up my journal for today, I climbed inside my sleeping bag while Frazer was listening to a tape on my cassette player while laid out on his bunk bed, which is directly above mine. When the lights went out, I was ready for another good night's sleep. I wonder if Bob has received my letter. Only a dozen weeks of our six-month tour remain but still we are working flat out every day which is good, and the results can be seen by anyone who visits Kelly's Garden.

Afternote

My hope to one day return to the Falkland Islands and re-visit Kelly's Garden, San Carlos Settlement, and Blue Beach Military Cemetery is realistically just that, a hope.

From what I gather from satellite images, all that survives of the Defence Base are dirt tracks and some old rusting PSP trackway panels that lead down to Bonners Bay, and the odd broken concrete base on which the portakabins once stood, and an old electrical junction box. The camp has all but disappeared and I find it sad to see how derelict and unforgotten the site has become. Thankfully for me, I will never forget how it looked when I flew out for the very last time because I took several photographs for my journal. I fully accept that nothing stays the same for ever, and that all things must pass as George Harrison once famously sang. In the case of East Falkland Island immediately after the war, the recovery and repair of its infrastructure was crucial and the project of establishing a Defence Base at Kelly's Garden was expedited, at significant cost to the British government. Today, the only large permanent military base on East Falkland Island is RAF Mount Pleasant which was opened in 1985, and will continue to operate indefinitely.

Many lessons were learned from the Falklands War such as the importance of helicopters in military conflict, the potential harm created through leaked information and intelligence by the media, and the need for accurate reconnaissance reporting to name just a few.

Improvements made to military clothing and equipment were much needed following the horrific injuries sustained by British personnel during Argentine air strikes on shipping such HMS Sheffield, Sir Galahad, and Sir Tristram. Significant medical advances were made in fields such as maxillofacial in the case of burn injuries and skin grafting, the recuperation and rehabilitation of wounded personnel, and the recognition and treatment of those suffering with severe psychological and emotional conditions such as Post-Traumatic Stress Disorder, or PTSD.

In Argentina, changes were introduced to recruitment and training of military personnel and the treatment of conscripted soldiers, following investigations into the military leaders and their subordinates.

In the United Kingdom, there was a considerable resurgence in national pride and identity, and also a renewed recognition and understanding of the need for a sufficiently sized and highly trained professional military fighting force, both in peacetime and at times of armed conflict.

For some years now, two countries that seem to increase global unease are undeniably China and Russia, with the first frequently repeating its absolute resolve to reclaim Taiwan and bring it back under Chinese administration and rule, just as it did with Tibet in 1949 and more recently Hong Kong in 1997.

For its part, Russia remains determined to annex parts of Ukraine having launched an illegal invasion which was carried out under the nonsensical justification that it was a 'Special Military Operation' in its programme of de-Nazification. Putin's deluded objective to have regions reinstated under Russian influence is very real, as is Russia's frequent breaches of British waters and air space that continue on an unprecedented regularity. And within Russia itself, the people are denied the freedom to speak out against Putin and are punished by extreme terms of imprisonment.

As a founding member of NATO and sitting member of the United Nations Security Council, I remain convinced that having a British army of just under 73,000 regular troops and a trained reserve of only 30,000 by 2025, as announced on 22 March 2021 by British Secretary of State for Defence Ben Wallace, is as dangerous as it is crazy.

The numbers are staggeringly low for a nation that has a population of almost 69 million people, and to explain my line of reasoning then just consider this. The reduction will result in an army that will only have a ratio of 1 soldier to every 699 citizens (1:699) whereas in the case of Russia, it has an army of over 1 million plus 2 million in reserve. Her population in 2023 is approximately 146 million which is a ratio of 1 soldiers to every 48 citizens (1:48).

Whilst I appreciate the overall standard of Russia's military and equipment is not high, is it not obvious that the British government has gone too far during a time of deteriorating geo-political tension?

Chapter Nineteen
No Stopping Now

Foreword

By the latter part of March 1983 and in the knowledge that 3 Troop would be relocating to Port Stanley on completion of the Rubb project, there was a growing sense of melancholy among some of my colleagues which I could fully understand, and so I thought it best to inform my troop commander and staff sergeant that I would happily stay behind as part of the Rear Party, and for as long as was necessary. Some of my colleagues on the other hand were understandably keen to return to Port Stanley, because they were experienced in runway repairs and enjoyed that aspect of combat engineering and also, Kelly's Garden was just a little too quiet and isolated for their liking.

Working conditions at the Defence Base remained challenging for most of the time we there, mainly because the weather kept changing one extreme to the other. It was also becoming abundantly clear that the southern hemisphere winter was not too far away, and the air temperature would get much colder as the weeks passed by. Military personnel kept arriving and leaving almost every day and at times, even the helicopter traffic flying in and out of Kelly's Garden was virtually nonstop, or at least that was how it seemed at the time.

The situation in 1983 clearly demonstrated the armed forces' capabilities in dealing with frequent upheaval and relocating from one operational theatre to another, and especially at short notice. When the British military puts its mind to something, it usually gets it right first time and that boils down to two main principles. The first is its exceptional ability to always plan ahead and determine exactly what it is it that needs to be achieved, and in what timescale. The second is the sound preparation and practicing of manoeuvres or procedures until they can be perfectly executed, and sometimes blindfold.

A good example was 30 April 1980 at Princess Gate in South Kensington, when 22 Special Air Service responded brilliantly to the Iranian Embassy siege that took London and the British government by surprise. After six days of intense negotiations, the six terrorists made the fatal mistake of murdering one of the hostages, and in the eyes of the government and the British people, enough was enough when television cameras and the media captured images of the body being thrown out of the building.

22 Special Air Service was put on standby and without the terrorists knowing, they covertly unlocked a skylight on the embassy roof on 3 May as a pre-measure just in case they needed to access it during Operation Nimrod. This was the codename assigned to the mission to rescue all hostages, and either capture or eliminate the terrorists as circumstances would dictate. On 5 May 1980, millions of television viewers tuned in to watch the events unfold live on air. What followed was one of the most daring and superbly controlled rescue operations in modern history, and it lasted just 17 minutes from start to finish.

Monday, 21 March 1983

Working through part of night resulted in 3 Troop assembling, erecting, and anchoring two more arch frames to their support legs which were then secured to the foundation footings, and this was followed by connecting both arches to the main free-standing structure using two pairs of axial beams. This meant that in total, we have already erected six individual panels which technically make up five sets of arches, and these will be covered by the green PVC sheets. Today's morning parade and equipment inspection was unexpectedly cancelled at the last minute and as such, everyone headed across to the Rubb site to be briefed on the day's tasks.

Beneath a low hanging cloud, 3 Troop began the work of assembling arch frames Number Seven, Eight, and Nine which we laid across the hangar floor and adjacent to their support legs. Out of the blue the weather changed and we were again working in the warmth of a glowing sun that was shining down on the Defence Base, the Verde Hills, Bonners Bay, and San Carlos Settlement. The Coles Crane proved invaluable because without it, there was no way we could have erected all three heavy alloy frames that each has a span of 25 metres, and so quickly.

The sheer size and weight of each assembled arch is considerable and as the structure grew in size, so did 3 Troop's morale and each stage was now being photographed by me and my colleagues, and others who were visiting the Defence Base. In fact, two locals came across from San Carlos Settlement on horseback because they could see the Rubb frame growing from their homes on northern bank of Bonners Bay, and they too were mightily impressed.

Hoisting Arch Number Five

Kelly's Garden had a surprise visitor today and it was none other than the most inspirational and highly respected senior staff officer I have met, namely Major General Sir David Thorne who is Commander British Forces Falkland Islands, or CBFFI. I heard him speak on board *Cunard Countess* and he last visited us here at Kelly's Garden on 14 February. In 1979 and whilst serving as Commander 3rd Infantry Brigade in Northern Ireland, it was the then Brigadier Thorne who had the terrible duty of informing Prime Minister Thatcher of the Provisional Irish Republican Army's two ambushes on British troops just outside Warrenpoint, in County Down.

In the deadliest attack on the British Army by the PIRA, a total of 18 soldiers were killed and many more injured when two roadside incendiary devices exploded. Also on that same day Lord Louis Mountbatten, 1st Earl Mountbatten of Burma and distant cousin of Queen Elizabeth II was also assassinated by members of the PIRA. The Gazelle helicopter carrying Major General Thorne arrived at Kelly's Garden around midday, and his presence delighted everyone on site.

A gifted two-star officer, he made time for as many of the troops as he could and our admiration for him increased, because he has an infectious personality that we all warmed to. He is a remarkable commander who smiled non-stop throughout his time with us, and this is precisely what the troops need right now, a British commander who communicates well and oozes inspiration and positivity. What I liked the most about him was the manner in which he expressed his obvious appreciation for what was being done by the troops, to help protect these islands such as building the Defence Base and throughout his visit, not once did he fail to answer a question. This was true leadership at its very best.

Around 11.45 and shortly after Major General Thorne flew back to Port Stanley, our troop commander visited the Rubb site said was astonished at how much we had achieved over the past 24 hours. Clearly the incentive of a having whole day off if we assemble and erect all 13 arches within four days is working. One of the welding team reported sick after lunch as he was suffering from arc-eye, a condition which is also called 'welder's flash' and is a painful inflammation of the cornea brought on by over-exposure to arc-welding. We were also visited by a staff sergeant who served with us in Canada last year. Our work continued without disruption up until close of play and the progress we have made is plain for all to see. We are almost at the half-way point of completing the Rubb frame and in our estimation, despite this being the most challenging phase, we should have it completed within three days. We finished work at 19.15 and while walking across to the cookhouse for dinner, a few of us looked back at the structure which now towers above the other buildings, and it makes quite a sight.

CBFFI's Gazelle helicopter at Kelly's Garden

Just one hour later and as I was strolling across to the Ablution Block for my nightly shower and shave, I stopped to look back at the Rubb frame and this time it was lit by the two lighting towers and the sight literally took my breath away. We managed to catch up with the staff sergeant who we knew in Ontario over dinner, and enjoyed our conversation but sadly he told us he would be flying back to Port Stanley first thing the very next day. Tonight, for a change there will no movie shown anywhere in Kelly's Garden and so I wrote up my journal while listening to Bach's haunting composition 'All Men Are Mortal,' performed magnificently by the brilliant organist Virgil Fox.

His playing always reminds me of my mother Enid, who herself is a highly accomplished organist and pianist, and made a public performance at a London exhibition at the age of just 14. It is she who gave me my love for most types of music, and I fondly remember her playing the organ at Christ Church in Llanelli when I was a young choir boy with David Banahan, Janet Protheroe, Colin Spencer and others. I read more of Gerald Durrell's delightful novel 'Rosy Is My Relative' which is a short yet highly amusing story of a young man by the name of Adrian, who inherits an alcoholic elephant from an oddball relative of his. The book is probably one my favourites by Durrell because it never fails to make me smile. Outside and high in the darkening night sky, tens of thousands of silver stars flickered and sparkled in the incredible vastness of our galaxy called the Milky Way. This forms just a tiny part of the universe which ironically, is another subject I am extremely interested in. It was totally silent and again, I started to dread the thought of leaving this place.

Tuesday, 22 March 1983

At 07.30 precisely, 3 Troop was again excused kit inspection which told us in no uncertain terms that our focus and priority right now is to have the Rubb hangar frame completed at the earliest opportunity, hence our troop commander's incentive which is now down to just three days. The weather thankfully was in our favour and in the background, I could see the majestic Verde Hills blend perfectly into the panorama that surrounds Kelly's Garden. Behind me stood the impressive structure that is the Rubb frame and although it is huge and secured firmly to the foundation anchor footings, it does rock ever so slightly whenever the wind is high.

This is only to be expected given it is still incomplete at this stage and for the first time ever, Helipads Number Two and Three were both occupied by RAF Boeing CH-47 Chinook helicopters. Each aircraft weighs over 25,000 pounds and has a speed of 170 knots. They cost in excess of £3 million and here at Kelly's Garden, we have a total of six with two normally airborne at any one time during the day, and as well as these incredible workhorses the RAF ChinDet has a full complement of pilots, loadmasters, aircraft technicians, and supporting ground crew.

Today and purely by chance, I met a sergeant who served as a JNCO Instructor when I was attending my Basic Military Training in 1977 however, he was assigned to another Training Party but we had a great chat which lasted some 20 minutes. We exchanged stories about Southwood Camp and it was hilarious to hear what the instructors got up to. Throughout the day, 3 Troop worked tirelessly on the Rubb frame and we completed and erected two more sets of arches and supporting legs which were Number Ten and Eleven.

This now leaves just two more arches and sets of supporting legs to be assembled, and when these are secured to the anchor points and attached to the main frame, this phase of the project will be complete. Three members of 2 Troop failed to turn up at Kelly's Garden today as did the essential engineer stores and equipment we were expecting from Port Stanley. To make best use of my free time, I checked my personal equipment and took a pile of dhobi across to the Laundry Building, before returning to the Rubb hangar site to take more photographs for my journal and as I stood on Helipad Number One, I could see the progress we have made over the past week. It is quite remarkable. Several head of cattle somehow managed to find their way onto the Defence Base even though there is no actual perimeter fence of any kind, and so an urgent message was sent to their owner who lives in San Carlos Settlement to have them removed, and as a priority.

The Chinook pilots need to start their engines and also we are expecting incoming aircraft that need to land here at Kelly's Garden. Cattle straying onto the Defence Base is becoming a general nuisance which we suspect is not being fully appreciated by some locals, and today it was visible that the RAF were unhappy with the situation. Who can blame them? There is no doubt in our minds that recent incidents will now need to be officially reported to RAF Command back in Port Stanley, and the matter passed to the Governor's office. The one consolation ironically was that the wind picked up and so helicopter flights were temporarily suspended, however, the high wind on the other hand was bad news for 3 Troop. We only have a couple of Rubb arch frames remaining that need assembling and erecting before we can begin the next stage, which is to cover the entire structure with the green PVC membrane.

A storm was clearly brewing and so I decided to take a quick stroll down to Bonners Bay, and from the water's edge I could see the Rubb hangar rise high above the rooftops on the Defence Base. I crossed my fingers in the hope that the wind would die down overnight because tomorrow we need to work at height, in order to complete the erecting and securing of the last sets of arch frames. This could prove to be a very long and tiring night shift working in the rain, and under the light of the two lighting towers.

Stray cattle roaming through Kelly's Garden

Wednesday, 23 March 1983

3 Troop went for breakfast this morning as a team, and we dried ourselves in the heat of the cookhouse because outside it had been raining heavily for most of the night, and we were soaked. We shared our concerns over the changing weather conditions and high winds, but also our personal safety. This was calmly discussed and after several minutes of contemplating and considering the risks involved, it was accepted that it would be foolish to work on the Rubb frame under current circumstances. As we finished our discussion and prepared to leave the cookhouse, yet again the weather changed and suddenly the clouds broke and the wind died.

The weather here really does test a person's patience and so with the decision to stand down now cancelled, and after a thumbs up was given for 3 Troop to proceed with its work, everyone reported to the Rubb site in their sections. Within minutes of arch frame Number Ten being assembled, it was hoisted and made ready for connecting to the supporting legs but just then, a message was received that one of the bolts was cross-threaded. A replacement was obtained and both Paul and Kevin were safely inside the Coles Crane within minutes, and lifted to the top of the frame along with the replacement bolt and hammer, and two large spanners. The original bolt was removed and replaced and so once again, the frame's rigidity and stability was recovered without fuss or bother.

Three members of 2 Troop arrived today and brought with them the essential stores that we have been waiting for, and they told us that they had been tasked with dismantling a burned-out Gazelle helicopter some 5 miles away from our location, which had been brought down during the Falklands War. More troops arrived today as did the Commanding Officer of 37 Engineer Regiment (FI) and his Regimental Sergeant Major (RSM), because both wanted to see the Rubb hangar project after hearing of the progress we had made since their last visit. After speaking with members of 3 Troop for about 20 minutes, they were obviously impressed by what they had seen and began to take photographs as we continued with our work.

After a lengthy meeting with our troop commander and staff sergeant, they left for Port Stanley and in a very short space of time we had assembled arch frame Number Eleven, and hoisted and secured it to its supporting legs. As soon as this was completed, the weather again changed for the worse and temporarily stopped 3 Troop from working at height, but the camp is definitely looking more like a fully established Defence Base with every day. Two sacks of mail and parcels arrived from back home but I did not receive a letter, and so I consoled myself by thinking that no news is good news.

To my surprise, the newly arrived tools which I signed for earlier were not up to the standard I had expected and could not be issued. I reported my observations to our troop commander who agreed with me on each account. It was arranged for all items to be returned to Port Stanley along with a request that they be replaced as a priority, and this time each item needed to be examined before being dispatched to Kelly's Garden. Suddenly the clouds began to break and drift away, and sunshine returned.

After finishing work for the day, I headed across to the Ablution Block and on my way back to the portakabin, two colleagues and I went to join others from 3 Troop who were watching the recently released Paul Newman movie 'Fort Apache The Bronx.' Some decided to spend their evening inside the Ant Hill because a member of another troop from 52 Field Squadron by the name of Geordie was visiting Kelly's Garden, and had brought along his acoustic guitar.

He would often play the guitar on board *Cunard Countess* and to his credit, he is an excellent singer and it was nice to catch up with him again after the movie. Everyone enjoyed the evening but soon I was ready to say goodnight, because I needed to write up my journal before getting inside my sleeping bag. There must have been an electrical supply issue somewhere on camp because the lights inside several portakabins kept flickering from time to time, including number 24, while outside we could see others cutting out. These were mostly along the southern edge of Kelly's Garden.

The outside air temperature dropped significantly during the late evening and even though the rain had stopped falling, some parts of the Defence Base were marked off because of the depth of the mud. More paved foot paths are needed at Kelly's Garden if truth be known but this is not on our schedule of work, but instead will most likely be mentioned during our handover to the incoming Royal Engineers.

Arch Frame Nine being hoisted

Thursday, 24 March 1983

Today is 52 Field Squadron's 68th day in the Falkland Islands and it began with the most spectacular sunrise ever. Not everyone has been counting down our remaining days at Kelly's Garden but for some of us, we believe this is important and especially as we approach the completion of our tasks. I genuinely have no desire whatsoever to leave because the Verde Hills to the east looked as impressive as ever, and they sit proud and majestic while overlooking the open water of Bonners Bay. There is absolutely nothing that makes me look forward to leaving this location and I could happily remain here for the rest of my life.

There is no more peaceful or remote a location that I know of, and the constant serenity and sense of calm that exists here is truly wonderful. Suddenly and in that precise moment, I felt an urge to go and visit Blue Beach Military Cemetery and pay my respects again to the fallen, and hopefully in the years to come I will return and spend more time here, even if only for a few hours. I will miss my walks through San Carlos Settlement and along the edge of Bonners Bay, and I know that this place has quite literally become a huge part of me.

On the grassed slopes some six-hundred metres away, a herd of cattle lazily grazed and were oblivious to the sound of Chinook helicopters flying in and out of

Kelly's Garden, and so for these creatures and for the foreseeable future, this is how their life will be in this part of East Falkland Island. As much as this saddens me, it is nevertheless essential that a permanent military presence be established here to protect the islanders and their homes.

It was my turn to have the morning off and so I decided to do my dhobi over at the Laundry Block along with Frazer, and as we made our way past the RAF accommodation, we heard the powerful roar of a fighter jet aircraft flying low over Ajax Bay. Chatting with a member of the Royal Artillery as we tried to get a better view of the aircraft, we were told that it was part of a defence exercise and the jet was on its way back to Port Stanley.

One hour later and after a stroll along the edge of Bonners Bay, Frazer and I returned to our portakabin via the Rubb hangar site and we could see that 3 Troop had almost completed the first stage of the project. There were now just two more arch frames to assemble and erect and these are Number 12 and 13, and they will form the rear aspect of the hangar frame, so we decided to cut short our morning and go and help our colleagues. Very quickly we both got changed into our works dress and prepared ourselves for a full shift.

Before reporting for work, I quickly wrote an entry into my journal while listening to a short piece of music and by 10.30 both Frazer and I were back on site and assembling the final two arch frames. Lunch was taken as a short break and at 13.45 everyone in 3 Troop paraded at Helipad Number One, where we were briefed by our staff sergeant and informed that our officer commanding would be visiting Kelly's Garden the very next day. We returned to work and by 15.45, the final two arch frames were at long last assembled, inspected, and made ready for hoisting and securing to their support legs and finally to the main frame.

With both legs fully secured to their anchor points, all that remained was for the Coles Crane to hoist each arch and connect them to the legs, and then secure the final axial tubes to the frames. This would strengthen the entire structure and that would be it, the Rubb hangar frame would finally be assembled and free-standing however, for reasons unknown to us it was decided that this task would be postponed until the next day. As we walked back towards our portakabin after enjoying a wonderful hot dinner, a few of us decided to walk down to Bonners Bay where in total silence we gazed at the spectacular sunset which was starting to come alive. I felt a sudden tightness in my throat as my emotions once again got the better of me, and in that moment, I felt an indescribable feeling of elation yet sadness. I could sense that Gareth was looking at me and as if knowing how I was feeling, he said "I now understand why you don't want to leave Kelly's Garden."

We stayed as a group for about one hour and chatted about anything other than work, and as we laughed and shared our stories as we used to do in Canada, we were once again enjoying each other's company so very much. It was then that we reflected on how demanding our tour had been to date, and how our friendship had bonded us even further despite the obstacles we had overcome such as the weather and the delays, yet through determination and solid team play we had come through it all as a true band of brothers. It was a very special moment in time.

I decided to have an early night and so I showered at 21.00 after which, I climbed inside my sleeping bag in the warmth of our portakabin, and in no time at all I could feel myself starting to drift off to sleep. I thought about my parents and friends who I dearly miss and around 04.00, I awoke from a deep sleep and opened my eyes only to see a silver light shining through the small portakabin window just above my bed space. I climbed out of my sleeping bag and standing by the window, I quietly slid open the glass to smell and enjoy the fresh sea-air outside.

The stars were sparkling in their thousands and so I got dressed and very quietly, I let myself out of the portakabin and walked down to the southern edge of Kelly's Garden, and from there I walked along the short track that leads to Bonners Boy. It was much colder than I had expected and when I reached the water's edge, I looked up at the night sky and was totally captivated by the most beautiful and incredible cosmic sight a person could ever wish to witness. I felt as though I was the luckiest person alive and no matter where I looked, I was enchanted by the absolute beauty around me, and I did not want that moment to end.

Writing my journal at Kelly's Garden

Friday, 25 March 1983

The sun shone down on Kelly's Garden as we reported for morning parade and in a single word, it was a scorcher, and it was also our staff sergeant's birthday. For Kevin and me, we spent the first hour some 35 feet up in the Coles Crane basket checking the two final sets of cross beams that had been fitted yesterday to the end arch section, and when we completed our checks the Rubb frame was officially freestanding. The next phase of the project would be to assemble the two large door frames and insert the rollers into the tracks that are yet to be secured to the foundation.

Once we have done this, we can then start to cover both doors and the entire Rubb hangar frame with the heavy green PVC bundles that are stored inside the G1098 Store. The Rubb hangar right now is one enormous skeletal structure and from inside the safety of the Coles Crane basket, I could see out in the distance a British Naval Type 42 Destroyer which I thought was *HMS Exeter*. She was slowly making her way south along San Carlos Water while accompanied by two other naval ships which neither of us could recognise. Today a section of Irish Rangers arrived at Kelly's Garden as did two bags of mail, and I received a letter from my mother's youngest sister Aunt Mair and my Uncle Michael, who is a retired Royal Artillery Colonel and former Managing Director of Girling and Lucas at Cwmbran in South Wales.

I adore them both and when I was aged 16, I visited them for one week at their magnificent home called Hollington House in Tiddington near Stratford-upon-Avon, and while I was there it was arranged for me to watch the British Grand Prix at Brands Hatch as a member of the Girling Support Team. My uncle also arranged for me to meet several Formula One racing drivers including Ronnie Peterson, James Hunt, Emerson Fittipaldi, and Stirling Moss. But the most exciting experience was meeting Graham Hill who visited my aunt and uncle at Hollington House one evening, and he came across as a perfect gentleman with panache and presence in abundance.

I also received a letter from my parents along with a document I must sign before I visit Morocco in July. Several members of the Army Air Corps arrived at Kelly's Garden around 11.50, and there was constant air traffic and troop activity on the ground, and the Defence Base is now becoming very busy. The two sets of Rubb door panels were laid out for assembling but at 19.00, the decision was made to finish work for the day and so 3 Troop headed for the cookhouse. Over at the Ant Hill some of my colleagues were celebrating our staff sergeant's birthday by presenting him with a plaque, while our corporal chef provided a large and varied selection of sandwiches together with sausage rolls, pasties, and cakes.

I popped in for a few hours but then returned to the peace and quiet of my portakabin however, that quickly changed when others returned much later. Those who had been drinking over at the bar began to play cards and music, but they were quickly reminded of the agreement we had made not to have any noise disturbance after 22.30. I wrote up my journal as I listened to Queen's 'Flash Gordon' through my earphones, and then I relaxed as best I could. Earlier this evening one of my colleagues handed me an article that had been written by his sister-in-law, and published in his local newspaper. The article was entitled "Lonely Soldier Needs Friend."

I read the article in full and at one point could not help but chuckle when I asked him which minefields he had cleared. In all honesty his sister-in-law has done us bachelors here in Kelly's Garden a favour and who knows, just maybe we will receive letters from single women in his hometown near Shepton Mallet.

Saturday, 26 March 1983

Today's weather was superb and with the air temperature far higher than normal for this time of year, the sky yet again looked incredible. After morning parade 3 Troop reported to the G1098 Store to sign out tools and engineering equipment which we needed for today's work. Wasting no time at all, the teams were tasked with preparing the new laundry site for further construction work, undertaking maintenance work at other sites, general minor repairs under the leadership of one of our corporals, and the remainder working on the Rubb site.

Watching colleagues scramble over the frame at height was not only impressing those who were looking on, but also making fantastic photographs as they passed tools and equipment around the structure without so much as a blink of an eye. All they were doing in all honesty was carrying out final checks on the tightness of the nuts and bolts, and even the RAF personnel and other troops looked on in astonishment at the height at which they were working. The first two PVC bundles to be placed on top of the arch frames would be sited at the rear aspect and around 10.00, they were lifted into place using the Coles Crane basket, and secured to the Rubb frame in readiness for being lowered and draped all the way down to the ground. This task looked all the more dangerous and difficult when we considered the large open gaps that are between each arch panel, and it was agreed that the Coles Crane alone would not be able to lift these PVC bundles with two men inside the basket at the same time.

Two teams of four began to attach tension strops to the Rubb frame while others helped my section check and prepare the individual bundles of heavy and neatly folded PVC membrane. These will form the waterproof skin that will cover the entire structure and there are nine bundles in total with each weighing several hundred pounds however, there was one problem we needed to address before we could even think of progressing to the next phase. That problem was how to lift these incredibly cumbersome bundles of PVC onto the top of the arch sections safely, and secure them to the frame? At a height of around 50 feet and more importantly without any of them falling through the gap between the arch frames presented us with a challenge, and there was only one realistic solution which was to request assistance from the RAF.

Even with the aid of a helicopter there were still crucial factors that needed to be discussed, such as the effect of the downdraft from the rotor blades on those working on top of the structure, and those who were acting as guides while standing of the frame itself at height. Also, how close should the pilot approach an arch frame before lowering the bundle, and from which direction should the aircraft approach and exit during each manoeuvre, and finally what words of command should be used by the teams while directing the pilot. There was also the question of how best to secure each bundle to the frame overnight and how to safely unfold and lower each bundle, during the draping procedure.

A meeting was convened between our troop commander, staff sergeant, and the Scout helicopter pilot who had been assigned to assist 3 Troop and at midday, that meeting took place in 3 Troop Office. Four two-man teams were selected to work with the Scout pilot from inside the safety of the Coles Crane basket, and one of these teams would be Paul and Kevin. Meanwhile, two of our colleagues were out in San Carlos Water in their Combat Support Boat as the rest of 3 Troop were fully occupied with preparing the PVC bundles and just after lunch, the news that I was dreading was received. We will return to Port Stanley by no later than 12 April irrespective of whether the Rubb hangar project is completed, or not.

There were mixed feelings at hearing this news because by returning to Port Stanley, 3 Troop will have to move into the Coastel at Whalebone Cove and from what we are hearing, it is not as pleasant as first reported because of its narrow corridors, lack of windows and natural light, and cramped cabins. Furthermore, by being accommodated in a garrison we will have other duties assigned to us in addition to our routine work but nevertheless, as soldiers we must carry on regardless.

Work carried on after lunch and as the weather conditions started to change and RAF helicopter activity continued, and the most impressive of all as ever was the

Boeing Chinook which quite simply is an incredibly versatile aircraft given its size and twin set of rotor blades. Our welding team was kept busy with making minor repairs to the slightly damaged steel gabion baskets which when filled with heavy rocks, will act as anchor points for the hangar tensioning strops. The rear section of the frame and two large doors were tested and both passed their inspection, and the management team was more than satisfied with what we have accomplished.

Around 19.00 all tools were cleaned, oiled, and returned to the G1098 Store and secured for the night, and it was then back to the portakabin to prepare for dinner. With conditions still damp and drizzly, we were lucky to catch a glimpse of the moon from time to time as it broke through occasional breaks in the cloud, and lit up the Defence Base in ghostly shades of silver and grey. For the second night running there was no movie to watch, and so I went for a shower which completely refreshed me, and with food in my stomach and now smelling of shampoo, I was more than ready for an early night. Before I climbed into my sleeping bag I enjoyed a conversation with my colleagues inside the warmth and comfort of portakabin number 24.

I wanted to read another novel by Gerald Durrell but sadly there were none available which was disappointing, because I have become so fond of his style of writing which is amusing and engaging, and these qualities have truly made him one of my favourite authors. In a mood of sweet serenity, Kelly's Garden sat silent at the edge of Bonners Bay and as I reflected on my many walks along the craggy path that leads to San Carlos Settlement, for the first time I finally accepted that I would be leaving Kelly's Garden on 12 April. After this date, my chances of ever seeing this place again will be remote unless I am posted back at some point in my career. As much as I hope this will happen, I do believe that realistically it will never happen if I am successful in my application to transfer across to the Army Air Corps, or to a new trade should I remain with the Royal Engineers. Who knows what lies ahead?

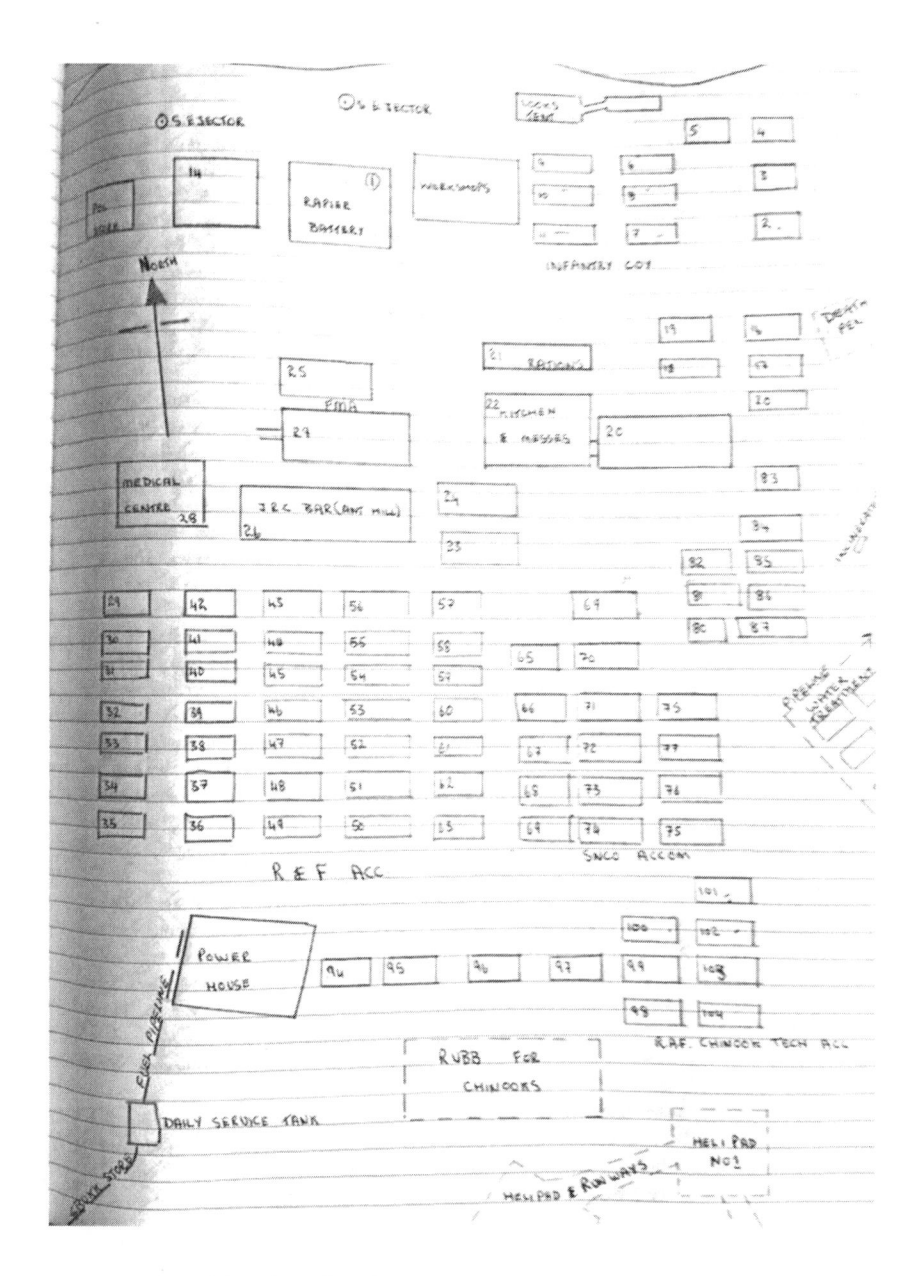

The plan of Kelly's Garden I drew in my journal

Afternote

With the Rubb project so close to completion, the days at Kelly's Garden were beginning to grow shorter as the southern-hemisphere winter slowly approached and over the course of the next four weeks, the air temperature dropped even further and weather conditions noticeably deteriorated. Having never experienced Arctic or Antarctic winters, I have often watched television documentaries and programmes that absolutely fascinate me as to how cold, hostile, and treacherous such places can become, and at times they are quite frightening. Knowing that our operational tour would end on 11 June 1983, and that 10 days later we would be back on the tropical Ascension Island just south of the equator, I must confess I was actually starting to look forward to feeling hot sunshine on my body again.

The Rubb project was by now well and truly nearing its completion but there was still the matter of covering the frame with the large green PVC bundles. These were extremely heavy and somewhat cumbersome to work with and for once, some of 3 Troop were losing sleep over the task ahead because of the risks it would present. Working at height did not bother us but it was the high winds that always gave cause for concern, and especially when it rose above 30 miles per hour, and so this would need to be very closely monitored at all time. Thankfully for us, the RAF would prove a great help as would the Scout helicopter that was assigned to 3 Troop, and when it arrived it immediately reminded me of my first flying experience in 1976, when I flew to the Brecon Beacons in an Army Air Corps Scout helicopter flown by a Territorial Army pilot.

The one thing I will always remember was the view from the top of the Rubb frame. For as far as the eye could see it was just simply breathtaking, spectacular, and wild. Unfortunately, and due to an experience which I will cover in more detail later, I developed a fear of heights and water that has lived with me ever since the return sea journey from Port Stanley to Ascension Island, in June 1983.

Chapter Twenty
Sooner the Better

Foreword

Life can often have moments and experiences that we will never want to forget because quite simply, they were extraordinary and so very special, and for me the two tours to Canada stand out in particular. The first was on Exercise Medicine Man 4 at BATUS in Alberta in July 1981 and the second, was on Exercise Waterleap at CFB Meaford in Ontario in July 1982 but the time I really miss the most, has to be the four months I served at Kelly's Garden in 1983. That period of my life will live with me forever but as the 14th century poet Geoffrey Chaucer wrote in Troilus and Criseyde, "all good things must come to an end." I appreciate these words were written many centuries ago and in an ancient style of English yet nevertheless, what Chaucer wrote is still very true.

When I closed my portakabin door in Kelly's Garden for the very last time on Wednesday, 13 April 1983, I genuinely had to fight back the tears as I walked across to the waiting RAF Sea King helicopter that would fly me back to Port Stanley, because I was saying farewell to a place that I had come to love so very much. Up until that precise moment in time, it was one of the most difficult and emotional situations I had ever encountered and dealing with it proved not only tough, but it was extremely upsetting. I felt completely at home in this remote part of East Falkland Island and I would have done anything to stay.

When I reflect on my time at the Defence Base as I do from time to time, I not only feel an emptiness in my stomach but also a sadness in the knowledge that it no longer exists, and that I will probably never meet any of 3 Troop ever again. The portakabins are all gone and so too has the Rubb hangar and three helipads, and also the Cookhouse, Generator House, REME Workshop and Ablution Block. There is now only the track that once encircled the Defence Camp and apart from this, nothing else exists.

Some years later while serving again at Dennis Barracks in Munsterlager, I was informed that the camp was decommissioned in 1986 and the Rubb hangar was apparently never used as a Chinook workshop and so naturally, I found this quite baffling and questioned why so much time, money, and effort had been spent on establishing a military base that would only operate for three years. I can but pray that one day, Kelly's Garden will be remembered for the part it played in post-Falklands War history and that some form of information notice boards showing maps and images be permanently placed on site, to tell its story. As an historian, I passionately do not think it right or proper for post-war bases such as Kelly's Garden and others to be forgotten.

In September 2022 and along with my son David, I had the privilege to be part of a Welsh Guards Association Battlefield Tour of Belgium and France during which we visited important World War One battle sites and cemeteries including Hechtel-Eksel, Ypres, Somme, Arras, Vimy Ridge, and Beaumont-Hamel. Each was immaculately preserved as reminders of the Great War and with an abundance of information, photographs, and artefacts.

I do not exaggerate when I say I yearn to return to Kelly's Garden to quietly retrace my footsteps, and visit once again Blue Beach Military Cemetery, and San Carlos Settlement.

My final day at Kelly's Garden was literally filled with mixed emotion. Firstly, there was sadness at saying goodbye and secondly, not many of us looked forward to being accommodated on the Coastel. There was also trepidation at the thought of crossing the South Atlantic on board a former Sealink Cross Channel car ferry, but there was excitement too over my visit to Morocco and trekking part of the Atlas Mountains. In a strange kind of way I began to realise that the quicker we left Kelly's Garden the better it would be for 3 Troop, or as I said at the time "the sooner the better."

Sunday, 27 March 1983

Before being medevacked to Port Stanley this morning, a colleague from 3 Troop helped the welding team load the RAF Chinook with empty gas bottles and several heavy boxes of loose stores, all of which had been packed and prepared earlier for handing back to our Squadron Quartermaster Sergeant (SQMS). This was a sure sign of our pending departure from Kelly's Garden and while standing on Helipad Number Three, we had an amazing view of Bomb Valley and Bonners Bay where *HMS Exeter* was anchored out in the distance.

A sleek British Naval Type 42 Destroyer, she brought down three Argentine aircraft during the war. Our colleague who is from Glasgow had asked not to be medevacked but was refused, as he has been diagnosed with having an acute ear infection which requires medical treatment as quickly as possible. Unfortunately, we only have a basic medical facility here at Kelly's Garden at present, however it is planned to convert portakabin number 28 into a manned Medical Centre very soon, and it will be operated by a Royal Army Medical Corps (RAMC) sergeant. Before flying out at 13.00, the RAF pilot heard that I had applied for transfer across to the Army Air Corps and he very kindly offered to show me inside the Chinook cockpit, and while sitting in the pilot's seat he talked me through the instrument panel that had a cruise guide indicator, altimeter and airspeed indicator, marker beacon lights, attitude indicator, rotor tachometer and much more.

Then moving across into the co-pilot's seat, I was shown the radar altimeter, turn and slip indicator, the radio call-sign plate, vertical gyro indicator, and then he explained how to operate the radio system and flight control pedals. It was an incredible insight into how complex the Chinook helicopter actually is, and I was particularly intrigued by how the cyclic pitch lever, collective, and anti-torque pedals work. Those 20 minutes motivated me to try and speed up my transfer application.

HMS Exeter

Over at the Rubb hangar and new Laundry sites, some members of 3 Troop were busy finishing minor snagging because we have been forewarned that as of tomorrow, we may be tasked with commencing preparatory work for a possible second Rubb hangar and with that, the remainder of the troop took delivery of a new stock of Rubb equipment that included nuts and bolts, washers, axial braces, and anchor plates. Surely, they cannot be considering another helicopter hangar at Kelly's Garden because first of all, where would it be sited? While we tried to understand the logic behind this decision and indeed, if it is to go ahead, then we simply cannot see any suitable area that is close to the existing taxiway and three helipads.

As I approached the hangar site, I was asked if I would lead one of the two teams that had been tasked with securing the last of the tensioning strops along the northern side of the Rubb hangar frame, to ensure that these were fastened correctly to their respective gabions. With Gareth, John, and Kevin, we completed the task in no time at all and after carrying out a final check of each shackle and strop, I confirmed that the equipment was safe and ready for tensioning the next day.

Two members of 3 Troop spent most of the afternoon checking the Command Support Boat which had been repaired and returned to Kelly's Garden, and they decided to take the craft out on the water and head towards the far end of Bonners Bay. Between them they took excellent photographs of the Defence Base and said that the Rubb hangar looked much taller than they had expected, and during their time out on the water they got close to *HMS Exeter*.

When the sea started to turn choppy, they sensibly decided to tread on the side of caution and returned to shore. They also confirmed that the craft showed no sign of damage or loss in performance and when they put it through a sharp U-Turn, it handled well so they will pass their report on to our troop commander and to the REME Workshop. This will then be fed back to Port Stanley and also to the team who carried out the repairs on the CSB.

Having finished our tasks for the day, over at the cookhouse my colleagues were surprised to discover how heavily rationed the meals had become in the space of 24 hours, and soon comments were being made to the Duty Officer (DO) of the day who just happened to be our very own troop commander. I popped over to the Ant Hill with Kevin and Frazer after food, and watched two movies namely the science fiction film 'Prophecy' starring Robert Foxworth, and the David Hamilton film 'Laura.' This evening was very pleasant and it would appear that the additional Rubb hangar panels and accessories that we have received recently, have nothing at all to do with a second helicopter hangar, and indeed it was confirmed that they have only been delivered to Kelly's Garden purely for storage purposes.

Over at the Ablution Block I enjoyed a long hot shower which I have now come to appreciate more than ever and especially after working long hours, and I wondered if we will have such excellent facilities on board the Coastel in Whalebone Cove. Walking back to my portakabin, I could appreciate just how much the partly covered Rubb hangar has changed the skyline here at Kelly's Garden, and so I went to find the photograph that I took three days after I first arrived while walking along the path around Bonners Bay, and leads to the jetty and San Carlos Settlement.

The difference between then and now is nothing short of remarkable to say the least, and inside my portakabin later in the day I logged this entry in my journal as I listened to Queen's 'Greatest Hits' on my cassette player. After a conversation with colleagues, I climbed inside my sleeping bag while feeling ready for a good night's sleep and although there is no moon this evening, the night sky looks as amazing as ever as I peered through the open window just to my left, and some five feet above me. I could smell the strong scent of salt sea-air and for me life does not be any better than this.

Monday, 28 March 1983

The warm air temperature of yesterday well and truly deserted us today and instead, we were met with a cold fresh breeze. Thankfully the sun did eventually come out and conditions were perfect for another day's work on the Rubb project. Today it is planned to have seven green PVC bundles airlifted to the top of the frame and secured to the cross sections, which will leave just the front aspect bundle and this will be lifted by the Coles Crane after all the other panels have been lowered, draped, and secured to the frame. Our planning and preparation has paid off because from now on the work should be pretty straight forward, and as long as the wind and rain keep away we do not expect to come up against any serious issues.

Today's morning parade was put to one side to allow 3 Troop to begin its work on the Rubb hangar, while a section of four colleagues reported to the site of a possible second Laundry Block to begin installing wooden foundation shuttering. Meanwhile, the Rubb section of which I am a member began the task of carrying out our final checks on the PVC bundles before being airlifted to the top of the hangar frame, using the Scout helicopter that arrived at Kelly's Garden this morning at around 10.00. Two smaller teams were then formed with the first being responsible for radio communications with the helicopter pilot, while the second would work from inside the safety of the Coles Crane basket and secure, then drape each PVC bundle over the Rubb frame.

The first airlift was planned for 13.30 and just after midday, we downed tools and headed over to the cookhouse for an early lunch. Together with the pilot, we had a briefing on how the drops would be made, the direction in which the helicopter would approach and exit on each airlift, the height at which the aircraft would hover above the team working inside the Coles Crane basket, and the radio communication protocol to be used throughout the manoeuvres.

The Scout helicopter

With lunch over, Team One returned to the Rubb hangar site and secured the first underslung PVC bundle to the undercarriage of the Scout helicopter, under the expert guidance of the pilot and when he was satisfied that the first airlift could begin, he gave a thumbs up. Slowly and cautiously, the first bundle was airlifted to the top of the frame and it was an exciting spectacle to watch as the aircraft climbed to a height of around 70 feet, and then started to lower the bundle down onto the first arch section. The task required clear and concise communication between Team One who were on the ground, Team Two who were inside the Coles Crane basket, and the Scout pilot.

Precise positioning was critical because just a couple of inches out in any direction would result in the bundle either not sitting correctly on the cross section, or not fully covering the arch frame when draped which would leave a gap between adjoining sheets. After the first PVC bundle was secured to the top of arch frame Number Two and the lifting harness was released, the Scout helicopter slowly climbed and banked to the left, so as to avoid creating a downdraft on Team Two.

The helicopter then carefully approached Team One to collect the second PVC bundle and this process was repeated until 18.45, at which time the final bundle was collected by the pilot. For everyone involved, this would prove the most difficult one to lower onto the Rubb hangar frame because it was very close to front aspect. The pilot and the two teams did an incredible job between them, and everyone watched with apprehension and great relief when the last bundle was finally lowered onto the frame at exactly 18.53. This was the best team effort ever, and the whole exercise had proved a total success.

Just before the helicopter left for Port Stanley, we thanked the pilot and waved him off as the aircraft climbed to an altitude of around 100 feet, and then pitched forward and flew off as an incoming RAF Chinook was diverted away from the Rubb hangar site, just in case its downdraft disturbed the PVC bundles. After the Chinook landed and the two turboshaft engines were shut, we walked across to the aircraft and explained the situation. Immediately the pilot acknowledged our reason and to our delight, he described how perfectly lined each PVC bundle looked from the air. It was exactly what we needed to hear. The Chinook delivered several sacks of mail and parcels, and one of our colleagues collected his letters before leaving Kelly's Garden to undertake plumbing work over at Ajax Bay. As he left, we noticed he was packed to the hilt with tools and personal equipment, and so we suspect he would not be returning for at least a couple of days. It was at this point in the day that Kevin told me the good news that he had found a copy of James Herriot's novel 'Vets in Harness' and had left it on my sleeping bag.

By 19.30 all work sites had been prepared for the following day and the names of the Laundry and Rubb teams were announced, printed, and placed on 3 Troop's Notice Board. Kevin and Paul were paired off to form one of the teams that would work inside the Coles Crane basket, and it would be their responsibility to ensure that each bundle was correctly positioned in the first instance before the retaining straps were released, and ensure that the membrane unfolded correctly. Once fully draped over and down the side to the two teams below.

Only then could the PVC sheets be fastened and secured to each arch frame while at the same time, two members from Team One and Team Two would fasten the bottom of the bundle to the supporting legs and attach the tensioning straps to the gabion anchor baskets, that now lined each side of the structure. As soon as one side was completed and secured, the process would then be repeated on the opposite side, and we estimated that each bundle would take approximately two hours to be fully draped, secured, and tensioned.

Everyone hoped for good weather the next day, because the last thing we need is rain and high winds. I suggested to Kevin that he and Paul go up in the Coles Crane basket there and then to make sure they both knew what to expect the following day, and also to check that each bundle was still fully secured to the top of the Rubb arch sections. As Kevin manoeuvred the basket into position some 45 feet above ground, he radioed me to say that he could see out in the distance the requisitioned Townsend Thoresen *MS Baltic Ferry* as it sailed into San Carlos Water.

I last saw this ship in Port Stanley Harbour back in January and on the first day we arrived in the Falkland Islands. With the sea looking calm and without any sign of a cross wind, Kevin and Paul felt confident that tomorrow's weather conditions would allow them to complete their task albeit, they did have slight reservation over low cloud that was approaching from the west.

They quickly carried out their inspection of the first four PVC bundles and to their relief they were all in perfect position. As Kevin lowered the Coles Crane basket to the ground, Paul gazed out once again at the incredible scene that lay below them and took some photographs for my journal. Later in the evening, a few others and I sat in silence inside our portakabin as we wrote letters to family and friends back home, while some read magazines and books, and others cleaned their personal kit. One or two grabbed a quick nap and at 21.00, we all decided to visit the Ant Hill where two of the worst movies ever made were being shown, which were 'Zoltan: Hound of Dracula,' and 'Dolemite.' I returned to my portakabin to read the final pages of Gerald Durrell's delightful novel 'All Creatures Great and Small,' and then I wrote this entry. Tomorrow's morning parade is to be held at 07.00 and so I decided to have an early night and as I lay inside the warmth and comfort of my sleeping bag, I closed my eyes and thought of the incredible scene outside, and how much I truly enjoy being here at Kelly's Garden. Having written up my journal it was soon time for sleep.

PVC bundles on top of the Rubb frame and two sappers at the far end

Tuesday, 29 March 1983

Today's morning parade took place at 07.00 in freezing cold conditions and thankfully it was all over within minutes, and as soon as we were dismissed Kevin, Paul, and I reported to the Rubb hangar along with Team One and Team Two who will both be working on the ground. We examined the tools and equipment before carrying out a final check on the wind and general weather conditions, and noticed that the sky was slowly beginning to cloud over and that an easterly breeze was growing in strength. Although these conditions were not a concern at first, they would nevertheless need to be monitored throughout the day.

The welding team were kept busy with carrying out checks and minor repairs while the rest of 3 Troop were preparing a concrete mix over at the Laundry Block site. Kevin and Paul climbed into the Coles Crane basket and in no time at all, they were level with the top of the first arch where their first task was to wipe dry the tubular alloy frame as best they could. They then radioed a report that the entire structure was soaking wet and quite slippery to the touch, and so with only a small support team available, they had no other option but to return to the safety of the ground.

With that, we returned to our portakabins to stay warm and already some members of the concreting team were sitting inside, and told us that they had decided to stagger their lunch break due to the deteriorating weather conditions. As for dropping the PVC bundles, I agreed with Kevin and Paul that it was a definite 'no-go' and with that I went with one of our corporals to 3 Troop Office to inform our troop commander.

As we arrived at the office, two members of the concreting team were concluding their report when out of the blue, we were all told to carry on with our tasks and that dropping the first PVC bundle was to go ahead, much to our surprise. This was totally unexpected given the poor weather conditions, and the fact that the Rubb frame was now probably more hazardous than ever, however, we both went back to our portakabin where Kevin and Paul were awaiting our return.

As we walked across to the Rubb hangar site, we quickly chatted about the decision to proceed with dropping the first PVC bundle of the day, and it was clear that all three of us were feeling uncomfortable. With the PVC bundles safely secured on top of the arches, Team One and Team Two were waiting for us dressed in their waterproofs and wearing safety belts, white helmets, and gloves. We updated them on our troop commander's decision and slowly they started to climb the Rubb hangar frame, then took up their positions at the point where the supporting legs on either side of the frame were bolted to the arch frame.

Me and Kevin (right) at Georgian Bay, Ontario 1982

With daylight beginning to fade and rain still falling, Kevin and Paul began to lower the first PVC bundle and as they looked down, they could see two members of Team One walking off site. They radioed to ask what was happening, and I explained that they had gone to speak with our troop commander again over safety concerns that everyone shared regarding the poor conditions. Kevin gave me a thumbs-up to acknowledge he had received my message, and also to the members who were positioned at the top of each leg below him, and together he and Paul slowly began to release the retaining straps on both sides of the bundle.

This allowed the PVC sheet to slowly unfold under its own weight, and then slide evenly across the width of the arch frame and it proved a perfect execution. The support teams wasted no time in fastening the sheet to the alloy structure and very soon the first section was fully secured, but right then we sensed something was not right. To everyone's disbelief and horror, the bundle had been folded incorrectly prior to being delivered to Kelly's Garden and as such, the inner surface was facing outwards as it lay over the Rubb hangar frame. Immediately the teams began to untie the sheet, then very carefully and with quite a degree of effort, they all started the difficult task of flipping the membrane over itself as it sat loose on top of the frame, and thankfully the manoeuvre worked and it proved a much easier task than they had anticipated, despite the weight.

After fully reversing the PVC sheet and re-securing it to the frame, Kevin and Paul decided to check all the other bundles and it transpired that they had all been folded correctly. By now, the numbers on the ground had increased because the Laundry Block concreting team had joined us to lend a hand, and with the two tower floodlights switched on, 3 Troop had managed to rectify what could have potentially turned out to be a major problem. It was an excellent team effort and all tools and equipment were cleaned, oiled, checked, and returned to the G1098 Store.

As we returned to our portakabins we were told that the Defence Base had passed the camp commandant's inspection which in all honestly, we had totally forgotten given the drama we encountered earlier with the PVC bundle. I wrote letters to my parents and friends back home, and then chatted for a while with colleagues and to help pass away the time, we shared music cassettes until 22.00. Some of us ventured across to the Ant Hill to watch the Australian movie 'Mad Max' but after only half an hour, three of us returned to the warmth and comfort of our portakabin to get an early night's sleep.

To my delight, someone had kindly left a copy of the Sunday Times on my sleeping bag and inside was a schedule of live classical concerts being performed at the London Barbican in August, so somebody in the team knew just how much I want to go to a concert before the end of the year. One particular concert includes my favourite piece of classical music by Edward Grieg which is his piano concerto in 'A' minor Op 16. I simply must try and get a ticket because it begins with the most wonderful and exciting piece of piano playing I have ever heard, and at the end is a haunting and evocative cadenza and each time I hear this concerto I am filled with an emotion I cannot begin to describe. For me, it is quite simply a very beautiful piece of classical music and so to hear it performed live by a full symphony orchestra, would be a dream come true.

Just before we turned out the lights in the portakabin, we were informed that our colleague who is still in Port Stanley and suffering a bad ear infection will not be returning to Kelly's Garden this week. Also, there was an update on 3 Troop's possible trek back to Port Stanley when our time here comes to an end, and it was agreed that this would be a great challenge. For me personally, it would also be an excellent test for my left knee which was badly injured during a rugby match in Germany

At some point I know I will require surgery because there is a tear to the medial meniscus but for now, it seems to be holding its own and thankfully without pain of any kind. I wrote up my journal and just before I climbed inside my sleeping bag, I looked out at the dark night sky outside as the air temperature dropped further. The wind was again blowing but not as hard as it had been during the day, and the

Defence Base was in darkness as there were no lights working anywhere from what I could see. It crossed my mind to take a quick stroll down to Bonners Bay, but I decided against that idea as it would not be fair to my colleagues to switch the light on and off, and then open and close the door while the wind was blowing.

Wednesday, 30 March 1983

With a cold wind gusting through Kelly's Garden, and in the knowledge that our time here is quickly coming to an end, I am of the persuasion that our troop sergeant has finally picked up on the increasing sense of melancholy throughout 3 Troop. I say this because he has tactfully eased off somewhat on the pressure he normally puts us under when wanting tasks completed on time, and his patience is appreciated. I suspect he too has some reservations over our pending return to Port Stanley because today, he mentioned during the morning parade that he will be flying there later to visit the work sites that have been assigned to 3 Troop.

After the parade, some of my colleagues began the task of stripping out random sections of damaged PSP flooring, while over at the Laundry Block others were making excellent progress on finishing the last section of the concrete foundation shuttering. Just then and without warning, the thick cloud started to break and we all felt the warmth of the sun once again. Around 11.30 we were told that our surveyor would be leaving Kelly's Garden on Friday and on promotion to Lance Corporal. We were all thrilled for him but sadly we will be saying farewell to a colleague who has been a true team-player, and one of the nicest persons you could ever hope to meet. He has been attached to 3 Troop since we first arrived in the Falklands and gelled with us all from the very beginning. He will be missed.

There was no mail today so we hope our staff sergeant will bring this with him when he returns from his visit to Port Stanley. During the course of the morning and whilst working on covering the Rubb hangar frame, we saw the last of our Ghurkha colleagues board a RAF Chinook helicopter which will take them back to Port Stanley, before they return to their parent unit at Aldershot in Hampshire. Our numbers are slowly starting to dwindle, and with the departure of the Gurkha Rifles came the arrival of a company from the Irish Rangers who recently deployed from the United Kingdom.

Due to the volume of work we still have to complete before our time here comes to an end, the planned three-day trek to Port Stanley has been cancelled and the news came as no surprise as it was generally considered the only sensible thing to do. This afternoon saw a continuation of stripping out damaged PSP panels while over at the G1098 Store, a colleague and I began the work of preparing the engineering equipment ready for handing over to our relief squadron. This job did not take long to complete and around 18.50, I walked across to the cookhouse for dinner after which I went for a stroll around the eastern edge of Bonners Bay. Draping the last of the PVC bundles over the Rubb frame has been delayed until we receive a delivery of additional tensioning strops however, this should not impact too much on the project's completion date.

After writing up my journal, I wrote a letter to my parents to inform them that I will be returning to Port Stanley in the coming days, and after that I headed across to the Ablution Block for a hot shower before getting myself ready for an early night's sleep. I read 'All Creatures Great and Small' and cannot wait to watch the television series when I get home because the story is quite simply wonderful, and I am confident it will be a real pleasure to watch as Herriot's stories are so appealing.

With the portakabin lights switched off, the room fell into darkness and the temptation to gaze once again at the moon and stars was too powerful for me to disregard, and so I stepped out into the quiet of the night. I walked towards the edge of Kelly's Garden and looked to outline of the Verde Hills and stared at their beauty and magnificence. I am so happy to be here and cannot describe just how much this location means to me. There is something mystical and mesmerising when I look up at the night sky because there is no light pollution here of any kind, and I always feel blessed that I have been given the opportunity to see and know this place for myself.

For me, being here and helping in some small way to restore the security and infrastructure of these islands, has been a total joy and privilege. Back inside my portakabin I quickly wrote up this entry and I hope that I am posted here again however, I do not put too much hope on that. I am beginning to sense that I may be posted back to Munsterlager after my post-tour leave, because I have heard from former armoured engineering colleagues that my old regiment is heavily undermanned and as such, REMRO are trawling for trained armoured engineers to be posted back to strengthen numbers.

Thursday, 31 March 1983

For the first time in almost three months, I left Kelly's Garden and flew the six miles north to Port San Carlos and even though its name gives the impression of being a large community and shipping port, nothing could be further from the truth. It is roughly twice the size of San Carlos Settlement and has an old weathered shipping pier, a number of buildings and wooden houses, and a small store which is located on the edge of what looked like a small village green. I am told that few settlers and their families live there and yet there was something quite unique about Port San Carlos, and it grabbed my fascination from the first moment I set foot there.

The settlement's name originates from the shipping vessel *'San Carlos'* which sailed to East Falkland Island in 1768. I am also told that some of the settlers witnessed for themselves the first landing of British troops in 1982. The aircraft in which I flew to Port San Carlos today was the same RAF Chinook that first landed there last year and is codenamed *'November,'* but even more remarkable is the fact that it was the only Chinook to survive the sinking of the British Merchant container ship *'SS Atlantic Conveyor,'* whilst on tow on 28 May 1982. The only other helicopter to survive was a Westland Wessex.

As I roamed around Port San Carlos, the store coincidentally opened for business and so I went inside and what intrigued me was its rudimentary layout, and the limited stock that was on the shelves. At the end of a small counter was a cash till, and standing next to it was a very friendly and chatty lady by the name of Helen who told me that she was the owner. During my time inside the shop, several customers purchase goods and left without saying a single word which for me was somewhat surreal, yet I was totally absorbed by their reclusive attitude.

They made me think that quite possibly they did not take easily to strangers and who could blame them, after the events of 1982? Nevertheless I enjoyed my conversation with Helen and the one scruffy young child who seemed completely bowled over by my presence, because I was a British soldier and all on my own. The child talked continuously right up until the time she left.

I said goodbye to Helen and walked across to a small deserted area where I came across several weathered army tents inside which were folded camp beds, and items of deserted military equipment that must have been there ever since the invasion. This was the main purpose of my visit because when military stores are either lost or in short supply, it is not uncommon for soldiers to search for 'buckshees' which is the military term for free items that have been discarded, such as rations, clothing, and spare parts.

My visit came about after I had been informed by a RAF sergeant loadmaster back in Kelly's Garden that Port San Carlos was well worth visiting, because there were small amounts of abandoned military equipment from the days of the war. I accepted his invitation to fly across on the next available helicopter and the flight took approximately 15 minutes and en route, we flew over the requisitioned Townsend Thoresen ship *'Baltic Ferry'* which was quite an experience.

The RAF loadmaster said his name was 'Baxo' and as I disembarked the Chinook, we arranged a return flight back to Kelly's Garden in exactly one hour's time. This would give me the opportunity to salvage as much equipment as I could carry however, after 20 minutes all I had managed to find were four shovels and at 18.40 precisely, the RAF Chinook returned to pick me up. I was flown back to Kelly's Garden and after securing the shovels inside the G1098 Store, I went across to the cookhouse for a hot dinner with colleagues who informed me that they had spent most of the day on stripping out and replacing PSP flooring panels. I told them about my trip to Port San Carlos and how small yet fascinating the settlement was, and also how private the settlers were.

I was very grateful to the RAF ChinDet and in particular to Baxo, for getting me across to Port San Carlos and returning me safely. Unfortunately, I never got to see him again to say how much I appreciated his kindness. 3 Troop's departure from Kelly's Garden is now another day closer and over dinner at the cookhouse, we were informed that our numbers would start reducing over the course of the following seven days, and that we would eventually be down to just three.

Most of the troop would be airlifted to Port Stanley on 18 April but right then, I was offered the one opportunity that I had been hoping for ever since first arriving here, and that was to be the last member of 3 Troop to leave Kelly's Garden. How could I refuse? This meant that I would be able to fulfil my wish of being allowed to say my final goodbye to Kelly's Garden alone, and to pay my respect to those who laid to rest in Blue Beach Military Cemetery one last time, and in complete privacy. It also meant I could trek to the ridge on the Verde Hills to shed a farewell tear, and all of these special moments will forever be so very precious to me, and for that alone I am already eternally grateful.

Afternote

Although I enlisted into the Corps of Royal Engineers in July 1977, I have always had a natural aptitude and flair for accounts and administration management, and this was frequently observed by senior officers. I believe I inherited these skills from my mother Enid who herself was incredibly gifted in accounts and served as a pay sergeant during her time with the ATS during World War Two, and then as an accounts manager in her civilian career in Llanelli.

I particularly enjoyed designing, creating, and setting up new office systems, writing directives, instructions, and policies, leading administrative projects and clerical teams, auditing, and heading inspection teams. While serving with Headquarters Squadron at 32 Armoured Engineer Regiment in Munsterlager in 1984, these abilities were recognised by the Adjutant, Regimental Paymaster, Staff Assistant and also my Officer Commanding, and during an annual appraisal interview it was invited to consider changing my career path. I was told I had the potential to quickly progress in GI matters, and that I would secure far greater career opportunities and advanced promotion if I became a Military Clerk RE.

After looking into the advantages of taking up this new career, I agreed and after qualifying as a Clerk RE Class 3, I was transferred across to the Royal Engineer Clerical Stream and within months, I was making my mark and gained promotion to corporal. Within one year I was given my first appointment as a Chief Clerk albeit it was of a Headquarters Squadron, and I thrived on the new challenges this role presented. Attending as many clerical and specialist courses as I could, I went on to gain as much experience as I could and over a short period of time, I could see that my development as a military clerk was progressing at an unprecedented pace and with it, I was being selected for key roles and appointments that exceeded my own expectations. More crucially, my annual appraisal reports and gradings improved considerably and I was regularly gaining the highest grading of Outstanding.

On 6 April 1992 and following a British Military Defence Review, a new branch was formed in the British Army and it was called the Adjutant General's Corps (AGC), and this was created through the merging of the following:

- Army Legal Corps.
- All military clerks.
- Military Provost Staff Corps.
- Royal Army Educational Corps.
- Royal Army Pay Corps.
- Royal Military Police.
- Women's Royal Army Corps.

In 1993, all Royal Engineer clerks and military clerks from across the rest of the British Army were transferred 'en masse' to this newly formed Adjutant General's Corps and at first, and quite understandably, loyalty to parent corps and regiments remained strong. Literally overnight, everyone was re-branded and belonged to a new corps that had its own identity, uniform, cap badge, and motto. Furthermore, we were now administered and managed by a completely new Manning and Records Office manned by officers and civil servants we did not know.

In short, I and my fellow sapper military clerks were no longer Royal Engineers which hurt quite a lot, because we knew absolutely nothing about the AGC and we were not alone. Belonging to the Royal Engineers had always been a personal choice and an honour, yet for me this had been taken away without any of my colleagues having any say in the matter, and this understandably resulted in many not feeling any sense of loyalty or belonging to the new corps. This was not a situation of our making and many were extremely unhappy at the time, because if memory serves me right, there was no formal parade or ceremony of any kind to mark this significant change in career circumstances, and there were no meetings in which we were introduced to our new corps.

There was one consolation however. As former Royal Engineer Chief Clerks, we visited the Royal Engineers Manning and Records Office at Kentigern House in Glasgow on numerous occasions, either to attend the annual Chief Clerks' Conference or on regimental business and as such, we all knew each other quite well and also the officers and civil servants who worked at Kentigern House. I spoke with them daily over the phone on matters such as manning requirements, postings, promotions, vetting, careers courses, and so much more that over time excellent working relationships were established. Indeed, we were on first name terms with many of the civil servants.

I could phone REMRO at any time and so when the mass transfer across to the AGC was implemented, this naturally generated an incredible sense of empathy and understanding on the part of the REMRO officers and civil servants who knew how we were feeling at that time. The support they gave to each and every one of us was *as remarkable as it was unprecedented, and wherever and whenever possible, they liaised closely with the AGC (SPS) MRO in an attempt to have former Royal Engineer military clerks continue to serve with sapper units worldwide.*

Between 1993 and 2000, only once was I posted to a non-sapper unit and for that alone I will forever be thankful to both MROs. Furthermore, by being allowed to serve with Royal Engineer units I could continue to wear my Royal Engineer Mess Dress uniform at formal functions, which in itself was incredibly important to me.

There was one officer in particular to whom I will forever be grateful, and that was my Commanding Officer at 36 Engineer Regiment in Maidstone in 1995. I thoroughly enjoyed working and serving as his Regimental Administrative Office Warrant Officer and on his promotion to Colonel just a few years later, he was appointed Commander Royal Engineers (CRE) 3 (United Kingdom) Division.

On taking up his new post at Bulford in Wiltshire, he kindly wrote to the Divisional Commander AGC SPS to request that I be appointed his Warrant Officer Staff Assistant and to my absolute delight, the request was approved.

Chapter Twenty-One
Goodbye Kelly's Garden

Foreword

With just 17 days remaining before 3 Troop was due to leave Kelly's Garden and return to Port Stanley where we would rejoin our parent 52 Field (Construction) Squadron, I started to notice a change in some of my colleagues and realised that both they and I were possibly going through a grieving process. It was obvious we were slowly coming to terms with our inevitable departure and so in some kind of way, I took this as small consolation that I was not alone in not wanting to return to a garrison environment. A huge part of me could not wait to see my friends and parents again and visit Morocco, a country I had read so much about since childhood and always wanted to trek part of the northern region of the Atlas Mountains.

Looking back 40 years later, I now appreciate that this was a relatively short yet somewhat unsettled time in my army career but I had dealt with it as best I could. Afterall, five months before deploying to the Falklands I had spent four incredible months in Canada with my colleagues, and we had shared many wonderful moments and experiences together at CFB Meaford, Toronto, the Algonquin Provincial Park, and Owen Sound.

Canada and the Falkland Islands by their very nature are worlds apart, yet this was one reason behind me wanting to join the British Army in the first instance. I was seeking excitement and adventure in my life, to travel and see the world from different perspectives and observe cultural diversity, to meet and integrate with people, and visit places of historical importance and interest.

Variety is the spice of life and I needed to change the manner in which I dealt with moving from one place to another, to learn how to let go and not become too attached to just one location, and I soon felt the better for it. My passion for Bonners Bay, Kelly's Garden, San Carlos Settlement, and the Verde Hills still runs through my veins and always will and I now concede that just maybe, I was being a little too naive by wanting to stay there forever, but that is how I genuinely felt in April 1983. When I look back, I think the best thing that could have happened would have been to be immediately posted back to the Falklands on a second tour, if only to get it out of my system but it never happened. Had I served another six months in or near to Port Stanley, then I genuinely believe that things would have turned out very different and again, this is why I advocate that things happen for a reason.

During the early stages of writing my memoir, I was reflecting on my situation in April 1983 and suddenly realised why I had felt so passionate about not wanting to leave Kelly's Garden. It all made perfect sense because I would have probably felt the same no matter where I was serving at that time, as long as I was as far away as possible from the chaos and mayhem of modern-day life.

Both CFB Meaford and Kelly's Garden were two isolated and secluded military establishments that had stunning backdrops, such as Lake Huron and San Carlos Water, no large communities but extensive wide-open space all around, and it was this that left its mark on me. No longer did I like the hustle and bustle of modern life or want to live in the world we call the 'rat race' but instead, I sought the peace and quiet of a remote and secluded location, and still I feel the same as I did in 1983.

Kelly's Garden felt safe and every day had a sense of calm about it instead of chaos, and nothing ever seemed to bother me or my colleagues. To this day, I believe this was down to the fact that we had become indifferent to materialism, keeping up with others when it came to worldly possessions, and being away from the likes of the media. Instead, enjoying our friendship with each other quickly became our main priority because it made us feel happy and very positive about life.

Having no streetlights, loud noise, heavy traffic, or air pollution had its benefits because each day you would wake up to the beautiful aroma of fresh sea-air, the majesty of the Verde Hills, and the sight of tiny red and white houses in San Carlos Settlement just across the bay. There was not a single tree to be seen anywhere, or indeed a tarmac track or any road signs yet all of this made life so very pleasant and enjoyable.

And it was while at Kelly's Garden that I discovered new values and principles by which I wanted to live the rest of my life. I wanted to broaden my knowledge on so many fascinating subjects including history, space, travel and ancient cultures, and to understand the true purpose of life so that hopefully one day, I could become a more complete individual. To that end I embraced three simple rules and made myself a promise to live by these as best I could, and they are:

Things happen for a reason: *Avoid regrets and always look forward.*
Never give to receive: *Give from your heart and not your needs.*
Accept who you are: *Self-belief trumps self-doubt every time.*

Friday, 1 April 1983

Today is April Fools and pranks are traditionally played out on folk back home and in many countries across Europe, but there is no time for tomfoolery of any kind here at Kelly's Garden, and it is just as well because it was my turn to have the morning off. Waking up around 08.30, instead of following my usual early morning routine of visiting the Laundry Building or going for a walk down to Bonners Bay, I had a good stretch and went back to sleep for an extra hour. When I finally got out of my sleeping bag, it was for a quick shower and shave before reading more of 'All Creatures Great and Small' but within minutes of opening the book, I found myself back inside my sleeping bag ready for another sleep.

After a light lunch over at the cookhouse with several of my colleagues, I reported to the Rubb hangar site and was soon applying mastic sealant to the Rubb supporting-leg anchor bases as this would allow for a small margin of expansion or contraction in the joints, as and when air temperatures changed. At precisely 14.35, another Air Strike Alarm was sounded by a Royal Artillery Rapier missile team located some 700 metres south of Kelly's Garden and with it, a hasty and well organised procedure was followed as troops grabbed personal webbing and camouflaged combat helmets.

On reporting to our designated rendezvous points, we waited and went through the drills we had carried out on previous occasions and again, not a single Argentine aircraft was sighted and several minutes later, we received the instruction to 'stand down'. With another false alarm out of the way, 3 Troop went back to the Rubb site and carried on with its work while RAF helicopter activity resumed and others went about their daily tasks.

With something to talk about later today, we all headed across to the Ant Hill at around 16.00 for a tea break, after which Paul helped me apply the remaining tubes of mastic sealant to the Rubb anchor bases. We finished around 18.50 and with the both of us smelling strongly of resin, we headed across to the G1098 Store and returned our tools and equipment. Between the two of us, we had done a fine job and today was extremely productive for 3 Troop as a whole, because most of the smaller remaining tasks have now been completed including a clearance of the Rubb hangar site itself, and landscaping over at the southern edge of the Defence Base.

As I secured the G1098 Store, I looked out towards Ajax Bay to my left and glimpsed the start of another outstanding sunset low in the western sky. Quite unexpectedly, our colleague who had suffered with an ear infection returned from Port Stanley at around 19.05, and thankfully he was much improved and brought with him a large sack of overdue mail amongst which, was a letter from my parents.

Over at the Ant Hill some watched David Bowie's video 'The Man who fell from Earth'. I am a fan of Bowie's creative work but sadly, I found this film to be a little too bizarre to appreciate what he was trying to portray and a few of my colleagues described it as confusing and odd. Tiredness was now taking its toll on my body and as I crept inside my sleeping bag, I looked out of the portakabin window and up towards the night sky. I quickly wrote this entry in my journal and wondered if Bob has replied to my letter. I do hope he has as it would be good to catch up with him again.

Saturday, 2 April 1983

3 Troop finally said goodbye to our surveyor who should have returned to Port Stanley two days ago, but he is happy because he is being promoted to Lance Corporal. After he flew out, we continued with our work of covering the Rubb frame and eventually the next PVC sheet was being carefully released and draped into its correct position by Kevin and Paul, who were again working from inside the Coles Crane basket. In no time the two ground teams below were busy fastening the sheet to the supporting legs and it was hanging perfectly, and adjacent to the first sheet.

We all felt relieved that the final phase of the project was now well and truly underway and for some reason, this particular sheet genuinely made the entire structure look even bigger. This was a sight for sore eyes and with the weather on the turn yet again, and after a short struggle with a rising wind, the PVC sheet was finally tensioned as low dark clouds appeared on the horizon. As they slowly approached Kelly's Garden I watched the dramatic sight of a RAF Chinook slowly emerge from a thick dark cloud to the south, with its powerful landing lights shining directly down onto an area of land at the southern edge of the Defence Base. I could not resist taking a photograph for my journal because this really was exceptional flying by the pilot, and made such a great picture.

The approaching Chinook

Along with the arrival of mail came our Royal Army Pay Corps sergeant who cashed cheques and resolved pay queries inside the Ant Hill. Over at the second Laundry Block, some of my colleagues cleaned their concrete mixers while at the Rubb hangar site, a four-man section was busy filling the rear left-hand corner gabion basket with heavy rocks using the Muir-Hill Dumper Truck.

The first PVC bundle that had been draped required a minor repair however, this took just a few minutes to complete and the task was finished by 19.00, but by now the entire team was beginning to feel the cold and everyone was extremely hungry and tired. When I returned to the portakabin, some were frantically drying themselves and getting changed into warm clothing and after writing up my journal, I decided to retire for the night. I do not know why but many found it impossible to sleep this evening. For me, my mind was still filled with the anticipation of visiting Morocco and although I only have a few more months to wait, the experience feels like a light year away.

Sunday, 3 April 1983

By 09.00 on this sunny April morning, 3 Troop had managed to drape the next green PVC sheet over the Rubb hangar frame but typical of Sod's law, what should have been a straight forward task turned into one almighty challenge when the wind yet again suddenly picked up, and the weather turned blustery. Eventually, and only through dogged determination and a certain amount of good fortune, Kevin and Paul managed to tension and secure the heavy membrane to the Rubb hangar frame.

A number of comments and concerns were made with regards to the deteriorating weather and dangers of working at height, and having climbed every inch of the giant 45-foot-high frame, some now considered it to be too risky even though it had become second nature. Since the project first started, we have literally spent many hours defying cold temperatures and rain, but when the wind blows, it becomes far more precarious yet nobody complains. That said, today the frame became exceptionally slippery with every PVC sheet we draped, and so we waited for our troop commander's decision whether or not to continue with the task. Our concern quite understandably, was the decreasing amount of Rubb panels that the teams could safely harness themselves to, while working at height and standing on the frame itself. This concern was genuine and we felt it needed to be addressed.

Talk of an early finish was mentioned, but this was quickly put to bed when an unexpected mishap occurred while working with the next PVC bundle. As the sheet was slowly draped, the wet surface of the panels caused the bundle to partially drop down between two arch frames and it hung some 30 feet in the air. This was not a total disaster by any stretch of the imagination however, it needed to be rectified before any long-term damage was done to the membrane but because we could not afford to waste any more, we allowed it to drop safely to the ground. All blame was down to the weather and general working conditions.

Without allowing the incident to deter the teams, the PVC sheet was checked for damage, re-bundled, lifted back onto the frame, and through a lot of hard effort it was eventually re-draped over the arch. Kevin and Paul managed to secure the sheet as Team One and Team Two fastened the bottom to the supporting legs, and finally with a huge sense of relief, it was fully tensioned and secured to the gabion baskets on both sides of the hangar. By now the weather had deteriorated even further but out of the blue, word was received that 3 Troop's working days would finish no earlier than 21.00 as opposed to 19.30, and worse still all lay-ins were immediately cancelled. These had no negative impact whatsoever on troop morale and indeed, I believe it strengthened our sense of team spirit even further, and I felt extremely proud to be part of such a remarkable group who took such decisions on the chin.

It has been suggested by others on the Defence Base that living conditions have started to decline, such as the standard of catering yet in all fairness to the chefs, troops were now arriving and leaving Kelly's Garden nearly every day and in increasing numbers, so this may very well be part of the reason. 3 Troop carried on regardless, and our main concerns right now were the deteriorating weather and safety implications of working at height in high winds and rain, and the fact that there were still a number of PVC sheets that need to be draped and secured to the frame, in order to complete this phase of the project.

We had no option today but to finish at 17.15 due to the weather and so we waited inside our portakabins until it was time to go for dinner, which was now over two hours away. Several of my colleagues chatted amongst themselves while others read books and wrote letters to families and folk back home. Two of the topics discussed were our pending return to Port Stanley and the various tasks we could expect to be assigned, because there are quite a number of engineering projects underway both on and off the runway at Port Stanley Airfield. Our conversation continued all through dinner and around 22.30, I went across to the Ablutions for a piping-hot shower and then wrote up my journal but by 23.20, I was ready for sleep while outside the rain was pouring down as a strong easterly wind howled its way through Kelly's Garden.

The partially covered Rubb

Monday, 4 April 1983

Everyone was woken by a powerful wind slamming against the side of our portakabin and again, we knew that the task of covering the Rubb hangar frame was either going to be postponed, or made painfully slow if it was allowed to go ahead because the conditions outside were now seriously unsafe. This gave 3 Troop the opportunity to quickly re-inspect the other completed work sites and check the PSP matting that had been laid between the Rubb hangar and three helipads, and so with the help of others who should have been working on other projects, we completed the inspection inside two hours.

Usually low morale and despondency can often be recovered through various characters coming to the front and making others laugh, but today this was not going to happen because everyone was too focussed on braving the persistent high wind while working in cold damp conditions. We had started our working day just before 07.00 and by midday, everyone was chilled to the bone and soaked to the skin, and understandably feeling a little frustrated.

Today was certainly proving to be the most testing of days we have known since first arriving at Kelly's Garden, and it was most definitely not fun for any of us. While taking a well-earned tea break over at the cookhouse, I was asked if I would take part in the forthcoming Squadron March and Shoot Competition that was being organised back in Port Stanley, and without hesitation I agreed. There is nothing I enjoy more than a good challenge and with that, several others put their names forward as well.

Thankfully by mid-afternoon we experienced another complete change in the weather, and this meant that the drop of the next PVC bundle over the Rubb arches could go ahead, and in no time all teams were back on site and in position. The first drop was planned for 15.25. Kevin and Paul needed to be in the Coles Crane basket by no later than 15.15 to allow for sufficient time to carry out a final check of the PVC bundle. As they started to loosen the retaining straps, quite frustratingly the weather looked as if it was going to take yet another turn for the worse, but Paul radioed to the teams below to say that he and Kevin were going ahead and within a matter of minutes, the large green PVC sheet was untied and slowly draped over the arch frame and supporting legs. It was another perfect execution and inside one hour, the sheet was fully secured and fastened to the alloy frame, then tensioned and anchored to the next pair of steel gabion baskets.

After this had been completed, some colleagues on the ground were justifiably voicing concern over the troop's safety and just as they did, the heavens literally opened and everyone on the Rubb site was caught in a severe hail storm. Those who were harnessed to the frame had no option but to ride it out as best they could, while Kevin and Paul crouched down inside the Coles Crane basket as much as they could until the storm finally passed, which was some several minutes later. It was agreed that completing just one PVC drop today was better than nothing, and what lifted spirits was the knowledge that we now only had four more PVC bundles remaining.

During the course of this evening, members of the RAF ChinDet were invited to join us in the Ant Hill to watch the movie 'Blue Max.' After the film finished, 11 members of 7 Field Squadron Royal Engineers arrived from Port Stanley and were issued camp beds by Frazer, while I and others headed back to our portakabin. I read the remainder of James Herriot's novel 'All Creatures Great and Small' and once again, I found myself fully immersed in the story which is quite simply a delight to read. We are to start work tomorrow at 07.00, and so I decided on an early night but first, I needed to quickly write up my journal and place it back inside my suitcase which is under my bunk bed.

Tuesday, 5 April 1983

Today started with Paul and Gareth helping me prepare the G1098 Store ahead of its forthcoming airlift back to Port Stanley, and the task took no more than two hours to complete, but it was yet another sure sign that our departure from Kelly's Garden is now fast approaching. I really will miss this location and in particular, the panoramic views and sense of solitude. Throughout the morning and early afternoon the high wind and dark clouds continued to plague 3 Troop, plus everyone else on the Defence Base.

Our main challenge now is the hanging around we have to endure while we wait to drop the rest of the PVC bundles, and to nobody's surprise the weather conditions yet again had the better of us. We sat in the freezing cold chatting away as the minutes slowly ticked by and over lunch in the cookhouse, we received word to stand down immediately. After finishing our food we returned to the portakabin to wait until the weather improved, no matter what time of day that would be and so in essence, the next PVC bundle was going to be dropped today, regardless. With that the two lighting towers were towed back into their position by the Coles Crane, just in case the work went into the late hours of the night, or possibly the early hours of tomorrow.

The welding team inspected more steel gabion baskets while some minor landscaping continued late into the afternoon, and another section carried out a final clearing up on each of the completed work sites, before signing these over to the RAF ChinDet. Meanwhile, the remainder of 3 Troop waited for the weather to improve. Some slept while others wrote letters to their friends and families back home, and a few watched 'The Secret Policeman's Other Ball' which is the fourth benefit concert held to raise funds for Amnesty International. British stars from the world of comedy such as Monty Python, Victoria Wood, Rowan Atkinson, Jasper Carrot, Marty Feldman, and Tim Brooke-Taylor each performed sketches to a live audience, and musicians including Sting, Eric Clapton, Pete Townsend, and Donovan sang some of their greatest songs.

At 20.15, approval was finally given for us to proceed with the next PVC drop and with that, all three teams quickly got changed into our cold weather clothing and made our way over to the Rubb site, which by now was quite dark. As the two lighting towers were switched on, the hangar frame instantly transformed into a spellbinding and ghostly looking structure that reached up to the night sky above, and again it reminded me of the spectacular photograph of Shackleton's ill-fated ship *Endurance*, as she sat ice-locked in the Weddell Sea in 1915.

With no wind or rain, the weather conditions were just perfect as Kevin and Paul reached the top of the arch frame in the Coles Crane basket, and over the next two hours they successfully dropped two more PVC bundles, and both were tensioned and secured to the frame without issue. These took far longer to drape because the work was now being carried out at night. At around 23.00 it was suggested to our troop commander that we go ahead and drop the third PVC bundle however, after some discussion common sense prevailed and it was decided to call it a day.

Checking the secured Rubb PVC coverings

With six PVC sheets now draped and fully secured to the Rubb frame, we only have two more sheets and the front section remaining, so 3 Troop was more than satisfied with what we had achieved this evening. Instead of going for a shower, everyone decided to play a quick game of football under the partly covered flood-lit Rubb hangar. Two teams of tired and dirty Royal Engineers played a game of football in one of the most bizarre environments ever, and it proved great fun and a much-needed release of pent-up frustration and relief, and most definitely the best way to end this day.

After almost completely tiring ourselves out, some of my colleagues headed to the Ant Hill which had been opened especially for them, and there they enjoyed a free can of McEwan's Export beer. Meanwhile, I and a few others decided to give the bar a miss and instead we went to the Ablution Block for a steaming-hot shower and by 01.30, our portakabin was silent except for a quiet card school that was taking place at the far end. The 22.30 house-rule for once was allowed to be broken and it was well deserved. I wrote up this entry while listening to the rock album 'Business as Usual' written and performed by the Australian band Men at Work. I suddenly felt ready for sleep while outside in the cold night, our welding team to their credit were still hard at work making minor repairs over at the floodlit Rubb site. Just then and without exaggeration, the rain began to fall heavily down on Kelly's Garden.

Wednesday, 6 April 1983

Waking up at 06.45 not a single person inside my portakabin was looking forward to today's work, especially after yesterday's extremely long shift. If we were civilians then we would be earning a small fortune through overtime, danger money, and other allowances. After a quick wash over at the Ablution Block, I hurriedly got changed into my works dress and quickly polished my boots, then reported for morning parade. 3 Troop was promised an early finish if we could repeat what we had achieved yesterday. This was good news given the recent decision to not finish work before 21.30.

Although this sounded fair and was warmly welcomed, unfortunately things did not exactly work out that way. Four of my colleagues checked the tension strops and ties that were attached to the steel gabion baskets last night, and also the PVC sheets that had been draped, while I and others began the work of battening down the bottom sections of the PVC to the anchor points along the foundation runs. Progress was slow but by lunchtime we had completed the work and to a very high standard, but just then we were told we were to go for another PVC drop without delay.

We all got into our respective teams and received a briefing from our troop commander, during which we were informed that according to the RAF here at Kelly's Garden, more bad weather was heading our way. We plodded on regardless and eventually Kevin and Paul went up in the Coles Crane basket, and started to lower the penultimate arch frame PVC bundle to the team below. They secured the membrane to the Rubb hangar frame before fully tensioning the strops, which were attached to their anchor points and everything went according to plan. It was another excellent effort by everyone concerned.

One of our colleagues however was put on immediate bed rest after suffering what could have been a very nasty injury to his foot, after a sharp ragged length of steel broke loose from one of the gabion baskets, and pierced his boot. As a result, he was limping badly at first and clearly in pain and discomfort. The accident brought his time here at Kelly's Garden to a premature end and the RAF will medevac him to Port Stanley first thing tomorrow. Meanwhile, we were informed that the majority of 3 Troop will return to Port Stanley over the next few days, and that I am to remain at the Defence Base as the Rear Party representative. I will then return to Port Stanley on 13 April.

As the weather deteriorated, we began the work of strengthening each gabion basket with additional steel stapling, and this involved turning these heavy metal cages through 180° using the heavy plant machinery we have, before reshuffling them back into their original position. The Muir-Hill did its work well and proved a life-saver. A small works party was assigned to Blue Beach Military Cemetery to quickly re-coat the white crosses that mark all 14 graves, and also the wooden perimeter fence and gate. This is being done in preparation for the forthcoming visit by wives and families of those who are laid to rest, and I feel for them all because this will be their first opportunity to visit their loved ones who they never expected to lose in battle. How does anyone come to terms with such loss?

As the rain started to fall on Kelly's Garden at around 18.30, we finished for the day because word was received that the RAF helicopter that was assigned to airlift the final PVC bundle was no longer available. The team felt relief that we would not be required to work through another night, and so there was nothing for it but to go for dinner and then enjoy a hot shower. Back inside the portakabin, my haircut was also postponed because the hair dressing equipment had given up the ghost. Instead, I joined my colleagues over at the Ant Hill and watched the amazing 1979 film 'Quadrophenia', which is based on the rock band The Who's incredible opera of the same name.

After the movie finished, we walked back to our portakabin and I could see that the Rubb frame was again illuminated by the lighting towers, so we walked across to take a closer look. For several minutes we stood transfixed to one of the most incredible sights ever. It is one I will never forget for as long as I live.

Orders have now been received that confirm and outline our scheduled return to Port Stanley and the preparations will commence immediately. The one thing we know for sure is that we will be working non-stop from now on, and this will continue right up until the moment 3 Troop flies out of Kelly's Garden. After reading more of James Herriot's enchanting novel 'It Should Never Happen to a Vet,' I wrote up my journal and then climbed inside my sleeping bag, while outside the rain continued to fall and I felt so tired.

Thursday and Friday, 7 and 8 April 1983

During the course of these two days, 3 Troop's work at Kelly's Garden was unrelenting and Friday was without doubt the more difficult of the two, because we started work at 06.30 and continued right through until 04.00 the following morning. 3 Troop's strength has been reduced by 10 and they are now all back in Port Stanley, supporting fellow Royal Engineers in the quarry where large rocks are being crushed for use in repairing the war damaged runway at Port Stanley Airport.

The Rubb project was fully completed and we were presented to a visiting senior officer who showed a lot of interest in how the structure had been assembled and erected, and how the PVC bundles were draped over the frame. I bumped into an old friend today by the name of Billy who served with me out in Canada, and he will now occupy Frazer's old bunk above mine. He has not changed one bit since I saw him last year, and it was wonderful catching up with him.

Saturday, 9 April 1983

Later today we will get to see some very well-known faces from the world of television and show business, because there is yet another Combined Services Entertainment show visiting the Falklands Islands, and they are coming to Kelly's Garden. I was working with a colleague near the Rubb site at around 11.00 when a RAF Sea King helicopter landed close to our location, and after the rotor blades stopped and the door opened by the loadmaster, out stepped British comedian Ken Goodwin and the comedienne Faith Brown. They were followed by Bob Carolgees of 'Spit the Dog' fame and a girl duo called Lips.

We casually waved to them and very excitedly they waved back. Meanwhile, out in Bonners Bay the *Cunard Countess* was anchored and on board were members of the British media, civic dignitaries, politicians, senior military officers, and the wives and families of some of those who were tragically killed during the Falklands War. *Cunard Countess* looked splendid and seeing her again brought back happy memories of my time on board her, while sailing south from Ascension Island. Over lunch, I sat with colleagues on the table immediately next to our celebrity performers and we could see by their faces that they were somewhat surprised by the basic facilities we have here. The Irish Rangers have a rock band and they have been invited to perform some cover songs during the concert.

It was around 19.00 when Ken Goodwin took to the stage, and as he did, an almighty gust of wind suddenly slammed against the portakabin which visibly unsettled him. The expression on his face was an absolute picture, and stopping dead in his tracks he looked up to the ceiling and muttered over the microphone "what the hell was that?" Everyone laughed as he continued his act and within minutes, he had the concert in full swing and quite genuinely, it was one of the best I have seen under such conditions. After the finale, the performers and audience walked across to the bar where we stayed for the remainder of the evening, chatting and drinking with the stars. They were a great bunch who genuinely wanted to know how we were coping. Their kind words of support touched us all and we took a lot of encouragement from them.

| Ken Goodwin | Bob Carolgees | Faith Brown |

Sunday, 10 April 1983

Back in Great Britain, television news programmes and the media covered the visit of British families to the Falkland Islands and Blue Beach Military Cemetery, and I found it quite heart-breaking to think that they had to wait until now to finally visit the final resting place of their loved ones, but what else could the British government do? Their safety was of paramount importance and we are after all, still under the threat of a possible Argentine air-strike at any given time. As the ceremony took place in the cemetery near San Carlos Settlement, *Cunard Countess* remained anchored out in Bonners Bay but by now, she was accompanied by five other ships including three Royal Naval gunships.

I had the good fortune to be invited to fly in a RAF Chinook helicopter to take aerial photographs of the finished Rubb hangar, Kelly's Garden, and the visiting flotilla that was out in Bonners Bay. The view from the air was simply unique yet moving. I thought of how those families must have been feeling during their memorial service, and my heart went out to each and every one of them.

Looking down on Blue Beach Cemetery from the Chinook is a moment I will never forget and always cherish. Quietly I said a prayer because below me, something very special was taking place. Back on the ground, a few of my colleagues continued preparing the G1098 Store for its pending air-lift back to Port Stanley while near the Generator House, the task of dismantling all three welding marquees took some time because these needed to be correctly packed. Also, our personal equipment was called forward and secured inside the G1098 Store before being signed over to the RAF.

By now 3 Troop was almost ready for its departure however, there were still a number of small jobs that cropped up around the Defence Base and these were completed as and when they were reported. I received a letter from my parents today which I read while sitting on a boulder at the edge of Bonners Bay, and out to the west an incredible sunset was splashed across the sky in colours of red, gold, and yellow. My colleague Marty was sat next to me and we chatted for some time and also back in our portakabin, after we returned from Bonners Bay. We decided to pop over to the RAF ChinDet lounge but it was not long before we returned to our portakabin, where before climbing inside my sleeping bag I wrote up this entry and then relaxed.

The photo I took of Kelly's Garden and the flotilla

Monday, 11 April 1983

Today was extremely cold, gusty, and not at all pleasant. Teams worked through the day from 07.30 until 22.50 on the PSP track that runs down to the edge of Bonners Bay, the tension straps on the Rubb hangar, the secondary Laundry site, and also the steel gabion baskets. The G1098 Store was finally air-lifted back to Port Stanley at midday and in it were the welding bay marquees and welding equipment, all of 3 Troop's engineering stores and tools, personal belongings, and finally spare items we had accumulated during our time here. I have only recorded a few lines because the work has taken up the entire day and I am now so ready for sleep.

Tuesday, 12 April 1983

We began our day's work at 06.00 which was our earliest start since first arriving here back in January, and we were relieved to hear that the Rubb hangar had officially been signed over to the RAF. The wind still blew hard but at least it was not as cold as yesterday, and so we decided to work on our final task which was to finish laying the last couple of rows of PSP panels that runs down to the edge of Bonners Bay. Ironically, this was one of the first tasks that had been assigned to 3 Troop when we first arrived but because of the Rubb hangar project, it was postponed and thankfully with the help of eight Irish Rangers, it was finally completed today.

They told us it had been the hardest day's work they had done in ages, and we warmed to their sense of humour and honesty but the fact is, working with PSP genuinely is hard work because the panels are made of steel, and those that have even the slightest of twists can prove difficult to interlock with others.

One of the Rear Party cleaned the Troop Office which was then signed over to the RAF and after that was completed, the paperwork and records were secured inside a large wooden box that would now serve as our temporary office. I was meant to be the sole member of 3 Troop to stay behind as Rear Party but I will now be accompanied by four colleagues including Kevin and Paul, and I will be glad of their company. Furthermore, I have been informed that the Regimental Quartermaster has asked for me to take over the Explosives' Store when I report to the quarry, which is situated at the far western end of the runway at Port Stanley Airport.

Around 19.30, we noticed *Cunard Countess* and the flotilla had quietly sailed out of Bonners Bay. During the evening, 3 Troop packed for its pending departure as did Billy and after that, we all went for a final drink together in the ChinDet Lounge after which I wrote up my journal.

Wednesday, 13 April 1983

At 14.00, our colleagues in 3 Troop left for Port Stanley and we were now suddenly a small group of just five Royal Engineers left on site, and at first it felt quite strange. With no tasks assigned, we wasted no time in setting up a video in the former Ant Hill and watched the film 'Animal House' and then relaxed while we had the chance. Tomorrow morning, we too will bid farewell to Kelly's Garden and I know that it will be a difficult time for me, and I am absolutely dreading that moment. The weather was good and so I trekked to the ridge of the Verde Hills for the very last time, and sitting there alone and looking out across the panoramic view that was before me, I admit I shed a tear or two. I reminisced on my time here and my walks across to San Carlos Settlement and Blue Beach Cemetery, yet I felt so very blessed to have spent a small part of my life here in this remote and isolated location which in all honesty, I would not even know existed had it not been for the tragic events of 1982.

Suddenly everything began to feel strange and surreal, and almost as if it was not happening at all and after one final look across to San Carlos Water out in the distance, I started to make my way down to the track at the edge of Bonners Bay from where I would walk across to San Carlos Settlement, and Blue Beach Cemetery for the very last time. As I made my way through the tiny community, I did not see or speak with a single soul while inside the cemetery, the absolute silence was so very beautiful and overpowering and as strange as this might sound, I genuinely did not want to leave.

Slowly the seconds ticked away until eventually, it was time for me to say a final goodbye and return to Kelly's Garden, and as I closed the cemetery gate behind me it was then that the tears flowed. I could not hold back because in truth, I had waited for so long to let the sadness out and in private. As expected I was overcome with a profound sadness and felt as though I had known all 14 who were laid to rest yet in truth, we would have been total strangers. I knew I needed to go through this experience and I thanked God that He had given me the opportunity.

On my return to Kelly's Garden, I was told by colleagues that we are to fly out tomorrow morning at 10.30 and although I am dreading that moment, it can no longer be avoided. I could not utter a single word but instead, walked back to Bonners Bay where I remained for quite some time alone and with my journal and pen, and that is where I am now writing this entry. This beautiful yet remote and rugged spot has won my heart and will forever live in my mind and soul, and I do not know if I will ever return. The sweet salt smell from the sea wafts through the air like a heavenly fragrance and so all I can do is pray that I will return one day.

Farewell Kelly's Garden.

Afternote

Some years after my tour in the Falklands and while serving again in the former West Germany in 1985, I heard that the Rubb hangar at Kelly's Garden had been dismantled just eight months after 3 Troop completed the project in 1983, but I was unsure if this true. Furthermore, I was informed that the structure had never been used as a helicopter hangar and if this was indeed the case, then why on earth was it was built in the first place? It made no sense whatsoever and so at first, I regarded both accounts to be inaccurate yet in saying this, I did hear similar reports from others who served in the Falklands post 1983. Still to this day I do have no knowledge of what really happened to the Rubb hangar other than the fact that today, it no longer exists.

My time at Kelly's Garden was finally over and some days after relocating to Port Stanley, in a strange kind of way I was once again happy and excited at the thought of returning to Tidworth, seeing my parents and friends, and visiting Morocco. Deep in my heart though, and without ever mentioning it to colleagues, I missed the Defence Base so very much and far more than I could have ever imagined. My silence was acting like a sticking plaster and it helped to some degree.

I thought it would be fitting to close this chapter with the last photograph I ever took of Kelly's Garden, and it was as I the RAF Chinook gained height before heading back to Port Stanley. The hangar did look impressive from the air, as did the three helipads and connecting taxiway but what was truly ironic, was that each helipad had a Chinook helicopter parked on it as we flew out, and for me it was though they had come to say a final farewell.

For me it made the most prefect photograph and the path which I used to walk down to the edge of Bonners Bay can clearly be seen to the right.

Kelly's Garden

Chapter Twenty-Two
Val and Rose

Foreword

*T*he only word to describe my time at Kelly's Garden is 'unforgettable'.

I have always had a burning desire to return even though as mentioned in the previous chapter, practically nothing of the former Defence Base exists and so to most people, my yearning makes no sense of any kind, and I accept this.

However, as an historian and a former soldier with a personal connection to the location, I believe my sentiment is more than justified and completely transcends nostalgia. It was here that I served with such wonderful colleagues and together we shared many experiences and indeed, I have often imagined how I would have coped had I remained there after the tour, and as a civilian. Every time I think about it, my heartfelt belief is that I would never have been truly, so why then do I still have this burning desire to return?

In 2020, I watched a television series called 'New Lives in the Wild' presented by the British broadcaster and adventurer Ben Fogle, and in each episode he revisits individuals and families who just a few years earlier, opted out of everyday life to begin a new lifestyle in a remote or secluded location. Almost all were off-grid and self-supporting, and the series included people who moved to different countries such as Iceland, India, and Canada but each had one thing in common, and that was the desire to begin a life that was as far away from modern day society as possible.

I found series quite fascinating and a testament to the courage and determination that some people have, and one episode in particular was called 'Fair Isle'. In it, Ben Fogle re-visited an American artist last saw five years earlier and his name was Tommy. Having left his native United States after a failed relationship Tommy bought an off-grid cottage on Fair Isle, a small island between Orkney and mainland Shetland and with a population of only 60. When asked if he ever felt lonely, Tommy instantly answered 'yes' and then went on to explain why. He said he regularly experienced extreme loneliness which I thought was refreshing to hear, because of his honesty on living alone in a remote location. As the American diplomat and politician George Ball once famously wrote "nostalgia is a seductive liar."

The older I have become, the more I realise that human beings are very much a social animal and no matter how private or secluded we choose to live our lives, we all at some point need human contact. Would I be truly happy if I had stayed at Kelly's Garden after the camp was decommissioned? My answer is no, but the one thing I do know is that I would still like to return if only for a few hours.

As the RAF Chinook gained height before heading back to Port Stanley, I looked down one final time on Bonners Bay, San Carlos Settlement, and the Defence Base, and gradually they grew smaller and disappeared from sight. There were only a handful of us on board the aircraft and yet I could sense the sombre atmosphere that lasted throughout the flight. The tie had finally been cut.

This chapter centres on the entries I wrote during the final two months of my 1983 Falklands Tour, and it was 52 Field (Construction) Squadron's role to support Royal Engineers from other units with repairing the damaged runway at Port Stanley Airport. Airfield damage repair is highly complex work and can only be undertaken by specialists and without bias, British Royal Engineers are among the best.

For my part, I was commander of a four-man section that would work in the nearby quarry where along with another section, we operated a pair of large rock-crushing trains that would provide airfield repair teams with the required vast quantities of crushed rock, around the clock. As mentioned in chapter three, seven long-haul bombing missions by RAF Vulcan bombers took place during the Falklands War under the codename Operation Black Buck.

The purpose of these sorties was to attack Port Stanley Airport runway to deny Argentine fighter aircraft use of this facility and each run was heavily fraught with danger, and to return safely to the United Kingdom was considered nothing short of miraculous. The aircraft took off from RAF Waddington in Lincolnshire and carried seven 1,000-pound bombs each on what was the longest sorties in British military aviation history. Ascension Island was used as a staging post and opinions as to the overall effectiveness of the operation were divided with some claiming that they were not worth the effort.

When 3 Troop arrived at the Coastel, the number of sappers working on Port Stanley Airport runway was approximately 1,000 and this included all those working on the runway itself, on new roads, inside the quarry, and the drivers operating the fleet of heavy plant equipment in support of the whole project. 42 days had been assigned to making good the runway damage and when completed, it would be used by aircraft such as RAF Phantom fighter jets and C-130 Hercules transporter planes, and for civil long-haul flights. Logistically it was a military engineering project of epic proportion with high importance placed on protection of the islands, and reinstating international flights and as such, an unprecedented demand was placed on equipment, manpower, resources, and military engineering capability.

Meanwhile inside the quarry, a small team of Royal Electrical and Mechanical Engineers (REME) provided crucial support to maintaining and repairing the two Goodwin Barsby Goliath Rock-Crushing trains, and these were required to work non-stop around the clock. With all of this in mind, 3 Troop understood that we were in for an exhausting final eight weeks, and that there would be no free time given that our work would continue until all runway repairs were fully completed.

The two rock-crushing trains were named 'Val' and 'Rose' and each comprised of a tall control bridge that overlooked a primary and secondary chamber, as well as a long belt-driven conveyor system, and when both were in full operation the noise the generated was deafening. Each train vibrated heavily and shook every bone in your body. Large boulders of quartzite rock were delivered to the quarry by a fleet of Volvo Haulamatic Dump Trucks, and tipped into the deep metal vaults before being crushed to the required size by solid cast-steel jaws.

The crushed rock then be passed along the conveyor belt and through a Loader Screen, before finally being stockpiled onto the ground at the far end of each train. From there, the crushed rock would be transferred to several designated holding sites near Port Stanley Airport runway, and also to other locations as and when required.

As Team Leader Two, I was put in charge of Val and my two main responsibilities were to ensure the train worked to its maximum capacity, while at the same time preventing electrical power overloading by monitoring the chambers when filled with rock.

Every mechanical or electrical breakdown had potential to stop rock-crushing production for up to five hours which put considerable pressure on the REME, as parts such as cast-steel jaws were incredibly expensive and took time to replace, but when I asked the REME corporal for advice on how best to operate the train without overloading the electrical motor, he replied "keep going until it happens," and that is exactly what I did.

After briefing my section before the first shift, we went across to the Quarry Store to collect our white safety helmets, safety gloves, ear defenders, and protective goggles. As we were working night shifts only, I forewarned each member that we would be working under flood lights which meant we needed to be mindful of their glare and strain on our eyes. I also told them that they were to look after each other at all times, and not to hesitate hitting the Emergency Brake should a team member be seen to be in potential danger. I also told them not to take any risks but looking back at it now, I still wince when I recall some of the close shaves we encountered *and yet, it was all part and parcel of operating such a large and powerful industrial piece of machinery.*

Thursday to Sunday, 14 to 17th April 1983

These past four days have been mentally and physically challenging for everyone in 3 Troop and already the non-stop activity, crammed living conditions, and unrelenting pace has taken its toll on most of us. Indeed, some events have completely eluded me because of the demand placed on my section which at times has been brain draining, yet I need to write up my journal as regularly as I can despite there being hardly any free time.

After flying out of Kelly's Garden and taking my last photograph of the Defence Base, the RAF Chinook flew at low altitude across East Falkland Island until it approached Port Stanley from the north-west. Throughout the flight the deteriorating weather and low clouds were a constant concern to the pilot and his crew, but when Port Stanley Harbour finally came into view, it improved significantly and I began to look forward to my final two months of this tour. As we flew low across Port Stanley Harbour and with the rear door lowered, we could hear the loud thundering wokka-wokka sound of the helicopter's twin sets of rotor blades.

It was at this point that I suddenly remembered I had not heard anything about my transfer application to the Army Air Corps. We landed on the same grassed helipad that we took off in the RAF Sea King back in January, and as we boarded the transport that would take us to the Coastel, it was then that I was informed I would be working my first shift as Team Leader Two in the quarry that same night. My crew is made up of Kevin, Paul, Jock, and Rocky and for some reason, I have lost all sense of time and these final two months will certainly test my team's character and strength. As such, I will regularly encourage each to keep smiling. They are a good bunch and I feel blessed to have them on my team.

By the end of our first two 12-hour night shifts, both rock crushing teams were feeling the need for a break of some kind, as these will be essential if we are expected to keep working at this pace for the remainder of the tour. The accommodation we have been assigned is the floating Coastel which has been featured on newspapers and television news programmes back home. Whilst it may be comfortable and warm, the cabins are small and confined, and they heat up quickly to the point where you desperately need fresh air yet we have no windows of any kind. It all feels somewhat claustrophobic and the cabins are so unlike the portakabins we enjoyed at Kelly's Garden.

With the end of our tour now in sight, I can already sense a growing desire from my colleagues that they just want to get the work finished as quickly as possible, and return to Tidworth. Kelly's Garden was absolute heaven compared to what we have here on the Coastel, and we live with the constant roar of RAF Phantom fighter jets flying overhead. There is also the heavy pounding of troops as they walk past our cabin door when we are trying to sleep, and these are the narrowest corridors I have ever encountered on any floating vessel. It is abundantly clear that this is not going to be an enjoyable way in which to end our six-month tour and yet, I am confident everyone will get on with their work and pull together. Of that I have no doubt.

Monday, 18 April 1983

The blue and white Coastel is berthed in the sheltered waters of Whalebone Cove, which is at the far eastern side of Port Stanley Harbour and approximately 500 metres from the western end of Port Stanley Airport runway. 300 metres to the north of Whalebone Cove is the deserted yet stunningly beautiful Yorke Bay which I am reliably informed, is still littered with Argentine anti-personnel mines that were planted during the Falklands War. Not too far away is the eerie rusting shipwreck from the past called *Lady Elizabeth*, a three-masted iron hull trading barque that first captured my imagination when I was a child and yet, here she sits almost within touching distance. Launched on 6 June 1879 in Southwick, she regularly sailed the seas until one day in 1912 and after setting sail from Vancouver with a cargo of timber on board, she rounded Cape Horn at the southernmost point of South America.

Severely damaged during a storm in which four crew were washed overboard, her skipper Captain Julius Hoegh altered course and set sail for the safety of Port Stanley where he planned to have the ship repaired. However, tragedy struck a second time when just 15 miles off the coast of the Falkland Islands, the ship crashed heavily onto a small group of rocks causing the *Lady Elizabeth* further damage to her hull, and she was considered to be beyond repair. Miraculously and despite taking on water, the ship eventually reached Port Stanley where she lay moored for the next 23 years. In 1936 she broke free, and drifted dangerously across Port Stanley Harbour to Whalebone Cove where to this day, she remains a remarkable and impressive piece of maritime history.

The Coastel with quarry road far left

    Our location is four miles by road from Port Stanley yet at times we feel as isolated as we were in Kelly's Garden, and it is strange to see street lights at night from across the harbour. It is all work and no play and the scale of post-war repairs is considerable. On the runway we can see RAF McDonnell Douglas Phantoms, Harrier Jump Jets, and Lockheed C-130 Hercules Transporter planes. Inside the quarry, the two rock-crushing trains each has a control bridge that overlook a large feeding chamber which at first appear intimidating, due to their depth and capacity, and the thunderous noise they make when crushing large boulders of rock.

    Each has large heavy cast-steel jaws that produce a horrendous screeching sound when in full operation, and the vibration generated by the train makes standing on the operating platform both difficult and unpleasant. Both trains are huge and surprisingly long, and frustratingly they break down far more than we expected due to electrical power failures that are brought on by operating the machines non-stop.

    Quartzite boulders are delivered to the quarry by dumper trucks and stockpiled immediately next to Val and Rose. These boulders are then scooped up by tracked loaders and dropped into the feeder chamber and as the platform vibrates, the boulders are shuffled closer towards the crushing chamber until they eventually fall inside. Once inside the chamber, they are grinded into smaller pieces of rock before being fed onto the conveyor belt, and then carried along to the farthest end where they are dropped onto the ground.

From there the crushed rock is collected and loaded onto a fleet of yellow Volvo Haulamatic Dump Trucks by a Terex Loader, and then transported to a holding site some 500 metres outside the quarry. The entire operation runs on an industrial scale which we are informed, must not be allowed to stop at any cost due to the constant demand for rock at various sites around Port Stanley Airport. Today we had an unexpected shortage of boulders. No deliveries were made to the quarry so we were not required to stay on site however, one member of the team will remain behind just in case further supplies are sourced and delivered. The weather remains good and thankfully we have hardly had any rain.

Coastel

52 Field (Construction) Squadron's headquarters is situated at the southern side of Port Stanley Airport and today, we heard that the new Commander British Forces Falkland Islands (CBFFI) namely Major General Keith Spacie has arrived on the island, and will take over from Major General Sir David Thorne. The RAF is responsible for controlling the Coastel and so far they are doing a splendid job. I do miss the tranquillity and rugged beauty of Kelly's Garden and the mesmerising view across to San Carlos Settlement, and I would warmly welcome any opportunity to return to the Defence Base before I return to Tidworth in two months' time. The chances of that ever happening is now extremely unlikely.

This afternoon my team watched the movie 'Southern Comfort' and around 18.30, we made our way through the maze of corridors on the Coastel that led to the restaurant where we enjoyed a hot dinner, and I was pleasantly surprised at the size of the cookhouse and excellent standard of catering. I have no idea as to how many troops are accommodated but it has to be in the hundreds, and around 19.15 I wrote this entry in my journal while listening to classical music on my headphones. It is now just seven weeks before we set sail for Ascension Island and return to Tidworth in Wiltshire. These Falkland Islands really have taken me by surprise and of that there is no doubt, because they have a desolate yet natural beauty that can only be found in remote locations such as this, and the abundance of wildlife that thrives here is quite simply staggering.

Had Argentina won the war in 1982, I dread to think what would have ensued because I do not believe for one second that Galtieri or his military junta would have shown any consideration or respect to the islanders for their allegiance to Great Britain. Indeed, how many would have been deported to mainland Argentina against their will, or put on trial to face false and politically fabricated charges? How many properties and pockets of land would have been confiscated by Argentina, or detention centres established for those the junta considered undesirable, both here and on the mainland? In truth, Britain needed to win this war and all cost and thankfully Prime Minister Thatcher made sure of that. Realistically, Galtieri never stood a chance and indeed it was absolute madness that he even contemplated invading a British Overseas Territory however, as history will forever show it was political suicide on his part.

Tuesday to Wednesday, 19 to 20 April 1983

The two quarry teams paraded each night at 18.30 outside the Coastel, dressed in green overalls and carrying white safety helmets, safety gloves, and packed meals, before being driven in the back of a Bedford Four Ton lorry. The evenings so far have been kind to us and comparatively cool, and there was hardly any wind or rain to hinder us or our work inside the quarry which at times, was one large dust bowl. Out in the distance and from the ramp at the entrance of the Coastel, we have an incredible view of Port Stanley Harbour, the capital Port Stanley, the wreck of *Lady Elizabeth*, and the two prominent geographical features called Sapper Hill and Two Sisters which sit to the north-west. The drive to the quarry takes approximately 10 minutes and as soon as we arrive, both fellow team leader John and I dispatch our sections to the Rest Marquee to prepare for work, while we report to the Control Tent for a debrief from the day team.

On Wednesday evening, one of the lighting towers was an absolute 'no-goer' and after a quick search with John, we managed to change it with a lighting tower from the Load Screen Section. He and I spent time with the REME Maintenance Team learning how to alter the speed of the Primary Chamber, adjust the clutch and belt tensioners, carry out basic maintenance checks, and by midnight both Val and Rose between them crushed some 40 loads of rock. The noise of boulders being broken apart by the cast-steel jaws was not only sickening, but it was also highly ear-piercing because the screech of steel scraping against rock sounded exactly like fingernails being dragged across an old school chalkboard, but much louder.

Around 02.00 on the Tuesday night shift, I had no option but to shut down Val due to two secondary jaw springs shattering and also, because of another temporary shortage of boulders. I sent my team to the Rest Marquee as blasting for rock took place at another site near the quarry, and with that all we could do was to wait. Frustrated by this situation, I radioed through to my troop commander to update him on the lack of rock and as we spoke, Team One also stood down as they too were waiting for further supplies. John and I decided to drive the Welder's Tractor to the Blasting Site Office to see for ourselves what was causing the delays and as we arrived, to our surprise we were told that there would be no further blasting for the remainder of our night shift.

We returned to the quarry and around 05.15, both teams started to walk back to the Coastel and as we made our way along the long dusty track, I mentioned that it reminded me of the old telegraph road at CFB Meaford in Canada and that brought a smile to our faces. Walking with colleagues at dawn with Port Stanley Harbour to our right was indeed a wonderful way in which to welcome the new day.

Over these past 48 hours, I have spent some of my spare time reading 'Shogun' which is written by Australian author James Clavell. Paul has loaned me the book and it is a fascinating story set in 17th century Asia, and I am thoroughly enjoying it. Others watched the 1965 movie 'That Darn Cat' starring Hayley Mills and Dean Jones which was being shown in the bar, and this was immediately after a Yellow Air Attack alert was stood down. Standing near the edge of Whalebone Cove and on a large boulder, I watched with others as a pair of RAF Phantom Fighter Jets scrambled and what an exhilarating spectacle it made.

Tonight was extremely cold and only one Team Leader plus one team member was required to work the night shift, because both crushing trains are still out of action due to the lack of quartzite boulders. John and Martin drew the shortest straws which meant that my team was not needed, and as they left the Coastel at around 18.30 and headed towards the quarry, I offered to cover the next shift should a similar situation arise. I then headed to the cookhouse to get myself a mug of coffee after which I wrote up my journal.

Since our return to Port Stanley, updating my journal has suffered somewhat due to working 12-hour night shifts in very dusty conditions and as such, any free time we now have is considered precious to each and every one of us. On top of this, the living conditions inside Coastel are not exactly ideal and for reasons unknown to 3 Troop, there is a lot of noise coming from certain corridors which we are told has been reported to our troop commander and staff sergeant.

This noise is interrupting both our sleep and free time in between night shifts, and something needs to be done to rectify the situation before things get out of hand. We were warned back in Kelly's Garden of noise disturbances inside the Coastel and that we would find it far more rowdy than living in the portakabins on the Defence Base. Sadly, this is turning out to be true and it really is not nice being on board the Coastel but that is how it is, and so we will have to deal with it one way or another.

Thursday, 21 April 1983

At 08.15 and after a delicious breakfast, both night teams got together to watch a recording of the WBA World Welterweight title fight that was fought at the Reno Convention Centre in Nevada just two days ago. The contenders were Welshman Colin Jones who was born in Gorseinon near Swansea, and the American Milton McCrory. They were fighting for the vacant title after Sugar Ray Leonard retired from boxing due to suffering a detached retina.

The contest ended in a split decision after Jones who is nicknamed 'The Punch' gave a sterling performance inside the ring, and was a credit to his country. The remainder of my morning and afternoon was spent reading the last two chapters of 'Shogun' which now has me totally captivated. Thankfully my roommate Paul was at work in the quarry, and so I was left to finish the book in peace. These days we treasure each and every opportunity we get to have some kind of peace and privacy, and all because of the conditions we now live in. I wrote a letter to my parents and updated this journal.

During tonight's shift, several 'blinds' occurred in the quarry which resulted in Val and Rose having to be shut down for over an hour. A 'blind' is an explosive charge that fails to detonate and in addition to these unforeseen incidents, inside the quarry the rock crushing was proving much slower than we had anticipated despite both trains being fully operational. This in part was due to the essential maintenance work that needed to be carried out by our REME Support Team, who also had to replace three badly damaged sets of cast-steel jaws.

What was also frustrating were the increasing delays between each delivery of boulders, and the sudden drop in air temperature which made tonight one of the coldest of the tour so far. Everyone froze as we stood on the control bridges of Val and Rose and as often as we could, John and I would send one member from our team to the Rest Marquee for a 15-minute break to stay warm. Not too far away we could see and hear RAF Phantom jets deploy throughout the night from Port Stanley Airport, and it was all very inspiring to watch these aircraft soar into the night sky at such incredible speed.

Standing on the bridge of the rock crunching trains gave us the best view possible and it certainly helped to pass the time. We pressed on until it was 06.00, and then walked back to the Coastel for a well-earned hot shower and breakfast, and much needed sleep. After a 12-hour night shift working in a cold dust filled quarry while being shaken for hours on end on a giant vibrating platform, and then from time to time having to dislodge heavy rocks blocking the crushing chamber, there is no better way to relax than to enjoy a long piping-hot shower. After that, I wrote up this journal and I am now ready for sleep. We have been informed that one of our troop corporals has been bedded down with a heavy cold and as such, he is recovering inside his cabin which he now has all to himself because we cannot afford to have others catch the virus from him.

Friday to Saturday, 22 to 30 April 1983

In the introduction I wrote at the beginning of my journal, I made the pledge that I would record events of each and every day of my operational tour no matter what happens, but unfortunately this past week has proved to be so busy that I have been unable to keep that promise from time to time, and because of reasons beyond my control. Some entries have been shorter than usual and this has naturally frustrated and concerned me, yet in saying this, I do believe I have managed to keep on top of my writing as best I can and will endeavour to do so. With the persistent heavy work load and lack of sleep, and all the other obstacles we now have to contend with here on the Coastel, and indeed inside the quarry, it has all had an impact of some kind on the members of 3 Troop. Because of this and in order to keep on top of my writing, I have decided to adopt an alternative process which is to record the events of the past week in one single entry.

In keeping true with British tradition, let me first talk about the weather. Over the past nine days we have enjoyed dry conditions which have helped immensely in maintaining high troop morale, and this is despite the long night shifts when the air temperature has dropped significantly. The one good thing about these cold nights is the excellent air quality it has provided which in turn, has given us the most wonderful close-up views of British military aircraft flying low overhead, and also of the southern hemisphere night sky.

The quarry on the other hand, has been a constant dust bowl and at times both Val and Rose have between them given us our fair share of unwanted headaches, and especially in the form of blockages inside the large crushing chambers. Such instances for some reason always seem to give our visiting officers cause for concern and dread, so clearly, they too must be under considerable pressure to meet fixed targets and within rigid timeframes.

Often such demands can appear to be somewhat unworkable and yet everyone appreciates that we are working in a post-war operational theatre, and under difficult conditions and for this reason alone, we remain determined to stay focussed on repairing the island's infrastructure, runway, and establishing a permanent military presence. During my Basic Military Training at Southwood Camp in 1977, it was emphasised over and over that an efficient sapper will always come up with a workable solution to a problem, and the golden rule in achieving this is never to panic, but instead to calmly identify and assess the situation, weigh up the options, and then come up with the best plan.

One afternoon I was asked by colleagues to speak with a friend and member of 3 Troop about his recent 'out of character' attitude towards others, which they had only noticed since leaving Kelly's Garden. I visited his cabin and explained what I had heard but unfortunately for him, he made the mistake of personalising the issue and proceeded to undermine my authority, and this left me no other option than to put him straight there and then. Normally an enthusiastic and solid team player, something had clearly unsettled him because overnight he had become a completely different person and what made it a more difficult meeting, was the fact that we had always been good friends up until that point.

I talked him through the concerns that others had brought to my attention but sadly, he rejected their claims and said he had nothing to apologise for. Suddenly, I could see for myself his character change. He became argumentative and unreasonable, so I stopped him dead in his tracks and the conversation immediately became one-way on my part, and I gave him an official warning and firm advice on what he needed to do. After a couple of minutes he was back to his normal self and sheepishly acknowledged that he had been in the wrong, but before I concluded our meeting I told him to think long and hard about the way he had behaved both before and during our discussion, and I left the matter at that.

He took my advice and apologised to the others, but I will need to keep a close eye on him for the remainder of the tour. When you are in charge of a team you will only earn respect if you yourself show respect to others, and listen to what they have to say and always keep promises made. Maintaining integrity and setting good values and examples is also needed. What will never earn you respect is trying to be 'one of the lads' because it is the team leader or commander who wags the tail. With this in mind, I remembered a sound piece of advice I was given by a sergeant instructor during my JNCO Cadre back in Munsterlager in 1980. His advice to me was "always be Fair, Firm and Friendly".

The two rock-crushing teams continued to work hard inside the quarry and braved the harsh and deteriorating weather conditions in a manner that impressed 3 Troop's management, but it was obvious that winter is now fast approaching. A colleague and I decided to take a walk into Port Stanley on Saturday 23 April because the weather for once was good, and this would be our last opportunity.

We agreed it would be far more enjoyable than staying on board Coastel, and so we walked the four miles following Airport Road and the views across the harbour were wonderful. We declined several offers of a lift from passing military vehicles and instead we chatted away and during our walk around Port Stanley, we again visited and photographed Brunel's famous Mizzen Mast from *SS Great Britain* that rests on its side along the harbour front, and also Government House. We also visited the General Store and Christ Church Cathedral before taking a stroll along quiet streets behind Ross Road.

As we approached the harbour front, we came across a colleague from another troop who was making his way to the Royal Military Police (RMP) Station in Port Stanley. He told us that while acting as Duty NCO on Coastel the previous night, he had helped a Royal Military Police patrol deal with a minor incident and now needed to provide a written statement. Inside the General Store, I bought a set of 11 Falkland Islands first day cover stamps for my mother and a Falkland Islands' tie for my father. I also bought two music cassettes by the American rock band Billy Squier who I saw perform at Maple Leaf Gardens in Toronto last year, when they supported Queen on their 'Hot Space' world tour.

As we continued our walk around Port Stanley, we discussed how basic the island's infrastructure appeared even though it had suffered and survived a military invasion the previous year. East Falkland Island reminds me a lot of the Scottish Islands and after eating lunch on a bench next to the Mizzen Mast, we went to see *RFA Sir Tristram* for the last time and took more photographs. I first saw *Sir Tristram* on the day I first arrived in the Falklands back in January, and she was still moored to the quayside east of Christ Church Cathedral.

Our return to Coastel was made much quicker by Sapper Williams who gave us a lift in his Haulamatic Dumper Truck, and along the route we passed several newly erected huts along a stretch of road which we were told was called The Narrows. We also caught sight of the requisitioned hospital ship *SS Uganda*, the sister ship of *SS Nevasa* on which I sailed with schoolchildren on an Educational Cruise to Lisbon, Gibraltar, Madeira and Tenerife in June 1967. I have very fond memories of that adventure and seeing *SS Uganda* so close brought them flooding back.

On Thursday 21 April, my team rested before deploying on night shift and I read the four letters I had received over the course of the past nine days, and it was so good to hear that everyone back home is keeping well. Since leaving my hometown of Llanelli in July 1977, I have come to realise that my ambitions in life have changed considerably and I feel more balanced and content as a person. The time is now passing by very quickly and soon it will time to leave these islands.

Afternote

The remainder of my time in the Falklands was spent supervising 12-hour night shifts inside the quarry, and this proved to be very demanding and tiring work right up until the end. The weather was growing increasingly wintery with every day and what follows in this chapter, is the final entry I wrote in my journal which covers the period Sunday, 1 May to Saturday, 7 May 1983. After that the writing stops.

I can also recall vividly the cramped living conditions on Coastel and the preparations for our pending departure, and the concerns many of us held over our imminent sea voyage back to Ascension Island on board HMS Keren.

As time wore on, it took a solid team effort from 3 Troop to see the tour through to a successful conclusion but then word was received that 52 Field (Construction) Squadron had been earmarked for another six-month tour either in late 1983, or early 1984. Belize in Central America was mentioned but not confirmed. At that time and across the British Army, this was considered an unprecedented demand on any married member of the Armed Forces because of the relatively short interval between two successive operational tours of duty. As my career progressed and over time, back-to-back tours would become normal for most members of the British Armed Forces, and the hardship it placed on both single and married personnel was proving considerable.

Sunday to Saturday, 1 to 7 May 1983

Over the course of the past six weeks, life on the Coastel and working each and every night for 12 hours continued as it had done, ever since we returned from Kelly's Garden on Thursday 14 April. One incident in particular that shocked many was a staggering fine of £340 which was imposed on a genuinely quiet colleague for alleged drunken behaviour which some, including independent witnesses, claimed was unfair.

Despite understanding the 'two can rule' on any military operational tour, this particular charge was pressed by a RAF sergeant who while on duty on Coastel one evening, had clearly overreacted to a petty exchange of cross words over a matter that many who were present, deemed extremely trivial. One of the most polite members of 3 Troop, our colleague was accused of being drunk and verbally rude to the RAF sergeant. Our colleague was far from drunk and despite pleas for him to reconsider his decision, he refused. Huge support was shown to our colleague and from members of the RAF who also asked the sergeant to drop the charge.

Our work was highly demanding and the challenges and mechanical problems we encountered inside the quarry were becoming increasingly frustrating, with ongoing blockages in the feeder chambers, and damage being caused to the cast-steel crushing jaws. Everyone worked hard and 3 Troop showed a dogged determination not to allow anything to discourage or deter us, or to cause upset. I have watched and witnessed individuals grow in character and maturity throughout this tour, and as it draws ever closer to its conclusion 3 Troop has gelled into the finest group of soldiers I could ever wish to serve with.

Each member has won my utmost admiration and respect because of the true grit they have shown, and in instances where situations were at times worrying and dangerous, we have come through it all as a team. It has been an absolute privilege.

I have now been informed by my staff sergeant that there is a realistic chance I will be returning to 32 Armoured Engineer Regiment in Germany by 9 August, because the unit needs experienced AVLB crewmen to form a brand-new squadron. I would dearly like to return to Dennis Barracks in Munsterlager as I hold many fond memories of my time there, and it would be wonderful to meet up with former colleagues and friends such as Bob and Jim Pridding, but in truth I would also like to serve on the six-month tour to Belize with 52 Field Squadron, which I hear is likely to happen but not until 1984. Belize is a Caribbean country on the northeast coast of Central America that sits south of Mexico and north of Guatemala, and has large areas of jungle and forest. It is a theatre I would very much like to see for myself however, I suspect there is more chance of me returning to Germany due to my armoured engineering background and experience.

It also looks as though my application to transfer across to the Army Air Corps will not progress due to the lack of vacancies and yet, I feel no sense of sadness whatsoever because as mentioned earlier, I am a firm advocate that things happen for a reason. My Glider Pilot Course may also be cancelled if I am to be posted back to Germany. The weeks slowly pass by and without too much to write about, unlike my time at Kelly's Garden.

We now await the arrival of 48 Field Squadron from 39 Engineer Regiment who are stationed at Waterbeach in Cambridge, and will serve as our relief squadron, but they have our sympathy because they will be here for the duration of the coming winter. We are told they are sailing south on board *HMS Keren* and this again raises concern, because this is the ship that will take us back to Ascension Island on a journey we genuinely dread after hearing nothing but dreadful reports about her.

Frazer showed me a video that the singer and songwriter Justin Haywood of the Moody Blues rock band made especially for him, and in it he sent a personal message. It is so humbling to know that such people still think of the troops here in the Falklands, and appreciate the way we are serving our country by supporting this British Overseas Territory. Such gestures always reduce the distance that separate us from those we love and miss so very much.

Afternote

It was at this point that I stopped writing entries in my journal because it had been stored away with the remainder of my personal belongings, and as such all I could do until my return to Swinton Barracks in Tidworth was to write notes on scraps of paper. These sadly over the years have become lost. Thankfully, I have a good memory and so this and my notes allowed me to record in detail many of my recollections of that unpleasant sea voyage to Ascension Island, as well as 3 Troop's return to Swinton Barracks in Tidworth and my visit to Morocco.

**Chapter Twenty-Three
June 1983 to October 1988**

Foreword

As mentioned at the end of Chapter Twenty Two, the last written entry in my Falkland's journal was dated Saturday, 7 May 1983.

Approximately two weeks prior to leaving the Falklands Islands, it was officially confirmed that we would be returning to Ascension Island on board the former Sealink Cross Channel Ferry St Edmund. This ship had been purchased by the Ministry of Defence in May 1982, and after several changes were made such as fitting two helipads to her top deck and completely changing her colours, she was renamed HMS Keren. Her reputation for being unstable while at sea preceded her arrival, and there was 3 Troop's experience of her lack of comfort and facilities after we spent our first night sleeping on her car deck, when we first arrived on 15 January 1982.

As our departure date drew closer, a number of newly arrived troops who had sailed on board HMS Keren expressed their views of the ship, and these were neither reassuring nor comforting. As expected, the voyage was at times alarming and as a person who has never been good on water, I genuinely feared for my own safety for reasons that will become clearer in this chapter. Such was my experiences on that return voyage across the South Atlantic in 1983, I have had a fear of the open sea ever since.

The remainder of my 23 year career with the British Army proved far more exciting than I could ever have wished for, and not only did I deploy on further operational tours of duty but also my career path changed completely and as a result, it brought accelerated promotion, new and exciting challenges, and opportunities where I could put my administrative and managerial skills to best use. More importantly, it prepared me for a rewarding career in business administrative and accounts management after I left the British Army in 2000, and in 2013 I established a self-employed bookkeeping business.

Saturday to Monday, 11 to 20 June 1983

My final day in the Falklands was Saturday, 11 June 1983 and it was by far the coldest day of the six-month tour and with the official start of winter only 10 days away. By now, 3 Troop was ready to return to Tidworth and that journey would begin this very day. Along with the remainder of 52 Field (Construction) Squadron, we paraded outside the Coastel at 09.00 precisely and while standing in three rows, my colleagues and I braved an icy-cold easterly South Atlantic breeze that blew across the open water of Port Stanley Harbour, and quite literally made everyone's eyes water. All around me cheeks turned red and many blew hard on clasped hands as the air temperature dropped even further. It was absolutely freezing!

After roll call we all climbed onto a fleet of Army Bedford Four Ton lorries and were transported in convoy from Whalebone Cove to Port Stanley, via Airport Road and along Fitzroy Road until finally we arrived at to our designated drop-off point which was at the top of Philomel Street. This is one of the very few streets in Port Stanley that has a steep incline. We disembarked and wearing our army-issue gloves and combat smocks which were fully fastened to the neck, each member of 3 Troop collected his military backpack and then lined up again in three ranks, but this time with the harbour below us and directly to our left. The time was around 09.40 and as the icy South Atlantic breeze continued to blow through the capital, the freezing cold air literally stung our faces and so everyone turned their back to the wind to face uphill to try and avoid getting any colder. I thought to myself that this had to be the coldest I had felt in years and began to shiver. 52 Field Squadron remained silent for what seemed an eternity and as we braved the elements, we waited patiently for the command to come to attention.

The order finally came and all three ranks reacted in an instant by smartly stamping our left foot hard onto the road, and then stood perfectly stiff with fists clenched and thumbs pointing down towards the ground along the seams of our trousers. The next order that was given was "by the left, left turn!" and with it, all three ranks turned and were now facing Port Stanley Harbour and there out in the distance, to everyone's horror was our worst nightmare namely *HMS Keren*. As the squadron slowly marched down Philomel Street, ironically the first Falklands' snow of 1983 began to fall and this made the road leading down to East Jetty much more slippery, and especially as we were weighed down by our heavy backpacks.

Thankfully, all our army suitcases and holdalls had been collected the previous night and these were already loaded onto *HMS Keren*, and as we marched into the ice-cold wind we all knew that we were leaving the Falkland Islands at the best possible time of the year. Chilled to the bone, we stood on the corner of Ross Road still apprehensive over the thought of crossing the South Atlantic on board *HMS Keren*, and there we waited for at least another 20 minutes.

HMS Keren was built by the Cammell Laird Shipping Company in 1973 and was launched at Birkenhead on Merseyside. Nowhere near the size or class of the ocean-going luxury liner *Cunard Countess*, the ship was taken over by the Royal Navy in 1982 for use as a troop carrier between Port Stanley and Ascension Island. Compared to *Cunard Countess* which was some 537 feet in length and weighed 17,600 tonnes, *HMS Keren* was dwarfed at just 429 feet in length and weighed only 8,987 tonnes.

Such significant differences spoke volumes as did the non-existence on board *HMS Keren* of standard facilities such as a swimming pool, gymnasium, theatre, shopping mall, and fully furnished ensuite cabins. 52 Field Squadron was transferred across Port Stanley Harbour to *HMS Keren* by Royal Navy Kiwi landing craft, and once moored alongside the stern door that was lowered to just above the waterline, 3 Troop eventually stepped onto the main car deck where we were greeted yet again by the putrid aroma that would linger throughout the 10 day sea voyage. This added even further to our sense of discomfort and I can honestly say that *HMS Keren* was not a nice ship, not by anybody's standard. Most fellow passengers seemed to think the same over the cramped conditions on board. The car deck had boxes and stores piled everywhere and the first impressions we were given her being a troop carrier, were not good.

After 3 Troop was fully accounted for, Paul and I were assigned to share a cabin just as we had on board *Cunard Countess* however, we both agreed that what we had been allocated this time on *HMS Keren* was absolutely dreadful. The thought of spending the next 10 days crossing a potentially rough South Atlantic Ocean in a former cross channel car ferry, was now a serious concern for many and you could see it on their faces. After changing into our 'at sea' uniform, Paul and I made our way to the restaurant for our first meal and although the furnishings were basic, the overall standard of catering was in fact very good.

After lunch everyone returned to their cabin and rested until it was time for our first briefing from the ship's First Engineer which took place on the Gallery Car Deck. Action on fire at sea, muster reporting points, alarm drills, and all other safety procedures were explained and pointed out and around 20.00, the ship's engine kicked into life and we watched as crew members made their way to their stations without hardly a word being spoken. Paul and I joined our colleagues on the top deck to say farewell to Port Stanley and the Falkland Islands, and in no time at all *HMS Keren* slowly made its way east towards Whalebone Cove. Some minutes later the ship turned sharply to port and headed north towards the narrow bottleneck that leads directly into Blanco Bay, and from there she sailed east and out into the open waters of the South Atlantic Ocean.

Suddenly, a voice was heard over the tannoy informing everyone on board that the ship was travelling at a speed of 15 knots and by 17.30 it was almost dark and I was chilled through to the bone. However, I could not bring myself to go below until the lights of Falkland Islands were finally out of sight and so with my emotions somewhat jumbled, I watched as the last light eventually disappeared out of sight and I realised that I would never see these islands again. All I wanted now was to get back to Tidworth as quickly as possible, and then go on my trip to Morocco.

Crossing the South Atlantic Ocean on board a cross channel ferry that swayed from side to side was no fun, especially for those of us who had not found our sea legs, and nor was it for the faint hearted or anyone who had genuine concerns over their safety. I truly believe there were many on board who were now just as anxious as I was over what lay ahead, and on one particular occasion which I have never forgotten to this day, even some of the restaurant crew looked worried when the ship suddenly listed while sailing through rough seas.

By day four, many were suffering with sea sickness and the ship's doctor was prescribing tablets at an alarming rate but for those of us who were not feeling unwell, our physical training continued as normal, and indeed their frequency increased because there was little else to do. Hurricane season in the South Atlantic is normally between 1 June and 30 November and around mid-afternoon on Wednesday 15 June, bad weather started to blow hard from the west and the sea conditions quickly deteriorated.

It even crossed my mind if these were in fact the notorious Roaring Forties I had read about as a child, because the waves literally tossed *HMS Keren* from side to side while inside the restaurant, tables and chairs were starting to slide back and forth across the polished floor, with some crashing into each other. A safety announcement was made over the ship's tannoy along with a request that all passengers return to their cabins, and this worried Paul and I.

Within just a few minutes many of us thought it best to return to the restaurant but by the time we arrived, there was hardly a free chair to be found. I looked around and could see others looking quite anxious as *HMS Keren* battled her way through the raging storm, and again among them were members of the crew who were peering out through the window. Suddenly and without warning the ship was buffeted by a powerful wave and with it came the loud sound of crockery and cooking crashing to the floor from inside the galley.

In all my life I had never experienced such fright and at one point I genuinely thought my worst nightmare was about to come true, and I do not exaggerate when

I say that even members of the crew were struggling to remain calm. After a couple of hours the storm slowly began to subside, and it was only then that Paul and I felt it safe to return to our cabin and by early morning, the ocean was once again like a mill pond but I made myself a promise there and then that I would never go on a sea voyage ever again, unless I absolutely had to.

Another incident that alarmed 3 Troop during our voyage north took place when we were just two days from Ascension Island. It was a sunny afternoon and the South Atlantic was very calm as we played football on the main car deck, when without warning a large motor suddenly kicked into life and we all stopped in an instant. Some of my colleagues were standing close to the stern door when quite unexpectedly it started to lower, and soon it was listing at quite an angle.

As it dropped even further we gasped when we realised that we were actually looking at the open South Atlantic, and with that we shouted to our colleagues to run and join us further along the car deck. When they reached us, we stared in disbelief at seeing the ocean stare right back at us but just then, the door started to raise and was soon fully closed. Without hesitation we returned to the upper deck and reported the incident to our seniors. Quite literally, the sea voyage from Port Stanley to Ascension Island on board *HMS Keren* was the most frightening and unsettling experience I had ever encountered, and it is one I would never want to repeat.

Monday, 20 June to Friday, 24 June 1983

At around midday on Monday 20 June, *HMS Keren* eventually arrived at Ascension Island and everyone on board breathed a huge sigh of relief, having endured a frightening sea voyage. For me, the Falkland Islands were now a long way away and while basking in glorious sunshine, it felt as though I was in a completely different world because for the first time in six months, I was wearing shorts. 3 Troop was informed that our return flight to RAF Brize Norton would depart Ascension on Thursday 23 June, which meant that we had three days in which to relax, sunbathe, and put the past six months behind us. Our operational tour of the Falkland Islands was a success because we had completed every single task assigned to us and for that achievement alone, we were proud and extremely privileged to have played our part. Deep down inside though, I was missing Kelly's Garden so much.

It is now time to start thinking about my four-week post-tour leave. Should I travel to Morocco and then visit my parents in Llanelli, or should I visit my parents first? Eventually, I decided to fly to Morocco on Friday 8 July for one week, and then visit Llanelli before returning to Tidworth to start preparing for my posting back to 32 Armoured Engineer Regiment in Munsterlager. Because the posting order had already been issued by REMRO in Glasgow, I was informed that my Glider Pilot Course had been cancelled and instead, I would be taking part on a 10-day Offshore Sailing Course in the Baltic which was being organised by the British Army Yacht Club in Kiel, West Germany. Was I scared? Yes, I genuinely was.

We would be visiting the time-locked Danish island of Aeroskobing, the historic and picturesque harbour town of Faarborg on the island of Funen, and the old port of Sonderberg in Southern Denmark. On successful completion of the course I would be qualified as a Competent Crewman and hopefully the experience would restore my lost confidence of being out at sea.

Throughout the three days we were moored at Ascension Island, 3 Troop relaxed as much as we could in glorious sunshine just south of the equator, and it was most definitely the best way to start recovering from our six-month tour of duty. There was quite literally no better way to spend our time and it passed very quickly. On Thursday 23 June at around midday, 3 Troop paraded on the main car deck of *HMS Keren* and from there we were transported across to Wideawake Airfield, which gained its name from the noise made by the Sooty terns that occupy the nearby cove.

It was this very airfield that the British RAF Vulcan bombers used as their staging point during Operation Black Buck in 1982. Our flight was scheduled to depart Ascension at 16.00 and while boarding the aircraft, I felt proud yet sad that our tour was now almost over and I do not know why, but that is how I felt at the time. I can still recall taking my seat in the central aisle and towards the rear of the aircraft, and fastening my seatbelt and closing my eyes in the hope that when I opened them next, I would be back at RAF Brize Norton.

I remember it as if it were yesterday. Our tour was almost over but first, we would need to cross the equator for a second time and refuel at Dakar-Yoff International Airport in Senegal, West Africa. Thankfully the return flight to Brize Norton was much quicker than we expected and it was extremely comfortable, and for the most of it I slept soundly until just before 06.00 on Friday 24 June. This was the date and time when we eventually touched down and as I disembarked the aircraft, I felt a sudden rush of cool yet soothing morning air, and I knew that we were now just one bus ride away from Tidworth. After that, our tour would be over.

3 Troop checked-in at the Arrivals' Desk and collected our personal belongings, then boarded a small fleet of white Royal Corps of Transport buses and soon we were on the road and heading for Reading, Basingstoke, and eventually Swinton Barracks in Perham Down. We arrived at the main gate on time and as expected, the married soldiers' families were waiting for them as we drove into camp. The buses pulled up immediately outside the single soldiers' accommodation block from where we departed back in January, and when the driver turned off the engine and opened

the door, for me the tour was officially over and with it a most memorable six-month experience which I will never forget.

As our married colleagues kissed and hugged their wives and children, tears were shed at their homecoming but for me, Paul, Kevin, and the other single soldiers, we just grabbed our belongings and headed for our rooms in the accommodation block. It was as simple as that and there was no nonsense of any kind. As I entered my room I was met with a silence and perfect stillness and it felt quite surreal because nothing had changed.

Our lockers were still padlocked and my bed was exactly the same as I had left it in January, except for a couple of letters that were placed on my pillow. Ismael and the Rear Party had done their job well and after a hot shower, I headed to the regimental cookhouse with others for a much-welcomed late breakfast. As we took our seats and began to eat, we were informed that because the next day was a Saturday, it had been decided that we would be given an extended weekend to do with as we please.

Saturday, 24 June to Friday, 8 July 1983

What am I going to do with my first long-weekend off in six months? Normally, I would do my dhobi and prepare for Monday's First Parade but I have no such plans this time around, and so I seriously considered driving to Llanelli to spring a surprise visit on my parents. Instead, I phoned home and when my mother answered I gave her the news that I was safely back in Tidworth, and that I would soon be on four weeks' leave. It was so wonderful and comforting to hear her soft voice again, and I could tell that she was excited and relieved that my tour was finally over.

As we chatted I leaned against the same glass panel inside the same phone box from which I rang her the night before I deployed to the Falkland Islands. I explained that I would be flying to Morocco on Friday 8 July for one week, but as soon as I return I would be driving straight to Llanelli to stay for two weeks. She was so delighted to hear this news and said she could not wait but then, I had to give her the news that I was being posted back to Germany in August for three years, and this was immediately followed by a long and painful pregnant pause.

As their only child, I knew this would upset them and yet they accepted how much I wanted to travel and so I had their full blessing. By being posted back to Munsterlager, we would only see each other for approximately four weeks each year and over a period of three years, at least.

The next two weeks at Tidworth quickly passed and I managed to book myself flights to and from Morocco on the dates I had planned. I would fly with Dan-Air to

Tangier-Boukhalef Airport and stay at the Hotel Africa which was just 20 minutes' drive from the airport. For the rest of my time with 52 Field (Construction) Squadron, 3 Troop serviced every item of military engineering equipment and restocked and audited the entire G1098 Store. We also carried out minor tasks around camp and worked in the same sections as we had in Kelly's Garden and finally, I prepared for my forthcoming posting back to Germany.

This involved a lot of personal administration. First, I had to report to the Movements' Clerk to collect a copy of my posting order and my rail ticket to Luton Airport, and a RAF Air-Trooping flight ticket to Hanover Airport. I then had to have my Clearance Certificate fully signed before I could leave Swinton Barracks, and this involved me having to report to the Part Two Order Clerk to make sure they notified REMRO in Glasgow of my exact posting date, because this would ensure I no longer paid Single Soldier Accommodation and Food Charges in the United Kingdom.

I was also issued with one Movements Forwarding Office (MFO) Box by the Quartermaster Department, which was the free service provided to military personnel who needed to have personal possessions and equipment delivered to a new unit. I also had to report to the Dental and Medical Centres, Clothing Store, Armoury, Pay Office, RSM, Guardroom, Gymnasium, and other departments. The last thing I had to do was sell my Ford Cortina which thankfully I managed to do just days before my actual flight date.

I would never get to serve with 22 Engineer Regiment again during my military career and yet for some reason, despite having thoroughly enjoyed both my tour to CFB Meaford in Canada and also the Falkland Islands, and having forged incredible friendships with members of the squadron, I felt it was the perfect time for me to move on. By now I was really looking forward to returning to Munsterlager where hopefully many of my former friends and colleagues would still be serving, and everything felt so very right with what was happening in my life. I could not have been any happier as I was at that moment in time.

Afternote

In July 1983, my visit to Morocco materialised and I got to trek part of the northern region of the Atlas Mountains and the experience was exactly the kind of adventure that I had hoped for. To a large extent Morocco did turn out to be the country I had read about but what did take me by surprise, was the extent of poverty I discovered in the outskirts of Tangiers and in particular, the shanty town which I was strongly advised against visiting. I could clearly see this from my window in the Hotel Africa and it was extensive. I was also surprised at the number of tourists who were forever being hounded by local children begging for money in full view of the Moroccan police, yet it was allowed to happen.

In 1983, Morocco was ruled by King Hassan II and not long after my visit, the government had lost much of its territory in the north. I visited the Kasbah Tangier and quite a number of shops that were close to my hotel, and I also walked around much of the city against the advice of hotel staff, but after just one day I felt I had seen everything I needed to see, and that was when I headed south to the Atlas Mountains for three days. My expectations of Morocco quickly jaded and in no time at all, I was so eager to leave that I purchased a one-day ferry ticket to Gibraltar.

Within a couple of hours I had crossed the Strait of Gibraltar and was in yet another British Overseas Territory but this time, at the bottom of the Iberian Peninsula. It was such a relief to be back on British soil and I visited the magnificent Saint Michael's Cave, the Naval Docks and border crossing to Spain, the British Governor's Residence, finally and the Gibraltar Parliament. On my penultimate day in Morocco, I visited the Caves of Hercules and Ceuta, the infamous Kasbah for a second time, the Grand Mosque, and Saint Andrew's Church. I flew back to the United Kingdom courtesy of Dan-Air which was an airline that ceased operations in 1992, and I have never had the desire to visit Morocco ever again.

9 August 1983 to 28 May 1986
32 Armoured Engineer Regiment, Munsterlager – Lance Corporal

Being posted back to Germany, and in particular to Dennis Barracks in Munsterlager was not only something I had wanted so much but also, it proved to be a blessing in disguise and another reason why I believe that things happen for a reason. Having served there for three years after completing my Basic Military and Trade Training in 1978, I knew both the camp and town intimately and also the beautiful surrounding region and because of this, I literally settled down overnight and was reunited with old friends and former colleagues.

Nothing had changed and without realising it at the time, my posting brought with it a brand new career that opened new doors, and provided many exciting opportunities. I was given completely new roles, appointments, and increased responsibilities that would accelerate my promotion and from the very beginning, I showed a burning ambition and determination to succeed and very soon, I could see that my prospects had improved beyond my wildest expectation.

On my first day of duty, I reported to the Regimental Headquarters where I was informed by the Regimental Chief Clerk that I would be employed within the Headquarters Troop. I was no longer going to fill the post of Lance Corporal AVLB crewman with the new Armoured Engineer Squadron as published in my posting order, but instead, I was to be assigned to an office environment which up until then was completely alien to me. For some reason this unexpected change did not bother me one bit and in fact it actually thrilled me.

Despite having no military administrative or clerical experience of any kind, I was employed within the Regimental Headquarters (RHQ) in a number of varying roles including Regimental Mail and Postal Orderly, Clerical Assistant to the Regimental Chief Clerk, and Technical Librarian. My role and responsibilities included the maintaining and updating of service and personnel records, military documentation, producing Regimental Part One Orders, re-organising the Regimental Library, and overseeing the control and management of classified documents within the Regimental Headquarters.

This work was totally new to me yet I thrived on the challenges and responsibilities that it presented, and also on the authority I was given, and the culture within a Headquarters' environment. I could not have been happier and did not want to be anywhere else, because I felt extremely comfortable working in administration and support of a Commanding Officer, Regimental Second-in-Command, Operations Training Major, Adjutant, Regimental Sergeant Major, Staff

Assistant, and Regimental Chief Clerk. Furthermore and most surprisingly of all, it felt completely natural to me and not at all overwhelming.

I also regarded my military administrative work and clerical duties to be both extremely interesting and stimulating, and soon I had no desire whatsoever to remain in either the Armoured or Combat Engineer career streams. These no longer appealed to me and deep down inside I knew exactly which career I wanted to pursue, and so with that I threw myself into my new role. I focussed heavily on learning more about army regulations, the procedures and protocols of working in a Headquarters, learning from senior clerks and officers the art of liaising with external agencies and higher authorities such as a Divisional Headquarters. In no time at all my effort and development was being noticed by my Officer Commanding, Regimental Chief Clerk, and most importantly the Warrant Officer Class One Staff Assistant who was the senior clerk in 32 Armoured Engineer Regiment. On being invited and agreeing to change my career path from Armoured Engineer to Military Clerk, I was fast-tracked to attend a Class Three Clerk All Arms course at the Employment Training School RAOC in Deepcut, Surrey. On 6 July 1984 I qualified and was transferred across to the Royal Engineers' clerical roster with immediate effect.

Main Gate and Guardroom at Dennis Barracks, 1983

RHQ 32 Armoured Engineer Regiment, 1983

Just four months after returning to Munsterlager, I was promoted to Corporal and deployed on Exercise LIONHEART between 3 September and 5 October 1984. LIONHEART was the largest NATO military exercise to be undertaken in Europe since the end of the Second World War, and my role was to provide clerical and administration support to the Regimental Headquarters in the field. Over 131,000 NATO troops took part in a four-week exercise during which three personnel were tragically killed. Immediately after Exercise LIONHEART, I was recommended for employment as a Chief Clerk and because I had lost my place on the Glider Pilot Course, I took part on an Off-Shore Sailing Course that was run by the British Army of the Rhine at Kiel Yacht Club, as promised by my previous unit namely 52 Field (Construction) Squadron.

After completing the seven-day sailing expedition in the Baltic, I gained the Royal Yachting Association Competent Crewman certificate and other sporting activities in which I participated included rugby union, tennis, and road-running. I competed in German Volkslauf races right across Lower Saxony and often with three other members of the Regimental Headquarters Troop. Our best achievement as a team was in 1984 when we competed in the Berlin City Race that attracted over 30,000 competitors. The elation I felt as I crossed the finish line inside the Berlin Olympic Stadium was beyond words, because this was the same arena in which the black American track and field athlete Jesse Owens won four gold medals in 1936, and destroyed Adolf Hitler's dream of Aryan power in sport.

It was also around this time that a brand-new Information and Administration Computer Programme was introduced into the British Army worldwide, and its name was PAMPAS which stood for Personnel Administration Micro Processing ADP System. Next to the Regimental Post-Room on the ground floor of the Headquarters at Dennis Barracks, a PAMPAS Cell was set up and I formed part of a team of 15 military clerks from across the regiment whose were tasked with inputting all personnel data from paper records. The project took over four months to complete and the work proved very demanding on the eyes, as well as on the individuals' attention to detail and powers of concentration. Unsurprisingly by the end of the project, almost every team member including myself needed to wear glasses because of the strain on the eye, and brought about by working 10 hours each day with old black and green monochrome monitors.

In December 1985 and following my first 18 months as a Royal Engineer Military Clerk, I was upgraded to Class 2 and formally appointed as Headquarters' Troop Chief Clerk in place of the incumbent sergeant. This earned me a recommendation for early promotion to sergeant and I attended and passed the mandatory four-week Education Promotion Certificate (EPC) Course on 4 February 1986. Through achieving this qualification, my new career was now in a very good place and it was up to me to compete and prove that I was ready for further promotion.

Open Day at Munsterlager, 1985

With hidden colleagues at Munsterlager

For me personally, Dennis Barracks was always a special and fascinating military barracks and not only because of its Second World War history, but because I served there during the Cold War on two separate tours and I experienced at first-hand how friendly and hospitable the German people truly are. Munsterlager had many traditional features such as an old watermill and an historic barn, but at the edge of the town was a German Panzer Training Area and I could never understand why live firing was permitted so close to a heavily populated town. Shells were often fired and heard overhead and on one occasion in 1985, there was a report of an incident in which a residential property had allegedly been struck and several civilians injured.

At the 1985 Open Day in Dennis Barracks, I happened to meet up with a friend and colleague who I had served with in 3 Troop whilst at Kelly's Garden just two years earlier. He had been posted to Munsterlager as an Armoured Engineer despite having no previous experience, and so we spent most of the afternoon socialising and catching up on old times.

My development as a military clerk was helped considerably by excellent guidance and instruction from the Regimental Chief Clerk and Staff Assistant, and I remained with 32 Armoured Engineer Regiment until 28 May 1986. I was issued a posting order to a Headquarters in the United Kingdom that was unknown to me and would serve as the Assistant Chief Clerk.

Based at Minley Manor near Farnborough, it was one mile from Hawley Training Area where I completed my Final Training Exercise (FTX) at the end of my Basic Military Training in 1977. The world could not get smaller and as hard as I tried, I could not recall ever seeing Minley Manor or the Headquarters while in training, and so I could not wait to report to my new unit and when I eventually arrived, I was overwhelmed and speechless by the building that greeted me.

29 May 1986 to 10 October 1988
CVHQ RE, Minley Manor – Assistant Chief Clerk – Corporal

After a 24-hour car journey all the way from Munsterlager in the former West Germany to Farnborough in Hampshire, and via a DFDS Hamburg-Harwich ferry crossing I finally arrived at the main gate of Gibraltar Barracks in Blackwater on Thursday, 29 May 1986. I was informed by the two armed military guards that my new unit namely Central Volunteers Headquarters Royal Engineers (CVHQ RE) was in fact on the opposite side of the main road, and that the entrance was 300 metres on the right.

Within minutes I arrived at a pair of tall palatial looking black wrought-iron gates that had gold tipped spikes, and was met by a smartly dressed Ministry of Defence security guard who directed me to a car park at the end of an impressive yellow gravelled drive. Everything about this place was magnificent and regal and as I slowly drove past an old church to my left, to my right I saw an old red-brick walled garden in which fruit and vegetables grew. This was no ordinary military establishment. As I turned right at the end of the drive I could see to my left an archway that led into a cobbled-stone courtyard in which two peacocks freely roamed. I was completely captivated as I made my way to the Security Office where I was met by an elderly Mod security guard called Fred who gave me the warmest of welcomes and escorted me to CVHQ RE's offices. Immediately I felt at home because this was my kind of place and I could not wait to meet the team.

Minley Manor, 1986

    Minley Manor was a magnificent red-brick Grade II listed Gothic-style chateau designed by Henry Clutton, an English architect between 1858 and 1860 and later upgraded by Raikes Currie who served as Member of Parliament for Northampton for 20 years, between 1837 and 1857. Connected to nobility through marrying the daughter of John Wodehouse, 2nd Baron of Kimberley in 1825, Raikes Currie was also a wealthy partner of the family run Curries & Co Bank which it is said, had some involvement with the slave industry.

    In 1934 the estate which boasted orchards, an orangery, stables, and a Grade II listed water tower was requisitioned by the British War Office as an annex to the Staff College at Camberley. Since 1971 it served as the Officers' Mess for the Royal School of Military Engineering and in 1986, it also became the official home of Headquarters 11 Engineer Group (HQ 11 Engr Group) and Central Volunteers HQ RE (CVHQ RE).

    My office looked directly out onto the main courtyard which in 1969, was featured in the movie 'Mosquito Squadron' and several other movies were filmed there over the years. Minley Manor was quite simply the most lavish and imposing of British Army establishments anywhere in the United Kingdom, and its shock value was always mind-blowing. The estate was extensive and within its boundary was part of Hawley Military Training Area, two farms, a 600-metre-long avenue of Wellingtonia trees which were the tallest in the country, several red-bricked country cottages, a tennis court, and 2,500 acres of prime Hampshire countryside.

Nearby and along Minley Road was the Brigadier's residence, and the well-known Crown and Cushion public house with its splendid cricket pitch immediately outside, and to its side was the 16th century Meade Hall in which I enjoyed many a fine meal.

To my surprise during the initial interview with the commanding officer, I was informed that my post was that of Assistant Chief Clerk to a Staff Sergeant Chief Clerk however, no such post actually existed because the Staff Sergeant was in fact a 'black economy' appointment only, on the Establishment Table. This meant that in reality I was the Chief Clerk and as such, I would have full responsibility for the administrative management and control of all Regular Permanent Staff and Territorial Army Officers and Soldiers serving with CVHQ RE. Furthermore, I would oversee all other GI matters that normally would be assigned to a Staff Sergeant Chief Clerk. At first this all sounded extremely heavily imbalanced because as a corporal I was two ranks below a staff sergeant and the difference in salary, status, power, and privileges were considerable.

I decided against mentioning this during the interview and instead I assured my new commanding officer was that I was extremely excited by my new appointment, and that I looked forward to the challenges and working with the rest of the team. These would all give me the opportunity to prove myself as a team player, and as a Military Clerk who had ambition and drive and so I left the meeting believing I had already made my mark. What I particularly liked about my new role was the authority I had been empowered with by my commanding officer, and the diversity of work and responsibilities which formed part of my new role.

I fully immersed myself into dealing with the huge backlog of unfinished work I had inherited and other matters that needed addressing as a priority, as well as working my way through a stack of papers, forms, and correspondences that were piled in the in-tray on my desk. Within less than a month everything was up to date and I was confidently on top of my game, and thriving on the progress I had made within such a short period of time.

CVHQ RE was the Administration and Training Wing of 111 Engineer Regiment (Volunteers) which comprised of 120 and 130 Field Squadron, 198 Park Squadron, and a number of Specialist Teams Royal Engineers (STRE) that were spread across the southeast of England. Headed by a lieutenant colonel commanding officer, CVHQ RE also had a major Quartermaster, a captain SO3 Engr, a captain Training Officer, one Warrant Officer Class One Sergeant Major Instructor (SMI), two staff sergeant Permanent Staff Instructors (PSIs), a full MT Section, and a RAPC staff sergeant and corporal.

The team was further supported by a Non-Regular Permanent Staff (NRPS) and everyone was required to work most weekends, in addition to our normal working week and from time to time, we would deploy on military training exercises and manoeuvres with the territorial officers and soldiers who were recruited from across the country. The hours were long and the work challenging, but the rewards were worthwhile and plentiful and between 7 and 26 September 1986, I qualified as a Military Clerk Class One at the Army School of Clerical Training, Worthy Down which is near the historic city of Winchester in Hampshire.

Back at Minley Manor in September 1987 and whilst walking along the Wellingtonia Avenue one sunny Sunday morning, I challenged a man who was clearly not a member of the British Army judging by the length of his hair. Practicing his golf swing, I introduced myself and asked to see some form of identity and if he had permission to be on military property. Instantly, he looked shocked and apologised.

We chatted a while and he kept going back to the subject of football, which I had no interest in, nor still do, and suddenly he asked if I knew who he was. I replied that I had no idea and with that he smiled and looking somewhat relieved, he told me that he was Andy King the former Everton midfield footballer and ex England international, and that he was now playing for Aldershot Football Club. Over the next year we became the closest of friends and Andy was married to a professional dancer who had performed on many national television programmes such as The Kenny Everett Show. I often drove Andy to Aldershot FC to watch him play as his guest, and he introduced me to the Club President who at that time was Arthur English who starred in the TV comedy series 'Are You Being Served?' He also introduced me to international footballers including Joe Jordon, Dennis Law, and Lou Macari. Sadly one day after I left the British Army, I learned that Andy passed away on 27 May 2015 after suffering a second heart attack at his home in Luton.

My office is the small window next to the bush on the left

I experienced many memorable and wonderful times while serving with CVHQ RE including a two-week Army Recruiting Campaign on Jersey and Guernsey in the Channel Islands, in 1987. CVHQ RE also took part in the Remembrance Day Parade in Saint Helier on Jersey, and we recruited several new territorial officers and soldiers. At Saint Peter's Port on Guernsey, we were invited to the island's Administration Offices and met several dignitaries as well as touring the island and visiting World War Two historical sites. At Weymouth during a training week, I met the comedian Brian Connolly at the mayor's palace.

Other responsibilities I undertook at CVHQ RE included training Territorial Army clerks, carrying out documentation inspections on all three squadrons, writing reports for audits, liaising with Manning and Records Offices, controlling confidential reports and manning establishments, and acting as the Classified Documents' Custodian.

It was in 1988 that I first underwent surgery at the Cambridge Military Hospital in Aldershot for a torn knee cartilage injury, which I incurred during a rugby match in Munsterlager in 1981. After a very quick recovery, I took part in Adventure Training Exercises in the Lake District and in Snowdonia National Park. On one occasion in Great Langdale, our five-man team completed a fifteen-mile-long trek during which we were caught up in a heavy storm and had no option but to stay overnight at a campsite near the famous Old Dungeon Ghyll. On Snowdon, we trekked the Ranger's Path to the summit and the following day completed a hair-raising 12-mile canoe challenge from Llanrwst to Conwy which almost ended in disaster.

An increasingly turbulent incoming tide near the mouth of the River Conwy almost capsized all seven canoes but by sticking together, we completed the course safely at the slipway next to the Liverpool Arms, and near the smallest house in Wales. We camped at Capel Curig Military Training Camp and it was on this particular exercise that I and others, had the opportunity to retrace part of the route I covered during the Welsh 1000 Peaks Race in 1976, and they agreed it was extremely demanding.

On 6 October 1988, I signed my confidential report at CVHQ RE prior to being posted back to Germany on promotion to sergeant, and this time as a Squadron Chief Clerk with 26 Engineer Regiment at Corunna Barracks, Iserlohn in North Rhine-Westphalia. To my pleasant surprise and as a reward for the hard work I had put into my role at CVHQ RE, I received my first recommendation for commissioning. At that time, I wanted to gain promotion to Warrant Officer Class Two before I applied for a Late Entry (LE) Commission and also, there were other ambitions and goals I wanted to fulfil because time was on my side, and I was in no rush.

Snowdon, 1988

Recruiting in the Channel Islands, 1987

Afternote

In November 2021 and after writing this particular chapter, I was curious as to what had become of Minley Manor and whether or not the British Army still had ownership. I also wanted to know what had become of the two farms and former Raikes' family church as well as the three cottages that were dotted around the estate, and the magnificent meadow that swept its way down towards the edge of what was once the Brigadier's residence. It was with sadness but no surprise that I discovered Minley Manor was sold by the Ministry of Defence in 2014, and to a property developer who had plans to convert the estate into a 5-star hotel with a spa and conference centre. More recently I read that Minley Manor is an exclusive wedding and individual events venue, and so I hope to visit it again one day and hopefully walk around the beautiful grounds and inside the actual manor house.

Similarly, Dennis Barracks in Munsterlager was sold at some point in the 1990s and today it serves as an industrial business park and private housing estate, as indeed have most former British military bases and stations across Germany. This all happened because the Cold War ended in 1991 and as such, there was no justifiable reason for the British Armed Forces to continue its military presence in a country that was now re-united after the fall of the Iron Curtain.

One day, it is my intention to revisit my former barracks in Munsterlager and also in Iserlohn, just to see how these have changed. Since leaving the British Army in 2000, I have visited several of my former camps and garrisons in the United Kingdom and I have to say that in most instances, I have genuinely been disillusioned and saddened by what I have seen. Two in particular were complete shadows of their former self and clearly lacked strict military order and organisation. I accept that nothing lasts for ever and just maybe, both these establishments were awaiting refurbishment of upgrading because there were still troops serving in them. I had no idea of their status in 2022 but there did seem to be a general lack of care and investment in both.

Whenever a military unit or establishment is shut down or the size of our Armed Forces reduced, the costs involved to re-establish and recruit more troops will be staggering in terms of training, equipping, accommodating and returning facilities to even the most basic of level and standard and quite possibly, it could prove unaffordable. Yet it is an undeniable fact that we live in a time of very worrying geopolitical tension and in which the use of nuclear warfare is not being ruled. Right now in 2023, a war is being fought in Europe which nobody would have thought possible after the end of the Cold War in 1991.

Chapter Twenty-Four
October 1988 to August 1995

Foreword

As I left CVHQ RE on 10 October 1988, I was confident that my career was on track and progressing at a pace with which I would make it to Warrant Officer. Furthermore, I was grateful for the appointments and postings that RE Manning and Records Office were choosing for me after I transferred across to the Military Clerk roster. At that time it was almost 10 years since I completed my Basic Military Training at Southwood Camp and I was now a newly promoted sergeant being posted back to Germany in the role of Squadron Chief Clerk.

Within nine months of arriving at 26 Engineer Regiment in Iserlohn, my rugby coaching was attracting a great deal of attention from the local German media, and also my commanding officer who made reference to it in my first confidential report as a SNCO Chief Clerk. This all came about when I took the German rugby team TVD Hagen through to the National Bundesliga in my first season as Head Coach, and on the back of this I also received a number of offers of contract from other German rugby clubs across the country. The one that stands out was the offer made by an agent to purchase my premature release from the British Army, and appoint me to a coaching position with the German National Rugby Union. I turned the offer down to protect both my military career and financial security.

Everything was going well in both my army and sporting careers, and I was achieving the highest grades in my annual confidential reports and recommendations for accelerated promotion. At the same time, my drive, motivation and ambitions increased to new levels and I became fiercely competitive. As the former US senator Bill Bradley once said, "ambition is the path to success."

Iserlohn is a small German city that sits in the Sauerland region of North Rhine-Westphalia, and its earliest history dates back to the 12th century. Surrounded by dense and extensive woodlands, it provided the ideal environment for cross country running and at weekends I would walk and run for miles at a time. German buildings for some reason have always intrigued me because of the wonderful variety of Gothic, Romanesque, and Medieval architecture and in Iserlohn, one in particular that really fascinated me.

The Danzturm is a 25 metre slender stone tower that stands on the highest point of a hill 384 metres above sea level that overlooks a small lake called the Seilersee, and I would often run up the ever increasing incline until I eventually reached the foot of the tower and gently make my way back to the main road. It is probably one of the most testing 10 kilometre runs I know of.

Less than an hour's drive from Iserlohn is the famous Möhne Dam which I flew over in the Harrier T-Bird Jump Jet whilst on Exercise CERTAIN ENCOUNTER in September 1981, and often I would walk across the dam while serving in Iserlohn. The city thrives academically and has two established universities that focus primarily on the applied science of engineering. I liked Iserlohn a lot but for me, it was Munsterlager that was always the more special given it was my first ever posting with the British Regular Army.

11 October 1988 to 30 March 1992
26 Engineer Regiment, Iserlohn – Squadron Chief Clerk – Sergeant

Rather than fly to Germany via Air-Trooping at Luton Airport, I decided to drive to Iserlohn which included a ferry crossing from Dover to Calais, and it took approximately 14 hours to complete. It was a pleasant journey but certainly not as eventful as my arrival at 26 Engineer Regiment which was around 14.15 on Tuesday, 11 October 1988. As a newly promoted sergeant and thrilled at taking up my first appointment as a Squadron Chief Clerk, I did feel somewhat apprehensive as I reported to Corunna Barracks which was located on the main road to Hemer, a military town some eight kilometres to the east. About one kilometre from Corunna Barracks was the British Military Hospital (BMH) Iserlohn while two kilometres further, was the Seilersee and Autobahn 46.

At the Guard Room I introduced myself to the Duty Officer and after registering my car for a vehicle permit, I was briefed on the layout of the camp and directed to the far end of the Regimental Headquarters where I was told I could park my car, and then report to the Staff Assistant whose name ironically was Warrant Officer Class One Thomas. I parked my car exactly where I was told to and gathered my posting documentation but as I did, the peace and quiet of the camp was completely shattered by someone bawling at some poor individual.

Immediately my heart went out to whoever was on the receiving end, and I thought to myself how embarrassing it must be to be singled out for such a public dressing down, and in broad daylight. I looked around to see who was shouting and to my absolute horror, it was none other than the Regimental Sergeant Major who was standing in an open window at the end of the Regimental Headquarters building, and the poor sod on the receiving end was me! He was in an absolute rage because without realising it, I was parked in his reserved car space and he was screaming for me to report to his office immediately. In my defence and as a newcomer to the regiment, I had only followed the instructions of the Duty Officer.

With a worried feeling in the pit of my stomach and extremely embarrassed and let down by the Duty Officer, I reported to the RSM who was on the ground floor and immediately next to the Adjutant and Staff Assistant's shared office. Standing alone in the corridor while waiting to be summoned, I heard the Adjutant say to the Commanding Officer "whoever the poor man is, he's in for it, sir!" Meanwhile, the RSM was shouting down the phone at someone else and so I felt small consolation that I was not the only person who had upset him.

Eventually I was called in and received an almighty dressing down as well as a punishment of three days' regimental duties without making any excuses, and I believe he respected this. Without my knowing it at the time he played for the Regimental Rugby XV, and because of my rugby background I was asked by the commanding officer to take over as coach. I happily agreed and very soon the RSM and I got on extremely well and we genuinely had a healthy respect for each other.

Both on and off the rugby field he was a man you would not want to get on the wrong side of but as his newly appointed rugby coach, I knew I would be safe. Looking back I can say with every confidence that he was an excellent RSM and the most immaculately dressed soldier I have ever known. He was also fun company and an entertaining story teller but best of all, he was a superb second row forward.

During my initial interview with the Staff Assistant, I was informed that I would take up the vacant post of Regimental Headquarters Troop Chief Clerk but by January 1989, and within just three months of taking up my new role I was double-hatted as Regimental Discipline SNCO and empowered with full responsibility for the conduct administration of 850 officers and soldiers. As such, I was now also called Regimental Liaison Officer and this involved communicating with external agencies and higher formations such as BAOR Divisional Legal Branch, Garrison (GI) Discipline Branch, Central Police Advisory Branch at Dusseldorf, Special Investigation Branch (SIB), Royal Military Police (RMP), and the District Courts Martial Office.

In late 1989, I was appointed 5 Field Squadron Chief Clerk and in doing so I had fulfilled one of my goals as a Military Clerk and I could not have joined a more historical sub-unit. 5 Field Squadron originated from the 5th Company Royal Engineers which in January 1879, had in its ranks a famous lieutenant by the name of John Chard who went on to win the Victoria Cross for his part in defending Rorke's Drift, during the Anglo-Zulu Wars in Natal. Senior to Lieutenant Gonville Bromhead of the 2nd Battalion, 24th Regiment of Foot by just a few days, Chad assumed command of 139 soldiers who were totally outnumbered by some 4,000 Zulu warriors who hours earlier, had won a decisive victory over Lord Chelmsford's column at the Battle of Isandlwana.

In my first year with 5 Field Squadron, I supervised and controlled the administration and clerical support needed to reorganise, train, and deploy the squadron on a four-month tour of Northern Ireland before taking on the role of Rear Party SNCO. The following year, I administered and deployed 108 Battle Casualty Replacements (BCRs) to the Gulf War as part of Operation GRANBY which was a military conflict that followed the Iraqi invasion of Kuwait in 1990. It was around this time that I was re-trained as a Chieftain AVLB Commander at the Armoured Engineer Wing of Bovington Camp in Wareham, Dorset due of an anticipated shortfall in Armoured Engineer SNCOs. I attended the course along with four others but remained in post as 5 Field Squadron Chief Clerk.

To say that life was hectic and somewhat chaotic in July 1991 would be an understatement, however, I also travelled to Norway for 12 days to attend a Unit Expedition Leader (UEL) Course at the British Mountain Training Centre (BMTC) near Kristiansand. Then in September 1991, I returned to the BMTC and was upgraded to Joint Service Mountain Expedition Leader (JSMEL) after co-leading a seven-day expedition along the Hovden Trail with a fellow SNCO from 5 Field Squadron. At the end of the 1991 annual reporting period, I was graded Outstanding by my officer commanding and recommended for early promotion to staff sergeant.

One physical challenge that 26 Engineer Regiment undertook every year was an event called the 'Sewer Run.' This was a race through the town's underground drainage system that began at one end of the town, and continued along a gradual incline until it reached an exit point some five kilometres away. Due to the restricted headroom, this race often involved everyone having to adopt the crouched walking and running position which was extremely demanding on your upper-leg muscle strength.

Another regular challenge began outside the gymnasium in Corunna Barracks and would involve running along the main road to a junction where a steep track veered-off to the left, and then followed another woodland track that went on for several kilometres. In winter this track was always covered in snow and eventually it levelled off before doubling back on itself. Iserlohn certainly kept the British troops fit all year round.

Throughout my time with 26 Engineer Regiment, my rugby coaching and refereeing commitments increased for both the British Army and also the German Rugby Unions, and in early 1989 I arranged and officiated a friendly rugby fixture between the regiment and a local German team called TVD Hagen. The match was first and foremost a public relations exercise because the opposition were players from Germany, France, Poland, the Former Yugoslav Republic, and there were several former British soldiers. 26 Engineer Regiment inflicted a heavy defeat on our German opponents and I was asked by their club captain if I would give his team two coaching sessions.

Although I was 26 Engineer Regiment's head coach and actively refereeing on a regular basis, I agreed to TVD Hagen's request simply because I wanted to help them improve their game. I could see that they had great potential but what heavily influenced my decision, was the determination they showed to become a better team. Throughout the game they never stopped working hard at the break downs and in the scrums, and they showed strength and power, and their team spirit was always positive.

After two evening training sessions, I was invited to become their coach and within one season TVD Hagen went on to win the 1991 North-Rhine Westphalia Regional Rugby Championship and with that, I had taken them into the National Bundesliga. Because of this, I was being contacted regularly by newspapers and local radio stations with invites to be interviewed, and one unexpected reward for the club's promotion were VIP tickets to the 1991 Rugby World Cup Final between Australia and England at Twickenham. Australia won the match 26 v 6 and after the match, we met with the director and players of Winchester Rugby Football Club in the White Swan public houses in Islington.

Corunna Barracks, Iserlohn 1991

Whilst at 26 Engineer Regiment I met and became good friends with a Royal Army Ordnance Warrant Officer Class One by the name of Tony Gardner, who had a wonderful sense of humour was very popular with everyone who knew him. Short in stature, he was affectionately nicknamed 'Titch' Gardner yet in life he was a giant of a man and had been an excellent scrum-half in his day, and represented his corps on numerous occasions.

I learned a lot from Tony because as a former coach himself, he knew the game inside out and very often he would come along and watch me coach the regimental team. Afterwards, he would constructively critique my performance over a beer and we respected each other very highly but sadly, while writing this memoir my son

David gave me the terrible news that Tony had passed away. Tony 'Titch' Gardner was a superb individual and a true gentleman.

One of the defining moments of the 20th century took place while I was serving with 26 Engineer Regiment in Iserlohn, and provided historic television footage that was broadcast across the world. Following the end of the Second World War military and geopolitical tensions between the United States, Soviet Union, and their allies continued until 1991. This period was better known as the Cold War.

The Eastern Bloc or Warsaw Pact as it was also known comprised of the Soviet Union (USSR) and her allies with China being the most notable, while the Western Block was made up of the United States of America and her allies, who were all NATO member countries including the United Kingdom. In March 1985, Soviet President Konstantin Chernenko died at the age of 73 and a new president was duly elected by the name of Mikhail Gorbachev. Free elections saw communist regimes lose power across Eastern Europe and after tens of thousands of German citizens attacked and climbed the Berlin Wall in protest, the beginning of the end of the Cold War was in sight.

The Berlin Wall was built by the German Democratic Republic (East Germany) in August 1961 and had divided the city for decades, but after mass protests and rebellious activity, sections of the wall started to give way until eventually it was breached on 9 November 1989. People and countries from across the globe watched on television screens as demonstrators broke through gaps in the wall and entered East Berlin, and completely unchallenged by East German guards. The reunification of Germany had begun and the reason I still recall those events so clearly is because it happened on a Thursday evening, and I had just finished a coaching session with TVD Hagen. Afterwards, the team and I went to a bar that was owned by one of the players named Ralph, and together we watched in silence as the events unfolded.

In March 1992, I received a posting order back to the United Kingdom and on promotion to staff sergeant.

6 April 1992 to 13 June 1993
78 Engineer Regiment (V), Southampton – Regimental Chief Clerk
Staff Sergeant

On 6 April 1992 I was posted to Southampton in Hampshire as part of a small start-up team tasked with establishing, equipping, and training a brand-new Territorial Army Regiment that had its Headquarters located at Blighmont Barracks on Millbrook Road. The new unit was named 78 Engineer (Fortress) Regiment

(Volunteers) and its role would be to support 3 (UK) Division, and we had just one year in which to ensure that the unit was fully set up, manned, and operational.

The start-up team was headed by a lieutenant colonel Commanding Officer, a captain Adjutant, an Operations Training Major, a Regimental Sergeant Major, two staff sergeant Permanent Staff Instructors, one REME staff sergeant, and me as the Regimental Chief Clerk. When I first arrived at Blighmont Barracks and met with the team it was evident from day one that this particular posting and the task we had ahead of us was going to be complex. It would also prove political and extremely challenging because the new Royal Engineer regiment was taking over from what had been up until then, a Royal Artillery unit and one retired SO3 who was stationed in Brighton was exceptionally unhappy.

From day one he was awkward and uncooperative, and I could empathise to some extent. Blighmont Barracks was located on the north side of the busy A33 dual-carriageway and directly opposite shipping offices and container holding areas that formed part of the Port of Southampton. The TA centre was immediately opposite the King George V Dry Dock and inside the building, we only had the most basic of furniture such as desks, several chairs, phones but hardly anything else. Living accommodation was also a problem because the nearest family married quarters were either at Marchwood Camp, or in the tiny seaside village of Calshot which was at the southernmost end of Southampton Water.

This was the main route used by shipping and cruise liners such as the *QE2* to access the Solent, and it was along this famous stretch of water that *Titanic* first sailed on her ill-fated maiden voyage in April 1912. Calshot was also home of the famous Sunderland Flying Boat that served during the Second World War as a patrol bomber aircraft. At first, I was accommodated in the Warrant Officers' and Sergeants' Mess at 17 Port and Maritime Regiment in Marchwood, on the western side of Southampton Water and some 10 miles south of Blighmont Barracks.

My first task was to plan, organise, and establish the Administrative and Pay Office of a regiment that would have under its command three squadrons, one sub-unit, and a REME Workshop as shown below. I was also responsible for ensuring that each was manned according to the Establishment Table.

- 560 (Hampshire) Headquarters Squadron based at Southampton.
- REME Workshops based at Southampton.
- 127 Field Squadron based at Dyke Road, Brighton.
- 227 Amphibious Squadron based at Shoe Lane, Aldershot.
- Sub-unit based at Tonbridge Wells.

During the initial interview with my commanding officer and adjutant, my roles and responsibilities were outlined and discussed in some depth and quite understandably it came as no surprise to me, to discover that not only was I going to be the first Regimental Chief Clerk of the new unit but also, I would be undertaking the additional duties of Staff Assistant. Both these roles would normally be assigned to a Warrant Officer Class Two and Warrant Officer Class One respectively. In reality and as a newly promoted Staff Sergeant, I was taking on the work of two Warrant Officers yet only receiving a Staff Sergeant's salary.

Furthermore, I was responsible for setting up an administrative and pay office in all four locations, and organising and controlling the purchase and installation of IT systems, office furniture, stationery supplies, telephone and filing systems, Queen's Regulations, technical library, typing pools, conference rooms, Classified Documents' cells, and more. In addition to all of this I would need to recruit supporting civil servants and liaise with the different Manning and Records Offices to ensure that all posts were. My commanding officer described my role as a huge tasking yet I saw it as another exciting challenge, and my immediate thought was that if I could deliver all of this within the given timeframe of just one year, then it would go a long way to setting me up for further promotion. This was despite the fact that I had to wait a minimum of two years to rise to make Warrant Officer Class Two, given I was a newly promoted Staff Sergeant.

My colleagues in the start-up team were also under extreme pressure because each needed to plan and organise their own department, create bespoke training courses and schedules, obtain directives and instructions, and source equipment and libraries. As a newly formed team made up of complete strangers, we all hit the ground running and the morale we generated was superb.

Because 78 Engineer Regiment (V) was a newly formed unit within 3 (UK) Division, a number of permanent and non-permanent staff who had served with the previous sub-units in all four locations were invited to remain in post. Many were transferred across to the new regiment accordingly including retired officers who held SO3 posts, civilians who were employed in stores and workshops however, it was noticeable that not all warmed to the changes that were being implemented.

It is widely accepted that most people do not like change, and so it was with 127 Field Squadron who were based in Brighton. Resistance and confrontation was soon being noted by members of the start-up team at meetings, in telephone calls, and correspondences, and it was all political. The team considered this to be nothing but a pointless and futile power struggle on the part of a certain individual however, through sensitive diplomacy and a necessary firmness that came from the very top, the situation was resolved and in no time at all, a more supportive and constructive working relationship was established.

Another of my responsibilities was the planning and arranging of a programme of military clerical training courses to be held at each location, and I would also act as instructor and although these were enjoyable and important, they were nevertheless adding to my workload. Soon it was all work and no play and clearly too much for just one person, and so I requested a meeting with my commanding officer and adjutant.

After sensitively outlining my concerns, I proposed workable options which were instantly approved and these included having a small team of TA clerks recruits assist me on a part-time basis. The meeting was a success and I assured them both that I was relishing my role, even though my working day still would not end until 23.00. By being based in Southampton, my job required me to make regular visits to each sub-unit and ensure that their administrative offices were running smoothly, and to their credit they were.

My time with 78 Engineer Regiment (V) was always going to be short-term as indeed was the case with the others in the start-up team, because as soon as we had fulfilled our purpose of setting up the new unit, we would be posted to new units which made sound common sense.

Determined not to lose focus on my rugby career, while serving at Blighmont Barracks I contacted and arranged a meeting with the Divisional Army Rugby Union Referee Controller for the South East of England, and he was extremely supportive. I was officiating matches at all levels in Winchester, Portsmouth, the Isle of Wight, and even at school seven-a-side tournaments but the most rewarding moment for me, was being selected to referee the South District Major Units Rugby Semi-Final at Warminster in 1993.

I also passed my Education Promotion Certificate (Advanced) at Worthy Down and gained full membership into the Institute of Supervisory Management. In June 1993, I received my final confidential report as a Royal Engineer because it was around this time that all military clerks in the British Army were transferred across to the newly formed Adjutant General's Corps (SPS) which included administrative and pay personnel.

Because of my proven experience in both planning and setting up a new military unit, and given that my original corps was the Royal Engineers, I was selected by the AGC Manning and Records Office to oversee the drawdown and closure of the administrative wing of the Army Apprentice College at Chepstow. AAC Chepstow was a well-known Royal Engineer Training Establishment based at Beachley which sits on the border with England and next to the Second Severn Crossing which today, is known as the Prince of Wales Bridge. On Sunday, 13 June 1993 I packed my car for the last time at 17 Port and Maritime Regiment in Marchwood ahead of a two-hour drive to Chepstow. I heard that the Adjutant General's Corps was delighted with my performance at Blighmont TA Cent and as such, I looked forward to a break from working seven days a week.

Two social events at Southampton which I really enjoyed was watching Richard O'Brien's cult musical 'The Rocky Horror Show' which I first saw in London, when I was aged 17. This time it was being performed at the Mayflower Theatre and I went with colleagues from the start-up team, and the water fights and rice throwing that had become part of audience participation was as enjoyable as ever.

The second was the meal we all had at a local public house which was used for filming the television series Worzel Gummidge, and starred Jon Pertwee in the leading role of Worzel Gummidge, Lorrain Chase as Dolly Clothes, and Una Stubbs as Aunt Sally.

As I headed for the flyover on my drive out of Southampton, there in the distance and to my right I could see a tower block of flats which was near Westrow Gardens, and this was where Benny Hill once lived.

14 June 1993 to 10 July 1994
Army Apprentice College Chepstow – College Chief Clerk – Staff Sergeant

By being posted to the Army Apprentice College Chepstow as Chief Clerk, without realising it at the time I was taking on yet another demanding role from day one of reporting to Beachley Barracks, and for three reasons. Firstly, the post had been gapped for over a year due to long-term sickness. When I heard this I was confused as to why a replacement had not been identified sooner, given that it had apparently been decided two years earlier by the Ministry of Defence to close the Army Apprentice College Chepstow by the end of June 1994. All I wanted to do was hit the ground running and get on with the job in hand, because quite simply there was no time to lose.

Secondly and from what I could gather, no planning, scheduling, or preparation of any kind had been put into the closing down the administrative departments of the college. Furthermore, it was obvious that nothing had been done in some other departments either and none of this was making any sense, but that was the status quo at the time.

Thirdly, because this was my first appointment as a member of the newly formed AGC (SPS), I was determined to make my mark from day one, yet there was no handover given or handover notes left. These play a crucial part in taking over any new appointment and more so if the unit is a training centre that is being permanently shut down. I would need to make a start immediately because there were overdue confidential reports, bundles of pending paperwork, and I was also responsible for administrating military personnel from the Army Physical Training Corps (APTC), Army Catering Corps (ACC), Royal Army Medical Corps (RAMC), and others.

As briefed during my initial interview with the camp commandant and subsequently written in my 1993/1994 confidential report, as College Chief Clerk I "was responsible for all clerical matters of a very busy unit that has been in a state of turmoil prior to closure." The report went on to say that I had inherited "numerous skeletons in the cupboard" and during the meeting with the commandant, I was forewarned to be prepared for what was to come because the administration of the entire college had been abandoned for over twelve months.

The backlog of missed deadlines, unfinished business, and general queries was breathtaking and indeed worrying and so I formulated a plan which was outlined to the commandant, adjutant, SO3, and head instructor. The meeting concluded with everyone appreciating that under such unprecedented circumstances, all I could do was my best during my 12 months with the college, and this to a large extent lifted a lot of pressure off my shoulders.

In a second one-to-one meeting with my commandant, I was assured that I would not be blamed for any shortcomings in careers that were a direct result of missed confidential report deadlines prior to my arrival, and this too was good to know.

Because I was a rugby coach and referee, the commandant then changed the subject and asked if I was interested in becoming College Rugby Head Coach, which I accepted. It turned out that he too was a rugby referee and so we had common ground. Before addressing the matter of a college administrative closure programme my number one priority was to assess the state of administration right across the establishment, and the commandant was not joking when he said that nothing had been done for over a year. With this in mind, I convened the first of many regular meetings with the Adjutant, Quartermaster, Education Officers, Senior Trade Instructors, Squadron Clerks, Pay Staff Sergeant, and others.

The meeting opened with my overall evaluation of how dire the situation was with regards to the college's administration, and this was followed by my running through a list of priorities that I had identified from my initial interview with the camp commandant. I then outlined my plan on how best to recover the situation and as such, I addressed each department in turn and explained in detail exactly what I needed from each, including deadlines, my expectations from each squadron clerk, and I pulled no punches. Also at that meeting was the Headquarters SO3 who had a wealth of experience, and key contacts, and I valued his advice and support throughout the whole time at Chepstow. I produced and distributed a 12-month schedule of meetings that would convene every two weeks and after summarising all the points I had covered, everyone around the table appeared relieved and eager to get on with the work.

My first priority was to have all confidential reports brought fully up to date and signed by the individuals and reporting officers, and these were dispatched to the relevant Manning and Records Offices and PBs, and the Divisional Commanders where applicable. There were also appraisal reports that needed to be raised for each member of the civilian permanent staff, as well as others working at the college. I also produced a comprehensive College Closure Directive that included objectives and target dates, and this were distributed inside two weeks. Most importantly, I arranged a two-day visit to the Royal Engineer Manning and Records Office in Glasgow to meet with the various officers and civil servants and discuss postings and preferences, career courses, outstanding matters, and any other business. Issues relating to the Royal Army Medical Corps, Royal Army Pay Corps and Army Physical Training Corps personnel were addressed and resolved through telephone calls to their MROs, and confirmed in written correspondences and copied to the Divisional Headquarters and very soon, things were beginning to come together.

Far sooner that I had expected, there was a renewed feeling of confidence throughout the college staff and this in turn, raised morale then one day the adjutant walked into my office with a serious look on his face. "The colonel would like a chief," he said and not knowing why he wanted to see me, I reported to his office with my diary, pen, and schedules in hand, and was prepared to answer any questions he wanted to ask relating to the progress being made.

To my surprise and out of the blue he asked, "do you think the college could win the Fern Cup?" I paused for a moment and replied with full confidence that in my opinion there had every chance and with that he smiled and replied, "excellent chief, give it your best shot!" Over the remainder of the season I took them through several rounds and eventually to the semi-final, but given the immense pressure we were under with the pending closure of the college, we played against a stronger team and was knocked out after losing by just a few points.

It was during one late evening training session for the tournament and while on the practice field just yards from the second Severn Crossing that I suddenly developed a tickly cough, and there and then I decided to give up smoking, and it proved to be very easy to do.

During the 1994 Five Nations Rugby Championship, the Scottish National Rugby Squad held their training camp at the Army Apprentice College in Chepstow ahead of their match against Wales, which was to be played at the National Stadium in Cardiff on Saturday 15 January. As College Rugby Coach, I was allowed to spectate from the touchline and the Scottish Head Coach at that time was none other than the great former back-row player, Jim Telfer. Here was a giant in the game of rugby and had won 21 caps for Scotland, and made 23 appearances with the British and Irish Lions during the legendary 1966 tour of Australia and New Zealand. He also made a further 11 appearances on the 1968 tour of South Africa.

On top of this he also played 8 times for the Barbarians and so for me, Jim Telfer was a star. Halfway through one of the sessions I was invited to assist the coaching team, and within minutes I was working with them and putting world class international players such as Gavin and Scott Hastings, Gregor Townsend, Kenny Logan, Andy Nicol and Craig Chalmers through various skill sets and set pieces, and the whole experience was incredible. What impressed me most were the handling skills, dynamic speed, and sheer physicality of these players, and the totally professional attitude they showed throughout. In appreciation for hosting the Scottish Team a few of the college players and I were given match tickets. Wales beat Scotland 29 v 6.

In July 1994 and as expected, I received a posting order and to my pleasant surprise, this time it was to the Ministry of Defence at Stanmore in Hertfordshire. My 12 months with the Army Apprentice College as Chief Clerk had been challenging but again a total success, and it helped enhance my career despite it only being a short time at Chepstow. I was more than happy to move on and undertake more challenges and greater responsibility.

11 July 1994 to 28 August 1995
Ministry of Defence Stanmore, Hertfordshire – Chief Clerk PB2
Staff Sergeant

After the experience I gained with CVHQ RE at Minley Manor, then 78 Engr Regt (V) at Blighmont in Southampton, and the Army Apprentice College at Chepstow, my confidence and self-belief soared and I genuinely felt there was nothing I could not turn my hand to if I really tried.

Several weeks before I left Chepstow, I was invited by AGC (SPS) Manning and Records Office to submit my three preferences of posting and after giving this a lot of thought, I included the Ministry of Defence because I thought this would test even further my working ability and broaden my knowledge, and that was how I came to be posted to Stanmore as Chief Clerk Personnel Branch 2 (Infantry). At that time, MoD Stanmore was located on London Road and formed part of the Military

Secretary's Department. It had the appearance of an old military style hospital which had two long adjacent corridors with numerous offices on both sides.

One of my immediate priorities was to find myself private accommodation and I managed to secure a room through the Ministry of Defence at a property in Borehamwood, which was very close to Elstree in northwest London where the BBC television series 'Eastenders' was filmed at that time. Often in the evenings I could see the lights of the film set as I drove into Elstree for a meal but eventually, I managed to find a more convenient property on Elms Road in Harrow which was much closer to Ministry of Defence Stanmore.

On my arrival on 11 July 1994, I parked my car and walked into the large single storey complex that stood on a incline, and the characteristics of a World War Two hospital was all around. There were two corridors that seemed to go on forever and branching off on both sides were former hospital wards that now served as Personnel Branches (PB) for the British Army. A Central Records Office was situated halfway along the right hand corridor and to the right, and this was where classified personnel files were stored and could be signed out by staff from each PB for management purposes, and each contained confidential reports, postings, performance reviews, course results, correspondences, promotion preferences, and other documentation.

No military personnel working at MoD Stanmore wore uniform and my role as Chief Clerk PB2, was to supervise the team of civil servants that supported and worked for the branch officers who were under the command of a retired colonel. PB2 managed the careers of British Infantry officers serving around the world and controlled their postings, ensured that confidential reports were correct and held on file for promotion boards, and liaised with regiments, headquarters and divisions, and carried out other sensitive business such as vetting. Again I needed to hit the ground running because during my interview with the colonel, a former Black Watch commanding officer, I was told that as well as doing my own work I would also be covering a Warrant Officer who was "less than satisfactory," as was later recorded in my confidential report.

The colonel said he had heard of my work while at Chepstow and when I confirmed what had happened, he smiled and leaned back in his chair and said, "that's why we wanted you." So yet again, I was going to be doing my own work plus that of a Warrant Officer.

My average working day at PB2 quickly turned into 12-hour shifts and one of my additional duties as a SNCO administrator working with the Ministry of Defence, was to periodically act as Duty Officer at the MoD Compassionate Cell in Empress State Building. This was a tall tower block on Lillie Road in West Brompton which up until 1962, was London's tallest commercial building.

My two lasting memories of working at Empress State Building are the incredible views of London's skyline and Stamford Bridge, home of Chelsea Football Club, and the time I looked down one day on Earl's Court 4 and watched as a fleet of articulated lorries carrying sound and stage equipment for Pink Floyd's 1994 'Division Bell' world tour were being unloaded at the rear of the building. The front of Empress State Building looked down on the historic Brompton cemetery where the suffragist campaigner Emmeline Pankhurst is buried, along with Princess Victoria Gouramma of India who was adopted by Queen Victoria, Sir Samuel Cunard who founded the famous Cunard shipping line, and the famous British actor and former wrestler Brian Glover.

Despite the high volume of work I undertook at PB2, the constant pressure of meeting strict deadlines for officer promotion boards, and the forward planning of postings and movement control of infantry officers worldwide, none of this proved taxing or stimulating. Instead it quickly became lacklustre, monotonous, and rather dull and I needed a role that would really challenge and test me, but this was not it. Two positives did come out of my time at Mod Stanmore and the first was 10 months after I arrived in July 1994, I was promoted to Warrant Officer Class Two and posted to 36 Engineer Regiment in Maidstone, Kent as Regimental Administrative Office Warrant Officer.

The second was the brief period I was Head Coach of Harrow Rugby Football Club. I was renting a room on Elms Road in Harrow and one evening by chance, I spoke with the captain of Harrow RFC while dining at the Leefe Robinson VC public house. After an interesting conversation which lasted over an hour, I was invited to go along and watch an evening training session at Grove Field which was just off Wood Lane, and after a drink and long chat with the club committee in the bar I was asked if would be available to coach the club through the 1994/1995 season. I mentioned to the chairman and secretary that my time at MoD Stanmore was going to be short due to my military ambitions and plans, however, they acknowledged this so I accepted the invite there and then.

I was not sad to leave MoD Stanmore because quite genuinely, I did not enjoy the lifestyle of living in a small rented room or the travel involved in getting back and forth to Empress State Building, and then working a full shift either side of a whole night's duty, and the weekly commute to Llanelli at weekends when I was not required to work. The Ministry of Defence sadly was not for me, nor was it for many who worked at Stanmore who I got to know through playing football during lunchtimes at a nearby RAF Station.

Often we would offload our feelings on each other over evening meals which we arranged at a nearby public house. One day as I was walking along the inclined corridor from PB2 (Infantry) to PB7 (Royal Engineers) in MoD Stanmore, I happened to bump into my former officer commanding when I was serving with 5 Field Squadron in Iserlohn, and we chatted for about 10 minutes

He mentioned that serving with the MoD would have a positive effect on my military career and ironically, it was just three weeks later that I was given the news by my colonel that I had been selected for promotion to Warrant Officer Class Two, and was being posted back to a Royal Engineer regiment. I could not have been happier and so ahead of a very hasty departure, I spent the following two weeks making sure that all my military uniforms were altered and new badges of rank fitted, and also I needed to book a room in the Warrant Officer's and Sergeants' Mess at 36 Engineer Regiment, Invicta Park Barracks in Maidstone. So short was the notice of my posting that there was little time for me to handover but thankfully a successor was found, and a short but comprehensive handover was completed on Friday 25 August. Later that day I drove out of MoD Stanmore for the very last time and headed for St Albans, and then the M25.

Afternote

On one occasion while serving at MoD Stanmore in 1994, instead of taking the public transport to Brompton to report for duty at Empress State Building, I decided to drive my car and after I finished my 24 hour weekend shift in the Compassionate Cell, on my way back I took a quick detour to visit a famous property at Logan Place in Kensington W8. The house was sat in the grounds of a high-walled garden and its splendour and grandeur was obvious as soon as I drove past. The property was called Garden Lodge. Easy to get to and even easier to park almost outside the side gate, I was surprised at the lack of security and the fact that I could get out and actually look through a tiny gap in the garden door. Behind the long brick wall was the house I had wanted to see for some time because this was where the legendary rock star Freddie Mercury lived, and died on 24 November 1991.

At long last I could pay my respect to the incredible front man of Queen who I watched perform live on three separate occasions. The first was 21 January 1979 at the Westfalenhalle in Dortmund when Queen were on their Live Killers world tour. The second was 2 August 1982 at the Maple Leaf Gardens in Toronto, when the band were on their Hot Space tour, and the third was 9 August 1986 at Knebworth in Hertfordshire, when they played the final concert of their Magic world tour.

This final concert was supported by Status Quo, Belouis Some, and Big Country and very sadly, it was the last time that Freddie Mercury performed live on stage. It was a quiet Sunday morning around 07.20 when I stood outside the green door of Logan Lodge, and through the tiny gap I could see the garden in which Freddie Mercury spent much of his time relaxing with friends and his treasured cats, and I could see the glass door at the entrance to the property. It was a memorable moment that I am so glad I experienced.

Although they were all only 12-month tours, my posting to the Army Apprentice College at Chepstow and 78 Engineer Regiment (V) in Southampton proved challenging and testing times in my military career, and for reasons I will explain. Firstly in the 1990s, after Staff Assistant or Superintendent Clerk, it was the Regimental Chief Clerk who was the most senior non-commissioned administrator of a Regular Army unit, and they would be supported by approximately 15 to 20 junior NCO clerks in the Headquarter Troop, plus sub-unit chief clerks who in turn would have at least two assistants. This was not the case at either Chepstow or Southampton.

Secondly, senior administrators would have a handover of at least 1 to 2 weeks and with guidance notes that included schedules of annual tasks and deadlines, meetings, an outline of responsibilities, contact lists, a breakdown of sub-units, details of key personnel such as OCs, Paymaster, QM, and a schedule of visits to each sub-unit for introductory purpose. Again, this was not the case at Chepstow or Southampton.

Thirdly, a handover would always be carried out with the predecessor in attendance so that it was 'controlled' yet this too, was not the case at Chepstow or Blighmont Barracks.

Personally, I would never have allowed any successor to take over from me without a handover, and I would always produce a comprehensive package of notes. In August 1995 and without realising it at the time, the best handover I would ever receive was just around the corner and it was at 36 Engineer Regiment. I was taking over as Regimental Administrative Office Warrant Officer from a fellow former Royal Engineer Military Clerk, and what Andy prepared in advance of my arrival was quite simply superb.

Chapter Twenty-Five
August 1995 to August 2000

Foreword

Most people enlist into the British Army between the age of 18 and 21 but in my case, I had already served one year as a Territorial before joining the Regular Army in July 1977. Just three months short of my 23rd birthday, this meant I was technically two years behind the average age for promotion to lance corporal but having every confidence in my ability and experience, I felt I could quickly make up for lost time. With that in mind I made it my goal to reach lance corporal either before or during 1980, and that is exactly what happened.

Being promoted to Warrant Officer Class Two in August 1995 fulfilled another personal goal in my career and it also fuelled my hunger to make it to Class One, the highest Senior Non-Commissioned Officer rank in the British Army. I knew the two years lost through not enlisting into the Regular Army until 1977 could possibly work against me and so I reviewed my circumstances, and after taking all factors into consideration and double-checking my conclusions, I determined that I had three options and each was a win-win situation. They were:

1. *Serve the full career of 22 years and retire with an immediate and full armed forces pension at the age of 45.*
2. *Apply for Late Entry (LE) Commission if promoted to Warrant Officer Class One.*
3. *Apply for 'Extended Continuance' if still a Warrant Officer Class Two at the 22-year point.*

All three guaranteed financial security but to make sure that these options were realistic and achievable, I had a telephone discussion with a SO3 at AGC (SPS) 3 (UK) Division. He confirmed that my first option was assured, my second was still possible but the chances of selection for Warrant Officer Class One were becoming increasingly less likely because of the timings of the next promotion board, and my third was very likely given the shortages at that time. I was more than happy with these and after speaking with a colleague who was in a similar situation, I decided to leave my future in the capable hands of the Adjutant General's Corps MRO. The bottom line was that I was still relishing my time with the British Army and I only had 22 months remaining before completing the full career and furthermore, if I decided to leave then my experience and qualifications would put me in contention for employment in business administrative management in civvy street. Feeling a renewed positivity about my future, I also felt re-energised and an increased sense of enthusiasm and motivation and overnight, I raised my game even further.

Looking back to the day when I first stepped inside the Drill Hall at Llanelli in 1976, I did not believe for one minute that what lay ahead of me was a 24 year adventure that would be filled with exciting moments, lots of travel, and memorable adventures shared with the most wonderful colleagues a person could ever wish for. Many of my experiences were exhilarating and breathtaking, while some were undeniably nerve-racking at times, yet they were all remarkable in their own special way and they all happened in countries and on continents that I do not think I would have visited had I not joined the British Army.

The friends and colleagues I served with and met will never be forgotten because they all played a part in my life, and in the story of my career with the Armed Forces and without them, there would be so much less to tell. In life, it is we who primarily choose which paths we follow and which people become our friends, and I often wonder if indeed I will ever see any of them again. This is not a question for me to answer but I will certainly continue to pray that one day this may happen, if it is truly meant to be.

The former American First Lady Eleanor Roosevelt famously once said that "life is what we make it," and I totally agree. Another saying about life which I like is "life is not a dress rehearsal, so make each day count." But the best adage of all is attributed to Samuel Clemens who wrote under the pen name of Mark Twain, "when our time is up, we will be more disappointed by the things we did not do rather than the things we did."

29 August 1995 to 11 May 1998
36 Engineer Regiment, Maidstone – RAOWO – Warrant Officer Class Two

My clerical experience and knowledge gained over the past 12 years gave me a good grounding upon which I could drive my career further forward, because much of it involved dealing with external agencies and higher authorities. I improved my 'People Skills' and learned how to conduct sensitive matters professionally and wisely, how to deal with people I did not know, and most importantly I learned the art of diplomacy which in essence, is the way we get others 'to let us have our own way.' At conferences and meetings, I would carefully observe negotiations and mediation being played out and I was intrigued by methods and techniques some would adopt and soon, I was doing the same and gaining good results.

In August 1995 I received my next posting order which was to 36 Engineer Regiment in Maidstone, Kent and as the new Regimental Administrative Office Warrant Officer (RAOWO). For me the timing was perfect. The past three years had proved far more challenging and demanding than first anticipated, and my individual development and career progression was exactly what I had hoped for.

After driving south along the M25 from Rickmansworth and then east to Dunton Green where it joins the M26, I was soon on the M20 and heading for Maidstone in Kent. Just one week earlier I had visited the outgoing RAOWO to discuss the role I would be taking over, and I was shown around Invicta Park Barracks which for me was the best start to a good handover.

My official reporting date was Tuesday, 29 August 1995 and on my arrival I was again impressed by the thoroughness and standard of the Guard Room and staff, the tidiness of the barracks and modern facilities that were inside the camp, the extensive open spaces of luscious green grass, and warm welcome. After a coffee in Andy's office, I was introduced to the Commanding Officer and Second-in-Command, the Operations Training Major, Adjutant, Intelligence Officer, and Regimental Sergeant Major. Their offices were all close to mine on the ground floor while on the next level was the Regimental Administrative Officer's office, the Regimental Administrative and Pay office, a central civilian typing pool, and in the far corner a Stationery Store and Technical Library.

As RAOWO of the general support engineer regiment in 3 (UK) Division, I was responsible for the management and control of all GI Admin business including postings, promotions, courses, discipline, discharges and for a unit that had a combined strength of some 745 officers and other ranks. There was also a sizeable contingent of civilian employees, such as typists, cleaners, caterers, ground maintenance workers, drivers, and bar staff.

36 Engineer Regiment was made up of the following:

- Regimental Headquarters
- 50 HQ Squadron
- 20 Field Squadron
- 61 Field Support Squadron
- 69 Gurkha Field Squadron
- REME Workshops

Just a short walk from Invicta Park Barracks was Her Majesty's Prison Maidstone in which London's infamous East End gangster Reggie Kray was serving a 30-year sentence, for the murder of Jack 'the hat' McVitie in a basement flat in Stoke Newington in 1967. The Member of Parliament for Maidstone at the time was Labour's Ann Widdecombe.

Within the confines of the barracks, each squadron had its own offices and a single road ran around the whole of the camp which was not an easy route to run in certain sections. The A229 which was adjacent to the barracks was ironically called Royal Engineer's Road and this branched off at a roundabout, and then led up an incline to the main gate and Guard Room. From there, a road called Flower Rise took you some 200 metres before it reached an incline that passed the REME Workshops, and continued up to a T-junction directly next to the NAAFI shop and immediately in front of the gymnasium.

It was at this T-Junction that Flower Rise joined Grapple Road. Here you could turn right and follow it to the Warrant Officers' and Sergeants' Mess, Officers' Mess, Married Quarters, playing fields, and eventually the Rear Gate. Turning left at the T-junction took you past 69 Gurkha Field Squadron, the Regimental Headquarters and 50 HQ Squadron, and along a short flat section towards the Education Centre.

Before reporting to 36 Engineer Regiment, I heard that Invicta Park Barracks had the most challenging Battle Fitness Test (BFT) route in the whole of corps, and troops would run this at least twice a month as part of their physical training programme. The BFT started on the road immediately outside the gymnasium and followed Grapple Road until it reached 20 Field Squadron's offices on Command Road. From there it gradually climbed its way to the bottom of a steep incline called Troodos Hill which eventually peaked on Malden Drive, some 700 metres further. The route then began to level before dropping gradually until it passed the assault course and NBC test chamber and from there, it headed towards the Rear Gate where the road turned sharply to the right, and followed Grapple Road all the way back to the gymnasium. This was a tough BFT route.

One lap was exactly one and a half miles and two laps made up the full Battle Fitness Test. The first lap was the 'warm up' and needed to be completed as a squad in no more than 15 minutes, and this was supervised by the Physical Training Instructor or PTI. The second lap was run as individuals and had to be completed in under 11 minutes 30 seconds for all those aged 45 years and below, otherwise it would be recorded as a 'Fail' and a re-test carried out within two weeks. My average time at the age of 40 was around 10 minutes 15 seconds.

My office was immediately next to the Adjutant and two doors from the Commanding Officer. During my initial interview with my new CO, I was briefed on what he expected of me, and from day one I just knew we were going to have a good and strong working relationship. Here was the officer I would come to respect more than any other during my entire time with the British Army, because he had exceptional skills, ability, talent, and oozed confidence in everything he undertook. He was quite remarkable and inspirational and even on road runs and at fitness training sessions, he was the most competitive of individuals. As his senior military GI administrator, he showed nothing less than total confidence and faith in me and my performance, and it was an absolute pleasure serving under his command.

36 Engineer Regiment had a full complement of AGC (SPS) personnel and they were competent and without doubt, the most efficient team I had led and so to be their RAOWO was not only a privilege, but it was also very special to me. My day-to-day responsibilities were the same as for any other RAOWO and additional roles included the provision of advice and guidance on matters of discipline and career progression, interviewing potential applicants for Special Duties in Northern Ireland, as well as acting as Staff Assistant which should have been the role of a Warrant Officer Class One. Although the workload was considerable and at times extremely demanding, I also gained an invaluable insight into dealing with complex issues and felt a sense of accomplishment that enthused and motivated me like no other appointment. I thrived on the authority that came with my post, and it was the best job ever.

On 19 April 1996 and after months of military refresher training and preparations for a six-month IFOR operational tour of duty in Bosnia, 36 Engineer Regiment deployed on Operation Resolute. After being transported by a fleet of white military coaches to RAF Brize Norton, the regiment was airlifted to Split Airport in Croatia and along with a senior echelon and command cell, I was stationed in a large disused foundry that was on the eastern edge of a war-torn town called Gorjni Vakuf. We were now 170 kilometres east of Split and 140 kilometres west of Sarajevo.

Bosnia-Herzegovina is a beautiful country in south-east Europe and that summer was officially one of the hottest on record, and at times the heat inside the offices and old foundry buildings was unbearable. Two of my AGC (SPS) sergeants were co-located with me at Gorjni Vakuf as well as three JNCOs, 69 Gurkha Field Squadron, and their corporal Chief Clerk. The set-up of the offices was the best we could organise given the available facilities and it functioned well, however, the telephone and communication system was at times appalling because of the war-damage inflicted on the country's infrastructure. Satellite communications were eventually installed but these soon proved unreliable, slow, and frustrating especially when connections were cut without warning. There was also the persistent problem of time delays when speaking with the United Kingdom.

My tour was interrupted by a six-week period between 8 July and 16 August when I returned to Maidstone on behalf of the commanding officer. He wanted me to ensure that the Rear Party was functioning smoothly and then visit REMRO in Glasgow, to discuss the schedule of queries and personnel matters that I had compiled such as promotions, postings, career courses, and any other business that could not be discussed from theatre. My visit to Glasgow lasted two days and proved invaluable and on my return to Invicta Park Barracks, I worked through my list and kept in daily contact with my colleagues back in Bosnia.

The C-130 Hercules at RAF Brize Norton

One story I have shared over the years was the time I returned to Bosnia on 16 August 1996 in a British RAF C-130 Hercules. Prior to leaving Maidstone, I booked a RAF helicopter to fly me from Split Airport to Gornji Vakuf because of the large bundle of documentation I would be carrying. I reported to the IFOR Helicopter check-in desk at Split Airport which was inside a portakabin close to the main terminal, and I was informed that I would be flying to Gorjni Vakuf courtesy of a Royal Netherlands Air Force helicopter, and I would be the only passenger. Eventually the helicopter arrived and landed about 100 metres from the portakabin and to my pleasant surprise, the pilot climbed out and began to walk towards me but something was telling me that this was no ordinary pilot.

It was the way in which the pilot walked that gave the show away because right then, the helmet came off and just like a scene out of 'Top Gun', an attractive young lady swished her shoulder length auburn hair from side to side, and then waved to me. We introduced ourselves and shook hands, and she smiled the most amazing smile you could ever imagine, and with that we entered the portakabin to finalise the flight documentation. As we walked across to the helicopter together, she put on her helmet and I noticed a label on the back that read "Please don't throw-up over the pilot."

Split Airport Croatia, 16 August 1996

We strapped ourselves into our seats and after completing pre-flight checks, the helicopter took off and headed for Gornji Vakuf and all through the flight, we chatted over our headsets and admired the beautiful scenery and countryside below. Again I struggled to understand why some world leaders choose to follow the path of war. Most villages and towns had been heavily shelled and subjected to ferocious gun fire and at times, it was heart-breaking to see the carnage that had been inflicted on this country and its people.

Days later I visited the 1984 Winter Olympic Stadium in Sarajevo and saw for myself the famous rings still hanging from the ceiling of the ice rink, and right above me. This creaking and pitiful-looking ruin was being used as a British Military Store and I was told that I was standing on the very spot that Torvill and Dean won their gold medal. The politics behind the Bosnian War are complex as I have already outlined, and on many occasions I spoke with official interpreters who worked for IFOR who told me so much more about the events that took place during the war. One of them said, "Bosnia is like Northern Ireland, peace will be short lived unless leaders on both sides let go of the past." The same could be said of most wars and one young female interpreter went further, and forecasted that the fighting in her country could rekindle within 40 years.

I thoroughly enjoyed serving in Bosnia-Herzegovina because of my role and the work it involved, and from day one of being in theatre everything went back to basics because we literally found ourselves working in a makeshift camp. We were also located near towns and communities that had almost been annihilated through fighting and shelling, and while trying not to get emotionally involved over what had taken place, we did nevertheless feel so sorry for these people. It was like being on a film set and at times it felt very surreal, with fortified defences and sentry posts established all around camp and incoming and outgoing armed patrols each and every hour of the day.

My view of Split from the Dutch helicopter

Gornji Vakuf

36 Regimental Headquarters, 50 Headquarters Squadron, 69 Gurkha Field Squadron, and REME Workshops were all based at Gorjni Vakuf however, the Regimental Administrative Officer (RAO) was stationed back at Split in Croatia and close to the international airport. Along with the Regimental Pay Office, I would often visit my teams in their locations which included 20 Field Squadron in Vitez, 61 Field Support Squadron in Tomislavgrad and Bugojno, but the most memorable visit was without doubt to the war-ravaged capital Sarajevo and the derelict Winter Olympic complex, where the concrete shell of what was once the bobsleigh run still stood.

I was told by an interpreter during my visit that during the war, certain parts of the Winter Olympic complex were used as execution sites including the bobsleigh run itself. Once a beautiful and proud city, immediately after the war Sarajevo was both shocking and pitiful to see at first hand, as indeed was the rest of the country because its people and communities had been torn apart by fierce fighting. As we left Sarajevo to return to Gorjni Vakuf, our Land Rover drove past the very place where Archduke Franz Ferdinand was assassinated on 28 June 1914.

Entrance to British Military Base at Gorjni Vakuf

Another experience I will never forget for as long as I live was the time I was running alone around a five-mile circuit that followed a dusty road, and it had become part of my regular fitness training. I was not armed because the local area was considered safe territory. Out of sight of the camp at Gorjni Vakuf and about two miles down the track, I suddenly heard a vehicle slow down behind and as it drew closer, I sensed I was being followed because every time I picked up the pace or slowed down, the vehicle did the same. Not wishing to show that I was concerned or bothered by what was happening, I continued my run and every now and then I moved to the other side of the track to allow the vehicle to pass.

At one point, I was waving my hand to tell the driver to pass me but again the vehicle maintained its distance and this continued up until I was back in sight of the camp. Thinking enough was enough, I stopped and turned to confront whoever was behind the driving wheel. The vehicle pulled up alongside me and sitting in the passenger seat was an unshaven cigar-smoking soldier who looked like a warlord, and he was armed to the teeth. In broken English he explained that he was the commander of the local militia and being concerned for my safety, he had decided to escort me back to camp. Relieved but still wary, I thanked him and the vehicle drove off but I never saw him again during my time at Gorjni Vakuf.

36 Regimental Headquarters at Gorjni Vakuf

Apartment block near Vitez

Road to Sipovo with destroyed houses

Standing next to a demolished road bridge

Former bunker from the war

Village I often drove through

36 Engineer Regiment returned to Maidstone on 4 October 1996 and my confidential report was graded outstanding. Despite receiving another unequivocal recommendation for promotion and commissioning, in February 1998 the AGC (SPS) MRO informed me that I was no longer eligible for Warrant Officer Class One. I had missed the selection board by just 7 days due to my age.

I did however receive another strong recommendation to attend a Short Service Commission (Late Entry) (SSC LE) Selection Course by my commanding officer, and this was fully supported by the Divisional AGC (SPS) Commander. I applied yet deep in my heart, I knew this was no longer something I wanted but two weeks later, I received a letter to say I had been selected for the next commissioning selection weekend at AGC (SPS) Regimental Headquarters in Worthy Down. I decided to give it a go as I was still highly competitive at that time, and I went along with a plan in mind that only I knew about.

A Late Entry (LE) commission is awarded to officers who are commissioned from the ranks and primarily they are Warrant Officers Class One and Class Two however, each regiment and corps has its own criteria for candidates. Having passed the 'Paper Board' I had to attend a two-day assessment and scored well on the written Military Knowledge Test, essay, group discussion and lecture, command tasks, and came first on the Assault Course and Physical Fitness Test.

Knowing I was in with a good chance of being offered a commission, all that was left was for me to sit before the selection panel yet my heart was not in it. Before attending the selection weekend, I sought advice from a fellow Warrant Officer who explained that during the final interview, I would be asked why I wanted to become an officer. If I answered that it was natural progression then I would instantly fail, because the correct answer is to start a new career. At the end of my interview I was asked this very question and after quite a long pause on my part, I looked at each of the three officers sitting on the panel and intentionally gave the wrong answer, and I have never looked back.

Kentigern House, Glasgow

One social occasion I really enjoyed at Maidstone was the town's annual Dragon Boat Race that took place on the River Medway, and being competitive as indeed the British soldiers always are, 36 Engineer Regiment entered a team. One person would act as the 'drummer' at the front, one would steer the boat at the rear, and the remaining 20 crew would row while working in pairs. As we paddled our boat to the starting line, the competitive spirit kicked in and everyone was giving advice and offering words of encouragement as though we all were seasoned competitors.

The two boats turned and lined up to await the starting gun and in the first race, we won by a considerable margin and could not get over just how fast we had covered the course as thousands of spectators on both river banks cheered us on. It was exhilarating and we qualified for the next round which again we won and by quite a margin, but there was one team from the local college who were clearly going to be our arch-rivals if we were ever to compete against them, which we did and that was in the final.

Both teams were raring to go but by now, some of our crew were wearing white kamikaze style head-scarfs with Japanese writing and so with adrenalin pumping, we rowed side by side to the starting line while exchanging healthy banter. We turned and waited. Everyone felt that this race was ours for the taking, and as the gun was fired the paddles hit the water perfectly and the acceleration of both boats was incredible. It was neck and neck right up to the final 50 metres, and the commentator on the river bank near the bridge had the crowd cheering at the top of their voice for both teams, but from nowhere the college found a final surge of power that took them past the finishing line just ahead of us. It was a close result and afterwards we all enjoyed the remainder of the day socialising into the late evening.

On 8 May 1998, I drove out of Invicta Park Barracks and headed to what should have been my last posting after being appointed Staff Assistant to the Commander Royal Engineers (CRE), Headquarters 3 (United Kingdom) Division in Bulford, Wiltshire. My abbreviated title was SA (G1) Engr 3 (UK) Div and again, to their credit the Adjutant General's Corps (SPS) Manning and Records Office had supported my request to serve with the Royal Engineers.

The truth is that the newly appointed CRE was in fact my commanding officer at 36 Engineer Regiment and he had just been promoted to colonel, but before he left Maidstone I mentioned to him during our farewell interview that I would be very keen to serve as his Staff Assistant, should the post ever become vacant. He fully supported this and just a few months later his request was approved, and I received a posting order appointing me to be the new SA (G1) Engr 3 (UK) Div.

12 May 1998 to 3 May 1999
HQ Royal Engineers 3 (UK) Bulford, Wiltshire – Staff Assistant (G1) Engr Warrant Officer Class Two

Extremely happy with my posting to HQ 3 (UK) Division, I was once again serving with my former commanding officer at 36 Engineer Regiment who was now the newly appointed Commander Royal Engineer (CRE). As his Staff Assistant within the Engineer Group, it was my responsibility to oversee and control all G1 matters including regimental manning levels, discipline, and personnel services across the Division's entire geographical area which included the South of England, and Ripon in North Yorkshire. Historically, 3 Division was first created in 1809 by Lord Arthur Wellesley, 1st Duke of Wellington and it was the first Division ever to be used in the fight against the French. It also saw action at the Battle of Waterloo, the Crimean War, and Second Boer War during the last year of the 19th century.

The headquarters was relocated from Germany to Bulford in late 1992, and it remained on a permanent state of operational readiness. The units that came under the command of CRE 3 (UK) Div included 22 Engineer Regiment in Tidworth, 36 Engineer Regiment in Maidstone, 38 Engineer Regiment in Ripon, and 9 Parachute Squadron Royal Engineers at Aldershot.

Among my day-to-day GI duties and other business, my role was to also act as liaison officer and central point of contact in respect of all Divisional trawls for Royal Engineer volunteers, managing Military Secretary (MS) matters relating to commissioned officers and warrant officers across the Division, carrying out Personnel Documentation Inspections on all units, and controlling the Confidential Reports for all officers and soldiers serving within the Division. In effect, I was carrying out the duties of a SO3 (captain) and responsible for in excess of 2,200 officers and soldiers across 3 (UK) Division.

But the one task I enjoyed the most was carrying out personnel documentation inspections in Tidworth, Maidstone, Aldershot, and Ripon and then subsequently having meetings with the commanding officers or their representatives in turn, which was usually the Adjutant.

On one particular documentation inspection, I had to travel to Ripon in North Yorkshire which was a return journey of over 540 miles and given that my schedule was extremely tight, I managed to book myself a Gazelle helicopter and pilot for the day. After breakfast in the Warrant Officers' and Sergeants' Mess at Bulford Camp, I went to collect my folder from my office and heard the aircraft hovering low above the headquarters as it made its approach to a landing site on the lawn immediately outside.

We followed a flight path that took us directly over the Derwent and Ladybower Reservoirs in the Peak District National Park in Derbyshire, and it was these that Guy Gibson and his Dam Buster crew used to practice their low level approaches in Lancaster bombers, in preparation for the famous attacks on the Ruhr Valley Dams in Nazi Germany in 1943. As we approached the first reservoir, I informed the pilot that I had flown over all three Ruhr Dams in a RAF Harrier T-Bird Jet when I was on a military exercise in Germany in 1981.

Clearly interested, he asked lots of questions and as I described to him how it felt to fly the exact route that Guy Gibson had followed, I added that sitting inside his helicopter was far more nerve racking than being in the T-Bird Harrier. He laughed and that experience still stands out as being one of fondest memories during my military career.

As the only Warrant Officer in HQ RE 3 (UK) Division, I also acted as Branch Sergeant Major and it was during my time at Bulford that I completed the full 22 year career. At the written request of the Commander Royal Engineer himself, both the Divisional AGC (SPS) Commander and AGC (SPS) Manning and Records Office approved a two-year period of 'Extended Continuance' which meant that I would continue in my post and in my rank.

This however was one of the three options I had come up with while serving with 36 Engineer Regiment and so I was more than happy, and especially as a number of fellow AGC colleagues from other Divisional branches had applied for 'Extended Continued' yet only two of us were successful. My time at Bulford was as exciting as it was fascinating, and I learned a lot about what goes on behind closed doors within a Divisional Headquarters and it was fascinating, particularly in respect of how individual branches and commanders work together in battle or conflict situations.

Once on a three-day Divisional Exercise for HQ staff only, I saw a completely different side to the Commander Royal Engineer as he led and guided his team through a TEWT, the acronym for 'Tactical Exercise Without Troops.' There is no doubt that he was a brilliant planner and military strategist who was quick at assessing situations and identifying options, the likes of which I had never seen before. To say that it was highly impressive is an understatement.

In April 1999 and completely out of the blue, I was contacted by my AGC (SPS) Divisional Branch and asked if I would consider taking up a post with a non-Royal Engineer unit that was in urgent need of an experienced RAOWO to take over and bring back to a high standard their RHQ administrative offices. 9 Supply Regiment RLC was based at a former RAF Station in Hullavington and their situation sounded dire yet familiar. I enjoyed this type of challenge and because the AGC (SPS)

Manning and Records Office had been so good to me ever since I was transferred across in 1993, I suggested to my Divisional AGC (SPS) SO3 that my first course of action should be to discuss the matter with the Commander Royal Engineer as this was only right and proper.

I briefed the CRE on the situation at Hullavington and outlined the request from Divisional AGC (SPS) SO3 that I consider helping the regiment out, and he fully agreed. I re-visited the AGC (SPS) SO3 whose office was literally above mine, and agreed to take up the posting. The paperwork was processed as a priority and on 7 May 1999, I drove out of Bulford Camp to join what would eventually be my final appointment with the British Army and ironically, for the first since joining the Regular Army in July 1977, I would not be serving with the sappers.

On my journey through Tidworth Garrison I stopped off at the Military Cemetery to spend more time at the grave of my old friend Warrant Officer Class Two Jim Pridding. It was a sunny afternoon and I am not ashamed to admit that while standing there alone and in total silence, I again shed tears over his loss because it was still difficult to come to terms with the fact that he passed away at such a young age. I had known Jim for over 20 years and we had become good friends, but my tears were also for Kevin Diable, another great colleague and friend who passed away back in 1983.

As I stood and looked out at the surrounding beautiful Wiltshire countryside, I suddenly sensed a warm comforting presence and it was as if they were both standing beside me, not smiling or looking sad and not even uttering a single word. They were just there with me in spirit, and that moment was so very private and special but it was soon time for me to say goodbye to them both. As I slowly drove towards the cemetery gate I looked in my rear view mirror but they had disappeared, and that reassured me that once again they were both at peace.

I headed for Marlborough and then Swindon, and eventually I joined the M4 westbound to Hullavington Barracks, a journey of less than one hour.

4 May 1999 to 31 August 2000
9 Supply Regiment Royal Logistics Corps, Hullavington – RAOWO
Warrant Officer Class Two

9 Supply Regiment RLC is very easy to find because it is literally less than one minute north of Junction 17 on the M4, and the entrance is directly opposite the village of Lower Stanton St Quinton which is some four and a half miles north of Chippenham in Gloucestershire. The barracks is a former RAF Station which closed

in 1992 and outside the rear perimeter fence, was a single runway with two taxiways leading off to several large hangars dotted around the airfield.

These now served as private industrial storage units, and the village of Hullavington itself was just a short walk from the married quarters that were situated directly opposite the runway. Without realising it at the time, I was taking up my final appointment with the British Regular Army and for once I felt completely relaxed, because I was now guaranteed an immediate pension whenever I decided to retire from army life, and that ironically would be a decision I would make in 12 months' time.

As a RAOWO serving on 'Extended Continuance' I knew that I was once again taking over a post that had been unfilled for over a year, and as my new commanding officer would later write in my final Confidential Report, "WO2 Thomas literally had to re-invent the wheel as there were no systems in place whatsoever," because "the appointment had been gapped for some time."

Why so many senior military administrative posts had become vacant right across the Regular Army was a concern for me and many of my colleagues, and even more so for AGC (SPS) MRO and Divisional Branches, because the message it was sending out was that retention was now a genuine dilemma, and it was getting worse. It had already become a topic of discussion while at 3 (UK) Division and many were openly saying that the situation needed to be addressed without delay.

But what was causing such a marked reduction in available personnel, and what could be done about it?

It was evident that far too many British military personnel were now serving on back-to-back six-month operational tours of duty, and that double-hatting was fast becoming the new 'norm' for an already overstretched regular army. Yet nothing was being seen to be done to resolve this situation and indeed, there was even talk of further cutbacks, redundancies, and reductions in defence spending at that time.

Thankfully, I inherited a full complement of AGC (SPS) Military Clerks at 9 Supply Regiment RLC and from what I saw they were efficient, hardworking, and competent in their work but again, I saw a need to start from scratch. I planned and implemented a new Administrative Office system and reviewed each and every Job Description while at the same time, reshuffling regimental personnel both within the Regimental Headquarters and the three squadrons on and off base. To their credit, every member of the clerical team adapted to their new roles and procedures and in no time at all, the Regimental Headquarters Administrative Office took on an entirely new dimension, and the standard of work improved.

Systems and office layouts were revamped, libraries reorganised, roles and responsibilities re-defined, deadlines set, and notices placed on boards in prominent places. As the bulk of the regiment was deployed on operational duty in Bosnia-Herzegovina, I assumed the role of Warrant Officers' and Sergeants' Mess Secretary as well as supporting my fellow Warrant Officers in ensuring that the Rear Party was running smoothly and carrying out its responsibilities efficiently. Communications between Bosnia and the Rear Party ran smoothly and this was observed by the Regimental Second-in-Command, the Regimental Administrative Officer, and the Regimental Quartermaster who were all based at Hullavington.

By May 2000, I began to wonder what life in the British Army and Armed Forces would be like if any of the changes in social attitudes were ever to be introduced, and it genuinely concerned me and my colleagues. I decided to circulate my CV through the Armed Forces Resettlement website and within weeks, I received a telephone call from a retired army major who asked if I would be interested in the post of Accounts and Office Manager with a logistical planning consultancy based at Dyer Street in Cirencester.

I just knew that this was the perfect time for me to consider retirement from military life and after two meetings with the Managing Director of LPC International, I was offered the post and accepted. I met with my Regimental Administrative Officer in Hullavington to inform him of my decision to retire, and he gave me his full backing. Immediately, telephone discussions were made between the RAO and AGC (SPS) Manning and Records, and also and 3 (UK) Division SPS Branch and fortunately for me, a workable plan was quickly identified and agreed and so I sent a Priority Signal (FAX) to my commanding officer out in Bosnia.

In the signal I explained that I had chosen to retire after 23 years with the British Regular Army using my 'Right of Free Premature Voluntary Release (PVR)' which I was entitled to, as a Warrant Officer serving on 'Extended Continuance'. I also informed my CO that a suitable replacement RAOWO had been identified by AGC (SPS) and after receiving a Signal from Bosnia agreeing to the plan, I booked a flight through RAF Air Trooping to Split for a farewell interview and to sign my Confidential Report, and finalise my release papers before returning to Hullavington.

The visit lasted longer than I had expected and my commanding officer proved to be one of the most accommodating and caring of commanders that any soldier could ever wish to serve under. Indeed, a small schedule of meetings was convened spread over two days so that I could bring my commander fully up to speed on what I had changed and implemented back at Hullavington, plus I wanted to discuss several areas of regimental administrative concerns that I felt he needed to address on his return to the United Kingdom.

He was more than pleased with the new systems and restructured Administrative Office, and at the end of our final meeting we both signed my discharge paperwork and Confidential Report, and then we went for a farewell lunch and drinks in the Warrant Officers' and Sergeants' Mess. The very next morning we shook hands and wished each other the best for both our futures, and I was driven to Split Airport from where I flew back to RAF Brize Norton. It could not have been a more organised or smooth transition.

Back in Hullavington Barracks a top-table farewell lunch was arranged by the Rear Party Sergeant Major during which speeches and toasts were made and washed down with fine wine. I was presented with my farewell gift which was a figurine of a black panther and the party continued at a local village pub, and on Thursday, 31 August 2000 I drove out of Hullavington Barracks for the very last time. Within the space of just a few minutes my British Army career had come to a perfect end. I was now a civilian once again.

The following Monday I took up my new post of Accounts and Office Manager with LPC International, and the relaxed environment in which I now found myself was so very different to my 24 years with the Armed Forces. I have never regretted retiring from the British Army when I did, and I genuinely have no idea if things have ever changed for military personnel. For me, serving with the Armed Forces was both a privilege and an honour and something I am extremely proud of. It was a chapter of my life that has now closed yet it still remains my favourite chapter of all, so what then lies ahead?

I firmly advocate that for something new to begin, something old needs to end and my decision to retire in August 2000 was absolutely the correct decision to make. As I may have mentioned at some point in this memoir, "things happen for a reason."

Afternote

Writing this memoir has at times proved more emotional than I could ever have possibly imagined, because it truly has been a walk down memory lane and a reflection on a period of my life that I fondly cherished. When I look back on it as I sometimes do, it brings back so many treasured memories of past friends, adventures, escapades, and achievements that have genuinely made me cry, laugh, and even gasp at times.

Indeed, I would go further and freely admit that it has also served as a therapy which I believe I needed after retiring from the British Army in August 2000. I say this because by writing my memoir I now realise that I had been denying a bereavement of some kind for over 22 years.

I owe a tremendous debt of gratitude to my son David because it was he who actually reconnected me with the military, by inviting me to a local Army Veteran's breakfast in 2022. And it was David who invited me to join the Llanelli Branch of the Welsh Guards Association as an associate member. What David did while possibly not realising it, was to make me realise that I really did miss the comradeship and the military far more than I care to admit.

I was once asked by a fellow veteran which three aspects of military life I miss the most and immediately I replied 'discipline', 'comradeship', and 'adventure'.

Military discipline has to be strict otherwise the whole system breaks down. Soldiers are trained to obey commands without challenge and this is drummed into them from day one of Basic Military Training. I am all for equality, liberalism, and people's rights to a certain degree however, when it comes to the military who are ultimately responsible for the defence of our nation, its border, and its people, then it has to be the dog that wags the tail. It cannot be any other way.

If a soldier is given an order by a superior then he or she should obey immediately and without challenge, and the example I always use to explain why is the scenario where a section commander of a patrol suddenly observes a sniper aiming a rifle directly at them. Instantly, that commander would shout "get down!"

or "take cover!" and it is the instant reaction to that order that will have possibly saved someone's life.

With regards to comradeship, I can vouch that soldiers thrive on this because I experienced it myself my first day. There were wonderful and different characters of all kinds throughout my career and none more so than those in 3 Troop 52 Field (Construction) Squadron. We served together in Canada and the Falkland Islands, and it was with these friends and colleagues that I experienced two memorable adventures in my life. The first was the expedition in Algonquin Provincial Park and the six-month operational tour of the Falklands. Both brought out the very best in me and my colleagues, and we bonded together to become one of the strongest teams I have ever had the privilege to be a part of.

As for adventure, quite simply this is an exciting experience that involves an element of daring, risk, and boldness. The British Army provides this in abundance.

To write my military memoir has taken three years and it fulfils an ambition I have had since 1983. The sense of closure satisfaction that it has given me is actually difficult to put into context, mainly because of its deep-rooted importance to me personally.

With that in mind, I would say that the last emotion I feel in ending this book is gratitude, for having managed to fulfil my writing ambition. I now have another book which I have wanted to write for many years but no matter what happens in the future, it is this memoir that will forever be my most treasured piece of writing.

FAREWELL MESSAGE FROM GENERAL WALKER
Chief of General Staff

ARMY

24423809 WO2 P THOMAS AGC (SPS)

23 Years Service

On the occasion of your retirement from the Army, I wish to thank you most sincerely for the loyal service you have given.

I recognise that, in carrying out your duties as a soldier, you will have had to make many sacrifices, putting the interests of your Country and the Army before your own.

This is very much appreciated and I wish, formally, to express my gratitude for the service you have given and for the excellent contribution you have made.

I wish you all the very best for the future and every happiness in the years to come. Good luck and thank you.

Michael Walker
Chief of General Staff

Testimonial

(Transcribed from my Discharge Records)

WO2 Thomas leaves the Army following 23 years exemplary service. A former Royal Engineer Clerk, he transferred across the Adjutant General's Corps following the Service's Defence Review. Throughout his career he has given nothing less than 100% loyalty and dedication at all times. He is without doubt the perfect example of a team player and leader and his administration skills are remarkable.

A thoroughly proactive and enthusiastic individual, he has served in numerous countries worldwide and has been an excellent ambassador for both the Service and his Corps: his integrity is without fault. He is a very active person and an experienced Joint Service Mountain Leader. He had led expeditions in Morocco, Norway and Canada. A former Harrow RFC Director of Coaching, he has also coached and refereed both in Europe and the United Kingdom. In 1992 he was selected to referee the Army Minor Units Rugby Cup Final at Warminster in recognition of his ability.

WO2 Thomas is a highly intelligent, polite, and smart individual who has managed his staff and personal life in a thoroughly professional manner. In 1992 he was awarded the Long Service and Good Conduct Medal. In 1998 he was selected for the appointment of Staff Assistant to the Commander Royal Engineer 3 (UK) Division. In 2000, he was awarded the Diploma in Administration Management (Distinction).

WO Thomas will be a very sad loss to both the Service and the Adjutant General's Corps but his future employer will gain a tremendous asset. I wish him every success in his future career.

Disclosure 1
MP 520
APC
65 Brown Street
Glasgow G2 8EX

Theatres

(Transcribed from my Discharge Records)

Place Of Deplanement	Date Arrived in Theatre	Date Emplaned This Theatre
Great Britain	04-Oct-1996	31-Aug-2000
Yugoslavia	16-Aug-1996	04-Oct-1996
Great Britain	08-Jul-1996	16-Aug-1996
Yugoslavia	19-Apr-1996	08-Jul-1996
Great Britain	31-Mar-1992	19-Apr-1996
Germany (Fed Republic)	09-Apr-1990	30-Mar-1992
Great Britain	30-Mar-1990	09-Apr-1990
Germany (Fed Republic)	19-Feb-1989	30-Mar-1990
Great Britain	27-Jan-1989	18-Feb-1989
Germany (Fed Republic)	10-Oct-1988	27-Jan-1989
Great Britain	29-May-1986	10-Oct-1988
Germany (Fed Republic)	15-Nov-1984	29-May-1986
Great Britain	01-Nov-1984	15-Nov-1984
Germany (Fed Republic)	10-Jul-1984	01-Nov-1984
Great Britain	07-Jun-1984	10-Jul-1984
Germany (Fed Republic)	09-Aug-1983	07-Jun-1984
Great Britain	24-Jun-1983	09-Aug-1983
Ascension Island	20-Jun-1983	23-Jun-1983
Seagoing	11-Jun-1983	20-Jun-1983
Falkland Islands	15-Jan-1983	11-Jun-1983
Seagoing	05-Jan-1983	15-Jan-1983
Ascension Island	04-Jan-1983	05-Jan-1983
Great Britain	02-Oct-1982	04-Jan-1983
Canada	05-Jul-1982	02-Oct-1982
Great Britain	13-May-1982	05-Jul-1982

Germany (Fed Republic)	01-Apr-1982	13-May-1982
Great Britain	01-Dec-1981	01-Apr-1982
Germany (Fed Republic)	04-Sep-1981	01-Dec-1981
Canada	09-Jul-1981	04-Sep-1981
Germany (Fed Republic)	10-Feb-1981	09-Jul-1981
Great Britain	30-Dec-1980	10-Feb-1981
Germany (Fed Republic)	23-Feb-1980	30-Dec-1980
Northern Ireland	04-Oct-1979	23-Feb-1980
Germany (Fed Republic)	23-Jul-1979	04-Oct-1979
Great Britain	31-May-1979	23-Jul-1979
Germany (Fed Republic)	15-Feb-1978	31-May-1979
Great Britain	27-Jun-1977	15-Feb-1978

Specialist Qualifications

(Transcribed from my Discharge Records)

Specialist Qualification	Effective Date
Driving Licence Category A	01-Jul-1993
Army Rugby Union Referee Class 1	10-Feb-1993
Army Rugby Union Referee Class 11	04-Mar-1992
Joint Services Mountain Expedition Leader (Summer)	19-Sep-1991
Summer Mountain Leader Training	03-Jul-1991
Army Rugby Union Preliminary Coaching	15-Mar-1991
Army Rugby Union Coach Award	15-Mar-1991
Army Rugby Union Referee Class 111	25-Aug-1989
Pampas Trained	23-Aug-1985
Royal Yacht Association Competent Crew	05-Oct-1984
Military Swimming Test Passed	25-Aug-1983
Driving Licence Group H (Formerly Group 5 & 6)	25-Jul-1979

(Note: The above are over and beyond trade and education qualifications.)

Philip Thomas